Growing in the character of a disciple

BOOK 2 IN THE REAL CHRISTIANITY SERIES

SEAN KEHOE

realchristianity.com

PUBLISHING DETAILS AND ACKNOWLEDGEMENTS TO BIBLE PUBLISHERS

© Sean Kehoe 2015   Published 2015

Growing in the character of a disciple – Book 2 in the Real Christianity series

Originally published online in May 2014 via our website. This first print edition of the book has been amended from that online version and is copyright 2015.

Sean Kehoe has asserted his right under the Copyright, Designs and Patents Act 1988 to be identified as the author of this work.

Published by Real Christianity of Box 5262, 6, Slington House, Rankine Road, Basingstoke, RG24 8PH, United Kingdom.

ISBN number 978-1-910968-01-7

Scripture quotations in this book are from a variety of translations. The Bible version used is indicated by the relevant initials at the end of each reference, as follows and the following acknowledgements are made to each of the publishers:

NIV = New International Version

KJV = King James Version

RSV = Revised Standard Version

NKJV = New King James Version

ASV = American Standard Version

NASB = New American Standard Bible

ESV = English Standard Version

Cover design by Kev Jones (kevdesign@me.com)

www.realchristianity.com

DEDICATION

This book is dedicated to my American friend, John Van Harn. He came to England as a missionary in 1978 to lead a ministry that aimed to contribute to the 'Great Commission' by making *disciples* of all nations, not just *converts.* His colleague, Dave Brown, was the one who led me to put my faith in Jesus Christ and be saved. However, from that point on, for more than two years, John Van Harn did more to disciple me than any other man, before or since.

That said, from the time when I graduated and moved on, I have not really had any human mentor. I simply never found anybody else able or willing to teach me how to be a disciple, other than for fleeting moments, or from afar, via teaching tapes and CDs. Therefore, from the age of 21 onwards Jesus has basically had to disciple me Himself, through my study of His written Word and from a long series of difficult and testing experiences.

Nevertheless, for those two years, 1981 to 1983, I had a genuine mentor in John Van Harn. He set me up for life, for which I am truly grateful. Accordingly, I dedicate this second book to him.

GROWING IN THE CHARACTER OF A DISCIPLE

BOOK 2 IN THE REAL CHRISTIANITY SERIES

CONTENTS

INTRODUCTION

If you have become a Christian then you are now under a duty to become a disciple. Being a follower of Jesus Christ involves far more than just believing in Him. We can be saved (in the sense of being justified) in a moment. We achieve that by repenting and believing in Jesus. But from that point onwards we need to spend the whole of the rest of our lives learning how to follow Him and obey Him on a daily basis. That requires discipline, which is the root meaning of the word 'disciple'. Of course, we are not saved, in the sense of being justified, by the quality of our discipleship. Justification is achieved in an instant, by faith alone, not by subsequently being a good disciple.

However, being *sanctified*, which is the second part of the overall process of being saved, requires that we live lives of obedience, self-sacrifice and discipline. So, our sanctification does require us to become disciples, and to remain so for the long term. The point is that Christian character cannot be formed overnight. Neither is it a *gift* that God gives to us. It is a *fruit* which has to be grown. It can only arise as the product of years, and even decades, spent as wholehearted disciples of Jesus. In this book I hope to introduce you to some of the key things that are needed if we are to see our characters change and to become more like Jesus.

So, in chapter one, we shall try to define what a disciple really is. We shall also look realistically at the cost and difficulty that Christian discipleship involves, rather than focusing solely on the benefits, as many churches do. Then in the remaining chapters we shall examine four vital subjects that we need to grasp if we are to grow as disciples. These are the qualities of thankfulness, faithfulness, truthfulness and forgiveness, i.e. our willingness to forgive others for what they have done to us. These are foundational character qualities, but they are not adequately taught in most churches.

Indeed, in many, they are hardly mentioned at all. But they ought to be emphasized strongly, because they play a major part in the whole process of becoming a disciple. So, by dealing with the above themes my hope is that a Christian will be helped to make a stronger start in their Christian life. Then they will be better placed to tackle a host of other important issues, topics and challenges, many of which are addressed in the remaining books in this series.

Sean Kehoe

8 September 2015

CHAPTER 1

WHAT IT MEANS TO BE A DISCIPLE AND HOW CHRISTIAN CHARACTER IS FORMED

25 Now great multitudes went with Him. And He turned and said to them, 26 "If anyone comes to Me and does not hate his father and mother, wife and children, brothers and sisters, yes, and his own life also, he cannot be My disciple. 27 And whoever does not bear his cross and come after Me cannot be My disciple. 28 For which of you, intending to build a tower, does not sit down first and count the cost, whether he has enough to finish it—

Luke 14:25-28 (NKJV)

So therefore, any one of you who does not renounce all that he has cannot be my disciple.

Luke 14:33 (ESV)

Whoever seeks to save his life will lose it, and whoever loses his life will preserve it.

Luke 17:33 (NKJV)

Know then in your heart that, as a man disciplines his son, the Lord your God disciplines you.

Deuteronomy 8:5 (RSV)

"......for those who honor me I will honor, and those who despise me shall be lightly esteemed."

1 Samuel 2:30(b) (RSV)

So Jesus was saying to those Jews who had believed Him, "If you continue in My word, then you are truly disciples of Mine;

John 8:31 (NASB)

12 and may the Lord make you increase and abound in love for one another and for all, as we do for you, 13 so that he may establish your hearts blameless in holiness before our God and Father, at the coming of our Lord Jesus with all his saints.

1 Thessalonians 3:12-13 (ESV)

By this all men will know that you are my disciples, if you have love for one another."

John 13:35 (RSV)

Jesus said to him, "No one who puts his hand to the plow and looks back is fit for the kingdom of God."

Luke 9:62 (ESV)

[40] So they took his advice, and when they had called in the apostles, they beat them and charged them not to speak in the name of Jesus, and let them go. [41] Then they left the presence of the council, rejoicing that they were counted worthy to suffer dishonor for the name.

Acts 5:40-41 (RSV)

There are many false teachings, wrong ideas and unrealistic expectations about what is involved in being a Christian

The main reason I wrote this chapter was to try to correct some of the misconceptions in the Western churches about what it means to be a Christian. In my own experience, over more than 30 years, I have heard very little preaching about the cost and difficulty of being a disciple. On the rare occasions when discipleship is mentioned at all, the impression is given that the Christian life is meant to be easy and comfortable, with little or no opposition.

Accordingly, most of us have no expectation of there being any price to pay for being a disciple. Most 'churchgoers' today are not taught to expect any affliction, pressure or testing. Instead, the general impression given is that the Christian life is meant to be non-challenging, uncontroversial and moderate and that we should fit in nicely with the unbelieving world around us.

Some leaders go even further and preach what has come to be known as a *"prosperity gospel"*. That is the idea that Christians should expect to prosper financially and that they should pray for and expect to receive wealth, property and prestige *in this life*. Indeed, the absence of such privileges is then portrayed as if it was evidence that one lacks faith, or that one is not living right, or not pleasing God.

There is actually an element of truth in such teaching about prosperity, but only an element. It is frequently taken much too far, until it becomes a dangerously false teaching. So, as a general rule, if we live in accordance with God's will, develop the fruit of the Holy Spirit, and put biblical principles into practice, then we will prosper. Moreover, that will often include financial success and promotion in one's career.

The problem is that that is very far from being the whole truth about what it means to 'prosper'. That is because, in addition to receiving such blessings, every real Christian must also expect to receive affliction, opposition, struggles, testing and also God's discipline. On top of all that, we also have to wage a lifelong war on three different fronts against the world, the flesh and the Devil. (See below for

2

more information about these three battles and see also Books Seven and Nine which address them in detail.)

Experiencing all of these things is not inconsistent with prospering. At least there is no contradiction if we correctly define prosperity. It really means being where God wants you to be, and successfully doing what He wants you to do. By that definition, even as Jesus hung on the cross, He was prospering, because He was achieving God's purposes, and on a massive scale.

In this chapter I hope to set out a more realistic picture of what we can expect to experience in our lives if we become a real Christian, as opposed to a nominal one. Then we can count the cost properly, ideally even before we are converted. If so, we will be much better placed to handle the struggles and persecution that later come our way, rather than be surprised or resentful when they arise.

That said, the average 'churchgoer' in the West does not receive much, if any, affliction, or at least not as a result of his beliefs. Many of us are not sufficiently recognizable as Christians to be seen as a threat by any of God's enemies, whether human or demonic. In fact, the average Christian does not even give the subject of affliction any thought, mainly because he has never been told that he ought to.

That, in turn, is because a lot of church leaders take the view (correctly) that if they told the truth about what the Bible actually tells us to expect, then many of us would leave their churches. They know that many of us would go elsewhere, so as to hear a more comfortable message. A large percentage of church leaders are hirelings, doing a paid job, rather than genuine shepherds.

They choose to limit themselves to saying what people *want* to hear rather than what they *need* to hear. (See Book Eight for more details of the differences between hirelings and shepherds) I will now attempt to summarize what the Bible actually tells a disciple to expect. However, for the reasons stated above, you may find that it is a message that you have not heard before.

Being a disciple involves a deep commitment to Jesus Christ and a determination to follow and obey Him for the rest of your life.

The word *'disciple'* is rarely even used in most Western churches today, let alone taught on. Therefore, many of us have no idea how radical the Bible is about the expectations Jesus has of His disciples. He actually commands that we follow Him, obey Him and devote our entire lives to Him. We are meant to hand over to Him all that we have and all that we are.

That includes our possessions, career plans, ambitions, relationships and even our own bodies. Too many of us think that a Christian is simply someone who believes in God, or perhaps someone who goes to church. We tend to recoil from the suggestion that we should be any more committed than that. It sounds 'over the top' to our modern ears to go any further than merely believing in Jesus.

Therefore, most Christians in the West settle for a life which is far less challenging, productive and adventurous than God intends us to have. He wants us all to aim very high and to seek to become the best disciple that we can possibly be. That should involve achieving great things for Him, i.e. relative to the level of talents we have been given.

Instead, most of us just want an easy life and to avoid inconvenience, hard work and discomfort. But, in taking the easy options, we are not experiencing the things that God wants us to face and overcome. Therefore we miss out on a great many blessings. In particular we would miss out on some or all of the rewards that Jesus will one day give out at the Judgment Seat of Christ to those who have served Him faithfully. (See Book 4.)

Those who choose the easy option, whether due to laziness, fear or lack of motivation, are going to miss out. They will not receive a host of blessings and rewards which Jesus wants to give to those disciples who serve Him with all their hearts. We therefore need to get really clear that becoming a disciple of Jesus Christ is a radical and costly step to take. It does bring blessings and advantages, and we must not overlook those either.

However, it also involves handing over your whole life to Him and agreeing to follow and obey Him, whatever the cost may be. It means a complete surrender of your own will to His, and to do what He wants, even if that clashes with what you want, as it often will. It may mean facing suffering, or even death, for His sake.

A real Christian must be willing to receive the whole package of what it means to be a disciple, both the good and the bad. Those are strange and extreme sounding statements to make. They will jar with most modern ears and sound excessive. We live in an age which has largely forgotten what discipleship is and we don't like to talk about duty, self-sacrifice or hardship.

We know what it is to be a fan, but Jesus is not looking for fans. He is not a celebrity or a pop star. He is the King. In fact, He is the King of kings and Lord of lords. He is also the Creator, Saviour, High Priest and Judge. Given all of that, He is fully entitled to expect complete loyalty and devoted service.

Moreover, Jesus is fully entitled to give us orders and commands. Again, those are words which sound odd to our Western ears. Today very few of us have had any military service. Therefore the very concept of giving absolute obedience to anybody's orders is unfamiliar to us, and even alien. But we need to grasp this. If not, we will have an inaccurate and unbalanced idea of what is involved in being Jesus' disciple.

4

Life as a Christian is not meant to be a holiday camp. A closer analogy would be to liken it to joining the army. When you become a soldier you give up all of your freedom and independence. You agree to go wherever you are sent and do whatever is required of you, however hard it may be, even if it means going to your death.

In much of the underdeveloped world, and especially in Islamic countries, becoming a Christian today may well involve losing one's life. More Christians were martyred in the twentieth century than in all the previous nineteen centuries combined. And it is getting even worse in this century, though our dishonest and politically correct media chooses not to report any of that. Their silence is primarily due to fear of being seen to criticise Islam. It is persistently portrayed as if it was a *'religion of peace'*.

In fact, it has always been spread and sustained by violence and intimidation, and it still is. For that reason, it is now by far the main persecutor of the Church. Moreover, the power and viciousness of Islam is growing and it is spreading into Europe and America, in which it previously had no foothold. Soon, even in the West, becoming a Christian will involve increasingly severe persecution at the hands of Muslims and also aggressive secularists.

Being a real Christian is not easy. It is going to involve difficulty, opposition and even suffering.

We need to abandon any illusions we may be under. Alongside all the joys and benefits of becoming a real Christian, seeking to live as a *genuine*, Bible-believing disciple will involve many forms of struggle. Every real Christian has enlisted as a soldier in a spiritual war and is going to be treated as such by all God's enemies, both human and demonic. They will certainly see you as their enemy, regardless of whether you see them as yours.

If we do not realise those facts from the outset, then we are likely to give up and fall away at the first sign of hardship. We will do so, not because it is particularly severe as such, but because it is unexpected. The remedy for that is that we must be realistic enough to expect turbulence. Then we will not be surprised by it when it comes:

[12] Beloved, do not be surprised at the fiery ordeal which comes upon you to prove you, as though something strange were happening to you. [13] But rejoice in so far as you share Christ's sufferings, that you may also rejoice and be glad when his glory is revealed. [14] If you are reproached for the name of Christ, you are blessed, because the spirit of glory and of God rests upon you. [15] But let none of you suffer as a murderer, or a thief, or a wrongdoer, or a mischief-maker;

[16] *yet if one suffers as a Christian, let him not be ashamed, but under that name let him glorify God.*

1Peter 4:12-16 (RSV)

When apostle Paul was converted God revealed to Ananias how much Paul would have to suffer for the sake of Jesus. Ananias must have told Paul about this, because Luke knew of it, which is why it is in the book of Acts. The point is that God made it clear to Paul, from the very start, that life as a Christian was not going to be easy:

[15] *But the Lord said to him, "Go, for he is a chosen instrument of mine to carry my name before the Gentiles and kings and the sons of Israel;* *[16]* *for I will show him how much he must suffer for the sake of my name."*

Acts 9:15-16 (RSV)

What Ananias was told proved to be entirely accurate. Years later, in his second letter to the Corinthians, Paul gives a list of just some of the things he had to endure:

[24] *Five times I have received at the hands of the Jews the forty lashes less one.* *[25]* *Three times I have been beaten with rods; once I was stoned. Three times I have been shipwrecked; a night and a day I have been adrift at sea;* *[26]* *on frequent journeys, in danger from rivers, danger from robbers, danger from my own people, danger from Gentiles, danger in the city, danger in the wilderness, danger at sea, danger from false brethren;* *[27]* *in toil and hardship, through many a sleepless night, in hunger and thirst, often without food, in cold and exposure.* *[28]* *And, apart from other things, there is the daily pressure upon me of my anxiety for all the churches.*

2 Corinthians 11:24-28 (RSV)

Apostle Paul also spoke very plainly to the church in Philippi about what being a disciple really involves. He describes it as being involved in a conflict which involves opposition and suffering:

[27] *Only let your manner of life be worthy of the gospel of Christ, so that whether I come and see you or am absent, I may hear of you that you are standing firm in one spirit, with one mind striving side by side for the faith of the gospel,* *[28]* *and not frightened in anything by your opponents. This is a clear sign to them of their destruction, but of your salvation, and that from God.* *[29]* *For it has been granted to you that for the sake of Christ you should not only believe in him but also suffer for his sake,* *[30]* *engaged in the same conflict that you saw I had and now hear that I still have.*

Philippians 1:27-30 (ESV)

Paul also told Timothy how his own life had involved a lot of persecution and that the same will happen to everyone who wants to live a godly life:

[10] Now you have observed my teaching, my conduct, my aim in life, my faith, my patience, my love, my steadfastness, [11] my persecutions, my sufferings, what befell me at Antioch, at Ico'nium, and at Lystra, what persecutions I endured; yet from them all the Lord rescued me. [12] Indeed all who desire to live a godly life in Christ Jesus will be persecuted, [13] while evil men and impostors will go on from bad to worse, deceivers and deceived.

2 Timothy 3:10-13 (RSV)

The problem is that we have to live as Christians in a non-Christian world which is crooked, wicked and often hostile to what we believe. Moreover, we are not only meant to live amongst such people; we are supposed to shine like lights for their benefit. What is more, instead of grumbling or complaining about this, Paul instructs us to be glad and to rejoice at the opportunities given to us to be such a light:

[12] Therefore, my beloved, as you have always obeyed, so now, not only as in my presence but much more in my absence, work out your own salvation with fear and trembling, [13] for it is God who works in you, both to will and to work for his good pleasure. [14] Do all things without grumbling or disputing, [15] that you may be blameless and innocent, children of God without blemish in the midst of a crooked and twisted generation, among whom you shine as lights in the world, [16] holding fast to the word of life, so that in the day of Christ I may be proud that I did not run in vain or labor in vain. [17] Even if I am to be poured out as a drink offering upon the sacrificial offering of your faith, I am glad and rejoice with you all. [18] Likewise you also should be glad and rejoice with me.

Philippians 2:12-18 (ESV)

Every disciple is regarded as being part of the spiritual war between God and His enemies. Therefore we all have a duty to learn how to fight effectively in that war

We are expected to see ourselves as being part of a huge worldwide battle:

"fight the good fight of the faith;…………… "
Timothy 6:12 (a) (RSV)

[10] Finally, be strong in the Lord and in the strength of his might. [11] Put on the whole armor of God, that you may be able to stand against the wiles of the devil. [12] For we are not contending against flesh and blood, but against the principalities, against the powers, against the world rulers of this present darkness, against the spiritual hosts of wickedness in the heavenly places.

Ephesians 6:10-12 (RSV)

[3] For though we live in the world we are not carrying on a worldly war, [4] for the weapons of our warfare are not worldly but have divine power to destroy

7

strongholds. [5] We destroy arguments and every proud obstacle to the knowledge of God, and take every thought captive to obey Christ,

2 Corinthians 10:3-5 (RSV)

God is training us for service in that war and the difficulties we face are meant to make us stronger and more ready for battle:

Blessed be the Lord, my rock,
who trains my hands for war,
and my fingers for battle;
Psalm 144:1 (RSV)

The war between God and His enemies has been going on ever since the Devil rebelled and led astray one third of the angels in Heaven. The scale of that battle grew even larger after Adam fell into sin. From then on human beings also became God's enemies, alongside the demons. Every Christian is part of that war and is expected to fight in it. Regrettably, that fact is not widely known.

Some of us may have heard of it, but we don't really believe it, or we won't accept it. Even if we do know there is a war, many of us see ourselves as non-combatants, or even neutrals. Those who think that way have no intention of fighting in any war or of getting caught up in it. However, whether you know it or not, you are already caught up in that war anyway. That is, provided you are a *real* Christian.

If you are, then Satan and his demons will regard you as a target, irrespective of what you may think of them. It is not a war against human beings, and it does not involve guns, bombs or any other such weapons. Neither can it involve the use of carnal methods and techniques which the world uses, such as deception, manipulation, domination or the control of other people. It is, nonetheless, a very real conflict, which is fought on many different fronts and in every part of your life.

We shall examine some of those aspects below. At any rate, God expects you to view yourself as a soldier in that spiritual war and to fight actively and effectively on His side. He also expects you to be alert and armed, i.e. spiritually, not militarily. We are instructed to wear the 'armour' that God provides. Apostle Paul refers to this in his letter to the Ephesians:

[13] Therefore take the whole armor of God, that you may be able to withstand in the evil day, and having done all, to stand. [14] Stand therefore, having girded your loins with truth, and having put on the breastplate of righteousness, [15] and having shod your feet with the equipment of the gospel of peace; [16] besides all these, taking the shield of faith, with which you can quench all the flaming darts of the evil one. [17] And take the helmet of salvation, and the sword of the Spirit, which is the word of God.

Ephesians 6:13-17 ((RSV)

In the book of Judges, we are told that God allowed some of the Canaanites to be left in the Land of Israel, even after the first generation of Israelites took possession of it after leaving the wilderness. He did so because He wanted the Israelites of the next generation to learn how to fight, just as the generation that won the land under Joshua had to learn:

Now these are the nations which the Lord left, to test Israel by them, that is, all in Israel who had no experience of any war in Canaan; ² it was only that the generations of the people of Israel might know war, that he might teach war to such at least as had not known it before. ³ These are the nations: the five lords of the Philistines, and all the Canaanites, and the Sido'nians, and the Hivites who dwelt on Mount Lebanon, from Mount Ba'al-her'mon as far as the entrance of Hamath. ⁴ They were for the testing of Israel, to know whether Israel would obey the commandments of the Lord, which he commanded their fathers by Moses.

Judges 3:1-4 (RSV)

In other words, God allowed some of those Canaanites to remain, so as to test His people and also to give them a need to fight, so that they could have the opportunity to learn how to do it. Although we are not called upon to fight human beings with military weapons, or even with carnal, worldly methods, the warfare analogy is still a valid one.

God still wants us to learn how to fight for Him today, albeit that our battles are mainly spiritual. As well as requiring *us* to take part in this war, Jesus Himself is involved in it. Contrary to the image most people have of Jesus, He is also a military figure. Indeed, one of Jesus' titles is the *'Lord of Hosts'*?

The word 'hosts' means armies. So, in effect, the title means that Jesus is the *"Lord of armies"*. We actually see a pre-appearance of Jesus in the book of Joshua, where He appears to Joshua with a drawn sword in His hand and gives orders to him in a military manner.

In this incident he is referred to as the *"angel of the LORD"*. That is another title that is used to refer to Jesus in the Old Testament, when He appeared in bodily form prior to His incarnation. In this incident the angel of the LORD, i.e., Jesus, describes Himself as the *"Commander of the army of the LORD"*. He has every appearance of being a military figure:

¹³ When Joshua was by Jericho, he lifted up his eyes and looked, and behold, a man stood before him with his drawn sword in his hand; and Joshua went to him and said to him, "Are you for us, or for our adversaries?" ¹⁴ And he said, "No; but as commander of the army of the LORD I have now come." And Joshua fell on his face to the earth, and worshiped, and said to him, "What does my lord bid his servant?" ¹⁵ And the commander of the LORD's army said to Joshua,

"Put off your shoes from your feet; for the place where you stand is holy." And Joshua did so.

Joshua 5:13-15 (RSV)

This Person who appeared to Joshua was obviously not just an angel, because Joshua bows down and worships Him, which he would never do to an angel. Indeed, no angel would allow anyone to worship them. Joshua is also told to take off his shoes because the ground on which he stands is now "holy" by virtue of God being present there. In the next chapter we see this same Person, who is now referred to as *"the LORD"*, tell Joshua what to do about attacking and taking the city of Jericho:

[1]Now Jericho was shut up from within and from without because of the people of Israel; none went out, and none came in. [2] And the LORD said to Joshua, "See, I have given into your hand Jericho, with its king and mighty men of valor. [3] You shall march around the city, all the men of war going around the city once. Thus shall you do for six days. [4] And seven priests shall bear seven trumpets of rams' horns before the ark; and on the seventh day you shall march around the city seven times, the priests blowing the trumpets. [5] And when they make a long blast with the ram's horn, as soon as you hear the sound of the trumpet, then all the people shall shout with a great shout; and the wall of the city will fall down flat, and the people shall go up every man straight before him."

Joshua 6:1-5 (RSV)

Later we again see the LORD (Jesus) speaking to Joshua and giving him further military instructions. This time it is about attacking and taking the city of Ai:

[1] And the Lord said to Joshua, "Do not fear or be dismayed; take all the fighting men with you, and arise, go up to Ai; see, I have given into your hand the king of Ai, and his people, his city, and his land; [2] and you shall do to Ai and its king as you did to Jericho and its king; only its spoil and its cattle you shall take as booty for yourselves; lay an ambush against the city, behind it." [3] So Joshua arose, and all the fighting men, to go up to Ai; and Joshua chose thirty thousand mighty men of valor, and sent them forth by night.

Joshua 8:1-3 (RSV)

[18] Then the Lord said to Joshua, "Stretch out the javelin that is in your hand toward Ai; for I will give it into your hand." And Joshua stretched out the javelin that was in his hand toward the city. [19] And the ambush rose quickly out of their place, and as soon as he had stretched out his hand, they ran and entered the city and took it; and they made haste to set the city on fire.

Joshua 8:18-19 (RSV)

We also see the LORD of Hosts accompanying King David. That largely explains David's tremendous military successes. He had the commander of God's army working alongside him and guiding him:

⁹ And David became greater and greater, for the Lord of hosts was with him.
1 Chronicles 11:9 (RSV)

The point is that in all of this, the angel of the LORD, i.e. Jesus, is seen as a military figure. He is referred to as the Commander of the army of the LORD and He operates in a military fashion, giving military orders about the conquest of a city. This illustrates the fact that, like Him, we are engaged in a war, albeit a spiritual one. That is evidently how God sees it, or He would have no need of any 'army'. Given that Jesus Himself is engaged in that war, leading all of God's armies, we have no valid basis to think that we can be excused from having to take part in His battles alongside Him.

Self-denial is a valid and essential part of a life of discipleship

Modern Western society is fixated upon self. We are continually urged to indulge ourselves, such that many of us have become habitually self-centred and even self-obsessed. Far from condemning such an approach, modern psychology encourages us to focus on ourselves, excuse ourselves and love ourselves more and more.

By contrast, the Bible takes it as a given that we love ourselves more than enough as it is. God never tells us to love ourselves, because He knows that we already do. Therefore none of us has any need to learn how to love ourselves. Instead, He tells us to love others in the same way that we already love ourselves:

"…..You shall love your neighbor as yourself"
Matthew 19:19(b) (RSV)

The Bible takes a directly opposite approach to that taken by the world. It urges us to *deny* ourselves. That goes against all our carnal instincts and cultural expectations, but it is a vital part of being a disciple. Look how Jesus put it:

And he said to all, "If any man would come after me, let him deny himself and take up his cross daily and follow me.
Luke 9:23 (RSV)

This life of self-denial and of taking up a cross and carrying it is not restricted to a selected few, such as apostle Paul. The verse quoted above was not a special message, which Jesus only said to a few hardy types. He said it to *"all"* and that it applied to *"any"* man who would come after Him. Therefore it applies to you, and to me, and to all other disciples, without exception. Apostle Paul spoke of how much he had to give up for the sake of the Gospel. Nevertheless, the sacrifices were worthwhile:

⁷ But whatever gain I had, I counted as loss for the sake of Christ. ⁸ Indeed I count everything as loss because of the surpassing worth of knowing Christ Jesus my Lord. For his sake I have suffered the loss of all things, and count them as refuse, in order that I may gain Christ ⁹ and be found in him, not having a righteousness of my own, based on law, but that which is through faith in Christ, the righteousness from God that depends on faith; ¹⁰ that I may know him and the power of his resurrection, and may share his sufferings, becoming like him in his death, ¹¹ that if possible I may attain the resurrection from the dead. ¹² Not that I have already obtained this or am already perfect; but I press on to make it my own, because Christ Jesus has made me his own. ¹³ Brethren, I do not consider that I have made it my own; but one thing I do, forgetting what lies behind and straining forward to what lies ahead, ¹⁴ I press on toward the goal for the prize of the upward call of God in Christ Jesus.
Philippians 3:7-14 (RSV)

If we are ever going to learn how to deny ourselves and make sacrifices for Jesus' sake we must also learn how to control ourselves. Self-control is an essential first step to becoming a disciple. It enables us to make choices, and impose things on ourselves which our flesh nature does not want. Therefore self-control is listed as one of the fruit of the Spirit in Paul's letter to the Galatians:

²² But the fruit of the Spirit is love, joy, peace, patience, kindness, goodness, faithfulness, ²gentleness, self-control; against such there is no law.
Galatians 5:22-23 (RSV)

If you don't have self-control then it will not be possible to achieve any of God's objectives for your life. That is because your flesh nature will never desire what God wants, or cooperate with anything that promotes your growth as a disciple. Therefore, doing God's will is never the natural choice that you will instinctively make. It has to be imposed on yourself by yourself.

The problem is you won't ever do that unless you can first learn to control yourself. That means that your will must make the decisions, rather than you acting in accordance with your fleshly desires, instincts and habits. Therefore the Bible has a lot to say in favour of self-control. In fact, it is the only acceptable form of control. We cannot, and must not, control anybody else, but we can, and must, control ourselves:

A man without self-control
is like a city broken into and left without walls
Proverbs 25:28 (RSV)

A fool gives full vent to his anger,
but a wise man quietly holds it back.
                    Proverbs 29:11 (RSV)

When you become a disciple it is as if you change your nationality and become a citizen of the Kingdom of God. That Kingdom and its ways and values must become your focus, in place of the values of this world.

Another way to express the radical nature of the change we have to make, from being an unbeliever to a mature disciple, is to speak in terms of us changing our nationality. We are no longer to view ourselves primarily as citizens of the country we live in, but as people whose real citizenship is in Heaven. Jesus expects our primary loyalty to be to Him and to His Kingdom:

But our citizenship is in heaven, and from it we await a Savior, the Lord Jesus Christ
                    Philippians 3:20 (ESV)

Therefore, while we are alive now, we are effectively aliens or exiles. We live *in* this world but we are not *of* this world. We are then required to live as such, abstaining from many of the activities of those around us:

Since you call on a Father who judges each person's work impartially, live out your time as foreigners here in reverent fear.
                    1 Peter 1:17 (NIV)

[11] Beloved, I beseech you as aliens and exiles to abstain from the passions of the flesh that wage war against your soul.
                    1 Peter 2:11 (RSV)

We are not to love the things of this world, i.e. the sinful, worldly things which are opposed to God and all that he stands for:

[15] Do not love the world or the things in the world. If anyone loves the world, love for the Father is not in him. [16] For all that is in the world, the lust of the flesh and the lust of the eyes and the pride of life, is not of the Father but is of the world. [17] And the world passes away, and the lust of it; but he who does the will of God abides forever.
                    1 John 2:15-17 (RSV)

The entire population of this planet is divided into two groups - those who believe in the real God of the Bible and accept Jesus Christ, and those who don't. All who don't are described as being *"of the world":*

[1]Beloved, do not believe every spirit, but test the spirits to see whether they are of God; for many false prophets have gone out into the world. [2]By this you know the Spirit of God: every spirit which confesses that Jesus Christ has come in the flesh is of God, [3]and every spirit which does not confess Jesus is not of God. This is the spirit of antichrist, of which you heard that it was coming, and now it is in the world already. [4]Little children, you are of God, and have overcome them; for he who is in you is greater than he who is in the world. [5]They are of the world, therefore what they say is of the world, and the world listens to them. [6]We are of God. Whoever knows God listens to us, and he who is not of God does not listen to us. By this we know the spirit of truth and the spirit of error.

1 John 4:1-6 (RSV)

Part of the war we have to fight is a lifelong battle between our *new self* and our *old self*. In other words, it is a battle between our *spirit* and our *flesh*

The battle or conflict that we have to face is not only external to us, involving other people and demons. It is also an internal battle between our 'old self', otherwise known as our 'old man', 'carnal nature' or 'flesh', and our 'new self', 'new man' or 'new nature'. That is our human spirit which is reborn within us when we become a Christian.

This aspect of our overall battle is like a civil war between the two very different natures that are both alive within us. They remain within us until we die. This part of our struggle means that we have to choose to do what our new nature wants and to refuse to do what our flesh or old self wants. See how apostle Paul puts it:

[5]For those who live according to the flesh set their minds on the things of the flesh, but those who live according to the Spirit set their minds on the things of the Spirit. [6]For to set the mind on the flesh is death, but to set the mind on the Spirit is life and peace. [7]For the mind that is set on the flesh is hostile to God, for it does not submit to God's law; indeed, it cannot. [8]Those who are in the flesh cannot please God. [9]You, however, are not in the flesh but in the Spirit, if in fact the Spirit of God dwells in you. Anyone who does not have the Spirit of Christ does not belong to him. [10]But if Christ is in you, although the body is dead because of sin, the Spirit is life because of righteousness. [11]If the Spirit of him who raised Jesus from the dead dwells in you, he who raised Christ Jesus from the dead will also give life to your mortal bodies through his Spirit who dwells in you.

Romans 8:5-11 (ESV)

[5]Put to death therefore what is earthly in you: sexual immorality, impurity, passion, evil desire, and covetousness, which is idolatry. [6]On account of these the wrath of God is coming. [7]In these you too once walked, when you were living in them. [8]But now you must put them all away: anger, wrath, malice,

slander, and obscene talk from your mouth. ⁹ Do not lie to one another, seeing that you have put off the old self with its practices ¹⁰ and have put on the new self, which is being renewed in knowledge after the image of its creator.

¹¹ Here there is not Greek and Jew, circumcised and uncircumcised, barbarian, Scythian, slave, free; but Christ is all, and in all. ¹² Put on then, as God's chosen ones, holy and beloved, compassionate hearts, kindness, humility, meekness, and patience, ¹³ bearing with one another and, if one has a complaint against another, forgiving each other; as the Lord has forgiven you, so you also must forgive. ¹⁴ And above all these put on love, which binds everything together in perfect harmony.

Colossians 3:5-14 (ESV)

This first part of our battle, which is against our own sinful, flesh nature, is usually our greatest and hardest struggle. We have an opponent who is actually living inside us. It's not a demon. It's part of you. It operates as a kind of traitor or fifth-columnist seeking to undermine you from within and lead you astray. See Book Seven for a fuller discussion of our battle against the flesh. Now let us look more closely at the second and third battles that we have to fight. These are against the world system and also against the Devil and his demons.

We also have to contend with the sinful world system which is all around us. We must also reject its values and separate ourselves from its influence.

Whereas our battle against our own flesh takes place within ourselves, our battle against the world and all it stands for is an external one. By 'the world' we mean all of the thinking, values, standards, ways, priorities, practices, obsessions and methods of the unsaved and sinful world around us.

It is a shorthand phrase for the whole way that this present evil age operates. This second part of our battle then is to resist the many temptations that this sinful world has to offer and to refuse to be conformed to it, or squeezed into its mould:

If then you have been raised with Christ, seek the things that are above, where Christ is, seated at the right hand of God. ² Set your minds on things that are above, not on things that are on earth.

Colossians 3:1-2 (RSV)

Do not be conformed to this world, but be transformed by the renewal of your mind, that by testing you may discern what is the will of God, what is good and acceptable and perfect.

Romans 12:2 (ESV)

Apostle Paul also tells us that when we become a Christian we must cease to live in the worldly, futile way in which unbelievers live. We have to turn away from all such values and live differently:

17 Now this I affirm and testify in the Lord, that you must no longer live as the Gentiles do, in the futility of their minds; 18 they are darkened in their understanding, alienated from the life of God because of the ignorance that is in them, due to their hardness of heart; 19 they have become callous and have given themselves up to licentiousness, greedy to practice every kind of uncleanness.

Ephesians 4:17-19 (RSV)

22 Put off your old nature which belongs to your former manner of life and is corrupt through deceitful lusts, 23 and be renewed in the spirit of your minds, 24 and put on the new nature, created after the likeness of God in true righteousness and holiness.

Ephesians 4:22-24 (RSV)

3 But sexual immorality and all impurity or covetousness must not even be named among you, as is proper among saints. 4 Let there be no filthiness nor foolish talk nor crude joking, which are out of place, but instead let there be thanksgiving. 5 For you may be sure of this, that everyone who is sexually immoral or impure, or who is covetous (that is, an idolater), has no inheritance in the kingdom of Christ and God. 6 Let no one deceive you with empty words, for because of these things the wrath of God comes upon the sons of disobedience.

7 Therefore do not become partners with them; 8 for at one time you were darkness, but now you are light in the Lord. Walk as children of light 9 (for the fruit of light is found in all that is good and right and true), 10 and try to discern what is pleasing to the Lord. 11 Take no part in the unfruitful works of darkness, but instead expose them. 12 For it is shameful even to speak of the things that they do in secret.

Ephesians 5:3-12 (ESV)

15 Look carefully then how you walk, not as unwise but as wise, 16 making the best use of the time, because the days are evil. 17 Therefore do not be foolish, but understand what the will of the Lord is. 18 And do not get drunk with wine, for that is debauchery, but be filled with the Spirit, 19 addressing one another in psalms and hymns and spiritual songs, singing and making melody to the Lord with your heart, 20 giving thanks always and for everything to God the Father in the name of our Lord Jesus Christ,

Ephesians 5:15-20 (ESV)

⁸ Finally, brothers, whatever is true, whatever is honorable, whatever is just, whatever is pure, whatever is lovely, whatever is commendable, if there is any excellence, if there is anything worthy of praise, think about these things.
Philippians 4:8 (ESV)

A real Christian is very different from the worldly people around him. He won't conform to their standards. Therefore the world will hate him. It hated Jesus and it will automatically hate, and oppose, anyone who rejects its ways and truly wants to follow and imitate Him:

Do not wonder, brethren, that the world hates you.
1 John 3:13 (RSV)

18"If the world hates you, know that it has hated me before it hated you. ¹⁹ If you were of the world, the world would love you as its own; but because you are not of the world, but I chose you out of the world, therefore the world hates you.
John 15:18-19 (ESV)

³ Let the time that is past suffice for doing what the Gentiles like to do, living in licentiousness, passions, drunkenness, revels, carousing, and lawless idolatry. ⁴ They are surprised that you do not now join them in the same wild profligacy, and they abuse you; ⁵ but they will give account to him who is ready to judge the living and the dead.
1 Peter 4:3-5 (RSV)

Conversely, being a friend of the world automatically makes you an enemy of God:

Unfaithful creatures! Do you not know that friendship with the world is enmity with God? Therefore whoever wishes to be a friend of the world makes himself an enemy of God.
James 4:4 (RSV)

Every disciple needs to lose his fear of people and learn not to be ashamed of Jesus

We all have a strong desire to be liked and approved of by others. Therefore we are prone to neglecting our duties as disciples, or even denying Jesus, in order to avoid being disapproved of or criticised by other people. That craving to be approved of, or at least not to be disapproved of, keeps many of us trapped and paralysed with fear. The Bible calls this *"the fear of man"* and says that it becomes a '*snare*:

Fear of man will prove to be a snare,
but whoever trusts in the Lord is kept safe.
Proverbs 29:25 (NIV)

17

If you can't conquer this fear of other people you will never get very far as a disciple of Jesus. You will always be the prisoner of other people's opinions. You will stay silent when you ought to speak, and you will also moderate the little that you do say, so as to avoid antagonizing the world around you. However, if you do that, you are effectively following those people and are their disciple, rather than Jesus'.

The answer is to meet your fear head on and to refuse to submit to it. When you do that you will find that your fear of other people will diminish, or even disappear. At any rate, whether we find it easy or hard, the fact is that God commands us not to fear other people:

> [7] *"Hear me, you who know what is right,*
> *you people who have taken my instruction to heart:*
> *Do not fear the reproach of mere mortals*
> *or be terrified by their insults.*
> [8] *For the moth will eat them up like a garment;*
> *the worm will devour them like wool.*
> *But my righteousness will last forever,*
> *my salvation through all generations."*
> *Isaiah 51:7-8 (NIV)*

We must also take active steps to rid ourselves of any sense of shame or embarrassment at being openly identified as being a disciple of Jesus. Many Christians feel reasonably relaxed about speaking about 'church' or even 'God'. However, there is something about the specific name of 'Jesus' and also about speaking of the cross or the Gospel, that makes even real Christians feel awkward and embarrassed.

So they avoid the use of the Name 'Jesus' and also avoid or tone down any reference to the Gospel. We need to resolve to overcome that sense of shame, as apostle Paul did, and be open about the whole Gospel:

> *For I am not ashamed of the gospel of Christ, for it is the power of God to salvation for everyone who believes, for the Jew first and also for the Greek.*
> *Romans 1:16 (NKJV)*

I once had a one to one meeting with the senior leader of a particular church. I asked him why he consistently avoids controversial or unpopular themes when he preaches. He admitted that he fears the reaction of the people in the congregation and that he is also afraid of people generally. I was actually impressed by his willingness to admit those things to me. Few other leaders would do so, even though many are just as fearful as him.

He impressed me further when he then asked: *"How can I get rid of that fear of people?"* My reply was that the best way would be to replace his fear of people

18

with an even stronger fear of God. That is that we need to develop such a strong fear of the LORD that it negates, or drives out, any fear of people that we might still suffer from.

He then asked *"But how can I develop the fear of the LORD?"* My reply was that he could develop it by making a series of small decisions, day by day, to do what God wants, rather than what people want. Therefore, I said he should resolve to preach and teach exactly what God's Word says and not to tone it down, or avoid, any part of it, even if it is controversial or contradicts current orthodoxy or political correctness.

I said that each time he does that, even if only in small ways, or in front of small groups, his fear of man will get slightly smaller and his fear of God will get slightly bigger. The increments might only be small, but they add up and make a profound difference over a period of time. By doing this, even the most timid person can eventually learn to behave in a remarkably bold way, which he might never have thought possible.

Imagine you were afraid of the school bully but were even more afraid of the Headmaster. What if they were both nearby and were telling you to do the opposite things? Your fear of the Headmaster would outweigh your fear of the school bully and therefore set you free from it. It is a little bit like that with the fear of the LORD. As it grows, it sets us free from all other competing fears.

I also said to this particular leader that we can develop the fear of the LORD by seeking to develop a fear for His written Word. Far too many of us are casual about God's Word and handle it as if it was the word of a mere man, i.e. as if we were reading a passage from Shakespeare or Charles Dickens. That is true of many preachers too. They have little or no fear of God's Word, because they don't fear God Himself.

However, the same is true in reverse as well. That is they do not fear God, because they do not fear His Word. We are meant to fear God's Word. It is meant to be awesome to us, because of *whose* Word it is and also because of its power. However, there is another reason why we should fear God's Word, which few of us ever realise.

That is that when we are judged at the Judgment Seat of Christ, one of the criteria by which we will be judged is the extent to which we have taken note of, and obeyed, God's written Word. (See Book Four for a fuller discussion of this theme). The point is that whenever we read God's Word, and even more so whenever we teach or preach from it, we will be held accountable, and one day judged, for how we handled it.

Jesus will hold us accountable for whether we believed it and also whether we took it seriously or treated it lightly. If we are in any position of leadership, such

19

that we teach or preach, then Jesus will judge whether we compromised and edited His Word, so as to avoid making ourselves unpopular or arousing antagonism, or whether we presented it fully and accurately.

Countless preachers do alter the meaning of God's Word, or they leave out parts of it, so as to avoid controversy. The same is true also of those who are not preachers. All of us face the same temptation to compromise God's message in order to preserve our own image and reputation. However, we have no right to do so and we will have to face the rebuke of Jesus Christ Himself if we do.

We should much prefer to be rebuked now by the world rather than be rebuked later by Jesus. That's because we should fear Him more than we fear them, and fear His Word more than we fear their words. The prophet Isaiah says that God is looking for people who actually tremble at His Word, i.e. because they take it so seriously and are so concerned to abide by it:

All these things my hand has made,
and so all these things are mine,
says the LORD.
But this is the man to whom I will look,
he that is humble and contrite in spirit,
and trembles at my word.
                    Isaiah 66:2 (RSV)

Our third battle is against the Devil and all his demons. They are doing all they can to undermine and destroy you.

If life as a Christian was not already complicated enough, with our own flesh and the ungodly world system to deal with, it is made much harder by the involvement of the Devil and his demons. They are all fallen angels who were thrown out of Heaven long ago, before this world was made. They have already been judged and have been sentenced to spend eternity in the Lake of Fire. Indeed, it was created for them. However, their sentence has not yet been carried out.

Until they are cast into the Lake of Fire, most of the demons are free to go where they wish and to interfere with us and oppose us. God actually permits them to do so, albeit within certain limits. Their primary objectives are to tempt us to sin, to get us to be afraid and discouraged, and to render us ineffective as disciples. They especially want to prevent us from telling others about the Gospel. Our battle against the Devil and his demons, is primarily a spiritual one:

For we do not wrestle against flesh and blood, but against the rulers, against the authorities, against the cosmic powers over this present darkness, against the spiritual forces of evil in the heavenly places.
                    Ephesians 6:12 (ESV)

The demons are well aware of the other two battles we already face, against our own flesh and against the sinful world system. They are watching us fight those battles and they make full use of both of those struggles in their attempt to further undermine us. So, these three battles are each distinct and separate. Yet, they are all being waged simultaneously and, in many ways, they are all inter-connected.

God wants disciples to bear fruit and do good works. That involves dying to oneself, which we do to ourselves, and being pruned, which God does to us. Both processes are painful, but essential if we are to be fruitful.

Being a disciple is not only about fighting battles. God also wants every Christian to do good works for Him. That is one of the reasons why we were created. God wants each of us to fulfil the purposes He has set for us and to make a difference in the lives of other people:

For we are his workmanship, created in Christ Jesus for good works, which God prepared beforehand, that we should walk in them.
Ephesians 2:10 (ESV)

We are also meant to bear fruit in the sense that the people around us benefit from our lives, and especially from our good works. Paul makes clear that that is what God wants from us:

[9] And so, from the day we heard of it, we have not ceased to pray for you, asking that you may be filled with the knowledge of his will in all spiritual wisdom and understanding, [10] to lead a life worthy of the Lord, fully pleasing to him, bearing fruit in every good work and increasing in the knowledge of God.
Colossians 1:9-10 (RSV)

[9] And let us not grow weary in well-doing, for in due season we shall reap, if we do not lose heart. [10] So then, as we have opportunity, let us do good to all men, and especially to those who are of the household of faith.
Galatians 6:9-10 (RSV)

Before we can become capable of bearing fruit of the right kind, we first of all have to change. We are not able to produce anything good in our own strength, or from our own carnal nature. The things that come from us naturally are just works of the flesh. The Bible uses some agricultural analogies to describe what therefore needs to happen to us if we are to become fruitful. Firstly, we are told that we need to die to ourselves and to all that our flesh nature stands for.

Jesus Himself spoke of this and likened each of us to a grain of wheat falling to the earth and dying. Apostle Paul also spoke of putting to death all that is earthly or carnal in our nature. In effect, we are called to be the 'executioner' of our own flesh nature. God does not do it for us. We have to do this to ourselves:

Put to death therefore what is earthly in you: fornication, impurity, passion, evil desire, and covetousness, which is idolatry.

Colossians 3:5 (RSV)

As we deny ourselves, and put our flesh nature to death, then we are like a grain of wheat dying in the ground. As a result it is able to produce far more grains of wheat than the single grain that it was to begin with. So, each believer must deny their own flesh by refusing to give it what it wants. We must be so severe in our self-denial that it is as if our flesh was being "put to death". If we are willing to do that to ourselves, like a seed which dies in the soil, then we will bear fruit:

[24] Truly, truly, I say to you, unless a grain of wheat falls into the earth and dies, it remains alone; but if it dies, it bears much fruit. [25] Whoever loves his life loses it, and whoever hates his life in this world will keep it for eternal life. [26] If anyone serves me, he must follow me; and where I am, there will my servant be also. If anyone serves me, the Father will honor him.

John 12:24-26 (ESV)

Another agricultural analogy which the Bible uses is to speak of pruning. A rose bush or a fruit-bearing shrub needs to be cut back every year in order to produce the maximum harvest the next year. Cutting back the branches enables that which remains to grow more vigorously and to be far more productive.

The same applies to us. If we want to bear fruit in our lives we have to be willing to be 'pruned'. That involves having certain things within our lives cut off, or at least cut back. Jesus compares Himself to a vine and says that we are the branches and that God the Father is the vinedresser or farmer who does the pruning:

"I am the true vine, and my Father is the vinedresser. [2] Every branch of mine that bears no fruit, he takes away, and every branch that does bear fruit he prunes, that it may bear more fruit.

John 15:1-2 (RSV)

Those branches that bear no fruit at all are cut off completely. So they have no future role. But even the branches that do bear some fruit are still pruned. That is done to cause that branch to grow back again and to be even more fruitful next time. So those branches that are pruned do have a future. God wants to take away all those parts of our life, character or possessions which would make us less fruitful if they were allowed to remain.

Preparing for persecution and suffering

We therefore need to start to see struggle, persecution and suffering as normal, rather than objecting to them, as though they were things which ought not to be happening to us. Far too many of us have been presented with a false, watered-down, manmade gospel. It is portrayed as being all about God's love and about enjoying a life of peace and prosperity. Then, when we actually encounter severe difficulties, we are surprised and even resentful, as if God has let us down. We feel He has not lived up to the image we had of Him, based on the way He was described to us.

In fact, far from promising us peace and prosperity, Jesus told us straightforwardly that Christians need to expect division. He also warned us not to be surprised when we encounter hostility from the unbelieving world, from apostate Christians within the churches, and even from our own families. In fact, far from being the exception, such opposition is often at its worst within our own families:

51"Do you suppose that I came to grant peace on earth? I tell you, no, but rather division; 52for from now on five members in one household will be divided, three against two and two against three. 53"They will be divided, father against son and son against father, mother against daughter and daughter against mother, mother-in-law against daughter-in-law and daughter-in-law against mother-in-law."

Luke 12:51-53 (NASB)

He also told us plainly that we would be like sheep in the midst of wolves and that people will persecute us simply for believing in Him, and for being His representatives:

16 "Behold, I am sending you out as sheep in the midst of wolves, so be wise as serpents and innocent as doves. 17 Beware of men, for they will deliver you over to courts and flog you in their synagogues, 18 and you will be dragged before governors and kings for my sake, to bear witness before them and the Gentiles.

Matthew 10: 16-18 (ESV)

21 Brother will deliver brother over to death, and the father his child, and children will rise against parents and have them put to death, 22 and you will be hated by all for my name's sake. But the one who endures to the end will be saved. 23 When they persecute you in one town, flee to the next, for truly, I say to you, you will not have gone through all the towns of Israel before the Son of Man comes. 24 A disciple is not above his teacher, nor a servant above his master.

Matthew 10: 21-24 (ESV)

The point is that the world hates Jesus. Therefore they will automatically hate His followers. We have all got to come to terms with that. Indeed, if we don't ever experience any hostility, rejection and opposition from the world, and from apostate Christians, then it is probably a sign that we are lukewarm and are not doing, or saying, what the Bible tells us to.

23

In other words, it may be that there is nothing in our lives for the unbelieving world to object to, because we are watering down our beliefs so as to make ourselves more acceptable to the world. Instead, we need to do the opposite and aim to be less like the world and more like Jesus. But, remember that if we are, then we will inevitably be persecuted:

¹⁸ 'If the world hates you, be aware that it hated me before it hated you. ¹⁹ If you belonged to the world, the world would love you as its own. Because you do not belong to the world, but I have chosen you out of the world—therefore the world hates you. ²⁰ Remember the word that I said to you, "Servants are not greater than their master." If they persecuted me, they will persecute you; if they kept my word, they will keep yours also. ²¹ But they will do all these things to you on account of my name, because they do not know him who sent me.

John 15:18-21 (NASB)

"I have said all these things to you to keep you from falling away. ² They will put you out of the synagogues. Indeed, the hour is coming when whoever kills you will think he is offering service to God. ³ And they will do these things because they have not known the Father, nor me. ⁴ But I have said these things to you, that when their hour comes you may remember that I told them to you. I did not say these things to you from the beginning, because I was with you.

John 16:1-4 (ESV)

Indeed, all who desire to live godly in Christ Jesus will be persecuted.

2 Timothy 3:12 (NASB)

³¹ Jesus answered them, "Do you now believe? ³² Behold, the hour is coming, indeed it has come, when you will be scattered, each to his own home, and will leave me alone. Yet I am not alone, for the Father is with me. ³³ I have said these things to you, that in me you may have peace. In the world you will have tribulation. But take heart; I have overcome the world."

John 16:31-33 (ESV)

²¹ When they had preached the gospel to that city and had made many disciples, they returned to Lystra and to Iconium and to Antioch, ²² strengthening the souls of the disciples, encouraging them to continue in the faith, and saying that through many tribulations we must enter the kingdom of God.

Acts 14:21-22 (ESV)

²² And now, behold, I am going to Jerusalem, constrained by the Spirit, not knowing what will happen to me there, ²³ except that the Holy Spirit testifies to me in every city that imprisonment and afflictions await me. ²⁴ But I do not account my life of any value nor as precious to myself, if only I may finish my course and the ministry that I received from the Lord Jesus, to testify to the gospel of the grace of God.

Acts 20:22-24 (ESV)

Therefore we really must not be surprised or discouraged when we meet opposition. Nor should we be intimidated by it, or allow ourselves to change our course because of it. Instead, we should endure it all and carry on regardless, blessing and praying for those who persecute us:

and we toil, working with our own hands; when we are reviled, we bless; when we are persecuted, we endure;

1 Corinthians 4:12 (NASB)

A genuine Christian will inevitably be persecuted, but he need not necessarily be defeated. Moreover, he is certainly not forsaken, no matter how severe his difficulties may become. God will always be with us, through it all, and will not allow us to be destroyed by the experiences we face:

[8] we are afflicted in every way, but not crushed; perplexed, but not despairing; [9] persecuted, but not forsaken; struck down, but not destroyed;

2 Corinthians 4:8-9 (NASB)

We can also take encouragement from the fact that Jesus Himself endured a huge amount of hostility from those who hated Him and His message. He is therefore our main example to follow:
Consider him who endured from sinners such hostility against himself, so that you may not grow weary or fainthearted.

Hebrews 12:3 (RSV)

Although any real Christian will certainly be opposed in this world, we can still be at peace, in the sense of being reconciled to the fact that such mistreatment is inevitable. We can take courage from the fact that, no matter how severe it gets, Jesus has already won the main battle. His overall victory is certain. Therefore we already know that we are on the winning side and are contending against an enemy whose eventual defeat is assured. Consider the following sample passages which illustrate Jesus' triumph over Satan and over all that is evil:

[33] "These things I have spoken to you, so that in Me you may have peace In the world you have tribulation, but take courage; I have overcome the world."

John 16:33 (NASB)

He disarmed the principalities and powers and made a public example of them, triumphing over them in him

Colossians 2:15 (RSV)

[12] But when Christ had offered for all time a single sacrifice for sins, he sat down at the right hand of God, [13] then to wait until his enemies should be made a stool for his feet.

Hebrews 10:12-13 (RSV)

[12] Then I turned to see the voice that was speaking to me, and on turning I saw seven golden lampstands, [13] and in the midst of the lampstands one like a son of man, clothed with a long robe and with a golden girdle round his breast; [14] his head and his hair were white as white wool, white as snow; his eyes were like a flame of fire, [15] his feet were like burnished bronze, refined as in a furnace, and his voice was like the sound of many waters; [16] in his right hand he held seven stars, from his mouth issued a sharp two-edged sword, and his face was like the sun shining in full strength.

Revelation 1:12-16 (RSV)

Then the seventh angel blew his trumpet, and there were loud voices in heaven, saying, "The kingdom of the world has become the kingdom of our Lord and of his Christ, and he shall reign for ever and ever."

Revelation 11:15 (RSV)

[7] Now war arose in heaven, Michael and his angels fighting against the dragon; and the dragon and his angels fought, [8] but they were defeated and there was no longer any place for them in heaven. [9] And the great dragon was thrown down, that ancient serpent, who is called the Devil and Satan, the deceiver of the whole world—he was thrown down to the earth, and his angels were thrown down with him. [10] And I heard a loud voice in heaven, saying, "Now the salvation and the power and the kingdom of our God and the authority of his Christ have come, for the accuser of our brethren has been thrown down, who accuses them day and night before our God.

Revelation 12:7-10 (RSV)

[11] Then I saw heaven opened, and behold, a white horse! He who sat upon it is called Faithful and True, and in righteousness he judges and makes war. [12] His eyes are like a flame of fire, and on his head are many diadems; and he has a name inscribed which no one knows but himself. [13] He is clad in a robe dipped in blood, and the name by which he is called is The Word of God.

[14] And the armies of heaven, arrayed in fine linen, white and pure, followed him on white horses. [15] From his mouth issues a sharp sword with which to smite the nations, and he will rule them with a rod of iron; he will tread the wine press of the fury of the wrath of God the Almighty. [16] On his robe and on his thigh he has a name inscribed, King of kings and Lord of lords.

Revelation 19:11-16 (RSV)

And the devil who deceived them was thrown into the lake of fire and brimstone, where the beast and the false prophet are also; and they will be tormented day and night forever and ever.

Revelation 20:10 (NASB)

While we wait for Jesus to commence His reign as King over all the Earth, we can be completely sure that, no matter what we are called upon to face or endure in the meantime, nothing can ever separate us from Him. All sorts of things may happen to us in this life, including death as a martyr.

However, He is still with us, even as we go through those experiences. Jesus does not promise to keep us *from* suffering or death, but He does promise to be *with us* during those bad experiences. We will not be separated from Him or have to endure the ordeals on our own:

³³Who will bring a charge against God's elect? God is the one who justifies; ³⁴who is the one who condemns? Christ Jesus is He who died, yes, rather who was raised, who is at the right hand of God, who also intercedes for us. ³⁵Who will separate us from the love of Christ? Will tribulation, or distress, or persecution, or famine, or nakedness, or peril, or sword? ³⁶Just as it is written, "for your sake we are being put to death all day long; we were considered as sheep to be slaughtered." ³⁷But in all these things we overwhelmingly conquer through Him who loved us. ³⁸For I am convinced that neither death, nor life, nor angels, nor principalities, nor things present, nor things to come, nor powers, ³⁹nor height, nor depth, nor any other created thing, will be able to separate us from the love of God, which is in Christ Jesus our Lord.

Romans 8:33-39 (NASB)

Endurance and perseverance

The character qualities of endurance and perseverance are not widely sought after. Perhaps that is because the only way to develop them is for us to endure and persevere regularly until we eventually get good at it. Doing that is not pleasant, but there is no other way to develop the ability to endure and persevere.

Therefore, if we are wise, we will pray for these qualities to be developed in our lives, even though the learning process will be painful, because it is undoubtedly worth it. We should therefore pray, as Paul did, to be strengthened in endurance and patience:

¹¹ May you be strengthened with all power, according to his glorious might, for all endurance and patience with joy, ¹² giving thanks to the Father, who has qualified you to share in the inheritance of the saints in light. ¹³ He has delivered us from the domain of darkness and transferred us to the kingdom of his beloved Son,

Colossians 1:11-13 (ESV)

The ability to endure things patiently, and to persevere come what may, are qualities which God wants us to have. They are two of the *fruits* of the Holy Spirit. That means they are not *gifts*. God does not *give* us patience, endurance or perseverance in the way that He gives us natural abilities or spiritual gifts. They have to be grown in us as fruits over long periods of time.

We can, of course, ask for God's help in developing these qualities, but it is still our responsibility to grow them. In other words, God will not give us Christian character as a gift. It cannot be imputed to us instantly, as Jesus' righteousness is transferred to us at the moment when we are justified.

We must choose to pursue these character qualities and to develop them over time. First of all, we must set our minds to want these things and to be determined to get them, because the Bible repeatedly tells us that we need these qualities:

For you have need of endurance, so that when you have done the will of God you may receive what is promised.
Hebrews 10:36 (ESV)

Be on the alert, stand firm in the faith, act like men, be strong.
1 Corinthians 16:13 (NASB)

for now we really live, if you stand firm in the Lord.
1Thessalonians 3:8 (NASB)

⁹ If anyone has an ear, let him hear:
¹⁰ If anyone is to be taken captive,
* to captivity he goes;*
if anyone is to be slain with the sword,
* with the sword must he be slain.*
Here is a call for the endurance and faith of the saints.
Revelation 13:9-10 (ESV)

Note that in each of the passages quoted above the responsibility is on us, not on God, to endure, stand firm, be strong etc. He will help us, but He will not do it for us. But we can still be encouraged, because these qualities really can be developed. It is not a hopeless task. We have Jesus' example to follow first of all.

We also have the example of all the people of faith who have gone before us and who have endured severe trials and achieved great things by doing so. The writer of the letter to the Hebrews describes these people who have gone ahead of us as being a 'cloud of witnesses'. That possibly implies that they are even able to see us and are cheering us on:

Therefore, since we are surrounded by so great a cloud of witnesses, let us also lay aside every weight, and sin which clings so closely, and let us run with endurance the race that is set before us, ² looking to Jesus, the founder and perfecter of our faith, who for the joy that was set before him endured the cross,

despising the shame, and is seated at the right hand of the throne of God. [3]
Consider him who endured from sinners such hostility against himself, so that
you may not grow weary or faint-hearted. [4] *In your struggle against sin you have*
not yet resisted to the point of shedding your blood.

Hebrews 12:1-4 (ESV)

Nobody has had to endure more than Jesus, or been more hated than He was. He
literally withstood everything that Satan himself had to throw at Him. Most of us
are only ever going to encounter much weaker and lower-ranking demons. Yet
Jesus endured suffering, while He was on this Earth in human form, just as we
must. We can do likewise with our own suffering, especially if we realise that we
need His help to persevere and ask Him for that help.

I don't often include quotations, other than from the Bible. However, this next
one is worth reflecting on. It was said by Calvin Coolidge, the 30th President of
the United States. He puts very well the vital importance of persistence if we are
to succeed in anything:

"Nothing in the world can take the place of persistence.
Talent will not;
nothing is more common than unsuccessful men with great talent.
Genius will not;
unrewarded genius is almost a proverb.
Education will not;
The world is full of educated derelicts.
Persistence, determination alone are omnipotent......."

President Calvin Coolidge

Some of the beneficial effects of hardship

Though it is hard to believe this while you are going through a period of hardship,
there really are many benefits that come from it. Some of these come to you
personally. Others are about making you more effective for the sake of others.
Therefore the benefit is also received by the cause we serve.

We become better soldiers and ambassadors for Jesus and achieve more for Him.
Jesus' half-brother, James, tells us that trials produce steadfastness in us. That,
in turn, leads to all sorts of further benefits. The end result is that we become
complete and lacking in nothing:

[2] *Count it all joy, my brothers, when you meet trials of various kinds,* [3] *for you*
know that the testing of your faith produces steadfastness. [4] *And let*
steadfastness have its full effect, that you may be perfect and complete, lacking
in nothing.

James 1:2-4 (ESV)

Hardship is also one of the most effective ways God has to get us to come back to Him when we have been wandering away or growing lukewarm. When times are easy we tend to forget God and become preoccupied with ourselves or our own ambitions or possessions. However, a dose of adversity soon brings us running back to God. It makes us rely on Him and become closer to Him:

⁴ But I am the Lord your God
  from the land of Egypt;
  you know no God but me,
  and besides me there is no savior.
⁵ It was I who knew you in the wilderness,
  in the land of drought;
⁶ but when they had grazed, they became full,
  they were filled, and their heart was lifted up;
  therefore they forgot me.
                    Hosea 13:4-6 (ESV)

Apostle Paul says that suffering produces endurance. That then produces character, which in turn produces hope. That hope then protects us from many things. Hope is therefore very important. That is why, in Paul's letters to the Ephesians and Thessalonians, we learn that hope is the 'helmet of salvation', which Paul tells us to wear.

By that he firstly means the specific hope that we are going to be saved and have eternal life. But he also means hope in general, in its fuller, broader sense. In both of those ways hope is the best protection for our minds. It keeps us from depression and despair and therefore makes all sorts of other things achievable.

We will also receive rewards at the Judgment Seat of Christ (see Book Four) for the level of endurance that we display in this life. Therefore another benefit of hardship is that it qualifies us to receive those rewards, such as the *'crown of life'* to which James refers:

Blessed is the man who remains steadfast under trial, for when he has stood the test he will receive the crown of life, which God has promised to those who love him.
                    James 1:12 (ESV)

Whatever circumstances we have to face, and however hard they may be, God wants us to learn to be *content*, even while in those circumstances

Another character quality which every disciple needs to seek to develop in himself is *contentment*. That is the ability to be calm, at peace and reconciled to facing any circumstances that we are called upon to deal with. Few people have endured more than Apostle Paul. Yet, he tells us that he learned to be content in whatever situation he faced. However, it is important to note the word 'learned'. Paul is not saying that he was always content, from the outset.

On the contrary, he is saying that he had to gradually learn how to be content, over a period of time. That should encourage all of us, who are not presently content, to believe that such contentment is truly possible. We can achieve it if we really want it, and are willing to persist in seeking for it:

[10] I rejoiced in the Lord greatly that now at length you have revived your concern for me. You were indeed concerned for me, but you had no opportunity. [11] Not that I am speaking of being in need, for I have learned in whatever situation I am to be content. [12] I know how to be brought low, and I know how to abound. In any and every circumstance, I have learned the secret of facing plenty and hunger, abundance and need. [13] I can do all things through him who strengthens me.

Philippians 4:10-13 (ESV)

When we become a Christian we also have a duty to learn the Bible thoroughly and to develop a broad and accurate knowledge of doctrine

When we become a Christian and set out on our life as a disciple we suddenly acquire a wide package of duties and responsibilities. It is as if we had joined the Army and become subject to military law and regulations. By that I do not mean that we should operate in a disciplined way and study diligently *in order to be* saved. We are to do so because we have been saved.

In other words, we are not justified as a result of our works. We are called upon to do good works as a consequence of our having already been justified. So, from the moment of conversion onwards, our greatest duty, and need, is to learn to understand and obey God's written Word, the Bible.

The true extent of your love for Him and your devotion to Him is shown by your devotion to reading, learning and abiding by the Bible. You do not love Jesus one gram more than you love and obey His Word. And you do not know Him any more than you know His Word. There is no use pretending otherwise. The Bible makes this very clear:

[21] Whoever has my commandments and keeps them, he it is who loves me. And he who loves me will be loved by my Father, and I will love him and manifest myself to him." [22] Judas (not Iscariot) said to him, "Lord, how is it that you will manifest yourself to us, and not to the world?" [23] Jesus answered him, "If anyone loves me, he will keep my word, and my Father will love him, and we will come to him and make our home with him.

31

²⁴ Whoever does not love me does not keep my words. And the word that you hear is not mine but the Father's who sent me.

John 14: 21-24 (ESV)

¹⁴ You are my friends if you do what I command you.
John 15:14 (ESV)

³ And by this we may be sure that we know him, if we keep his commandments. ⁴ He who says "I know him" but disobeys his commandments is a liar, and the truth is not in him; ⁵ but whoever keeps his word, in him truly love for God is perfected. By this we may be sure that we are in him: ⁶ he who says he abides in him ought to walk in the same way in which he walked.

1 John 2:3-6 (RSV)

⁸ This Book of the Law shall not depart from your mouth, but you shall meditate on it day and night, so that you may be careful to do according to all that is written in it. For then you will make your way prosperous, and then you will have good success.

Joshua 1:8 (ESV)

We are commanded to be obedient to Jesus and that means knowing and obeying His written Word. But how can we possibly do that unless we study it carefully? There is no other way. Therefore we are meant to become firmly rooted in the faith by knowing and obeying the whole Bible. That is also how we will avoid being led astray by false teaching and false prophets, of whom there are very many, especially in our own day:

Therefore as you have received Christ Jesus the Lord, so walk in Him, ⁷ having been firmly rooted and now being built up in Him and established in your faith, just as you were instructed, and overflowing with gratitude.⁸ See to it that no one takes you captive through philosophy and empty deception, according to the tradition of men, according to the elementary principles of the world, rather than according to Christ.

Colossians 2:6-8 (NASB)

It is your duty therefore to obey all of Jesus' commands, including those given to us via the prophets and apostles, because every one of those was writing under God's instruction and guidance. Therefore, what they said is what God was saying. You are also responsible for making sure that you are not deceived by false doctrines. As Paul says above, we are to "see to it".

You might perhaps imagine that Jesus would hold us blameless if we are deceived by false teachers. However, that is not necessarily so, because proper diligence on our part is able to prevent us from being deceived in the first place. Any person who sincerely and diligently studies God's Word will not be led astray.

32

At any rate, even if they are deceived for a while, it will not be permanent, because diligent study of God's Word will eventually identify and correct the error. However, that will only be the case if you are devoted to the Word of God itself, rather than to your own favourite teacher or denomination. However good they may be, they are not authoritative and they can never be relied on.

Only God's written Word is totally reliable. Everyone else, and everything else, is flawed, or potentially flawed. They can all lead you astray if you follow them and rely on them, rather than on what the Bible says. Therefore, as Paul says, you must "see to it" that you know the whole Bible really well, so that nobody is capable of deceiving you, or at least not for long. Be like the people of Berea who checked everything that any teacher told them by looking to see whether it was in the Scriptures.

They did so even if that teacher was Apostle Paul. By contrast, there have always been, and still are, many people who don't want to hear the real truth of what the Bible says. Such people prefer a pleasant, easy, reassuring message. They automatically reject anything which sounds critical of their lifestyles, or which calls upon them to repent. They prefer to believe comforting lies, rather than an uncomfortable truth. Isaiah spoke of such people:

⁹ For they are a rebellious people,
  lying children,
children unwilling to hear
  the instruction of the Lord;
¹⁰ who say to the seers, "Do not see,"
  and to the prophets, "Do not prophesy to us what is right;
speak to us smooth things,
  prophesy illusions,
¹¹ leave the way, turn aside from the path,
  let us hear no more about the Holy One of Israel."
¹² Therefore thus says the Holy One of Israel,
"Because you despise this word
  and trust in oppression and perverseness
  and rely on them,
¹³ therefore this iniquity shall be to you
  like a breach in a high wall, bulging out, and about to collapse,
  whose breaking comes suddenly, in an instant;
¹⁴ and its breaking is like that of a potter's vessel
  that is smashed so ruthlessly
that among its fragments not a shard is found
  with which to take fire from the hearth,
  or to dip up water out of the cistern."
                    Isaiah 30:9-14 (ESV)

What it means to "enter by the narrow gate" and to stay on the hard road, rather than take the broad, easy way

Another analogy which the Bible uses to describe the life of a real disciple is to speak of it as going through a narrow gate. That represents being saved. It then refers to continuing along a hard, narrow way. This represents the hardships faced by a disciple, rather than diverting onto any easy, broad path. The life of a real disciple is often difficult. Tough choices have to be made to deny oneself and to do one's duty, even when one really doesn't want to.

By contrast, the broad path, on which all unbelievers and false, compromised churchgoers travel, is very easy. On the broad path people can do whatever they want and always take the easy option. However, a disciple has to choose to do what Jesus wants, which is much harder:

[13] "Enter by the narrow gate; for the gate is wide and the way is easy, that leads to destruction, and those who enter by it are many. [14] For the gate is narrow and the way is hard, that leads to life, and those who find it are few.
Matthew 7:13-14 (RSV)

The narrow gate represents entering into the Christian life to begin with. It means believing the true Gospel, as set out in the Bible, rather than the lukewarm, compromised, counterfeit gospel which so many churches present to us. Their man-made gospel is deliberately designed to be easy. It basically amounts to: *"Jesus loves you and wants you to love Him"*.

There is little or no emphasis on sin, or God's judgment, or our need to repent and get right with God. Neither do they focus on the cost and hardship involved in a life of real discipleship. Such a realistic and accurate biblical message is not popular. Therefore a worldly church leader will not preach it. He fears being criticised for the things he says. He also fears offending people and therefore losing members. In particular, he fears losing their financial support.

So, vast numbers of people enter churches (at least in the West) with a very inadequate and inaccurate idea of what the Gospel is. Many of them are not saved at all. They have not been shown the narrow gate and they have not entered by it. That therefore puts them on the wrong path from the start. But, even if they do begin well, merely to *enter* by the narrow gate is not enough.

If we want to develop into a strong disciple we must then *stay on the hard way* and not give in to the temptation to leave it in favour of the easier and broader path which leads to destruction. It is your responsibility to find out whether you are on the hard path and, if you are, then to stay on it and not veer off onto the easy way. The responsibility for all of that cannot be delegated to anybody else. However, God will, of course, help you to stay faithful, if you are willing to be helped.

CHAPTER 2

A CLOSER LOOK AT HOW GOD DEVELOPS US AS DISCIPLES

Let us know; let us press on to know the Lord;.......
Hosea 6:3(a) (ESV)

⁶ Therefore, as you received Christ Jesus the Lord, so walk in him, ⁷ rooted and built up in him and established in the faith, just as you were taught, abounding in thanksgiving. ⁸ See to it that no one takes you captive by philosophy and empty deceit, according to human tradition, according to the elemental spirits of the world, and not according to Christ.
Colossians 2:6-8 (ESV)

Take heed lest your heart be deceived, and you turn aside and serve other gods and worship them,
Deuteronomy 11:16 (RSV)

And he did evil, because he did not prepare his heart to seek the Lord.
2 Chronicles 12:14 (NKJV)

then take heed lest you forget the Lord, who brought you out of the land of Egypt, out of the house of bondage.
Deuteronomy 6:12(a) (RSV)

²³ And he said to all, "If anyone would come after me, let him deny himself and take up his cross daily and follow me. ²⁴ For whoever would save his life will lose it, but whoever loses his life for my sake will save it. ²⁵ For what does it profit a man if he gains the whole world and loses or forfeits himself? ²⁶ For whoever is ashamed of me and of my words, of him will the Son of Man be ashamed when he comes in his glory and the glory of the Father and of the holy angels.
Luke 9:23-26 (ESV)

²¹ When they had preached the gospel to that city and had made many disciples, they returned to Lystra and to Iconium and to Antioch, ²² strengthening the souls of the disciples, encouraging them to continue in the faith, and saying that through many tribulations we must enter the kingdom of God.
Acts 14:21-22 (ESV)

¹ I therefore, a prisoner for the Lord, beg you to lead a life worthy of the calling to which you have been called, ² with all lowliness and meekness, with patience, forbearing one another in love,
Ephesians 4:1-2 (RSV)

He who has my commandments and keeps them, he it is who loves me; and he who loves me will be loved by my Father, and I will love him and manifest myself to him."

John 14:21 (RSV)

[8] For we do not want you to be ignorant, brethren, of the affliction we experienced in Asia; for we were so utterly, unbearably crushed that we despaired of life itself. [9] Why, we felt that we had received the sentence of death; but that was to make us rely not on ourselves but on God who raises the dead;

2 Corinthians 1:8-9 (RSV)

And I am sure that he who began a good work in you will bring it to completion at the day of Jesus Christ.

Philippians 1:6 (RSV)

Of all those who claim to be Christians, not everyone is genuine. We are not all real disciples

Another point about which we need to become realistic is the fact that not everybody who claims to be a Christian really is one. Many people are false. Many are deceivers and even more are deceived. So, we cannot safely assume that everybody who goes to church, or even all those who lead churches, are real Christians.

Many are not and it is your personal responsibility to identify those who are false and to avoid coming under their influence. One day Jesus will put the question beyond doubt by identifying all such false people. Then they will be publicly rejected by Him:

[21] "Not everyone who says to me, 'Lord, Lord,' shall enter the kingdom of heaven, but he who does the will of my Father who is in heaven. [22] On that day many will say to me, 'Lord, Lord, did we not prophesy in your name, and cast out demons in your name, and do many mighty works in your name?' [23] And then will I declare to them, 'I never knew you; depart from me, you evildoers.' [24] "Everyone then who hears these words of mine and does them will be like a wise man who built his house upon the rock; [25] and the rain fell, and the floods came, and the winds blew and beat upon that house, but it did not fall, because it had been founded on the rock. [26] And everyone who hears these words of mine and does not do them will be like a foolish man who built his house upon the sand; [27] and the rain fell, and the floods came, and the winds blew and beat against that house, and it fell; and great was the fall of it."

Matthew 7:21-27 (RSV)

There are many people who appear to be real, but they are not genuine. They may say the right things, but they do not truly believe it themselves:

36

Hear this, O house of Jacob,
who are called by the name of Israel,
and who came from the waters of Judah,
who swear by the name of the LORD
and confess the God of Israel,
but not in truth or right.
Isaiah 48:1 (ESV)

Of the people who claim to be Christians, they are not all real disciples. Many people in churches are false and you are required to try to learn how to identify them. You are to do so primarily by examining their fruit. You are also meant to learn how to identify their false teaching, by constantly comparing what they say with what the Bible says. There is literally no church member or leader, however eminent, upon whom you can safely and uncritically rely.

Whoever they may be, you are meant to check their teaching against the Bible. Moreover, if they don't like you doing that, then that in itself tells you something very important about them. It would probably be your cue to leave that church and go elsewhere. Consider also this very sobering passage from Luke, in which Jesus speaks of the need to enter by the narrow door and warns us against being complacent:

[22] He went on his way through towns and villages, teaching and journeying toward Jerusalem. [23] And someone said to him, "Lord, will those who are saved be few?" And he said to them, [24] "Strive to enter through the narrow door. For many, I tell you, will seek to enter and will not be able. [25] When once the master of the house has risen and shut the door, and you begin to stand outside and to knock at the door, saying, 'Lord, open to us,' then he will answer you, 'I do not know where you come from.' [26] Then you will begin to say, 'We ate and drank in your presence, and you taught in our streets.' [27] But he will say, 'I tell you, I do not know where you come from. Depart from me, all you workers of evil!' [28] In that place there will be weeping and gnashing of teeth, when you see Abraham and Isaac and Jacob and all the prophets in the kingdom of God but you yourselves cast out. [29] And people will come from east and west, and from north and south, and recline at table in the kingdom of God. [30] And behold, some are last who will be first, and some are first who will be last."
Luke 13:22-30 (ESV)

We see from the above passage that many who assume they are Christians, and thus saved, will one day discover that they are not, or even that they *never were*. They will hear Jesus tell them to depart, because He does not know where they come from. In other words, they do not belong to Him.

There is a high cost involved in being a genuine disciple. We must be realistic about that and be willing to pay that price.

Being a genuine disciple involves paying a high price. At any rate, the cost of real discipleship is far higher than most of us have been told to expect. Therefore we need to be much more realistic about that cost and be willing to pay whatever it takes. The truth is that Jesus makes very high demands of us at times. Here is a passage where Jesus makes these points in His own graphic way:

18 Now when Jesus saw a crowd around him, he gave orders to go over to the other side. 19 And a scribe came up and said to him, "Teacher, I will follow you wherever you go." 20 And Jesus said to him, "Foxes have holes, and birds of the air have nests, but the Son of Man has nowhere to lay his head." 21 Another of the disciples said to him, "Lord, let me first go and bury my father." 22 And Jesus said to him, "Follow me, and leave the dead to bury their own dead."
Matthew 8:18-22 (ESV)

Jesus means that when we choose to follow Him we need to give up any idea of having any rights, entitlements or expectations. We must hand over our entire lives to Him and follow Him, wherever He goes and whatever it costs. Consider this very frank statement by Jesus in Luke's gospel about the high level of commitment involved in true discipleship. He speaks of the need to 'hate' our father and mother etc. He does not mean that literally. It is a figure of speech.

We know that, because the fifth commandment tells us all to honour our father and mother. What Jesus means is simply that other people must all be put into second place, behind Him. He wants us to count the cost of following Him realistically, ahead of time, and to resolve to be willing to pay it, before we even begin. In fact, from the outset, we must renounce all that we have and see it as His property. We must then focus on following Him as our top priority, ahead of everything else and everyone else:

25 Now great crowds accompanied him, and he turned and said to them, 26 "If anyone comes to me and does not hate his own father and mother and wife and children and brothers and sisters, yes, and even his own life, he cannot be my disciple. 27 Whoever does not bear his own cross and come after me cannot be my disciple. 28 For which of you, desiring to build a tower, does not first sit down and count the cost, whether he has enough to complete it? 29 Otherwise, when he has laid a foundation and is not able to finish, all who see it begin to mock him, 30 saying, 'This man began to build and was not able to finish.' 31 Or what king, going out to encounter another king in war, will not sit down first and deliberate whether he is able with ten thousand to meet him who comes against him with twenty thousand? 32 And if not, while the other is yet a great way off, he sends a delegation and asks for terms of peace. 33 So therefore, any one of you who does not renounce all that he has cannot be my disciple.
Luke 14:25-33 (ESV)

For many of us the hardest thing to give up and to hand over to Jesus is our money and possessions. They can exert a terrifically strong hold over us. Nevertheless, we must be willing to give it all to Him and consider it all as being at His disposal. Indeed, some of us will be called upon to literally give it all away:

[18] And a ruler asked him, "Good Teacher, what must I do to inherit eternal life?" [19] And Jesus said to him, "Why do you call me good? No one is good except God alone. [20] You know the commandments: 'Do not commit adultery, Do not murder, Do not steal, Do not bear false witness, Honor your father and mother.'" [21] And he said, "All these I have kept from my youth." [22] When Jesus heard this, he said to him, "One thing you still lack. Sell all that you have and distribute to the poor, and you will have treasure in heaven; and come, follow me." [23] But when he heard these things, he became very sad, for he was extremely rich.

[24] Jesus, seeing that he had become sad, said, "How difficult it is for those who have wealth to enter the kingdom of God! [25] For it is easier for a camel to go through the eye of a needle than for a rich person to enter the kingdom of God." [26] Those who heard it said, "Then who can be saved?" [27] But he said, "What is impossible with man is possible with God." [28] And Peter said, "See, we have left our homes and followed you." [29] And he said to them, "Truly, I say to you, there is no one who has left house or wife or brothers or parents or children, for the sake of the kingdom of God, [30] who will not receive many times more in this time, and in the age to come eternal life."

Luke 18:18-30 (ESV)

Jesus did not come to bring peace to this present age. On the contrary, following Him and staying true to His Word will result in conflict and trouble.

Being a genuine disciple of Jesus Christ does bring you peace. However, that means in the Hebrew sense of being at peace within, or despite, difficult circumstances. The peace that Jesus gives us does not mean the absence of such difficulties. The Hebrew word for peace is *'Shalom'*. It is very different in meaning from the Greek word for peace, from which we get the girls' name *'Irene'*.

Shalom is a much broader and deeper word. It involves deep, overall wholesomeness, contentment, success and prosperity. One can experience Shalom even in the midst of severe difficulty or conflict. It is a much deeper and more far reaching concept than what is meant by the Greek word from which we get the word Irene.

The Greek concept of peace, which has been adopted by the entire Western world, simply means the absence of war, conflict, hostility etc. That is a very narrow definition of peace. So, a person can have peace in the sense of *Shalom* even in the midst of war, famine, conflict, persecution etc. But there would still not be peace in the Greek sense, i.e. *'Irene'*. In short, Jesus does promise His disciples that it is possible to achieve *Shalom* type peace. However, He does not promise *Irene* type peace.

Jesus spoke of us needing to take up our own cross, i.e. to carry a metaphorical cross and follow Him. He actually said this long before he Himself had to carry a cross. He was, evidently, referring to the many other people who were publicly crucified by the Romans. It was a regular sight. The image of someone carrying a cross would therefore have been familiar to His listeners before they ever saw Him having to do it.

The image is of each disciple preparing to die and being willing to put his own flesh to death in order to follow Jesus. That is a valid expression of what life as a Christian can sometimes be. It is not all easy and 'peaceful', i.e. in the Greek sense of peace:

34 "Do not think that I have come to bring peace to the earth. I have not come to bring peace, but a sword. 35 For I have come to set a man against his father, and a daughter against her mother, and a daughter-in-law against her mother-in-law. 36 And a person's enemies will be those of his own household. 37 Whoever loves father or mother more than me is not worthy of me, and whoever loves son or daughter more than me is not worthy of me. 38 And whoever does not take his cross and follow me is not worthy of me. 39 Whoever finds his life will lose it, and whoever loses his life for my sake will find it.

Matthew 10:34-39 (ESV)

It is important to get our expectations right as we enter the Christian life as a new believer. Too many of us have been given a false impression of Christianity by churches which try to present an attractive, positive image of what being a Christian is like. Therefore they make no mention of sacrifice, hardship, obedience, self-denial and so on. Those aspects of the Christian life are not seen as being easily marketable. They fear that to tell the plain truth about what the Bible actually says about being a disciple may put people off.

However, we have no right to alter or 'improve' the message so as to get more people to accept Christianity. If we do that we are just creating a false gospel and are not helping anybody. Any leader who preaches a lukewarm, easy gospel is not seeking to make disciples. He is just looking for more members for his church, without any regard as to whether or not they are becoming real and mature followers of Jesus.

It is the duty of a disciple to be "salt and light" in this world

Another of the many purposes and objectives of a real disciple is that they should learn how to be both "salt and light" in this lost world. Each disciple is like a lamp. We are supposed to bring light wherever we go, lighting up the darkness of sin and ignorance that is in the lives and minds of those around us. That involves being an influence for good and helping others to know the truth, but our duty as disciples extends beyond imparting truth to those around us.

We are also to be of practical help to the poor, the sick, the elderly, the weak, the dying and so on. Therefore, as well as preaching the Gospel, a disciple is also meant to make a difference to the world around them by helping to meet the material needs of those with whom he comes into contact. Here is how Jesus Himself made this point:

[13] "You are the salt of the earth, but if salt has lost its taste, how shall its saltiness be restored? It is no longer good for anything except to be thrown out and trampled under people's feet.

[14] "You are the light of the world. A city set on a hill cannot be hidden. [15] Nor do people light a lamp and put it under a basket, but on a stand, and it gives light to all in the house. [16] In the same way, let your light shine before others, so that they may see your good works and give glory to your Father who is in heaven.
Matthew 5:13-16 (ESV)

So, we are meant to share the Gospel and make a practical difference in the lives of the poor and needy. It is not one or the other. That needs to be emphasised because too many of us opt for doing only one of those things, at most, and then ignore the other. For example, some will focus solely on teaching and preaching, but they place little or no emphasis on doing practical things to help others.

Conversely, many people focus on giving such practical help, but they downplay the Gospel-proclaiming aspect of being a disciple. It is not up to us to choose those parts of Jesus' commands which we prefer. We cannot focus exclusively on those, ignoring the other counterbalancing things which He also said. If we do so we become at least unbalanced, and potentially even false.

For example many people follow the so called "social gospel". They under-emphasise, or even ignore, anything which has to do with preaching about the need to repent and believe in Jesus in order to be saved. Instead, they focus solely on helping people practically, or on working for charities.

That one-sided approach is not valid. It is a rejection of what Jesus also said about being a light. That has to involve spreading the truth about the entirety of God's Word in a balanced and accurate way. A disciple cannot pick and choose which of God's commands are to be obeyed and which can be put to one side.

One of Jesus' intentions for His disciples is to refine them, just as a jeweller smelts and purifies silver by exposing it to great heat. He is doing that now, in this life, but He will complete it at the Judgment Seat

Jesus intends to refine us, just as a jeweller smelts precious metals to purify them and to separate them from the worthless dross which is mixed in with them. He is doing this now during our lives. However, when Jesus returns in His glorified resurrection body and judges us at the Judgment Seat of Christ He will complete the refining process.

At the Judgment Seat He will assess our lives and He will take away all that remains of the dross. He will also burn up all the wood, hay and stubble. Then he will see how much, or how little, of value is left intact, after that process of smelting or burning is complete. Here are two passages which refer to this future event. The first is from Malachi:

² "But who can endure the day of His coming? And who can stand when He appears? For He is like a refiner's fire and like fullers' soap. ³ He will sit as a smelter and purifier of silver, and He will purify the sons of Levi and refine them like gold and silver, so that they may present to the LORD offerings in righteousness.

Malachi 3:2-3 (NASB)

We are all going to be judged in the end and we see here that one of the main criteria Jesus will use for judging us is how much real precious metal is left behind when the dross in our lives is burned away. The gold and silver represent those things we did in obedience to His Word, i.e. the things God wanted us to do and which were done in the right manner and with the right motives. The dross is everything else, i.e. the wilful, selfish, impetuous, carnal things we did which were not God's will and which He did not ask us to do. See how apostle Paul develops this theme:

¹⁰ According to the grace of God given to me, like a skilled master builder I laid a foundation, and someone else is building upon it. Let each one take care how he builds upon it. ¹¹ For no one can lay a foundation other than that which is laid, which is Jesus Christ. ¹² Now if anyone builds on the foundation with gold, silver, precious stones, wood, hay, straw— ¹³ each one's work will become manifest, for the Day will disclose it, because it will be revealed by fire, and the fire will test what sort of work each one has done. ¹⁴ If the work that anyone has built on the foundation survives, he will receive a reward. ¹⁵ If anyone's work is burned up, he will suffer loss, though he himself will be saved, but only as through fire.

1 Corinthians 3:10-15 (ESV)

At the Judgment Seat of Christ each of us will be individually rewarded, or not rewarded, praised or rebuked, and promoted or demoted. Some of the key factors that Jesus will evaluate in His role as our Judge are the extent to which we have been salt and light, our obedience, our faithfulness, how much fruit we bore and so on. See my Book Four for a much fuller discussion of the many and varied criteria He will use in judging us.

We already know in advance that we are going to be judged in this way by Jesus. Doesn't it therefore make sense to try, as far as possible, to bring that judgment process forward into the present? We can do that by judging ourselves frankly, in comparison to God's Word. Then we can simply alter our attitudes and behaviour now, wherever we see that they are wrong.

It can also come by praying for Jesus to expose your errors and sins, here and now, so that you can tackle them and repent of them before you get to the Judgment Seat. If you do that, and keep on doing it, then it may be difficult and uncomfortable for you now, but you will gain greatly on the Day when Jesus Christ judges you. You will already have dealt with and removed some of the dross or the wood, hay and stubble in your life, ahead of the Judgment Seat of Christ. Then there will be less for Jesus to have to burn up and less need for Him to have to rebuke you.

That self-examination must surely make sense. It is also enlightened self-interest for us to seek as much correction and constructive criticism as we can get here and now, so that we can change even more thoroughly. Then we will bear more fruit, amass more "gold, silver and precious stones" and receive a greater reward than we would otherwise have got. Whatever rewards we receive at the Judgment Seat of Christ, whether small, or large, or nothing at all, they will be eternal.

However, any embarrassment or discomfort we receive now by being corrected and changing our behaviour is only temporary. Therefore, one would be a fool to avoid such self-judgment and correction now, merely because we find it difficult or unpleasant. It is the eternal outcome that matters, not the temporary difficulties or embarrassments of this life.

When you become a disciple God will begin to treat you as His own child. That means He will discipline you and even punish you. He does it for your own good, to help you to grow up.

There is today a misguided over-emphasis on God's love in many Western churches. There is also a misunderstanding of what His love really means. That error causes many of us to assume that God would never rebuke or discipline a Christian. Actually, the opposite is the case. The very fact that God disciplines us is one of the things that proves that we really belong to Him and are His children.

No adult would go around chastising other people's children, but no right-thinking parent would fail to discipline their own child. Therefore, whenever you see an adult disciplining a wayward child, it indicates that they are related as parent and child. You would never think of it as evidence that they are not related.

Likewise, if we are real Christians, we need to expect to be treated as God's children. That means being disciplined and punished by Him when our attitudes and behaviour require it. If He did not do these things it would actually indicate that we are not His children:

⁵ Know then in your heart that, as a man disciplines his son, the Lord your God disciplines you. ⁶ So you shall keep the commandments of the Lord your God by walking in his ways and by fearing him.
Deuteronomy 8:5-6 (ESV)

⁵ And have you forgotten the exhortation that addresses you as sons?
"My son, do not regard lightly the discipline of the Lord,
nor be weary when reproved by him.
⁶ For the Lord disciplines the one he loves,
and chastises every son whom he receives."
⁷ It is for discipline that you have to endure. God is treating you as sons. For what son is there whom his father does not discipline? ⁸ If you are left without discipline, in which all have participated, then you are illegitimate children and not sons. ⁹ Besides this, we have had earthly fathers who disciplined us and we respected them. Shall we not much more be subject to the Father of spirits and live? ¹⁰ For they disciplined us for a short time as it seemed best to them, but he disciplines us for our good, that we may share his holiness. ¹¹ For the moment all discipline seems painful rather than pleasant, but later it yields the peaceful fruit of righteousness to those who have been trained by it.
Hebrews 12:5-11 (ESV)

So, the very fact that God disciplines us is proof that He does love us, because He knows we need it and benefit from it:
Blessed is the man whom thou dost chasten, O LORD,
and whom thou dost teach out of thy law
Psalm 94:12 (RSV)

"----that he might humble you and test you, to do you good in the end"
Deuteronomy 8:16(b) (RSV)

Accordingly, we need to expect God's discipline and cooperate with it. We should repent voluntarily, even before we are disciplined by Him for the wrong things that we do:

Those whom I love, I reprove and discipline, so be zealous and repent.
Revelation 3:19 (ESV)

44

God is very careful in His disciplining of us. He will chastise us, and sometimes it will need to be severe, but He will not usually bring our lives to an end. His aim is to change us and mature us. So He limits the chastisement to what we can stand and what will help us. He does not ordinarily go beyond that:

The Lord has disciplined me severely,
but he has not given me over to death.
Psalm 118:18 (ESV)

However it has to be said that there can be exceptional circumstances which arise if we become carnal and live in immorality, as some Christians do. If so, then God might reach a point where He chooses to take our lives in order to stop us continuing in such sins. Apostle Paul addresses this disturbing and controversial theme in 1 Corinthians:

[1] I want you to know, brethren, that our fathers were all under the cloud, and all passed through the sea, [2] and all were baptized into Moses in the cloud and in the sea, [3] and all ate the same supernatural food [4] and all drank the same supernatural drink. For they drank from the supernatural Rock which followed them, and the Rock was Christ. [5] Nevertheless with most of them God was not pleased; for they were overthrown in the wilderness. [6] Now these things are warnings for us, not to desire evil as they did. [7] Do not be idolaters as some of them were; as it is written, "The people sat down to eat and drink and rose up to dance." [8] We must not indulge in immorality as some of them did, and twenty-three thousand fell in a single day. [9] We must not put the Lord to the test, as some of them did and were destroyed by serpents; [10] nor grumble, as some of them did and were destroyed by the Destroyer. [11] Now these things happened to them as a warning, but they were written down for our instruction, upon whom the end of the ages has come. [12] Therefore let anyone who thinks that he stands take heed lest he fall.
1 Corinthians 10:1-12 (RSV)

Such a drastic response as this is rare. Even so, we do need to be aware that it is a valid part of what God sometimes does to discipline His own people. God caused the premature death of many of the Israelites when they were in the Wilderness. He also refused to allow the older generation to enter the Promised Land.

Many of those people who died in the wilderness, or who were even directly put to death or destroyed by God Himself, were believers and were saved. They had eternal life, but their lives were ended or shortened and they lost their inheritance, i.e. their right to live in the Promised Land.

That is, many of them were real believers who were saved and had eternal life. They were simply carnal, unbelieving and disobedient in their lifestyles and attitudes, as many of us are. So, God took away their lives because they disobeyed and displeased Him. In the book of Exodus, Moses sets out how God will deal with those Israelites who afflict widows or orphans. He makes clear that they will receive God's wrath and that God will actually kill the wrongdoer:

[22] You shall not afflict any widow or orphan. [23] If you do afflict them, and they cry out to me, I will surely hear their cry; [24] and my wrath will burn, and I will kill you with the sword, and your wives shall become widows and your children fatherless.

Exodus 22:22-24 (RSV)

Note how severely God dealt with the wicked sons of Eli, and also King Saul

Likewise, in 1 Samuel, we are told about the priest, Eli, whose sons, Hophni and Phinehas were wicked. They worked in the Tabernacle like their father, but they abused their positions and exploited people. Therefore the Bible says that it was God's will to put them to death:

Eli's sons were scoundrels; they had no regard for the Lord.
1 Samuel 2:12 (NIV)

This sin of the young men was very great in the Lord's sight, for they were treating the Lord's offering with contempt.
Samuel 2:17 (NIV)

[22] Now Eli, who was very old, heard about everything his sons were doing to all Israel and how they slept with the women who served at the entrance to the tent of meeting. [23] So he said to them, "Why do you do such things? I hear from all the people about these wicked deeds of yours. [24] No, my sons; the report I hear spreading among the Lord's people is not good. [25] If one person sins against another, God may mediate for the offender; but if anyone sins against the Lord, who will intercede for them?" His sons, however, did not listen to their father's rebuke, for it was the Lord's will to put them to death.
Samuel 2:22-25 (NIV)

Of course, the passage from Exodus, which we saw earlier, comes from the Law of Moses, which none of us are under. It was fulfilled, and therefore rendered obsolete, by Jesus' death and resurrection. So, the above passage from Exodus is no longer operative. Nonetheless, I still include it above because it illustrates this principle. It demonstrates the way God thinks and how drastically He is prepared to act in certain situations.

The Law of Moses is no longer in operation, but God does still sometimes do what He describes above. He still ends the lives of certain people, as He did with Hophni and Phinehas, the wicked sons of Eli. He does not do so today in order to comply with the Law of Moses. He does it because that is how He is.

We see another example of how God sometimes reacts to sin in the account of the deaths of Nadab and Abihu in Leviticus chapter 10. These two brothers were sons of Aaron, i.e. Moses' brother. Therefore, they were priests, as was their father, Aaron. It was therefore part of their duty to offer sacrifices and to burn incense in the Tabernacle. One day they did something which angered God. They disobeyed God's instructions in some way, the exact details of which are not given.

At any rate, they offered fire to the LORD in the Tabernacle in a way which God saw as unholy. In other words, they disrespected God by their actions, or by their neglect to do as He had commanded them. Therefore, as Nadab and Abihu were doing this, fire came forth from God and consumed them. God ended their lives Himself, there and then, at the very scene of their wrongdoing:

Now Nadab and Abi'hu, the sons of Aaron, each took his censer, and put fire in it, and laid incense on it, and offered unholy fire before the LORD, such as he had not commanded them. ² And fire came forth from the presence of the LORD and devoured them, and they died before the LORD.
Leviticus 10:1-2 (RSV)

Finally, look at what the Bible says about King Saul. He was appointed by God but he was unfaithful. Therefore, in the end, God did not merely demote or remove him. We are told that He "slew him":

¹³ So Saul died for his unfaithfulness; he was unfaithful to the Lord in that he did not keep the command of the Lord, and also consulted a medium, seeking guidance, ¹⁴ and did not seek guidance from the Lord. Therefore the Lord slew him, and turned the kingdom over to David the son of Jesse.
1 Chronicles 10:13-14 (RSV)

God also dealt severely with Ananias and Sapphira and that was in the New Testament, not the Old

In case anybody says that this only happened in the Old Testament, let us look at the book of Acts where we see the same thing happening to Ananias and Sapphira. They sold some land and gave some of the proceeds away to the apostles. They claimed that what they gave was the *entire* proceeds. In fact, they had held some back for themselves.

There was nothing wrong with that, in itself. The Bible makes clear that they were fully entitled to do as they wished with the money. They were under no duty to give away any of it, let alone all of it. The sin was not in holding some of it back, but in *lying* about it:

47

*¹ But a man named Anani'as with his wife Sapphi'ra sold a piece of property, ²
and with his wife's knowledge he kept back some of the proceeds, and brought
only a part and laid it at the apostles' feet. ³ But Peter said, "Anani'as, why has
Satan filled your heart to lie to the Holy Spirit and to keep back part of the
proceeds of the land? ⁴ While it remained unsold, did it not remain your own?
And after it was sold, was it not at your disposal? How is it that you have
contrived this deed in your heart? You have not lied to men but to God." ⁵ When
Anani'as heard these words, he fell down and died. And great fear came upon
all who heard of it. ⁶ The young men rose and wrapped him up and carried him
out and buried him.*

Acts 5:1-6 (RSV)

So, God took away Ananias' life because he had lied to the Holy Spirit. Then the
same thing happened to his wife:

*⁷ After an interval of about three hours his wife came in, not knowing what had
happened. ⁸ And Peter said to her, "Tell me whether you sold the land for so
much." And she said, "Yes, for so much." ⁹ But Peter said to her, "How is it that
you have agreed together to tempt the Spirit of the Lord? Hark, the feet of those
that have buried your husband are at the door, and they will carry you out." ¹⁰
Immediately she fell down at his feet and died. When the young men came in
they found her dead, and they carried her out and buried her beside her
husband. ¹¹ And great fear came upon the whole church, and upon all who
heard of these things.*

Acts 5:7-11 (RSV)

Some have argued that Ananias and Sapphira were not real Christians and were
actually unsaved unbelievers, who were only pretending to be part of the church.
However, I see no basis for saying that. The Bible does not say it, or even suggest
it. On the contrary, if they were not real Christians God would have had no reason
to discipline them. If God disciplined every non-Christian who ever told a lie,
there would be none of them left.

God fully expects unbelievers to lie, but His principal judgment of them will come
later at the Great White Throne, where they will be condemned and punished
eternally. The main reason why people argue that Ananias and Sapphira must
have been non-Christians is because they don't like the idea of God dealing with
real Christians in this way. However, whether we like a thing or not has nothing
to do with whether it is true.

We must therefore be guided by what the Bible actually says, not by what we
would like it to say. On that basis we have to conclude that discipline of this kind
can, and does, apply to real Christians. It ranges from rebuke to chastisement, and
all the way up to ending our lives. That would send us to our Judgment and take
away our opportunity to do any further harm.

What does Paul mean when he refers to "deliver(ing) a man over to Satan for the destruction of his flesh"?

If you are still unpersuaded that God can, and does, discipline us severely, and that He sometimes even takes away the life of a real Christian, then consider some further passages. Here apostle Paul speaks of *"deliver(ing) a man over to Satan for the destruction of his flesh"*.

¹ It is actually reported that there is immorality among you, and of a kind that is not found even among pagans; for a man is living with his father's wife. ² And you are arrogant! Ought you not rather to mourn? Let him who has done this be removed from among you. ³ For though absent in body I am present in spirit, and as if present, I have already pronounced judgment ⁴ in the name of the Lord Jesus on the man who has done such a thing. When you are assembled, and my spirit is present, with the power of our Lord Jesus, ⁵ you are to deliver this man to Satan for the destruction of the flesh, that his spirit may be saved in the day of the Lord Jesus.

1 Corinthians 5:1-5 (RSV)

"......By rejecting conscience, certain persons have made shipwreck of their faith, among them Hymenaeus and Alexander, whom I have delivered to Satan that they may learn not to blaspheme."

1 Timothy 1:19(b)-20 (RSV)

These are controversial passages and there are differing opinions as to exactly what Paul is speaking about. Some say that he merely means that such a person is put outside of the umbrella of protection of the Church. They then receive a buffeting of demonic attacks and eventually realize their error and stop behaving in a carnal way. It may well include all of that.

However, my own belief is that it can go far beyond that and even include the loss of that carnal believer's life. In direct terms, such a death could be caused by the severity of the demonic onslaught against him. However, the indirect cause is that God has permitted it, by removing His shield of protection. Then the carnal man dies and his sin and rebellion cease, but he himself can still be saved.

Conversely, if God had not intervened, then perhaps he may not have been saved in the end, i.e. if his life had continued and his sin had kept on increasing until it reached its full limits and he became apostate. It is a little bit like where a football manager can see that the behaviour of one of his players on the pitch is seriously out of order. Perhaps he has already had a yellow card, but he is continuing to foul other players, make reckless tackles and show dissent to the referee.

His own manager might look at that developing situation and be able to see that it is inevitably going to end with that player being sent off by the referee. If so, that would generate a further ban of one, or even three, whole games, in addition to the current match.

In that situation a sensible manager might choose to substitute that player right now, before he gets compulsorily sent off. That would be upsetting for that player, but it would save him from even worse consequences, which would have occurred if he had been allowed to stay on the pitch any longer. Plus, it could save other players from potentially serious injuries.

An example of this is the famous footballer, Paul Gascoigne ("Gazza") and his bizarre behaviour during the 1991 FA Cup Final between Tottenham Hotspur and Nottingham Forest. Gazza was in a strange mood that day and from the very first minute of the game he was lunging into wild tackles. One of those fouls nearly broke a Nottingham Forest player's leg. That was in the first few minutes of the game. At that point his own manager could, and should, have substituted him. Sadly, he didn't.

It was a shame because, later in the match, Gazza made yet another lunging tackle which caused him to tear his own cruciate ligaments very badly. He required surgery and had to miss a whole season to recover. All of that could have been avoided, if only he had been taken off the pitch by his own manager.

The point is that there are some Christians, even real ones, who get themselves into a severe mess. Their lives are sliding downwards so badly that they could cause harm to others, or even lose their own salvation, if they aren't stopped. My own belief is that God may look at that situation and conclude that the only practical solution is to take that believer home early, by ending their lives. If so, that would actually be a mercy, because the alternative would be to allow that person to continue declining until they pass the point of no return and become fully apostate. In that case, they could lose their eternal life.

What are we to make of the warnings in the letter to the Hebrews?

The letter to the Hebrews seems to make it clear that it is possible for a Christian, even a real one, to fall so far, and to become so apostate, that there is no way back for them. It would appear that such a person may then end up being judged as an *unbeliever* at the Great White Throne instead of being judged as a believer at the Judgment Seat of Christ. In other words, it seems that an apostate can lose their salvation and end up being condemned:

⁴ For it is impossible to restore again to repentance those who have once been enlightened, who have tasted the heavenly gift, and have become partakers of the Holy Spirit, ⁵ and have tasted the goodness of the word of God and the powers of the age to come, ⁶ if they then commit apostasy, since they crucify the Son of God on their own account and hold him up to contempt. ⁷ For land which has drunk the rain that often falls upon it, and brings forth vegetation useful to those for whose sake it is cultivated, receives a blessing from God. ⁸ But if it bears thorns and thistles, it is worthless and near to being cursed; its end is to be burned.

Hebrews 6:4-8 (RSV)

This next passage deals with the situation of a person who has believed the Gospel, and begun to be a disciple and to become sanctified. It indicates that he is in a worse position than an outright unbeliever if he then falls away and *"spurns the Son of God"*. What else can that mean, other than that he must end up in the Lake of Fire? That is where every unsaved person will end up. But how can a person be saved and yet be in a worse position than someone who is in the Lake of Fire?

²⁶ For if we sin deliberately after receiving the knowledge of the truth, there no longer remains a sacrifice for sins, ²⁷ but a fearful prospect of judgment, and a fury of fire which will consume the adversaries. ²⁸ A man who has violated the law of Moses dies without mercy at the testimony of two or three witnesses. ²⁹ How much worse punishment do you think will be deserved by the man who has spurned the Son of God, and profaned the blood of the covenant by which he was sanctified, and outraged the Spirit of grace? ³⁰ For we know him who said, "Vengeance is mine, I will repay." And again, "The Lord will judge his people." ³¹ It is a fearful thing to fall into the hands of the living God.

Hebrews 10:26-31 (RSV)

Also, what does John mean in 1 John 5 when he refers to "sin leading to death"?

Apostle John also addresses this theme in his first letter. He is discussing the different levels and types of sins that a *believer* might commit and how other believers ought to respond to that believer's sins. Because this is such an important and difficult issue, let us look at John's words in the New American Standard Bible. That translation is particularly accurate, and thus more suitable to use when one is dealing with highly controversial passages:

¹⁶ If anyone sees his brother committing a sin not leading to death, he shall ask and God will for him give life to those who commit sin not leading to death. There is a sin leading to death; I do not say that he should make request for this. ¹⁷ All unrighteousness is sin, and there is a sin not leading to death.

1 John 5:16-17 (NASB)

Apostle John is referring to fellow believers who commit the ordinary, day to day, sins that we all commit, even if we are seeking to do God's will and are maturing as disciples. For such fellow believers he says we are to pray, so that they cease sinning. That is because those sins are *"not leading to death"*. However, there

51

are other sins which do lead to death. For such grave sins John instructs us that it is not always the right thing to pray for that person.

That is because sin of that high level of seriousness may make it necessary for God to bring forward that believer's death. In other words, God may choose to remove them from this life and take them home early, so as to prevent them causing further harm to themselves or others.

This is a very complex and difficult area. Therefore we would need to think long and hard, and be very sure of our ground, before we ever come to the conclusion that a particular believer has gone so far into sin, and of such a grave nature, that God might intend to end their lives early. Nevertheless, I have briefly flagged the issue, because the Bible indicates that such situations can arise, and perhaps more often than we realise.

Knowing that that is a possibility, however remote, should cause us all to fear the LORD more deeply and to take care how we live. Please refer to chapters 21 and 22 of Book One of this series for a much fuller discussion of whether, and how, a real Christian might be able to fall away and end up being eternally lost.

However, for present purposes, let it suffice to say that we all need to have a genuine fear of God and to be in awe of Him. That includes having a very real fear of the consequences of drifting away from Him. In the context of all that, it makes sense as to why God ending the life of a believer prematurely can rightly be seen as a mercy, i.e. to prevent him from falling away completely and losing his salvation.

The furnace of affliction or *'the school of hard knocks'* – how God uses severe adversity to melt away the dross from our lives.

Not all of the difficult or unpleasant circumstances that we experience are due to God's chastening or punishment. Some of it has other causes and purposes. One of those is that God allows us to face adversity, struggle, opposition and difficulty as a way of changing us. He allows such things even when He is pleased with us.

As we saw above, it is as if the pressure we face has the effect of smelting us, just as precious metal is smelted by a jeweller to melt away the dross within the metal and to refine the silver or gold that remains. He does that to make it purer and better. It is also to test its genuineness. God does the same with us:

⁶ In this you rejoice, though now for a little while, if necessary, you have been grieved by various trials, ⁷ so that the tested genuineness of your faith—more precious than gold that perishes though it is tested by fire—may be found to result in praise and glory and honour at the revelation of Jesus Christ.
1 Peter 1:6-7 (ESV)

Moses also speaks of the time spent as slaves in Egypt as being a *'furnace'*. Evidently God used that time in Egypt to forge the Israelites into what He wanted them to be:

But the Lord has taken you, and brought you forth out of the iron furnace, out of Egypt, to be a people of his own possession, as at this day.

Deuteronomy 4:20 (RSV)

Job also spoke of this process. He faced more adversity than most of us ever will. Yet he was aware that it had a redemptive purpose. He knew that, in the end, after God had tested him by pressure, just as precious metal is tested by fire, he would emerge as pure gold rather than as a mixture of gold and dross:

"....when He has tried me, I shall come forth as gold"

Job 23:10(b) (NASB)

Therefore, instead of complaining about pressure or difficulty, as we often do, we ought to try to remember its valuable purpose. We should even find it possible to rejoice in our sufferings, because of the benefits they produce in us:

[3] More than that, we rejoice in our sufferings, knowing that suffering produces endurance, [4] and endurance produces character, and character produces hope, [5] and hope does not disappoint us, because God's love has been poured into our hearts through the Holy Spirit which has been given to us.

Romans 5:3-5 (RSV)

It is good for us if God's discipline can begin as early as possible, preferably while we are still young:

It is good for a man that he bear
the yoke in his youth.

Lamentations 3:27 (ESV)

At times the Christian life can be like a furnace in which we are 'tried' by being put under severe pressure. That is done firstly to see what we are made of and, secondly, to change us, so that we become better and purer. So, we must not assume that all pressure and difficulty is a departure from God's will, as if we were going the wrong way.

Neither does it always mean that God is punishing or chastening us. On the contrary, it is often evidence that we are on the right path, because some affliction is essential if we are to become a mature disciple. It is therefore God's policy to ensure that some of it will come our way, even if we are living well and doing what is right:

"Behold, I have refined you, but not as silver;

I have tested you in the furnace of affliction.
Isaiah 48:10 (NASB)

God does not adopt this approach of allowing us to face affliction because He is against us or because He wants to harm us. He is for us and He does it for our benefit, because He is wise enough to know that it is what we all need. Often it is these difficulties or restrictions that prevent us from doing things that would have destroyed us if we had been allowed to do all the things we wanted to do:

Surely it was for my benefit
that I suffered such anguish.
In your love you kept me
from the pit of destruction;
Isaiah 38:17(a) (NIV)

God takes no *pleasure* from our sufferings, or from putting us under pressure. He allows it because there are times when it is necessary and He does it all with compassion. Moreover, it is not permanent. God will only allow the affliction to continue for as long as it is needed in order to bring about the required changes:

[31] For the Lord will not
cast off for ever,
[32] but, though he cause grief, he will have compassion
according to the abundance of his steadfast love;
[33] for he does not willingly afflict
or grieve the sons of men.
Lamentations 3:31-33 (RSV)

Although God will allow us to face very severe crisis and difficulties at times, and even to be knocked down by people and by circumstances, He will not let us be permanently knocked down. He will raise us up again at some point, when He has achieved the changes in our lives that He is trying to bring about:

Thou who hast made me see many sore troubles
wilt revive me again;
from the depths of the earth
thou wilt bring me up again.
[21] Thou wilt increase my honor,
and comfort me again.
Psalm 71:20-21 (RSV)

for a righteous man falls seven times, and rises again;
but the wicked are overthrown by calamity.
Proverbs 24:16 (RSV)

One of the greatest benefits that comes from affliction and opposition is that it tends to drive us towards God's Word. When a real disciple is put under severe pressure, he will turn more and more to the Scriptures. The Bible will become increasingly important and precious to him. That fact alone makes the affliction worthwhile:

Before I was afflicted I went astray,
but now I keep your word.
                              Psalm 119:67 (ESV)

It is good for me that I was afflicted,
that I might learn your statutes.
                              Psalm 119:71 (ESV)

Be willing to *ask* God to put you into the furnace of affliction and to keep you there as long as is necessary

Obviously, most of us have no desire to suffer or to be put under pressure. Indeed, it would be perverse for us to actually *want* to suffer, or to gain any pleasure from it. We should not want it in that sense. Nevertheless, it is valid to be willing to pray that God would place us into His "furnace of affliction" if He wishes to, i.e. whenever He feels we need it.

It would be like an overweight person who has no actual desire to diet but who, nonetheless, *chooses* to go into a health farm or diet clinic for a period of time, where food intake is strictly controlled. It isn't what they want as such. They may well find it very difficult, but it is still what they choose to do.

Likewise, it makes sense that we should take that approach when facing affliction, because anything that God does is for the best, even when He is putting us through an ordeal. However, we need to think very carefully before we actually pray to *ask* God to put us into His furnace of affliction. You can make that prayer, and it is a good thing to do.

However, you need to do it with your eyes wide open, realising the full implications of what you are praying for. God will take you at your word and you will then be sent on a roller-coaster ride involving some white-knuckle moments of difficulty and pressure.

You will face incident after incident, and person after person, each of which God will use to test and stretch you to your limits. He will not take you past the point at which He knows you would snap. However, in my experience, He does seem to go fairly close to that point. At least it feels like that while you are going through it.

I draw attention to this concept of a Christian positively asking to be put into the furnace of affliction because it is a prayer I made myself many years ago. God certainly took me at my word and my life was turned upside down and inside out for more than a decade. I believe it was the direct result of my making that prayer. I asked God to put me into His furnace and not to let me out until He was satisfied that I had been in there long enough to deal with the dross in my life and character.

I made that prayer with my eyes open, fully meaning what I was saying, and knowing that it would lead to some difficulty. I got the idea from listening to a teaching tape in which the speaker recommended it, but warned that we should not pray it unless we really mean it and are willing to pay the price. I did mean it, and was willing to face whatever God saw fit to do with me.

However, I had no idea at the time how *long* that smelting process would take or how *arduous* it would be. It also never occurred to me that God would put pressure on me in my job and business. Somehow, I didn't expect Him to reach into those parts of my life. At any rate, the fact is I prayed that prayer and within a month a series of stress-inducing incidents began which went on for 13 years.

It all began with me discovering that one of my business partners at that time had forged an invoice on the firm's letterhead. It was typed up by him, rather than by the cashiers, and was not entered onto the computer system at all. He did it in order to get a client to pay him personally, rather than the firm. It was an attempt by him to divert money away from the firm and to have it all for himself instead.

I was a one third owner of that firm. I then went to the Senior Partner and reported this to him. He promised to support me when I confronted the partner who had done this. However, when we met to discuss it at a Partners' meeting, the Senior Partner said nothing.

He never backed me up and just stared at the floor when I turned to him and asked for his comments. He made no reply. I could see then that I was on my own and that the Senior Partner had decided to back the wrongdoer rather than me. From that moment, I realised that I needed to get out of that firm.

So I told the other two partners, shortly afterwards, that I wanted to de-merge the firm and leave, taking my own files and clients with me, plus my own staff. At that point the two of them turned on me aggressively and refused to cooperate or to permit me to leave. So, I appointed solicitors to act for me and then issued court proceedings to have the firm wound up.

I did so on the basis of the second partner's misconduct and the Senior Partner's refusal to do anything about it, or to allow me to leave. But they resisted those proceedings. Then, they went to the other extreme and held a further partner's meeting a few weeks later at which they expelled me from the firm. The two of them simply voted to expel me as a partner. I voted against, but they had two votes.

They expelled me on the supposed basis that I was causing 'disruption', and they drew up a list of bogus or exaggerated allegations. So, we ended up with the bizarre situation in which I was basically expelled for catching the second partner in an act of wrongdoing and for raising it at a partners' meeting. It was the sort of thing which you might expect to read about in a John Grisham book, but which you never expect to happen in real life, least of all to yourself.

In addition to that blow, we also learned, in the very same month, that my wife was being made redundant from her job which she had had for many years. Therefore we suddenly had no income at all. That said, it was also God's way of providing for us, because the redundancy payment helped us to start up the new firm. So, in quick succession, I was thrown out of my job and business and then my wife lost her job.

Another hammer blow was that my former partners then refused to pay me my one third share of the equity or capital in the business. The partnership deed required that they pay me, but instead of doing so, they made more allegations against me and argued that these amounted to 'counterclaims'. Those just happened to be equal to what I was owed by them. So they refused to pay anything.

I could have fought them in the courts, but it would have taken about two years, especially as they would have dragged it out by causing procedural delays. So, after fighting for a few months, I gave up and discontinued my claim. I could not afford the legal costs involved. In the space of the first three months I had already received bills from my own solicitors of over £20,000 and we had only just got started.

I had also realised by then that my former partners would make whatever further allegations were needed to spin out the case for as long as they wished so as to avoid, or at least delay, paying me. Moreover, I had to take into account that there was a high chance that they would not actually be *able* to pay me in the end, even if I eventually won the case and got a court order requiring them to do so.

You can perhaps imagine how painful that whole experience was. It was profoundly unjust and hugely disruptive to me financially. I was left with no option but to start again from scratch by opening a brand new law firm. It had no staff, no files, no clients, no furniture, no equipment, no anything. On day one I was literally the only person in the so called 'firm'.

The furniture consisted of a dining room chair from home and my mobile phone was the only phone 'system' that I had. Yet, only one day earlier, I had been the managing partner and Head of the Litigation department in a quite large firm.

Nevertheless, I then recruited staff, got furniture, and began to open files for new clients. However, it was very tough, especially as we had very little cash and banks refused to help me.

Consequently, for the first three years of the new firm's life I had to survive in an extremely difficult financial situation. It was emotionally exhausting, always being on a knife edge. I came close to going bust several times, but by one means or another, God always rescued me at the last moment. I therefore survived each crisis, in turn, though only for yet another one to arise within weeks or months afterwards.

On top of all that I began to experience severe problems with some of the staff that I recruited for the new law firm. Person after person came in and caused me great stress and difficulty due to their dishonesty, laziness, incompetence or malice. Again and again I had to go through the long and drawn out process of investigating, disciplining and dismissing them.

I found it all very wearing and debilitating, especially as so many of them were so devious and nasty to deal with. The problem was made worse by the fact that the new firm grew so quickly. At its peak, five years after I started the new firm, there were over 80 staff working in it.

That rapid rate of expansion helps to explain why so many bad people got in. But it still doesn't fully explain the very high numbers of bad staff. It was disproportionate, or statistically unrepresentative, in that I got far more than my fair share of devious and malicious employees. I now realise that God deliberately allowed this stream of bad people to get in. Firstly, He wanted to test me to my limits, but secondly, it was also to give me lots of experience of handling wicked people.

The various situations I faced in dealing with them gave me the material I needed to write Book Six in this series, which is about identifying wicked people and how to handle them. So, the long series of confrontations had great value in the end, but the learning process was an exhausting ordeal, which went on for many years.

One of the worst employees I had to deal with was a woman in her early thirties whom I recruited and made a supervisor. I unwisely gave her that role too quickly and she turned out to be both incompetent and disloyal. So we had to dismiss her after only five months in the job. She then issued proceedings in an Employment Tribunal and made up a ridiculously false story as to why she had been sacked. She said that it was because she had worn a short skirt!

That had nothing to do with it. Indeed, I hadn't even seen it. Or, if I had, I hadn't noticed it. She also went to the national media making these bogus allegations about me. One day a journalist actually came to the door of our house, while I was out, and upset my wife by questioning her. I defended the case, in which she was claiming over £100,000, but in the end she abandoned her entire claim and received no damages or costs at all.

She had assumed that I would be intimidated by the size of her claim, and by having my name in national newspapers, and that I would accept her demands. However, I refused to be intimidated, or to give in to her. Therefore, at the last moment, she dropped the entire claim because she didn't actually want it to go to a hearing. She knew all along that she had no case and was only bluffing.

Nevertheless, for several months I had to deal with the stress of false allegations being made by a malicious claimant and with it being heavily publicized in virtually every national newspaper. It wasn't easy, to put it mildly. In fact it really got me down. Yet I had no alternative but to fight it. I felt like the Psalmist in his dealings with false witnesses:

Give me not up to the will of my adversaries;
for false witnesses have risen against me,
and they breathe out violence.
                              Psalm 27:12 (RSV)

In addition to all these pressures, I was also kept very busy as a Borough Councillor and also as the Chairman of the Conservative Association. I had these two roles at the same time as running a law firm and they added a lot to my workload. However, perhaps the greatest pressure of all though came from something so obscure that less than 0.5% of the population have ever even heard of it. It was a legal issue which threatened my entire livelihood for about ten years.

It had to do with the client agreements used in litigation cases. They are called Conditional Fee Agreements ("CFAs") or *"no win, no fee"* agreements so far as the public are concerned. It is much too complex to explain in detail here, but the gist of it is that these CFAs were drafted to comply with very specific (and badly written) legislation. If they were correctly worded, and fully complied with all of the minutiae of the CFA regulations, then a law firm would be paid in full. However, if they were not, then the law firm would be paid nothing at all.

There were many cases being reported of law firms whose CFAs had been ruled to be non-compliant, and therefore invalid. In each case, it was for one or other of a variety of utterly trivial reasons. These reported cases came one after another, and caused major turmoil amongst law firms. Each time I wondered if my firm would be the next to be destroyed by having its CFA declared to have been imperfectly drafted in some obscure way.

Therefore, for nearly a decade, there was a "costs war". Insurance companies and other paying parties were searching assiduously for tiny defects in the drafting of these CFAs, which they could then use as an excuse to get out of paying. If a firm's CFA was held to be non-compliant, then nothing at all would be payable to that firm for all the work done on that file, for perhaps the previous 12-36 months. Moreover, it would not only affect that one file, but all subsequent files as well, because that insurer would then raise the same challenge with that firm on every other file from then on.

Furthermore, other insurers would also hear of the Court's judgment and then join in by refusing to pay. So, the consequences of having your CFA declared invalid in any way were potentially catastrophic. This costs war affected most law firms in England and Wales, but mine in particular, because nearly all our work was done through CFAs. Most other firms only did a small percentage of their work that way.

Thus, if my firm's CFA had ever been held to be technically in breach of the rules, and thus invalid, then I would have been financially wiped out overnight. I would have been bankrupt. I had that huge threat hanging over me for nearly a decade. I managed to fend off various temporary challenges for five years, but eventually the first serious legal challenge was made to me.

It related to some microscopically small details in our CFA. An insurance company challenged it on four different grounds and refused to pay us. We therefore had to go to Court in London to have a judge decide whether or not they should have to pay us, i.e. whether the drafting of our CFA was valid or invalid.

That case then lasted for five more years. That long delay was mainly because I deliberately slowed their challenge down in every way I could. We also redrafted my firm's CFA for all new clients from then on. I did so because I wanted to try to reduce the potential impact of losing the case by allowing as many as possible of the old ones to get completed and paid before this legal challenge reached the stage of a court hearing. My aim was to have as few old CFAs remaining as possible, in case I lost at that hearing.

Eventually, it all ended well. I won the case outright and our CFA was fully upheld and declared to be technically compliant on all counts. The insurer had challenged my CFA on four different points and they lost on all of them. However, during those ten years I had had to live with the constant prospect of being wiped out financially and of losing my whole business, all because a minor word or phrase in our CFA might be held to be technically non-compliant. It was like the sword of Damocles hanging over my head throughout all those years, on top of all the other work pressures that I had to face, plus the problems of dealing with bad staff.

If that wasn't enough, I also had to deal with some major problems in the church I was then part of. The leader, whom I will call 'Rick', was behaving very badly, including being a liar and a manipulator. I was the Chairman of the Trustees of that church and was therefore responsible for all the paid staff of the church. Therefore it fell to me to try to do something about the leader's misconduct. (See Book One and also Book Six for further details). Tackling him was very disorientating and stressful in itself, but he also did great harm to me by telling lies about me in order to defend himself.

On top of all these things there were also many other miscellaneous, one-off pressures and crises too. It was basically coming at me from all directions simultaneously and it was unrelenting. At any given time there would always be one, and usually two, three or even more, crises for me to deal with.

The pressure never stopped, throughout all those years, but God made good use of that sustained ordeal in order to break me and refine my character. I changed a great deal and learned very much. As far as I was concerned, it definitely met the definition of being a 'furnace'. I also believe that that long sequence of events was the direct result of my prayer that God would put me into His furnace.

God took that prayer far more seriously than I had. Even so, as I look back, I don't regret praying as I did. Neither do I regret any of the time spent in the furnace, despite its severity. It all served the purpose of melting me down and changing me for the better.

Therefore if I had my time again I would make the same prayer. I would also advise you to do so too, *provided* you are serious, really mean what you are praying, and are willing to stay in the furnace for as long as it takes. However, bear in mind that, realistically, it will probably mean *years* rather than weeks or months.

I say that because when metal is melted it requires very severe heat and for a long time. Ordinary flames would just heat the metal, but not melt it. In the same way, God is not merely seeking to heat you up; He wants to melt you down completely. So, be reconciled to the fact that it will take ages, due to the scale of the task He is attempting to accomplish.

Some might say that it is foolish to pray for additional difficulties, and that, as they say in the army, one should "never volunteer for anything". There is some sense in that. Most soldiers only do what they have to do and don't volunteer for any more. That's not unreasonable. However, there is also a school of thought that says that if you have to be in the army, then you may as well try to be the very best you can be.

It's that kind of reasoning that makes people apply to join the Marines or the Paratroops or some other equivalent. I was interested to hear, when watching a series about the American 101st Airborne Division in World War Two, that many of the men who applied to join it expressed that view. They had volunteered to join an elite unit because they wanted to be the very best they could be.

However, choosing to train to become a paratrooper, rather than remaining as an ordinary, conscripted infantryman, meant a much harder physical regime. Many volunteers had to drop out, or else they were weeded out by the Army, because they just couldn't cope with the rigour of it all.

Nevertheless, that minority who could endure it, became some of the very best and most effective soldiers in the army. For that reason, when there was a really difficult job to be done, General Eisenhower often sent the 101st Airborne Division to deal with it.

So, volunteering for a much harder training regime can be the right thing to do, provided you have thought it through beforehand, and are willing to pay the full price. Do bear in mind though that being put into God's furnace is not an entirely voluntary affair. He will put all of us into it, from time to time, and to a certain extent, even if we never ask for it.

Therefore, we can't escape God's training regime simply by never volunteering for it. The only question is whether you should deliberately seek to be given more of it, or just take whatever level of pressure God was going to give you anyway, without asking for any extra. It all depends on how committed you are and whether you want an easier life now, or a better life in the next world.

God will also test you from time to time to find out how you handle pressure and how you react in difficult situations

Another reason why God puts all of us through difficult experiences, whether we ask for them or not, is because He wants us to develop strength, stamina and hardiness. He wants us to be able to withstand a series of difficult experiences, over a sustained period of time, and to come through successfully, still persevering, and without fainting or giving in:

10If you faint in the day of adversity,
your strength is small
Proverbs 24:10 (RSV)

As part of that toughening up process, God needs to find out how well, or badly, we will react under the pressure of various tests and trials. An employer takes a similar approach with a member of staff. He will sometimes give an employee a difficult task, which he knows is harder than anything they have done to date, simply because he wants to find out how they will react to that challenge.

It is a way of finding out what that employee is really made of and how much potential they have to be promoted and to do even harder things in the future. It is effectively a quality control test to see what we are at present, just as a silversmith tests silver to find out how pure it is:

For you, O God, have tested us;
you have tried us as silver is tried.
                    Psalm 66:10 (ESV)

When you face such times of crisis and testing you will need to have resilience and the ability to bounce back. You will be greatly assisted in that if you can learn to encourage yourself, rather than having to rely on other people for encouragement, which may not be forthcoming. In other words, you have to learn how to build yourself up, restore your own morale, and reassure yourself.

You can do this best by digging into God's Word at such times, especially the Psalms. In particular you can do it by speaking God's promises out loud by way of proclamation. (See the later book in this series, on the subject of prayer and spiritual warfare, for details of what proclamation is and how to do it.)

King David is a classic example of a man who really knew how to encourage himself, and how to pick himself up and stay strong when facing a crisis. Here he is at a very grim moment. David's wives and children, and the wives and children of all his men, have been kidnapped by Amalekite raiders while he and his men were away.

When they learn of this disaster, David's men blame him for it and want to stone him to death, which is hardly a supportive response. Yet David does not panic. He gets a grip on his own emotions, encourages himself, and then gets himself ready to take practical action:

¹ Now when David and his men came to Ziklag on the third day, the Amal'ekites had made a raid upon the Negeb and upon Ziklag. They had overcome Ziklag, and burned it with fire, ² and taken captive the women and all who were in it, both small and great; they killed no one, but carried them off, and went their way. ³ And when David and his men came to the city, they found it burned with fire, and their wives and sons and daughters taken captive. ⁴ Then David and the people who were with him raised their voices and wept, until they had no more strength to weep. ⁵ David's two wives also had been taken captive, Ahin'o-am of Jezreel, and Ab'igail the widow of Nabal of Carmel. ⁶ And David was greatly distressed; for the people spoke of stoning him, because all the people were bitter in soul, each for his sons and daughters. But David strengthened himself in the Lord his God.
                    1 Samuel 30:1-6 (RSV)

David then launched a counterattack on the Amalekites and recovered all the hostages alive and well. This would never have been achieved if he had not had the self-control and resilience needed to regain control of his own feelings:

¹⁷ And David smote them from twilight until the evening of the next day; and not a man of them escaped, except four hundred young men, who mounted camels

63

and fled. ¹⁸ David recovered all that the Amal'ekites had taken; and David
rescued his two wives. ¹⁹ Nothing was missing, whether small or great, sons or
daughters, spoil or anything that had been taken; David brought back all. ²⁰
David also captured all the flocks and herds; and the people drove those cattle
before him, and said, "This is David's spoil."

1 Samuel 30:17-20 (RSV)

God is watching all of us all the time and testing us continually. This is true both
of genuine disciples and also unbelievers. All of us are being examined and tested
so that God can assess us and evaluate our attitude, work rate, calibre, character,
endurance, faithfulness, obedience and so on. He even tests the wicked in these
ways, not just disciples. Nobody is immune from this regime of examination and
testing:

⁴ The Lord is in his holy temple,
  the Lord's throne is in heaven;
  his eyes behold, his eyelids test, the children of men.
⁵ The Lord tests the righteous and the wicked,
  and his soul hates him that loves violence.

Psalm 11:4-5 (RSV)

God will even allow us to come into contact with false teachers, false prophets
and insincere leaders. That is partly for the simple reason that such people exist
in this world and in large numbers. Therefore they can't be avoided. However, it
is also because God wants to find out how we will deal with them. He wants to
know whether we will believe what His written Word says and remain faithful to
that, or whether we will choose to believe what mere men tell us, even when it
contradicts His Word:

"If a prophet arises among you, or a dreamer of dreams, and gives you a sign
or a wonder, ² and the sign or wonder which he tells you comes to pass, and if
he says, 'Let us go after other gods,' which you have not known, 'and let us
serve them,' ³ you shall not listen to the words of that prophet or to that dreamer
of dreams; for the Lord your God is testing you, to know whether you love the
Lord your God with all your heart and with all your soul. ⁴ You shall walk after
the Lord your God and fear him, and keep his commandments and obey his
voice, and you shall serve him and cleave to him.

Deuteronomy 13:1-4 (RSV)

**You need to accept that God will subject you to ongoing "quality control"
tests**

If you want to be successful as a disciple and to grow as quickly and as far as
possible, then you will need to come to terms with the fact that God carries out
these ongoing quality control tests. Stop being surprised, perplexed or annoyed

by them and just seek to pass them. Then seek to serve Him as faithfully as you can, while going through them. Seek to pass each of His tests and to graduate upwards to the next level.

However, be aware as well that the inevitable result of every such promotion is that you will then be required to take even harder tests. In short, do everything in the full knowledge that you are being continually tested. Also accept that that is a valid part of how God operates, because He wants to search you and find out what you are capable of. He also wants to find out what your real thoughts and motives are:

And you, Solomon my son, know the God of your father and serve him with a whole heart and with a willing mind, for the Lord searches all hearts and understands every plan and thought.......
1 Chronicles 29:9(a) (ESV)

And he who searches the hearts of men knows what is the mind of the Spirit, because the Spirit intercedes for the saints according to the will of God.
Romans 8:27 (RSV)

Therefore the fact that you are regularly tested and exposed to severe difficulties, even for long periods, is not a sign that God is against you or has abandoned you. Neither does it mean that He disapproves of you. Far from it. It is actually evidence that He regards you as being His. You are being treated as a disciple. That is the point, which far too many of us miss.

We tend to assume that difficulty and trials are obviously a departure from God's plan for us. In fact, much of the time, they *are* His plan. So we need to stop viewing these struggles as an aberration that ought not to be allowed to happen to a Christian. Instead, start to see them all as normal, and even advantageous.

You would never succeed in an army career if you never got the chance to experience living under canvas, or even sleeping under hedges, in arctic, desert and jungle conditions. Likewise, it would be a very inadequate training regime if they never let you go on assault courses or cross country runs or mountain climbs etc. The fact that you are subjected to such things is a sign that the senior officers take you, and your training, very seriously.

They would actually be letting you down, and letting your country down, if they did not regularly expose you to such arduous conditions and test you up to, and even beyond, your current limits. One of the reasons why the Royal Marines and Parachute Regiment did so well in the Falklands War, and defeated an Argentinian force which was many times larger in terms of numbers, was because they had been so well trained.

They were far hardier, both in mind and body, than the Argentinian conscripts. The British soldiers, all of whom are volunteers, were used to sleeping out all night on Dartmoor in the cold and wet. Therefore, the bleak terrain of South Georgia and the Falklands did not cause them any concern. It seemed quite familiar, after all they had been through in training exercises.

I also remember my Dad telling me about some of his Army training. In particular, he spoke of how they were required to crawl across the ground while live bullets were being fired horizontally, just two or three feet above them. The Army did that because they wanted them to get used to the experience of being fired at. Then they would not panic, or be fazed, by the whizz of bullets passing nearby in real battles later on.

Have I been painting an excessively negative picture of what it means to be a Christian, over-emphasising the struggles and under-emphasising the benefits?

I hope that what I have said in this chapter is balanced. I have attempted to emphasise the joys and benefits that come from being Jesus' disciple, both in this life, and also in eternity. However I have also gone to great lengths to try to remind you of the downsides as well. It could be that in my efforts to correct the imbalance in most present day Western churches I have made the mistake of over-emphasising the struggles.

To some readers I may have given the impression that those difficulties are continuous and unrelenting for all of us. They are not. In reality, for most of us, they come and go. That said, the truth is that for a real Christian, the opposition and the struggles come more often than we would like and they stay for longer than we would like. That is why the Bible speaks of these things so regularly and frankly.

What I have tried to do, therefore, is to draw attention to the warnings made by the apostles, and by Jesus in particular. The warnings are *theirs,* not mine. So is the level of emphasis they give to this theme. I have only emphasised these issues because the Bible does so. That said, the best way for you to gauge whether I am guilty of any imbalance is to read the whole New Testament right through.

Ask yourself, as you go along, how much of it is pointing to the *benefits* of being a Christian and how much is speaking about the *difficulties* it brings. Then you *can* decide for yourself what the overall message of the Bible is on this issue, and which of these things the Bible emphasises the most.

Having come to a conclusion on that point, then ask yourself whether the picture the Bible paints of what life will be like for a real Christian is the same as, or different from, what you may have been taught to expect by any churches you have been part of to date.

I suspect that you may conclude at the end of that process that it is in the majority of the churches in the West that the real imbalance is to be found. Their emphasis is usually on ease, comfort and prosperity, and they generally deny, or are silent about, anything which might alarm us.

Jesus is entirely realistic about what stage we are at. He is also patient with us as we gradually learn lessons and grow as disciples.

It is also possible that you have picked up the mistaken impression that because it can be difficult to be a disciple at times then it follows that Jesus must be a harsh taskmaster who is never satisfied with us. That is absolutely not the case. It is very true that Jesus always wants us to go further, get stronger, become wiser, bear more fruit etc. However, He is also entirely realistic about the current level of our maturity at any given time.

Remember that Jesus was, is, and always will be, a human being, as well as being God. He therefore grew up and learned things gradually, just as we do. He also faced the same struggles we face and He knows how hard life can be for us at times:

For we have not a high priest who is unable to sympathize with our weaknesses, but one who in every respect has been tempted as we are, yet without sin.
Hebrews 4:15 (RSV)

He can deal gently with the ignorant and wayward, since he himself is beset with weakness.
Hebrews 5:2 (RSV)

Therefore, if we are a two week old Christian who knows very little and has only just begun to take the first faltering steps as a disciple, then Jesus will expect very little from us. He will be pleased by the tiniest little steps forward. He will also fully expect us to make errors, misjudge situations, get into messes and fall flat on our faces. In fact, He will expect us to do all those things *regularly*.

That is what all new believers do. They are spiritual infants and have got to learn by trial and error and by making mistakes. There is no other way. That's how we learn anything in life, for example maths or playing the piano or riding a bike. We have no alternative but to start as absolute novices and gradually develop from there. Jesus is fully aware of that.

You do not become angry, or even feel dissatisfied, when your five year old falls off their bicycle when they first try to ride it without stabilizers. Likewise, Jesus is not angry when we try things and make mistakes. He fully understands and even sympathizes. He remembers that He too had to learn and develop gradually, as He grew up from a child to a youth to a young man.

He was always God, even as a child. Nevertheless, He chose to limit Himself, such that even He had to learn things step by step. In terms of His human nature, He did not begin with complete knowledge or understanding. We know that because the Bible says His wisdom *increased* over the years. Luke makes this clear when speaking of Jesus's upbringing:

And Jesus increased in wisdom and in stature, and in favor with God and man.
Luke 2:52 (RSV)

We should therefore make sure we get this very clear and be reassured and encouraged. A piano teacher expects less from a five year old beginner than from a ten year old who has reached grade 3 or 4. And he expects less of that ten year old than of a 16 year old who is preparing to take grade 8. Yet, despite the fact that they are at different levels, the piano teacher could be equally pleased with all three of those youngsters.

Relative to their age and length of experience, they might all be doing equally well in his eyes. Or they may not. It depends on each child's own diligence, commitment, work-rate and attentiveness etc. The teacher might, for example, be more pleased with the attitude and *relative* rate of progress of the 10 year old than with that of the 16 year old, even though the latter is further ahead in *absolute* terms.

We can all see that point very easily in the context of piano teachers and the like, but we need to grasp that it also applies to us as disciples. So, the fact that Jesus always wants us to go further, become better, and grow more like Him, does not mean that He is unreasonable or difficult to please. He may or may not be pleased with the current state of our attitude, or the level of our maturity relative to our age.

However, whether He is or not, He will still want us to go further, try new things, learn more, and take more risks for Him. Those will always be His ambitions for us, however much, or little, progress we may have made to date. But it absolutely doesn't follow that He is therefore against us, or impossible to please.

You have only to read the seven letters to the seven churches in Revelation chapters two and three, to know that there are some people with whom Jesus is very pleased, even though they may not realise it. So, we need to recognise that, whatever stage we are at, Jesus will always want us to become more mature. That is still the case, even if we have already been growing in maturity for 70 years and have come a long way.

Even so, it doesn't mean that He is against us, or that He is an endless critic who can never be satisfied. He is delighted with us at times and thrilled by any progress we make. Nevertheless, He still urges us to keep going, and never to stop growing and maturing. That is the right way to see Jesus. He is infinitely understanding and realistic, but also intensely ambitious for us, as any good parent is.

CHAPTER 3

CULTIVATE THE ATTITUDE OF THANKFULNESS UNTIL IT IS A HABIT

[4]Rejoice in the Lord always; again I will say, rejoice!
Philippians 4:4 (NASB)

[18] give thanks in all circumstances, for this is God's will for you in Christ Jesus.
1 Thessalonians 5:18 (NIV)

And now we thank thee, our God, and praise thy glorious name.
1 Chronicles 29:13 (RSV)

[1]It is good to give thanks to the LORD
And to sing praises to Your name, O Most High;
Psalm 92:1 (NASB)

[1]I will give thanks to the LORD with my whole heart,
in the company of the upright, in the congregation.
Psalm 111:1 (RSV)

[16] I have not stopped giving thanks for you, remembering you in my prayers.
Ephesians 1:16 (NIV)

[57] But thanks be to God! He gives us the victory through our Lord Jesus Christ.
1 Corinthians 15:57 (NIV)

[7]I will offer to thee the sacrifice of thanksgiving
and call on the name of the LORD
Psalm 116:17 (RSV)

[23]He who brings thanksgiving as his sacrifice honors me;
to him who orders his way aright
I will show the salvation of God!"
Psalm 50:23(RSV)

As children, most of us will have been told that we need to be thankful and to express it by saying so out loud. It is easy to see why. Firstly, it is good manners and it makes us more pleasant to be with. However, there is far more to it than that. Having an attitude of thankfulness towards God, and also towards other people, has a major bearing on how well we do in the Christian life and how far we progress as disciples. An ungrateful, complaining Christian will not get very far. Moreover, such grumbling and moaning will displease God and we will receive God's discipline as a result of it.

Consider the reaction of the Israelites after God had performed a whole series of miracles to get them out of Egypt. They were travelling away from Egypt and towards the Promised Land when they saw Egyptian soldiers pursuing them. It is understandable that they should feel afraid, but they went beyond that in their reaction. They began to *complain* about God and even said that it would have been better if He had left them in Egypt:

⁹The Egyptians pursued them, all Pharaoh's horses and chariots and his horsemen and his army, and overtook them encamped at the sea, by Pi-ha-hi'roth, in front of Ba'al-ze'phon. ¹⁰When Pharaoh drew near, the people of Israel lifted up their eyes, and behold, the Egyptians were marching after them; and they were in great fear. And the people of Israel cried out to the LORD; ¹¹and they said to Moses, "Is it because there are no graves in Egypt that you have taken us away to die in the wilderness? What have you done to us, in bringing us out of Egypt? ¹²Is not this what we said to you in Egypt, 'Let us alone and let us serve the Egyptians'? For it would have been better for us to serve the Egyptians than to die in the wilderness."

Exodus 14:9-12 (RSV)

The people grumbled on this occasion, but it wasn't the exception. It was the norm. They continued to complain about other things, and about the desert and the food in particular:

¹They set out from Elim, and all the congregation of the people of Israel came to the wilderness of Sin, which is between Elim and Sinai, on the fifteenth day of the second month after they had departed from the land of Egypt. ²And the whole congregation of the people of Israel murmured against Moses and Aaron in the wilderness, ³and said to them, "Would that we had died by the hand of the LORD in the land of Egypt, when we sat by the fleshpots and ate bread to the full; for you have brought us out into this wilderness to kill this whole assembly with hunger."

Exodus 16:1-3 (RSV)

Although things were difficult, God provided for all their needs. He gave them food in the form of manna, which He provided supernaturally. Even so, that did not prevent the people complaining on a subsequent occasion when they faced another difficulty. This time it was lack of water:

¹All the congregation of the people of Israel moved on from the wilderness of Sin by stages, according to the commandment of the LORD, and camped at Reph'idim; but there was no water for the people to drink. 2Therefore the people found fault with Moses, and said, "Give us water to drink." And Moses said to them, "Why do you find fault with me? Why do you put the LORD to the proof?"

³But the people thirsted there for water, and the people murmured against Moses, and said, "Why did you bring us up out of Egypt, to kill us and our children and our cattle with thirst?" ⁴ So Moses cried to the LORD, "What shall I do with this people? They are almost ready to stone me." ⁵And the LORD said to Moses, "Pass on before the people, taking with you some of the elders of Israel; and take in your hand the rod with which you struck the Nile, and go. ⁶ Behold, I will stand before you there on the rock at Horeb; and you shall strike the rock, and water shall come out of it, that the people may drink." And Moses did so, in the sight of the elders of Israel. ⁷And he called the name of the place Massah and Mer'ibah, because of the faultfinding of the children of Israel, and because they put the LORD to the proof by saying, "Is the LORD among us or not?"

Exodus 17:1-7 (RSV)

God felt hurt and angry when the people of Israel complained about these problems, and for focusing on what He had *not* done for them, instead of giving thanks for all the amazing things He *had* done for them. But it wasn't a one-off occasion. They kept on and on moaning. God felt it was so unacceptable that He eventually needed to punish them for it:

¹Now the people became like those who complain of adversity in the hearing of the LORD; and when the LORD heard it, His anger was kindled, and the fire of the LORD burned among them and consumed some of the outskirts of the camp.

Numbers 11:1 (NASB)

However, the grumbling didn't end there, and neither did God's anger. Therefore, when the people of Israel were still in the wilderness, God decided that all the people who were over the age of 20 at the time of leaving Egypt (except for Joshua and Caleb) would be allowed to die in the wilderness. He therefore made them wait in the wilderness for another 38 years while all those who had complained died off, one by one. They were never allowed to cross over and enter the Promised Land, all because they had complained repeatedly and been so ungrateful. That is how seriously God took this:

²⁹ In this wilderness your bodies will fall—every one of you twenty years old or more who was counted in the census and who has grumbled against me.

Numbers 14:29 (NIV)

God feels very strongly about ingratitude and complaining. He really doesn't like it. Therefore, if we have any sense, we will take note. What is the point of God telling us what does, and does not, please Him about our attitudes, if we then pay no attention and just carry on as we were? If we don't listen to Him voluntarily, then He will have to escalate to more drastic ways of correcting us. Why would any sensible person want that, when we could simply choose to listen willingly?

73

Ingratitude is the norm. Gratitude is the exception

We are selfish due to our sinful, flesh nature. Therefore the norm is for us to be ungrateful. Gratitude is exceptional. We have all experienced ingratitude from others and we don't like it. Yet we also know we have all been guilty of it ourselves. Jesus frequently encountered it. On one occasion He healed ten lepers of their leprosy, but only one of them thanked Him. The rest just walked away, without saying a word:

[11]While He was on the way to Jerusalem, He was passing between Samaria and Galilee. [12]As He entered a village, ten leprous men who stood at a distance met Him; [13]and they raised their voices, saying, "Jesus, Master, have mercy on us!" [14]When He saw them, He said to them, "Go and show yourselves to the priests." And as they were going, they were cleansed. [15]Now one of them, when he saw that he had been healed, turned back, glorifying God with a loud voice, [16]and he fell on his face at His feet, giving thanks to Him. And he was a Samaritan. [17]Then Jesus answered and said, "Were there not ten cleansed? But the nine--where are they? [18]"Was no one found who returned to give glory to God, except this foreigner?" [19]And He said to him, "Stand up and go; your faith has made you well."

Luke 17:11-19 (NASB)

I would like to be able to adopt a superior attitude concerning those nine lepers who never thanked Jesus, and to say that their ingratitude was astonishing. However, I have done the same thing myself, many times. I have often failed to thank God for His kindness to me and I have also failed to thank other people who have helped me.

As I look back now I can think of all sorts of people, especially teachers, bosses, and work colleagues, who have taught me, helped me, trained me or corrected me. Yet, while they were doing these things I did not always appreciate, or even recognise, what they were doing for me. I sometimes took such people for granted. There were times when I even resented them.

I have since found, having been a boss myself, that staff often took me for granted or failed to recognise the efforts I made to help them. That bothered me, but it also reminded me of how I had equally failed to appreciate my own bosses in the past. I cannot go back now and deal with those past events differently. But I can, at least, try to alter my attitude from now on.

The corrosive effect of grumbling and complaining

Ingratitude doesn't stay silent for long. It inevitably turns into grumbling out loud, which is an even worse problem. It has a corrosive and poisonous effect on everybody. It harms the person complaining. Plus it undermines those who listen

74

to it, and especially those who begin to join in with it. That's another dangerous feature of moaning. It is highly contagious.

Any member of staff in a workplace who is prone to complaining will soon cause others to join in. An atmosphere of discontent and resentment will then quickly spread all around that office or factory. Within weeks, a happy workforce can be turned into a sour, embittered group through the influence of just one or two regular complainers.

They will soon have most of the others focusing on every place where the "glass is half empty". They too will then start seeing things in the most negative light possible, rather than choosing to see those things as opportunities, learning experiences, or even privileges. I've come to the conclusion now, after many years' experience in business, that I will not recruit or continue to employ an unhappy, complaining person.

By that I mean someone who is habitually like that and who chooses to remain so. They are always unproductive, disruptive and divisive. They also drag down those who are around them and make them unproductive too. It would be difficult to over-state the harm that a regularly discontented person can do.

They would probably do less harm to your business if they went around pouring acid over the furniture and equipment. The harmful effect of that would probably be less expensive than the damage caused by allowing habitual complainers to work for you. The influence always seems to operate in only one direction. Complainers never get 'dragged up' to the level of the happy staff.

They always seem to bring the contented people down to their level. So, in my business, I learned to take it seriously, just as God does. I took decisive action to exclude, or even remove, such people. I prefer that they go to work for someone else, who is less particular about what type of staff he takes on.

Complaining and resenting will cause your personality or character to become sour

If you complain habitually and tend to resent people then your very nature will become sour over time. The effect is very marked. The person becomes like sour milk. It affects them to their core, and a sense of grievance overtakes them. For example, I can think of a man who works at a garden centre near my house. Whenever I have been there he seems bitter, reluctant and uncooperative.

On one occasion I overheard him speaking in a disparaging way about his boss, the proprietor of the garden centre. He was openly doing so in front of me, a customer. I don't think he cared that I could hear him. In fact, the expression of his reservoir of resentments had become so normal for him that he probably didn't even notice that he was doing it.

The net effect of it all was that he was obviously unhappy. Yet, what was the chain of causation? Was he bitter because of the circumstances of his life, or was his life the way it was because of his bitterness? It was probably both. That is where giving thanks can really change a person's life. To give thanks to God, and also to express one's gratitude to others, is not only a *symptom* of an already healthy heart-attitude. It is also the *cause* of it. In other words, we can cure ourselves of sourness, and even of selfishness, simply by learning to give thanks.

To complain is to lack gratitude

One of the things that most displeases God about complaining is that it indicates an underlying ingratitude. That is a very hurtful thing for anyone to have to deal with, even for God. Being a parent, and also running a business, has helped me to see why ingratitude is such a bad thing. It is a deep insult. It indicates that we care very little for the person whom we are failing to thank or appreciate.

I did not properly appreciate, or thank, my parents when I was younger. Now that I have children myself, it gets to me if they take me for granted, or don't appreciate what I do for them. We all feel wounded when we are used, or taken for granted, by other people. That is especially so where we have gone out of our way to help and yet the other person seems only to be aware of what we *didn't do* for them.

People have often done that to me. However, I can't easily condemn it, because I know that I have also done it to others. Even worse, I know that I have done it to God. And I've done it many times. I'd like to cut all complaining out of my life, but it isn't easy. Even so, that should be our aim.

To complain is to lack understanding

Whenever we complain we also reveal the fact that we lack understanding and a sense of proportion. Firstly, we are failing to remember all those countless things that God has done for us, or which He has protected us from. It indicates that we are focused excessively on something else, that we wish was not happening, or that we lack, but forgetting everything that we do have.

Or, at least, it means we are not keeping those good things in proper perspective and remembering them, even while we struggle with some difficulty. I have noticed that I tend only to get irritated and moan about small things, i.e. just the little delays and minor disappointments of life. When I've had to face much bigger crises, blows and losses, I've usually been much calmer.

It's possibly because when I face major problems I remember to pray and seek God's grace to help me to endure. However, when the problem is very minor, I tend to forget to pray. So, I am less likely to ask for His help and therefore have to deal with the problem on my own, in my own strength. That may explain some of it.

Complaining indicates that your sinful flesh nature is alive and well and has not been crucified.

When niggling little problems get under our skin and cause us to complain, they demonstrate that our sinful flesh nature hasn't been properly crucified yet. That's not a good sign, but there is at least this one advantage in being exposed to aggravating little problems. Our reactions remind us that we need to work harder to crucify our own flesh and die to self. Low level suffering or inconveniences, especially unexpected ones, are very good at exposing areas of uncrucified flesh, where the sin nature is still active within us.

There's a valuable lesson in that. Perhaps that is one reason why God keeps on allowing some rain to fall into our lives. It brings us down to earth and reminds us of our real condition, and the true level of our maturity, or immaturity. It also reminds us of our need for Him and of our need to do battle with our sinful flesh nature and to keep putting it to death. (See Book Seven for more detail).

So, one important thing which is revealed when we choose either to complain or to give thanks is whether the 'new man' or the 'old man' is in control of us at that moment. The old man is a name the Bible uses for our sinful flesh nature. The new man, conversely, is the phrase the Bible uses for our own spirit which is born again and comes to life when we become a Christian. The new man cannot sin, whereas the old man cannot do anything other than sin. Both are part of you and you will have that old man within you and causing problems until you die. Then you will, at last, be rid of him.

At any given moment, you have to decide whether you will let your old man or your new man be your 'spokesman'. The question is to which of them will you 'pass the microphone'? You always have a choice at any given moment. You can let the old man speak, in which case he will complain. Or you can let the new man speak, in which case he will give thanks. So, you can easily tell whether your new man or old man is speaking on your behalf, simply by listening to whether your mouth is giving thanks or moaning.

To complain is to demonstrate that we are self-centred

The fact that we complain also indicates that we are still self-centred, rather than focused on Jesus and on other people, as we ought to be. Again, that discovery is our cue to seek to change and to ask God for His help. When we do complain, thus indicating that we're preoccupied with self, then the best thing to do is to openly acknowledge it. Confess it to God as sin, rather than trying to justify it or deny it. Ask Him to redeem the situation by using those difficult circumstances constructively and profitably, so as to help us to see what we're really like, and to change.

God is never to blame for anything and He is never unjust. Therefore, whatever happens, you can never validly complain about Him

When we complain and grumble we can get to the point where we are actually blaming or accusing God for things. We might not say it out loud, but that could be what we are really thinking. Whenever we do that we are deluded. God is never to blame for anything, no matter what it is, or how it happens. Whatever you may have experienced, He is not at fault for it. God is perfect. He never does anything wrong or unjust. It is an impossibility, and we are foolish even to entertain the idea.

Therefore, don't even consider criticizing God or lashing out at Him. Don't even do it indirectly or by implication. You would be accusing the wrong person. If you have been blaming Him, then you have been falsely accusing the best friend you've ever had. Far from being the cause of your problems, He is your closest ally. He cares for you more than anybody else, no matter how bad your circumstances may be. He also has a plan for each of us which is for our good, not to harm us:

For I know the plans I have for you, says the LORD, plans for welfare and not for evil, to give you a future and a hope.
Jeremiah 29:11 (RSV)

Job had to suffer more testing than any of us are ever likely to face. He lost all his children and all his possessions in one day. Yet, he refused to blame God for it. That fact warmed God's heart because, although Job never knew it, the very reason he had lost everything was because the Devil had challenged God to test Job. Satan had said that if He did, then Job would curse God to His face. However, Job didn't. He refused to blame God, and that needs to be our attitude too:

20Then Job arose, and rent his robe, and shaved his head, and fell upon the ground, and worshiped. 21And he said, "Naked I came from my mother's womb, and naked shall I return; the LORD gave, and the LORD has taken away; blessed be the name of the LORD." 22In all this Job did not sin or charge God with wrong.
Job 1:20-22 (RSV)

At the end of the book of Job, God Himself speaks in response to the various explanations of his sufferings that had been put forward by Job's friends, and even by Job. The things they said did not accurately reflect the true facts, or represent God's actual views or motives. We all need to be so careful, because we are very limited in our understanding. We can only grasp parts of what is really going on at times.

We would therefore be seriously at fault if, with our severely limited minds and incomplete knowledge, we tried to be too emphatic about things we don't understand and which only God can. In particular, we must never speak, or even think, in such a way as to suggest that He is at fault, because He never is. If we think He is, we are just wrong and foolish, no matter what the circumstances may be:

⁶Then the LORD spoke to Job out of the storm: ⁷"Brace yourself like a man; I will question you, and you shall answer me. ⁸ "Would you discredit my justice? Would you condemn me to justify yourself ? ⁹ Do you have an arm like God's, and can your voice thunder like his?

Job 40:6-9 (NIV)

Thankfulness opens our eyes to see the world more accurately and in proper perspective

God tells us repeatedly to be thankful. When we are it has the effect of opening our own eyes. It enables us to see the world more realistically. It puts our circumstances into perspective and corrects the way we see God and the people around us. Expressing our gratitude in one area also helps us to see what else we have to be thankful for. So, don't wait until you already *feel* thankful. Express thanks now, regardless of how you feel.

Do it as a decision of your will, even if you don't yet feel thankful. Later on your feelings will follow your actions and come into line with what you are saying. Expressing thankfulness lifts your own spirit, changes your mood, and will help you to actually become thankful. It does so even if you weren't feeling that way when you began giving thanks.

Thankfulness helps us to endure things more patiently

Expressing thanks also helps us to grow in patience and endurance. It alters the way we see things and gives us peace and greater resilience. A thankful person can endure far more than a person who is ungrateful. That is partly because they see the world, and their situation, more accurately. They will take into account the positive factors which are so easily forgotten if we are focusing on what we lack, or on something which has annoyed or disappointed us.

This is so important. A thankful person will become, and remain, an encouraged person. If so, they will be very difficult to defeat. However, a complaining person will, inevitably, become discouraged. As such, they will be much easier to defeat. They will find it much harder to overcome their circumstances or to win the battles which life throws at all of us.

Thankfulness is good for our health, spiritually and physically

The habit of being thankful if, practised over a long period, will have a powerful effect even on our health. It will change us spiritually and physically. We know, even from our own experience, that that is true. I also know from a consultant I know who specializes in mouth and throat cancer that there is a distinct pattern among the patients they see. It tends to be men who are bitter, angry and unhappy that get most of these cancers. The Bible would support that general point:

A joyful heart is good medicine,
But a broken spirit dries up the bones.
Proverbs 17:22 (NASB)

Do not be grieved, for the joy of the LORD is your strength.
Nehemiah 8:10 (b) (NASB)

Thankfulness needs to be expressed out loud, not just in thought

You might convince yourself that you are a thankful person deep down, and that you feel thankful even if you don't express it. But that won't do. What really counts is what you *say*, not what you think, or believe you think. The way God has made us is such that our mouths have a vital role to play. We need to speak, not just to feel. Thankfulness needs to be expressed in words. It's not enough just to feel thankful inwardly, or to think thankful thoughts. We need to say it out loud to God and also to other people:

¹O give thanks to the LORD,
for he is good;
for his steadfast love endures forever!
²Let the redeemed of the LORD say so,
whom he has redeemed from trouble
Psalm 107:1-2 (RSV)

We cry out loud to God when we are in a crisis, rather than just thinking silent thoughts asking for His help. So too, our thanksgiving needs to be audibly expressed, either in speech or in song:

¹⁹Then they cried to the LORD in their trouble,
and he delivered them from their distress;
²⁰he sent forth his word, and healed them,
and delivered them from destruction.
²¹ Let them thank the LORD for his steadfast love,
for his wonderful works to the sons of men!
²²And let them offer sacrifices of thanksgiving,
and tell of his deeds in songs of joy!
                          Psalm 107:19-22 (RSV)

Moreover, our thanksgiving should frequently be in the presence and hearing of other people, not just when we are alone:

³¹Let them thank the LORD for his steadfast love,
for his wonderful works to the sons of men!
³² Let them extol him in the congregation of the people,
and praise him in the assembly of the elders.
                          Psalm 107:31-32 (RSV)

³⁰With my mouth I will give great thanks to the LORD;
I will praise him in the midst of the throng.
                          Psalm 109:30 (RSV)

We need to get into the habit of finding, and taking, opportunities to speak out loud to give thanks for our blessings. We must tell God and tell others. The very act of speaking in that way will improve us from the inside out and change how we think, feel, and act. Plus, it will affect other people and do them good. It will make us a positive influence, rather than a bad one.

Thankfulness and praise enable us to become closer to God and to gain access to Him

See how the Psalmist expresses this thought in this well-known verse:

⁴Enter His gates with thanksgiving
And His courts with praise.
Give thanks to Him, bless His name.
                          Psalm 100:4 (NASB)

The above verse contains an important clue as to how to get into God's presence. The clear implication is that the very act of giving thanks is what enables us to enter God's gates, i.e. at the outer edge of His presence. Then, praising Him enables us to go even closer and enter His inner courts. It refers to moving from the outer to the inner areas of God's dwelling place.

Giving thanks brings us closer to God, such that we can enter the 'gates' at the outer edge of His dwelling place. Praise brings us even closer, such that we can go in to His court, thereby having direct access to Him and being heard by Him, in much the same way as we might gain access to a King or President. Anyone can write to a President, but not everybody can have direct personal access to his office.

So, if we want to get closer to God we need to focus on both thanksgiving and praise. Set out to make both of these central to your whole way of life. Doing so will alter you and your attitudes, but it will also enable you to enter God's presence in your prayers and to relate to Him more intimately. This is not just some formula to manipulate God and get Him to do what you want. It means adopting a wholly new attitude and approach to God and persisting with it until it becomes the norm. Then it will seriously impact our relationship with God.

Thankfulness is primarily a decision, not a feeling

We often make the mistake of waiting until we feel like giving thanks before we do so. However, it doesn't work that way. Thanks are due to God whether we feel like it or not. We are to express our thanks as a decision of our will. It doesn't need to be the natural outpouring of an excited or happy mood. It's fine if it is, but it doesn't need to be.

The reality is that that is not always how we feel. Sometimes we are not naturally happy or buoyant. However, we cannot allow ourselves to be limited or controlled by our feelings. God is worthy of our thanks and praise at all times, regardless of our changing moods.

⁶As therefore you received Christ Jesus the Lord, so live in him, ⁷rooted and built up in him and established in the faith, just as you were taught, abounding in thanksgiving.

Colossians 2:6-7 (RSV)

The real reason for thanking God is not that we feel thankful. It is simply that He is worthy of being thanked, whether we feel it or not Our responsibility is to decide to be thankful and then to decide to express it, regardless of what our actual feelings might be. We are to offer thanks as a form of offering or sacrifice. That may well mean doing so when we do not feel like it and when, instead, we actually feel low or sad or anxious:

"Offer to God a sacrifice of thanksgiving
and pay your vows to the Most High;
Psalm 50:14 (NASB)

¹² I am under vows to you, O God;
I will present my thank offerings to you.
                    Psalm 56:12 (NIV)

He who brings thanksgiving as his sacrifice honors me;
to him who orders his way aright I will show the salvation of God!
                    Psalm 50:23 (RSV)

When the Bible refers to offering God a "sacrifice" of thanksgiving, the implication is that our offering of thanks is a decision or a step, rather than a spontaneous outburst. It's something we choose to do and to give. It's not just a feeling. It may even be difficult, and require us to overcome our feelings. We may even need to tell ourselves what to do:

¹⁷I will give thanks to the LORD
according to His righteousness
and will sing praise to the name
of the LORD Most High.
                    Psalm 7:17 (NASB)

Twice the Psalmist says "I will" when He refers to giving thanks. He is speaking of His will, not his feelings, and indicating that he is deciding to give thanks. It is a choice, or a resolve, not an emotion. In fact, he is actually speaking to himself and instructing himself to give thanks. The Psalmist quite often tells himself what to do. Here he is telling himself to bless the Lord:

1Bless the LORD, O my soul,
And all that is within me, bless His holy name.
²Bless the LORD, O my soul,
And forget none of His benefits;
                    Psalm 103:1-2 (NASB)

Presumably the Psalmist tells himself to do this because, at that moment, giving thanks is not his natural inclination. It is not what he feels like doing, but it is what he chooses to do, because he knows he should. We need to copy him in that approach.

Make a decision always to rejoice and give thanks, regardless of your circumstances

Make a decision that no matter what your circumstances may be, you will give thanks to the LORD anyway. Do it every day, indeed several times every day. Train yourself to give thanks. Set out to make it your habit. The more often you do it, the more habitual it will become. Then you will find it easier to continue to thank God by force of habit, even in hard times:

¹⁷ Though the fig tree should not blossom,
nor fruit be on the vines,
the produce of the olive fail
and the fields yield no food,
the flock be cut off from the fold
and there be no herd in the stalls,
¹⁸ yet I will rejoice in the Lord;
I will take joy in the God of my salvation.
Habakkuk 3:17-18 (ESV)

¹⁶Rejoice always; ¹⁷pray without ceasing; ¹⁸in everything give thanks; for this is God's will for you in Christ Jesus.
1 Thessalonians 5:16-18 (NASB)

Note that Paul says we are to give thanks "*in*" everything. He does not say we are to give thanks "*for*" everything. He means that however bad our current circumstances may be, we are still to give thanks *in them*. We are not necessarily giving thanks for the ordeal, or for our suffering. The point is that even in those adverse circumstances we should still look for things to be thankful for, such as our children, health, family, job, home etc.

Doing that puts the current difficulty into its proper context. We then realise that it is vastly outnumbered by the many blessings we also have. We still have much to be thankful for, however bad things may get. It is giving thanks in those painful situations that touches God's heart the most. That fact alone makes it worthwhile. However, it will also alter the way we see our situation and especially the way we react to it.

Sometimes giving thanks requires an effort of the will and can be a sacrifice

God is very realistic. He is well aware that at certain times, when we face tests and ordeals, it is difficult to give thanks. At such times to go ahead and give thanks anyway, despite not feeling like doing so, is a kind of sacrifice. It is something that you do as a decision of your will, from obedience rather than spontaneously. God values it very highly when we offer thanksgiving in that manner. As we saw above, the Psalmist refers to it as the "sacrifice of thanksgiving":

I will offer to thee the sacrifice of thanksgiving
and call on the name of the Lord
Psalm 116:17 (RSV)

Therefore, try to develop the habit of giving thanks daily, every time you pray. Let it become a natural and permanent fixture in your prayer life, regardless of how you feel. Indeed, if anything, it is particularly at difficult times that you most need to give thanks. Firstly it pleases God, but secondly, it also helps you to refocus your thinking onto God, and on to all that He does for you, rather than dwelling on whatever your current problem is. That's a good habit to have and will help you, in more challenging times, not to neglect to give thanks.

Develop the habit of reminding yourself about the ways that God has helped or rescued you in the past

Most of us tend to make the mistake of being overly fixated upon our current difficulties, whatever they happen to be, and forgetting the many times that God has helped us or rescued us in the past. For that reason, God regularly urged the Jewish people to remind themselves of the many ways that He had provided for them, or helped them, in the past and to believe that He would do so again. Here is a short passage where the Psalmist says that the people forgot what God had done for them in the past. He then begins to list some examples of God's help:

¹¹ They forgot what he had done,
the wonders he had shown them.
¹² He did miracles in the sight of their fathers
in the land of Egypt,
in the region of Zoan.
¹³ He divided the sea and led them through;
he made the water stand firm like a wall.
¹⁴ He guided them with the cloud by day
and with light from the fire all night.
¹⁵ He split the rocks in the desert
and gave them water as abundant as the seas;
*   Psalm 78:11-15 (NIV)*

It is good to do the same and remind ourselves daily of our own personal experiences of God's past provisions and the ways He has rescued us, even if they are not as dramatic as those provided through Moses. It will adjust our attitude, as well as pleasing God.

God is especially pleased and touched when we thank Him in difficult circumstances

If you are struggling to see why thankfulness matters so much to God, try to imagine a situation in a family involving a parent and a child. Imagine that a child has looked forward to a day out at a theme park such as Alton Towers. But then it cannot go ahead, because the weather is too bad, so it has to be cancelled. Instead, the parent can only take the child to a cinema instead. What if that night, when being tucked up in bed the child was to say "*Thank you for taking me to the cinema today*".

That remark would be very touching to the parent and would be remembered long afterwards. Contrast that however with a child who was to complain to the parent and blame them for the cancellation of the trip to Alton Towers. That would be painful. Isn't it just the same with us and God? He is a parent and He feels the same emotions that you or I would feel when faced with such grateful, or ungrateful, words from our own child.

Why the Devil and his demons hate it when we are thankful

We've seen some of the reasons why thankfulness and praise are so important to God and so beneficial to us. It follows, therefore, that the demons who are assigned to obstruct you will not want you to be thankful. They will try very hard to stop you. They know exactly how much it matters and how much depends on it. Be motivated, therefore, by the very fact that the demons *don't* want you to give thanks. Let that very fact spur you on, all the more. Resolve that if the demons don't want you to give thanks, then that is all the more reason to do it.

CHAPTER 4

THE MEANING AND IMPORTANCE OF FAITHFULNESS

Many a man proclaims his own loyalty;
but a faithful man who can find?
Proverbs 20:6 (RSV)

I will look with favor on the faithful in the land, that they may dwell with me;
he who walks in the way that is blameless shall minister to me
Psalm 101:6 (RSV)

[11]'None of the men who came up from Egypt, from twenty years old and upward,
shall see the land which I swore to Abraham, to Isaac and to Jacob; for they did
not follow Me fully, [12]except Caleb the son of Jephunneh the Kenizzite and
Joshua the son of Nun, for they have followed the LORD fully.'
Numbers 32:11-12 (NASB)

[7]"You are the LORD God, who chose Abram and brought him out of Ur of the
Chaldeans and named him Abraham.[8]You found his heart faithful to you, and
you made a covenant with him to give to his descendants the land of the
Canaanites, Hittites, Amorites, Perizzites, Jebusites and Girgashites. You have
kept your promise because you are righteous.
Nehemiah 9:7-8 (NIV)

What is 'faithfulness'?

We could define faithfulness as being trustworthy, reliable, dependable and taking one's responsibilities seriously. This applies to every task or duty and to every relationship we are in. If we had to give it a single word definition, we could say it is 'loyalty'. It means sticking to a task and doing the very best you can with it.

Likewise, it means sticking to a person and remaining true to them, no matter how inconvenient that may become. The main person with whom you need to be faithful is God. He is always your first priority. But He also wants you to be faithful in every area of your life and with every other person. Psalm 15 describes the kind of person God is looking for and it is a very demanding set of specifications:

[1] LORD, who may dwell in your sacred tent?
Who may live on your holy mountain?
[2] The one whose walk is blameless,
who does what is righteous,
who speaks the truth from their heart;

³ whose tongue utters no slander,
who does no wrong to a neighbor,
and casts no slur on others;
⁴ who despises a vile person
but honors those who fear the LORD;
who keeps an oath even when it hurts,
and does not change their mind;
⁵ who lends money to the poor without interest;
who does not accept a bribe against the innocent.
Whoever does these things
will never be shaken.
                                    Psalm 15:1-5 (NIV)

To become faithful is one of God's main aims for us

Faithfulness is so important to God that it is listed as one of the fruit of the Spirit in Galatians chapter five. It is listed there because it is one of the key defining qualities of God's own character. He Himself is totally faithful. He never breaks a promise and He never lets anybody down. God the Father wants you to grow to resemble the character and nature of His Son, Jesus Christ. That's a very ambitious project:

For those whom he foreknew he also predestined to be conformed to the image of his Son, in order that he might be the first-born among many brethren.
                                    Romans 8:29 (RSV)

Consider the extraordinary faithfulness Jesus showed when He stuck to His plan of going to the cross and allowing Himself to be crucified. He could have called it off or saved Himself from it at any time, but He never did. He voluntarily went through with all of it for our sake. That was faithfulness in its most extreme form. In considering how to grow in faithfulness yourself, please also refer to the chapter in this book on truthfulness. The two qualities are distinct, but closely related.

The first step in becoming a faithful person is to *want* to be one

Becoming a consistently faithful person, across every aspect of your life, is a major project. It will take a long time for your character to develop. However, it has to begin somewhere and the best place to begin is by wanting it. You need to set your heart to really seek for this character quality. It needs to be your own aim and your own desire, just as it is God's aim for you.

²I will give heed to the way that is blameless.
Oh when wilt thou come to me?
I will walk with integrity of heart within my house;

³I will not set before my eyes anything that is base.
I hate the work of those who fall away; it shall not cleave to me.
⁴Perverseness of heart shall be far from me;
I will know nothing of evil.
                                    Psalm 101:2-4 (RSV)

You need to pray persistently and sincerely that God would build these qualities into your character. Ask Him to help you to put the Bible into practice in your own life, so that His statutes can be made part of you:

⁴You have ordained Your precepts,
That we should keep them diligently.
⁵Oh that my ways may be established
To keep Your statutes!
                        Psalm 119:4-5 (NASB)

And ask God to remove every kind of falseness from you:

²⁹Remove the false way from me,
And graciously grant me Your law.
                        Psalm 119:29 (NASB)

Go further and ask God to help you to become a 'blameless' person:

⁸⁰May my heart be blameless in Your statutes,
So that I will not be ashamed.
                        Psalm 119:80 (NASB)

Being blameless doesn't mean that we are sinless. Nobody is sinless. It means being sincere, genuine, truthful, godly and committed to obey God's Word to the best of your ability. Some good examples in the Bible of extremely blameless men would be Job, Daniel, Noah and Nathanael. Seek to become like them. However, we do not have to rise to the dizzying heights that they reached in order to be classed as blameless. It is within the reach of ordinary people like us, if we really want it.

Faithfulness is what you do when nobody is watching

Another good definition of faithfulness is that it's the way you do a job when nobody is watching. It is the way you go about painting the back of a shed when you know that nobody is ever going to see it or check it. If you were given that job, would you do it properly and diligently, with all the required coats of paints? Or, would you cut corners and lower your standards? Actually, there never is a time when nobody is watching. God sees everything you ever do.

He not only watches, He takes a keen interest. He is continually looking for evidence of you growing in Christlikeness. And He always wants to either reward or correct what you do. He is committed to improving you and seeing you grow to maturity. So, don't ever imagine that God won't notice. He's interested in every part of your life and He wants you to become faithful in everything you do, including your job. There is no aspect of your life or character in which He is content to allow you to remain carnal, worldly or immature.

God is reliable but unpredictable; we are unreliable but predictable.

Being faithful, or reliable, is not the same as being predictable or dull. On the contrary, God is totally reliable and faithful but He can be very unpredictable. He frequently manages to surprise us by going about things in novel, creative, unusual, unexpected ways. By contrast, we tend to be unreliable and unfaithful, yet we are very predictable. We let people down or behave badly in the same old ways, time and time again. When a person lacks faithfulness and cannot be depended on, he becomes a hazard and a disappointment to those around him. Let that never be said of you:

19Like a bad tooth and an unsteady foot
Is confidence in a faithless man in time of trouble.
Proverbs 25:19 (NASB)

God is looking for disciples who are truly committed to Him and willing to take a stand

The main person with whom we need to be faithful is God Himself. That is a major part of what discipleship is all about. Jesus is looking for men and women who are willing to be truly committed to Him:

6My eyes shall be upon the faithful of the land,
that they may dwell with me;
He who walks in a blameless way
is the one who will minister to me.
Psalm 101:6 (NASB)

The LORD is continually looking around to find people whose hearts are completely His, not just partly so. That means people who are genuinely devoted to Him and determined to obey His commands:

9"For the eyes of the LORD move to and fro throughout the earth that He may
strongly support those whose heart is completely His......
2 Chronicles 16:9 (a) (NASB)

Moreover, God looks around in every generation for men and women upon whom He can rely. He wants people who are willing to take responsibility for their fellow men and to "stand in the gap" to plead for them before God, so that His judgment on them can be averted. However, such faithful, courageous people are so rare that in most generations God struggles to find them. In the days of Ezekiel God couldn't find anybody:

29The people of the land have practiced oppression and committed robbery, and they have wronged the poor and needy and have oppressed the sojourner without justice. 30I searched for a man among them who would build up the wall and stand in the gap before Me for the land, so that I would not destroy it; but I found no one. 31Thus I have poured out My indignation on them; I have consumed them with the fire of My wrath; their way I have brought upon their heads," declares the Lord GOD.

Ezekiel 22:29-31 (NASB)

It is essential to remain true and faithful to God and to represent Him accurately, no matter how isolated that may cause us to be. Even if we are surrounded by wicked people, we must remain true to what the Bible says and be loyal to God and to everything that He stands for. Likewise we must be opposed to, and appalled by, everything that God opposes or is appalled by.

Behaving in such ways will certainly cause us to be isolated at times and even persecuted, but it will please God. Moreover, it will actually bring us under His protection and cause Him to ensure, when judgment comes upon those around us, that we are kept out of it, just as faithful Lot was kept from the judgment which came on Sodom.

Consider this very disturbing passage from Ezekiel which serves as a great inducement to us to stay faithful, no matter how much it may cost us. The passage concerns Ezekiel, to whom God reveals that He is sending angels to act as 'executioners' of those who have engaged in idolatry and other abominations.

However, God specified that a mark should be put on the forehead of all those faithful people who had not engaged in such abominations and who had been appalled and grieved about them, as God was. Such faithful people were to be spared and were not to come under the judgment that was about to happen:

Then he cried in my ears with a loud voice, saying, "Draw near, you executioners of the city, each with his destroying weapon in his hand." 2And lo, six men came from the direction of the upper gate, which faces north, every man with his weapon for slaughter in his hand, and with them was a man clothed in linen, with a writing case at his side. And they went in and stood beside the bronze altar.3 Now the glory of the God of Israel had gone up from the cherubim on which it rested to the threshold of the house; and he called to the man clothed in linen, who had the writing case at his side. 4And the LORD said to him, "Go through the city, through Jerusalem, and put a mark upon the foreheads of the men who sigh and groan over all the abominations that are committed in it."

⁵ And to the others he said in my hearing, "Pass through the city after him, and smite; your eye shall not spare, and you shall show no pity; ⁶ slay old men outright, young men and maidens, little children and women, but touch no one upon whom is the mark. And begin at my sanctuary." So they began with the elders who were before the house. ⁷ Then he said to them, "Defile the house, and fill the courts with the slain. Go forth." So they went forth, and smote in the city.

⁸ And while they were smiting, and I was left alone, I fell upon my face, and cried, "Ah Lord GOD! wilt thou destroy all that remains of Israel in the outpouring of thy wrath upon Jerusalem?" ⁹ Then he said to me, "The guilt of the house of Israel and Judah is exceedingly great; the land is full of blood, and the city full of injustice; for they say, 'The LORD has forsaken the land, and the LORD does not see.' ¹⁰ As for me, my eye will not spare, nor will I have pity, but I will requite their deeds upon their heads."

Ezekiel 9:1-10 (RSV)

In the same way judgment is coming upon all people, including those amongst whom wc live and work. It may not take the same form, and it may not come today, but God's judgment will eventually come. Whenever it does come, we need to be counted among that minority who were loyal to God and who were appalled and grieved by the same things as God.

However much that approach might cause the world around us to scorn or despise us, it will gain us God's approval. Then an equivalent mark, whether literal or metaphorical, will be placed upon us. I want to receive such a mark and to keep it, no matter what difficulty that creates.

Sometimes God cannot find even one faithful person in a place or situation. Let that never be so wherever you are

When sin and rebellion are on the increase in a town, workplace, or organization God looks for people who are remaining faithful. Through such people God can, and does, make a difference. They can be used by God to turn the situation around, to 'rebuild the wall' and to stand in the gap while the wall is being rebuilt. Through them God can do great things.

Moreover, where He finds such a person, even if they are the only one, God will sometimes turn His anger away from everybody.

Then His judgment on that whole place is delayed, or even avoided, all for the sake of that one person. But there are times when God cannot find even one such

92

faithful believer, whose heart is true and brave and genuinely loyal to Him. In such a case, where there is not even one faithful person, God's judgment is likely to follow quickly:

28 And her prophets have daubed for them with whitewash, seeing false visions and divining lies for them, saying, 'Thus says the Lord GOD,' when the LORD has not spoken. 29 The people of the land have practiced extortion and committed robbery; they have oppressed the poor and needy, and have extorted from the sojourner without redress. 30 And I sought for a man among them who should build up the wall and stand in the breach before me for the land, that I should not destroy it; but I found none. 31 Therefore I have poured out my indignation upon them; I have consumed them with the fire of my wrath; their way have I requited upon their heads, says the Lord GOD."

Ezekiel 22:28-31 (RSV)

In whatever situation or place you may be, you could be that faithful person, perhaps the only one there. If so, your individual faithfulness could cause God's judgment on all of those around you to be delayed or avoided. That will, at the very least, provide more time for the people you know or work with to repent and turn to God

Growing as a disciple involves moving continually from one test to the next

I have slowly learned over the years how to be a manager of staff. In doing so, I have gained many insights into how God operates as a 'manager'. He has objectives for each of us for growth and development, mainly in character, but also in knowledge, skill and experience.

He wants to bring us forward and upward, but also to find out how far we've already come. Therefore He sets lots of little tests for us. You may not even realise that you are going through such tests, but you are.

He is watching very closely to see how you handle each of them. He also knows all your thoughts and motives and He is always searching your heart to see what you are really thinking in any situation that you face:

9 "As for you, my son Solomon, know the God of your father, and serve Him with a whole heart and a willing mind; for the LORD searches all hearts, and understands every intent of the thoughts. If you seek Him, He will let you find Him; but if you forsake Him, He will reject you forever.

1 Chronicles 28:9(NASB)

I know, my God that you test the heart and have pleasure in uprightness……..

1 Chronicles 29:17(a) (ESV)

It may be a test of your honesty. Or it may be a test to see whether you will keep a promise, even when it has become inconvenient or more costly than you expected. Will you still keep your word? Will you paint the back of the shed fully and carefully? Will you apply two coats of paint as you were asked to do, or will you skip the second coat and hope that nobody notices? Will you make the effort and turn up to give the help you promised to give someone?

Those are the kind of things God wants to discover about you. We see an example of this in the life of King Hezekiah. We are told directly that God tested him. God allowed the representatives of the King of Babylon to come to Judah and to threaten King Hezekiah. God wanted to find out how he would handle that exceptionally stressful situation:

And so in the matter of the envoys of the princes of Babylon, who had been sent to him to inquire about the sign that had been done in the land, God left him to himself, in order to test him and to know all that was in his heart.
2 Chronicles 32:31 (ESV)

Therefore be alert to the fact that life is full of these tests. Start to consider why God puts you through them and what He wants you to learn from them, or what He is trying to find out about you. You are much more likely to pass such tests if you are aware that they exist and understand their purpose. Sadly, most of us don't realise either of those things. It's like being at school and sitting down to answer a series of questions without even realising that you are in an exam. That's hardly the best way to do well in it.

There will be no promotion unless you are faithful at your current level

Until you pass the various tests that God sets for you, He will not allow you to be promoted or to take on any greater responsibility. What boss would be willing to put you in charge of a chain of shops if you can't even be faithful in running one shop? Likewise, God will not allow you to move up in your service to Him until you prove yourself to be faithful at your current level.

Surprisingly, most people never realise that there is any connection between faithfulness and promotion. A few people are aware that employers operate this way, but not many grasp that this is also the way God operates. In particular, they don't recognise the tests as being tests, or at least not while they are happening.

That's a shame, because if you don't pass these tests that God sets for you, He will simply keep on setting them for you, again and again, until you do. He won't let you skip any test and He won't let you go on until you pass each one. That is why some people never get beyond square one in their Christian life.

This principle, that there is no promotion until you are faithful at your current level, applies to all of us. We see it in operation in the life of King David. He was eventually promoted, by several stages, to be the King of Israel. However, that series of promotions began even before he was 17, when God saw how carefully and diligently the teenage David cared for his father's sheep:

⁷⁰He chose David his servant,
and took him from the sheepfolds;
⁷¹from tending the ewes that had young
he brought him to be the shepherd of Jacob his people,
of Israel his inheritance.
⁷²With upright heart he tended them,
and guided them with skilful hand.
Psalm 78:70-72 (RSV)

Why require yourself to retake the same tests repeatedly? Pass them and move on.

Given that that is God's way of deciding whom He should promote, why not just knuckle down, be faithful, and pass the tests God has set for you? If so, you will become eligible to move on to the next set of tests, at the next level up. Just knowing that your current situation is a test will help you to approach it in a much better way.

You will begin to realise that your current crisis, and others like it, are not just random events. They will suddenly acquire meaning and significance. In fact, you may start to see them as opportunities, which is what they really are. You can then become more focused on this project of being faithful in every task or test that God ever sets for you.

But remember, when God sets tests for us, He usually disguises them. For example, He tends to operate through other people, such as your boss, clients, customers, colleagues, neighbours, friends etc. He especially likes to use those people who make life difficult. Difficult people, and even wicked ones, are some of God's favourite agents for testing you. That is partly because we don't associate such people with God.

Of course, they themselves have no idea of the testing 'project' which they are assisting God with. But you need to learn to recognise when it's the case. A great deal of the testing that God does in our lives is done through such undisclosed agents. It makes no difference at all whether they are Christians or not. God uses the most surprising people, and in the most unexpected situations, as He pursues His development program for you.

Above all, we must be faithful to God

The most important thing of all is our personal commitment to God Himself. If we can get that right then other duties and relationships will also grow stronger. It is entirely possible to be unfaithful to God, to lie to Him and to let Him down, even if we believe in Him. The Jewish people did it, and so do we, quite regularly:

[35]They remembered that God was their rock,
the Most High God their redeemer.
[36]But they flattered him with their mouths;
they lied to him with their tongues.
[37]Their heart was not steadfast toward him;
they were not true to his covenant.
                    Psalm 78:35-37 (RSV)

[53]He led them in safety,
so that they were not afraid;
but the sea overwhelmed their enemies.
[54]And he brought them to his holy land,
to the mountain which his right hand had won.
[55]He drove out nations before them;
he apportioned them for a possession
and settled the tribes of Israel in their tents.
[56]Yet they tested and rebelled against the Most High God,
and did not observe his testimonies,
[57]but turned away and acted treacherously like their fathers;
they twisted like a deceitful bow.
[58]For they provoked him to anger with their high places;
they moved him to jealousy with their graven images.
                    Psalm 78:53-58 (RSV)

God is therefore on the lookout for blameless people who are genuinely and wholeheartedly faithful to Him. He wants people He can trust, who will not let Him down. To such people He will show favour. However, He will not allow deceitful people to be in His presence:

[6]I will look with favour on the faithful in the land,
that they may dwell with me;
he who walks in the way that is blameless shall minister to me.
[7]No man who practices deceit shall dwell in my house;
no man who utters lies shall continue in my presence.
                    Psalm 101:6-7 (RSV)

Moreover, God will respond to unfaithfulness when He sees it. Those who are unfaithful to God, or unfaithful in the tasks or roles that they are given, will be

96

brought down. In one way or another He will remove them, demote them or replace them:

For behold, those who are far from you shall perish;
you put an end to everyone who is unfaithful to you.
Psalm 73:27 (ESV)

King Saul of Israel was unfaithful and disobedient. Therefore he was replaced. God is no respecter of persons. Nobody is above being disciplined and nobody is too senior, or too important, to have to be faithful:

For God does not show favoritism.
Romans 2:11 (NIV)

Then Peter opened his mouth, and said, Of a truth I perceive that God is no respecter of persons:
Acts 10:34 (KJV)

[23] And whatever you do, do it heartily, as to the Lord and not to men, [24] knowing that from the Lord you will receive the reward of the inheritance; for you serve the Lord Christ. [25] But he who does wrong will be repaid for what he has done, and there is no partiality.
Colossians 3:23-25 (NKJV)

Since you call on a Father who judges each person's work impartially, live out your time as foreigners here in reverent fear.
1 Peter 1:17 (NIV)

We must also be faithful to God's Word, the Bible

We must obviously be faithful to God personally. However, one of the main ways we are expected to do that is by being faithful to God's Word. He has given us the Bible and it is intended to say what He wants to tell us. It would not be over-stating the position to say that we demonstrate our faithfulness to God most clearly by the attitude we adopt in relation to His written Word.

We cannot genuinely say that we love, respect or honour God any more than we love, respect and honour His Word. It is, in a certain sense, a proxy for Him. Our view of it indicates our view of Him. So, we must show our faithfulness to Him by being faithful to the Bible and, in particular, by obeying it:

[1] Blessed are those whose way is blameless,
who walk in the law of the LORD!
[2] Blessed are those who keep his testimonies,
who seek him with their whole heart,

97

³who also do no wrong, but walk in his ways!
⁴Thou hast commanded thy precepts to be kept diligently.
⁵O that my ways may be steadfast in keeping thy statutes!
Psalm 119:1-5 (RSV)

Therefore, if you want to become a faithful person, there is no better place to start than by seriously increasing your respect for the Bible and learning it thoroughly. There is no better way of demonstrating your loyalty to God.

The faithfulness of the prophet Daniel

If you are looking for a role model from whom to learn about faithfulness, then the prophet Daniel is one of the very best you will find, anywhere in the Bible. He faced far more pressures and problems than we are ever likely to face. There were also many temptations, and opportunities for him to become proud or corrupt or to compromise, but he never did. He was remarkably faithful to God, to the Kings he worked for, and to everybody he ever met. Therefore not even his enemies could find any fault in him, even though they wanted to:

¹It pleased Darius to set over the kingdom a hundred and twenty satraps, to be throughout the whole kingdom; ²and over them three presidents, of whom Daniel was one, to whom these satraps should give account, so that the king might suffer no loss. ³Then this Daniel became distinguished above all the other presidents and satraps, because an excellent spirit was in him; and the king planned to set him over the whole kingdom. ⁴Then the presidents and the satraps sought to find a ground for complaint against Daniel with regard to the kingdom; but they could find no ground for complaint or any fault, because he was faithful, and no error or fault was found in him. ⁵Then these men said, "We shall not find any ground for complaint against this Daniel unless we find it in connection with the law of his God."
Daniel 6:1-5 (RSV)

Daniel is best known for the episode where he ended up in the lions' den because of his refusal to stop praying to God, even when it became illegal to do so. He risked his life over that issue and never wavered in his faithfulness. That was a big test for anybody to face, even Daniel. However, we would be wrong to think that this huge, life or death crisis was the first test Daniel ever faced. That is very rarely the way that God operates.

He does not usually expose us to life or death situations as the very first test we ever face. God is practical and He knows that our faithfulness and courage have to be developed over time, like a muscle. Therefore He starts us off with small tests and builds up to larger ones, stage by stage.

98

The same was true of Daniel's three friends, who ended up being cast into the fiery furnace because they refused to worship the Nebuchadnezzar's image. That, likewise, was not the first test that they ever faced. The first test that we are told about arose shortly after they all arrived in Babylon, after being taken there as prisoners. All four of these young men, probably in their late teens, faced the test of what to do about the food that was being offered to them.

It did not meet the requirements of the Law of Moses. Today we would say it was not kosher. Instead of compromising by just quietly eating it, they asked to be given vegetables. This stance was less likely to get them into trouble with Nebuchadnezzar than was the case on later occasions. Indeed, there is no indication that he ever even knew of it. So, the risk was less intense.

However, the point is that it was that smaller test which prepared those four teenagers to take and pass the huge tests which they faced many years later. If we are not willing to take a stand on smaller issues and face things such as criticism, disapproval or ridicule, we will never develop the levels of faithfulness that are needed to face up to the threat of martyrdom. We won't even be able to handle the loss of our livelihoods or homes for Jesus' sake.

Many Christians have wondered whether they could be sufficiently faithful to pass the test of martyrdom if they ever had to face it. The real answer to that question is that if you are faithful *now* in the small tests you face at school or work and are willing to be disapproved of, or laughed at, for the sake of Jesus, then God will give you the grace you need to pass the life or death tests that might arise in the future.

So, not only do we learn that habit of faithfulness. It is also that our small acts of courage today qualify us to receive God's help in future when the stakes are much higher. It is God's nature to respond with loyalty to those who are loyal to Him. He also honours those who honour Him. Therefore, if you want to maximize the likelihood of your staying faithful to the end, no matter what, then take care to be faithful now in the small, day to day pressures that you currently face.

The one thing we absolutely must not do is to be presumptuous or over-confident. I say that because I once heard a man say that, if faced with a man pointing a gun at him, he had no doubt that he would *"definitely not deny Jesus."* Even as he said it, I was reminded of the over-confident bravado of apostle Peter as he 'talked big' on the night Jesus was arrested. He would have done much better if he had simply said: *"Lord, if I am tested today, please give me the grace and courage I need to stay faithful to you".*

Those are the kind of words that real martyrs say. Daniel was like the prophet Samuel, Job, Joseph, Moses, John the Baptist, Apostle Paul and other remarkable figures. They all refused to compromise with sin or to betray God by letting Him down or taking Him for granted. Now let's consider someone who was very different; a man who began well, but ended in failure because of his unfaithfulness.

King Saul was not faithful. Therefore he was removed from being King

Saul was the first King of Israel. He began well and showed great promise at the start. However, in the end, he was removed from power. God regretted making Saul King. That wasn't because he failed, made mistakes or lost battles. He could have failed and made mistakes repeatedly, and still have kept God's approval. The reason King Saul had his position as King taken away from him was because God was not satisfied with his level of personal faithfulness.

That was the issue, not his level of success. When he was under pressure he let God down and became disobedient and unfaithful. The prophet Samuel, who was a priest at the Temple, had told King Saul to wait for him and that he would meet him at Gilgal. At that time Samuel would have offered sacrifices and prayed for God's help in the battle against the Philistines.

However, Saul became impatient in waiting for Samuel to come. Therefore, he usurped Samuel's priestly role and gave the offerings himself, even though he was not a priest and had no right or authority to offer the sacrifices. King Saul acted impetuously and went beyond his proper authority. He did what he knew to be wrong because he was in a highly stressful situation and felt he could not wait any longer for Samuel. When Samuel arrived, immediately afterwards, and saw what Saul had done, he announced God's judgment on Saul for his disobedience and lack of faithfulness:

⁵ And the Philistines mustered to fight with Israel, thirty thousand chariots, and six thousand horsemen, and troops like the sand on the seashore in multitude; they came up and encamped in Michmash, to the east of Beth-a'ven. ⁶ When the men of Israel saw that they were in straits (for the people were hard pressed), the people hid themselves in caves and in holes and in rocks and in tombs and in cisterns, ⁷ or crossed the fords of the Jord[a] to the land of Gad and Gilead. Saul was still at Gilgal, and all the people followed him trembling. ⁸ He waited seven days, the time appointed by Samuel; but Samuel did not come to Gilgal, and the people were scattering from him. ⁹ So Saul said, "Bring the burnt offering here to me, and the peace offerings." And he offered the burnt offering. ¹⁰ As soon as he had finished offering the burnt offering, behold, Samuel came; and Saul went out to meet him and salute him.

¹¹ Samuel said, "What have you done?" And Saul said, "When I saw that the people were scattering from me, and that you did not come within the days appointed, and that the Philistines had mustered at Michmash, ¹² I said, 'Now the Philistines will come down upon me at Gilgal, and I have not entreated the favor of the LORD'; so I forced myself, and offered the burnt offering." ¹³ And

Samuel said to Saul, "You have done foolishly; you have not kept the commandment of the LORD your God, which he commanded you; for now the LORD would have established your kingdom over Israel forever. ¹⁴ But now your kingdom shall not continue; the LORD has sought out a man after his own heart; and the LORD has appointed him to be prince over his people, because you have not kept what the LORD commanded you."

1 Samuel 13:5-14 (RSV)

¹⁰ The word of the LORD came to Samuel: ¹¹ "I regret that I have made Saul king, for he has turned back from following me and has not performed my commandments." And Samuel was angry, and he cried to the LORD all night.

1 Samuel 15:10-11 (ESV)

God was displeased by Saul's ongoing unfaithfulness and disobedience. Things reached a head when Saul disobeyed God's commands in relation to how he was to deal with the Amalekites. God then decided to remove the kingship from Saul. God did so even though Saul attempted, belatedly, to repent.

The problem was that Saul's repentance came too late, even assuming that it was genuine. Note also that Saul's disobedience arose because he feared the opinions of his people and tried to please them rather than please God. That was a fatal error. Nobody can be faithful to God if they also aim to please people. You can please one, or the other, but not both:

²² And Samuel said,
"Has the LORD as great delight in burnt offerings and sacrifices,
as in obeying the voice of the LORD?
Behold, to obey is better than sacrifice,
and to listen than the fat of rams.
²³ For rebellion is as the sin of divination,
and presumption is as iniquity and idolatry.
Because you have rejected the word of the LORD,
he has also rejected you from being king."
²⁴ Saul said to Samuel, "I have sinned, for I have transgressed the commandment of the LORD and your words, because I feared the people and obeyed their voice. ²⁵ Now therefore, please pardon my sin and return with me that I may bow before the LORD." ²⁶ And Samuel said to Saul, "I will not return with you. For you have rejected the word of the LORD, and the LORD has rejected you from being king over Israel." ²⁷ As Samuel turned to go away, Saul seized the skirt of his robe, and it tore. ²⁸ And Samuel said to him, "The LORD has torn the kingdom of Israel from you this day and has given it to a neighbor of yours, who is better than you.

1 Samuel 15:22-28 (ESV)

Even worse, Saul also consulted a medium, (the witch at Endor) rather than seek God's guidance. God was not willing to tolerate that unfaithfulness. Therefore God took away not only Saul's throne, but also his life:

¹³So Saul died for his unfaithfulness; he was unfaithful to the LORD in that he did not keep the command of the LORD, and also consulted a medium, seeking guidance, ¹⁴ and did not seek guidance from the LORD. Therefore the LORD slew him, and turned the kingdom over to David the son of Jesse.
1 Chronicles 10:13-14 (RSV)

Saul could have continued as King if he had operated differently. He didn't need more skill or more cleverness. He just needed more faithfulness. In particular, he needed to repent quickly when he did wrong, instead of hiding or denying his sins. The next King, David, probably made just as many mistakes as Saul did. He also committed some major sins. The difference was that he knew how to repent and how to restore his intimacy and fellowship with God. That is why God thought so highly of David.

The faithfulness of King David - a man after God's own heart

God rejected King Saul, as we have seen, and looked for a man He could rely on to be faithful and who would be *"a man after (God's) own heart":*

¹³ And Samuel said to Saul, "You have done foolishly; you have not kept the commandment of the LORD your God, which he commanded you; for now the LORD would have established your kingdom over Israel forever. ¹⁴But now your kingdom shall not continue; the LORD has sought out a man after his own heart; and the LORD has appointed him to be prince over his people, because you have not kept what the LORD commanded you."
1 Samuel 13:13-14 (RSV)

God commanded the prophet Samuel, to appoint a new King to replace Saul and He told Samuel where to find him:

¹The LORD said to Samuel, "How long will you grieve over Saul, seeing I have rejected him from being king over Israel? Fill your horn with oil, and go; I will send you to Jesse the Bethlehemite, for I have provided for myself a king among his sons."
1 Samuel 16:1 (RSV)

Jesse had eight sons. All of them were impressive men, especially the older ones. However, the one God had chosen was the youngest, David. He was still only a teenager, probably about 16 or 17. God made it clear to Samuel that He was looking for a man with the right kind of heart, as opposed to talent, ability or strength. That is because faithfulness is an attitude of the heart, not a skill or ability:

⁶When they came, he looked on Eli'ab and thought, "Surely the LORD'S anointed is before him." ⁷But the LORD said to Samuel, "Do not look on his appearance or on the height of his stature, because I have rejected him; for the LORD sees not as man sees; man looks on the outward appearance, but the LORD looks on the heart." ⁸Then Jesse called Abin'adab, and made him pass before Samuel. And he said, "Neither has the LORD chosen this one." ⁹Then Jesse made Shammah pass by. And he said, "Neither has the LORD chosen this one." ¹⁰And Jesse made seven of his sons pass before Samuel. And Samuel said to Jesse, "The LORD has not chosen these." ¹¹And Samuel said to Jesse, "Are all your sons here?" And he said, "There remains yet the youngest, but behold, he is keeping the sheep." And Samuel said to Jesse, "Send and fetch him; for we will not sit down till he comes here."

1 Samuel 16:6-11 (RSV)

So, David was chosen and then secretly anointed by Samuel to be the next King of Israel. Saul was not told about it because he would have killed David if he had known. David then ended up making a name for himself when he volunteered to fight a giant called Goliath in one to one combat.

Goliath was a Philistine soldier who had been challenging Israel's army to select a man to fight him. He was also mocking the Israelite army, because nobody volunteered. Nobody but David was brave enough, or had enough faith, to fight him. He therefore told King Saul that he wanted to fight Goliath, despite being only about 17 years old:

³²And David said to Saul, "Let no man's heart fail because of him; your servant will go and fight with this Philistine."

1 Samuel 17:32 (RSV)

The duel took place and, contrary to what some people imagine, David went into it fully expecting to win. He trusted God and believed He would help him. David also felt outraged at the way that the heathen Goliath had been defying God and insulting His chosen people, Israel. His heart was so intensely loyal to God that he could not bear to hear such things. He wanted to vindicate God and to uphold His honour. He was therefore willing to face Goliath and to stop him:

⁴¹And the Philistine came on and drew near to David, with his shield-bearer in front of him. ⁴²And when the Philistine looked, and saw David, he disdained him; for he was but a youth, ruddy and comely in appearance. ⁴³And the Philistine said to David, "Am I a dog, that you come to me with sticks?" And the Philistine cursed David by his gods. ⁴⁴The Philistine said to David,

"Come to me, and I will give your flesh to the birds of the air and to the beasts of the field."

1 Samuel 17:41-44 (RSV)

Goliath had been insulting God's people, Israel. Now he was insulting David personally and making very intimidating threats. However, David's loyalty to God made him willing to take this great risk for the sake of God's Name. David showed great courage that day. That is true of all people who are faithful to God.

Faithfulness will inevitably lead us into situations of danger, where we have to put at risk our reputation, finances, status, or even our own lives. The courage we show at such times is a key indicator of our faithfulness. Look how much courage David showed, and with such boldness:

[45] Then David said to the Philistine, "You come to me with a sword and with a spear and with a javelin; but I come to you in the name of the LORD of hosts, the God of the armies of Israel, whom you have defied. [46] This day the LORD will deliver you into my hand, and I will strike you down, and cut off your head; and I will give the dead bodies of the host of the Philistines this day to the birds of the air and to the wild beasts of the earth; that all the earth may know that there is a God in Israel, [47] and that all this assembly may know that the LORD saves not with sword and spear; for the battle is the LORD'S and he will give you into our hand." [48] When the Philistine arose and came and drew near to meet David, David ran quickly toward the battle line to meet the Philistine. [49] And David put his hand in his bag and took out a stone, and slung it, and struck the Philistine on his forehead; the stone sank into his forehead, and he fell on his face to the ground.

1 Samuel 17:45-49 (RSV)

Once David had become famous, following his spectacular victory over Goliath, King Saul began to envy him. He became suspicious and paranoid. He saw David as a threat and tried to kill him. He sent men to hunt David down and so he had to go on the run for several years, hiding in the wilderness to get away from Saul's men. Nevertheless, even during this period on the run, David never did anything to undermine King Saul. He recognised that Saul was still the legitimate King of Israel and that, although Samuel had already anointed him, his own time as King had not yet begun.

Thus David refused to seize the throne, either by force or manipulation. He was sorely tested on one occasion when he was hiding in a cave from Saul's men and Saul came in to relieve himself. David had the perfect chance to kill Saul. His men urged him to do so, saying that it was obviously a God-given opportunity. But David refused. He stayed faithful to King Saul and chose, instead, to wait until God made him King, rather than grab power for himself:

¹When Saul returned from following the Philistines, he was told, "Behold, David is in the wilderness of En-ge'di." ²Then Saul took three thousand chosen men out of all Israel, and went to seek David and his men in front of the Wildgoats' Rocks. ³And he came to the sheepfolds by the way, where there was a cave; and Saul went in to relieve himself. Now David and his men were sitting in the innermost parts of the cave. ⁴And the men of David said to him, "Here is the day of which the LORD said to you, 'Behold, I will give your enemy into your hand, and you shall do to him as it shall seem good to you.'" Then David arose and stealthily cut off the skirt of Saul's robe. ⁵And afterward David's heart smote him, because he had cut off Saul's skirt. ⁶He said to his men, "The LORD forbid that I should do this thing to my lord, the LORD'S anointed, to put forth my hand against him, seeing he is the LORD'S anointed." ⁷So David persuaded his men with these words, and did not permit them to attack Saul. And Saul rose up and left the cave, and went upon his way.

1 Samuel 24:1-7 (RSV)

What a difficult test that was for David. We are unlikely ever to face one as severe as that. But note his extreme faithfulness to God, and also to King Saul himself, who was still the rightful King. David felt that as God had appointed Saul, he had a solemn duty to be loyal to the King, even though Saul was seeking to have him killed. David came out of the cave afterwards and shouted to Saul so that he could realise what had happened and that David had done him no harm:

⁸Afterward David also arose, and went out of the cave, and called after Saul, "My lord the king!" And when Saul looked behind him, David bowed with his face to the earth, and did obeisance. ⁹And David said to Saul, "Why do you listen to the words of men who say, 'Behold, David seeks your hurt'? ¹⁰Lo, this day your eyes have seen how the LORD gave you today into my hand in the cave; and some bade me kill you, but I spared you. I said, 'I will not put forth my hand against my lord; for he is the LORD'S anointed.' ¹¹See, my father, see the skirt of your robe in my hand; for by the fact that I cut off the skirt of your robe, and did not kill you, you may know and see that there is no wrong or treason in my hands. I have not sinned against you, though you hunt my life to take it. ¹²May the LORD judge between me and you, may the LORD avenge me upon you; but my hand shall not be against you.

1 Samuel 24:8-12 (RSV)

When Saul heard this he was convicted, He knew that he was acting wrongly and that David was a much more faithful man than himself:

¹⁶When David had finished speaking these words to Saul, Saul said, "Is this your voice, my son David?" And Saul lifted up his voice and wept. ¹⁷He said to David, "You are more righteous than I; for you have repaid me good, whereas I have repaid you evil. ¹⁸And you have declared this day how you have dealt well with me, in that you did not kill me when the LORD put me into your hands. ¹⁹For if a man finds his enemy, will he let him go away safe? So may the LORD

105

reward you with good for what you have done to me this day. ²⁰And now, behold,
I know that you shall surely be king, and that the kingdom of Israel shall be
established in your hand. ²¹Swear to me therefore by the LORD that you will not
cut off my descendants after me, and that you will not destroy my name out of
my father's house." ²²And David swore this to Saul. Then Saul went home; but
David and his men went up to the stronghold.

1 Samuel 24:16-22 (RSV)

However, although Saul really was convicted, and knew he was sinning, he still
did not repent. He continued, even after this, to pursue David, and to attempt to
kill him. Thus, he was still seeking to do to David something which he had asked
David to swear not to do to him. Saul was thus unfaithful to David, and to God
and he was also a hypocrite.

By contrast, David was remarkably faithful, both to Saul and to God. Therefore
his strength gradually rose. More and more men came to join David in the
wilderness and became his followers. In the end, the whole kingdom became his
and he reigned over it all with justice and equity:

¹⁵*So David reigned over all Israel; and David administered justice and equity to*
all his people.

2 Samuel 8:15 (RSV)

One of the main reasons why David's reign was so successful was that he had
entered into it well. He refused to grab the throne, which is what probably 99.9%
of other men would have done. Instead, he waited many years to be given Saul's
place as King. He was also totally faithful to his predecessor, despite grievous
ongoing provocation. Thus he reaped a good harvest from that faithfulness. The
'law of sowing and reaping' was at work in David's life.

However, the main reason for his success was that he was so faithful to God, to
his people, and to the men who served under him. There were a few spectacular
exceptions when David sinned badly, but he always repented for those. Overall,
he was unusually faithful, and God viewed him as *"a man after my (own) heart,*
who will do all my will":

²¹ *Then they asked for a king; and God gave them Saul the son of Kish, a man*
of the tribe of Benjamin, for forty years. ²²And when he had removed him, he
raised up David to be their king; of whom he testified and said, 'I have found in
David the son of Jesse a man after my heart, who will do all my will.'

Acts 13:21-22 (RSV)

Consequently, God viewed David as the best King that Israel ever had. God also
set out His assessment of the other Kings of both Israel and Judah. The Bible
records each reign, whether good or bad. When it does, it focuses not on the

abilities or successes of each King, but on the degree to which they were faithful. That was always the crucial thing in God's eyes, not their achievements.

That is where God's view of things is so very different to ours. We tend to assess other people on all the wrong criteria, such as their looks, fame, wealth, power and achievements, but God's view is very unlike ours. He considers to be successful a lot of men and women whom the world regards as failures. He also regards as failures many people whom most of us would admire as great successes.

CHAPTER 5

GOD'S ASSESSMENT OF THE FAITHFULNESS OF THE KINGS OF JUDAH AND ISRAEL

because David did what was right in the eyes of the LORD, and did not turn aside from anything that he commanded him all the days of his life, except in the matter of Uri'ah the Hittite.

1 Kings 15:5 (RSV)

[11]And Asa did what was right in the eyes of the LORD, as David his father had done. [12]He put away the male cult prostitutes out of the land, and removed all the idols that his fathers had made. [13]He also removed Ma'acah his mother from being queen mother because she had an abominable image made for Ashe'rah; and Asa cut down her image and burned it at the brook Kidron. [14]But the high places were not taken away. Nevertheless the heart of Asa was wholly true to the LORD all his days.

1 Kings 15:11-14 (RSV)

[22] In the time of his distress he became yet more faithless to the Lord—this same King Ahaz. [23] For he sacrificed to the gods of Damascus which had defeated him, and said, "Because the gods of the kings of Syria helped them, I will sacrifice to them that they may help me." But they were the ruin of him, and of all Israel.

2 Chronicles 28:22-23 (RSV)

[20]Thus Hezeki'ah did throughout all Judah; and he did what was good and right and faithful before the LORD his God. [21] And every work that he undertook in the service of the house of God and in accordance with the law and the commandments, seeking his God, he did with all his heart, and prospered

2 Chronicles 31:20-21(RSV)

How God graded the various kings of Israel and Judah

Let's look at some examples of both good and bad kings, according to how God assessed them. We cannot look at them all, as there are so many, but we will consider a number. In each case, note carefully the characteristics God focuses on, and also those that He *doesn't* focus on, when assessing people. We shall begin by looking at King Jehoshaphat of Judah:

[3]The LORD was with Jehosh'aphat, because he walked in the earlier ways of his father; he did not seek the Ba'als, [4] but sought the God of his father and walked in his commandments, and not according to the ways of Israel.

⁵Therefore the LORD established the kingdom in his hand; and all Judah brought tribute to Jehosh'aphat; and he had great riches and honor.⁶ His heart was courageous in the ways of the LORD; and furthermore he took the high places and the Ashe'rim out of Judah.

⁷ In the third year of his reign he sent his princes, Ben-hail, Obadi'ah, Zechari'ah, Nethan'el, and Micai'ah, to teach in the cities of Judah; ⁸ and with them the Levites, Shemai'ah, Nethani'ah, Zebadi'ah, As'ahel, Shemi'ramoth, Jehon'athan, Adoni'jah, Tobi'jah, and Tobadoni'jah; and with these Levites, the priests Elish'ama and Jeho'ram. ⁹ And they taught in Judah, having the book of the law of the LORD with them; they went about through all the cities of Judah and taught among the people.

2 Chronicles 17:3-9 (RSV)

Note also the positive consequences for the people of Judah that came from Jehoshaphat's faithfulness and also the rewards that came to Jehoshaphat personally:

¹⁰ And the fear of the LORD fell upon all the kingdoms of the lands that were round about Judah, and they made no war against Jehosh'aphat. ¹¹ Some of the Philistines brought Jehosh'aphat presents, and silver for tribute; and the Arabs also brought him seven thousand seven hundred rams and seven thousand seven hundred he-goats. ¹² And Jehosh'aphat grew steadily greater. He built in Judah fortresses and store-cities, ¹³ and he had great stores in the cities of Judah. He had soldiers, mighty men of valor, in Jerusalem.

2 Chronicles 17:10-13 (RSV)

That was God's verdict on the reign of the godly King Jehoshaphat of Judah. But, note that God never even mentions his abilities or his achievements, as almost all of us would do. Instead, God's attention is focused on the fact that:

a) he did not serve or worship the Baals. (These were the pagan gods that the Canaanites worshipped. Their occult practices had spread into both Israel and Judah)

b) he sought instead for God, i.e. he worshiped only the true God.

c) he walked in the commandments, i.e. he was obedient to God's written Word.

d) His heart was "courageous in the ways of the LORD"

e) He made it a priority to send out some of his best people to teach God's Word (the book of the law of the LORD) in all the cities of Judah.

Those are the things God focused on when evaluating the reign of Jehoshaphat. That speaks volumes about what our priorities should be. Now let's look at God's assessment of King Amaziah of Judah. He began well and showed some faithfulness. However, his problem was that his faithfulness was not sufficiently wholehearted:

Amaziah was twenty-five years old when he became king, and he reigned twenty-nine years in Jerusalem. And his mother's name was Jehoaddan of Jerusalem. ² He did right in the sight of the LORD, yet not with a whole heart.

2 Chronicles 25:1-2 (NASB)

God's assessment of the reign of King Amaziah

There were three main things that caused Amaziah to go astray in the end and to abandon his faithfulness:

a) He did not fully trust in God to help him. So, he formed an alliance with the idolatrous Northern Kingdom of Israel. God did not tell him, or want him, to do that, due to the wickedness of its kings:

⁶ He hired also 100,000 valiant warriors out of Israel for one hundred talents of silver. ⁷ But a man of God came to him saying, "O king, do not let the army of Israel go with you, for the LORD is not with Israel nor with any of the sons of Ephraim.

2 Chronicles 25:6-7 (NASB)

b) He had a military victory over the people of Seir and, after the battle was over, he brought their false gods/idols back to Jerusalem. He then ended up getting into idolatry, bowing down to those gods and burning incense to them:

¹⁴ Now after Amaziah came from slaughtering the Edomites, he brought the gods of the sons of Seir, set them up as his gods, bowed down before them and burned incense to them. ¹⁵ Then the anger of the LORD burned against Amaziah, and He sent him a prophet who said to him, "Why have you sought the gods of the people who have not delivered their own people from your hand?" ¹⁶ As he was talking with him, the king said to him, "Have we appointed you a royal counselor? Stop! Why should you be struck down?" Then the prophet stopped and said, "I know that God has planned to destroy you, because you have done this and have not listened to my counsel."

2 Chronicles 25:14-16 (NASB)

c) His heart became proud and over-confident because of his victories. As a result, he started an unnecessary war and also refused to listen to God's prophets:

¹⁹ You said, 'Behold, you have defeated Edom.' And your heart has become proud in boasting. Now stay at home; for why should you provoke trouble so

111

that you, even you, would fall and Judah with you?"[20] But Amaziah would not listen, for it was from God, that He might deliver them into the hand of Joash because they had sought the gods of Edom.

2 Chronicles 25:19-20 (NASB)

So, Amaziah began well, as so many of us do. His crucial failure was that but he did not keep it up. He allowed himself to slip into unfaithfulness and even idolatry and he turned away from following the Lord. That caused God to engineer his downfall, which is so sad, because if he had stayed faithful and been wholehearted he would have had God's help.

Instead, God arranged for the Northern Kingdom to bring Amaziah down and also for his own people in Jerusalem to turn against him. None of this would have happened if only he had remained faithful:

From the time that Amaziah turned away from following the LORD they conspired against him in Jerusalem, and he fled to Lachish; but they sent after him to Lachish and killed him there.

2 Chronicles 25:27 (NASB)

God's assessment of the reigns of King Uzziah and his son, King Jotham

Now look at Amaziah's son, King Uzziah of Judah. He too began well but then allowed himself to slip. He dropped his standards as a result of the same problems of pride, over-confidence and presumption:

[1]And all the people of Judah took Uzzi'ah, who was sixteen years old, and made him king instead of his father Amazi'ah. [2]He built Eloth and restored it to Judah, after the king slept with his fathers. [3]Uzzi'ah was sixteen years old when he began to reign, and he reigned fifty-two years in Jerusalem. His mother's name was Jecoli'ah of Jerusalem. [4]And he did what was right in the eyes of the LORD, according to all that his father Amazi'ah had done. [5]He set himself to seek God in the days of Zechari'ah, who instructed him in the fear of God; and as long as he sought the LORD, God made him prosper.

2 Chronicles 26:1-5 (RSV)

Here we see God's assessment of how King Uzziah *began* his reign. It focuses entirely on the fact that he:

a)   did what was right in the eyes of the LORD

b)   feared God

c)   sought the LORD

112

Again, none of these things have anything to do with Uzziah's abilities, achievements or victories in battles. They are all about his loyalty and faithfulness to God. That makes sense. Why should God praise us or reward us for our talents or abilities, when it was He that gave them all to us in the first place? Those things interest us, but not God, because our talents do not entitle us to any credit or reward.

Thus, in a certain sense, it would be inappropriate to praise Mozart for what he composed, given that the music usually just arrived, complete, in Mozart's head. All he had to do was to write it down. It was all given to him by God. So the credit for Mozart's music really belongs to God, far more than to Mozart.

However, what we could praise Mozart for is his diligence in writing it down, after he had received it in his head. That states the extent of Mozart's contribution more accurately. He was a diligent worker, for which he deserves credit, but the music itself was really God's, not his. The same principle applies to the Kings of Israel and also to us.

When we appear before Jesus at the Judgment Seat of Christ, He will not reward us for being good looking or clever or successful or powerful. If we have any of those things it is no credit to us, because they came from Him, not us. Jesus will limit Himself, therefore, to rewarding us for our faithfulness in terms of what we did with what He gave us.

So, at the Judgment Seat of Christ those who were given great talent have no advantage over those who were given very little talent. Once you stop to consider this, it becomes obvious that that would be how God would see things.

In the later part of his long reign, King Uzziah became less faithful and less obedient. God's blessings upon him for his faithfulness, and all the success that that brought him, started to go to his head and he became proud. He then usurped the role of the priests and became angry when they tried to stop him doing so.

God therefore punished Uzziah towards the end of his reign. What a shame for Him to spoil his good record in that way and to have his decline into unfaithfulness recorded in the Bible, for all of us to see for the next 3000 years. That failure must be seen as a lesson to us, especially as we approach the end of our lives or ministries.

That is when there is the greatest temptation to become self-satisfied and to rest on our laurels. We must never allow ourselves to become proud or complacent, such that Jesus revises downwards the 'grade' that He had been intending to give us:

15 In Jerusalem he made engines, invented by skilful men, to be on the towers and the corners, to shoot arrows and great stones. And his fame spread far, for he was marvelously helped, till he was strong. [16]But when he was strong he grew proud, to his destruction. For he was false to the LORD his God, and entered the temple of the LORD to burn incense on the altar of incense. [17]But Azari'ah the priest went in after him, with eighty priests of the LORD who were men of valor; [18]and they withstood King Uzzi'ah, and said to him, "It is not for you, Uzzi'ah, to burn incense to the LORD, but for the priests the sons of Aaron, who are consecrated to burn incense. Go out of the sanctuary; for you have done wrong, and it will bring you no honor from the LORD God."

[19]Then Uzzi'ah was angry. Now he had a censer in his hand to burn incense, and when he became angry with the priests leprosy broke out on his forehead, in the presence of the priests in the house of the LORD, by the altar of incense. [20]And Azari'ah the chief priest, and all the priests, looked at him, and behold, he was leprous in his forehead! And they thrust him out quickly, and he himself hastened to go out, because the LORD had smitten him. [21]And King Uzzi'ah was a leper to the day of his death, and being a leper dwelt in a separate house, for he was excluded from the house of the LORD. And Jotham his son was over the king's household, governing the people of the land.

2 Chronicles 26:15-21 (RSV)

However, Uzziah's son, Jotham did better. He avoided the sin that Uzziah had committed in the Temple. That was good but, despite speaking well of Jotham, God still notes in the end that he did not prevent the people from following corrupt practices. In short, Jotham did well, but he did not go as far as he should have gone to try to lead the people into the right path:

[1]Jotham was twenty-five years old when he began to reign, and he reigned sixteen years in Jerusalem. His mother's name was Jeru'shah the daughter of Zadok. [2]And he did what was right in the eyes of the LORD according to all that his father Uzzi'ah had done--only he did not invade the temple of the LORD. But the people still followed corrupt practices.

2 Chronicles 27:1-2 (RSV)

Nonetheless, because of the general faithfulness that he did show, God made King Jotham mighty:

So Jotham became mighty because he ordered his ways before the LORD his God.

2 Chronicles 27:6 (RSV)

God's assessment of the reign of King Ahaz

Next we see a King who received a wholly bad report from God. We are told that King Ahaz *"did not do what was right in the eyes of the LORD"*. Now note the things that God highlights which led to his downfall:

[1]Ahaz was twenty years old when he began to reign, and he reigned sixteen years in Jerusalem. And he did not do what was right in the eyes of the LORD, like his father David, [2]but walked in the ways of the kings of Israel. He even made molten images for the Ba'als; [3]and he burned incense in the valley of the son of Hinnom, and burned his sons as an offering, according to the abominable practices of the nations whom the LORD drove out before the people of Israel. [4]And he sacrificed and burned incense on the high places, and on the hills, and under every green tree. [5]Therefore the LORD his God gave him into the hand of the king of Syria, who defeated him and took captive a great number of his people and brought them to Damascus. He was also given into the hand of the king of Israel, who defeated him with great slaughter.

2 Chronicles 28:1-5 (RSV)

The sins of King Ahaz, which caused God to condemn his time as King, were that:

a) he did not do what was right in God's eyes (By that God means what he did morally and spiritually, not economically or militarily).

b) he walked in the ways of the Kings of Israel, i.e. in idolatry and unfaithfulness to God

c) he made molten images of the Baals and burned incense as part of idolatrous worship

d) he even burned his own sons as human sacrifices to the pagan gods.

The terrible sins of King Ahaz brought down the Southern Kingdom of Judah. God also brought judgment on Ahaz personally. As He did so, Ahaz turned towards the pagan gods even more thoroughly than before, seeking their help rather than God's. Instead of repenting when God brought him under such judgment, he continued, and even intensified, his sin. Thus he brought even worse judgment upon himself and also on his people:

[19]For the LORD brought Judah low because of Ahaz king of Israel, for he had dealt wantonly in Judah and had been faithless to the LORD. [20]So Til'gath-pilne'ser king of Assyria came against him, and afflicted him instead of strengthening him. [21]For Ahaz took from the house of the LORD and the house of the king and of the princes, and gave tribute to the king of Assyria; but it did not help him. [22]In the time of his distress he became yet more faithless to the LORD--this same King Ahaz. [23]For he sacrificed to the gods of Damascus which had defeated him, and said, "Because the gods of the kings of Syria helped them, I will sacrifice to them that they may help me." But they were the ruin of him, and of all Israel. [24]And Ahaz gathered together the vessels of the house of God and cut in pieces the vessels of the house of God, and he shut up the doors of the house of the LORD; and he made himself altars in every corner of

Jerusalem. ^{25}In every city of Judah he made high places to burn incense to other gods, provoking to anger the LORD, the God of his fathers.

2 Chronicles 28:19-25 (RSV)

God's assessment of the reign of King Hezekiah

Next we see a faithful King, Hezekiah of Judah. Note that the Northern Kingdom of Israel never had any faithful kings. Every single one of them was unfaithful and evil. King Hezekiah saw what the unfaithfulness of previous Kings of Judah had caused and also how the unfaithfulness of the people, and especially their idolatry, had brought them under God's judgment.

He was determined to put things right. His main focus was not on restoring the economy of Judah, or the power of its military. It was on leading the people into greater faithfulness towards God. What a striking contrast there is between his priorities and those of our political leaders today, or even our church leaders:

^{1}Hezeki'ah began to reign when he was twenty-five years old, and he reigned twenty-nine years in Jerusalem. His mother's name was Abi'jah the daughter of Zechari'ah. ^{2}And he did what was right in the eyes of the LORD, according to all that David his father had done. ^{3}In the first year of his reign, in the first month, he opened the doors of the house of the LORD, and repaired them. ^{4}He brought in the priests and the Levites, and assembled them in the square on the east, ^{5}and said to them, "Hear me, Levites! Now sanctify yourselves, and sanctify the house of the LORD, the God of your fathers, and carry out the filth from the holy place.

^{6}For our fathers have been unfaithful and have done what was evil in the sight of the LORD our God; they have forsaken him, and have turned away their faces from the habitation of the LORD, and turned their backs. ^{7}They also shut the doors of the vestibule and put out the lamps, and have not burned incense or offered burnt offerings in the holy place to the God of Israel. ^{8}Therefore the wrath of the LORD came on Judah and Jerusalem, and he has made them an object of horror, of astonishment, and of hissing, as you see with your own eyes. ^{9}For lo, our fathers have fallen by the sword and our sons and our daughters and our wives are in captivity for this.

^{10}Now it is in my heart to make a covenant with the LORD, the God of Israel, that his fierce anger may turn away from us. ^{11}My sons, do not now be negligent, for the LORD has chosen you to stand in his presence, to minister to him, and to be his ministers and burn incense to him."

2 Chronicles 29:1-11 (RSV)

Hezekiah took steps not only to put things right in Judah, but even to help to improve the situation in the Northern Kingdom of Israel:

¹Hezeki'ah sent to all Israel and Judah, and wrote letters also to E'phraim and Manas'seh, that they should come to the house of the LORD at Jerusalem, to keep the passover to the LORD the God of Israel.

2 Chronicles 30:1 (RSV)

However, despite his best efforts, not many people from the Northern Kingdom responded well to his invitations. Nevertheless, though he did not always succeed, God's overall verdict on King Hezekiah was very positive. In particular, we are told that he did what he did *"with all his heart"*.

Again, God's emphasis is on Hezekiah's wholeheartedness and faithfulness, even though he did not fully succeed in the things he was trying to do for God, because the people were not willing to obey. His abilities and the extent of his achievements are not even mentioned, let alone emphasised:

²⁰Thus Hezeki'ah did throughout all Judah; and he did what was good and right and faithful before the LORD his God. ²¹And every work that he undertook in the service of the house of God and in accordance with the law and the commandments, seeking his God, he did with all his heart, and prospered.

2 Chronicles 31:20-21 (RSV)

God's assessment of the reign of King Manasseh

Sadly, Hezekiah's son, Manasseh, was evil, at least for the majority of his reign. God's verdict on those wasted and misused years is very scathing:

¹Manas'seh was twelve years old when he began to reign, and he reigned fifty-five years in Jerusalem. ²He did what was evil in the sight of the LORD, according to the abominable practices of the nations whom the LORD drove out before the people of Israel. ³For he rebuilt the high places which his father Hezeki'ah had broken down, and erected altars to the Ba'als, and made Ashe'rahs, and worshiped all the host of heaven, and served them. ⁴And he built altars in the house of the LORD, of which the LORD had said, "In Jerusalem shall my name be forever." ⁵And he built altars for all the host of heaven in the two courts of the house of the LORD. ⁶And he burned his sons as an offering in the valley of the son of Hinnom, and practiced soothsaying and augury and sorcery, and dealt with mediums and with wizards. He did much evil in the sight of the LORD, provoking him to anger.

2 Chronicles 33:1-6 (RSV)

⁹Manas'seh seduced Judah and the inhabitants of Jerusalem, so that they did more evil than the nations whom the LORD destroyed before the people of Israel.

2 Chronicles 33:9 (RSV)

117

Strangely, at the very end of his reign, when God's judgment was already coming upon him for his wickedness and unfaithfulness, Manasseh repented. It is one of the very few examples we see in the Bible of a really wicked man repenting and genuinely turning back to God:

[10]The LORD spoke to Manas'seh and to his people, but they gave no heed. [11]Therefore the LORD brought upon them the commanders of the army of the king of Assyria, who took Manas'seh with hooks and bound him with fetters of bronze and brought him to Babylon. [12]And when he was in distress he entreated the favor of the LORD his God and humbled himself greatly before the God of his fathers. [13]He prayed to him, and God received his entreaty and heard his supplication and brought him again to Jerusalem into his kingdom. Then Manas'seh knew that the LORD was God.

2 Chronicles 33:10-13 (RSV)

After his repentance, King Manasseh changed and sincerely tried his best to put right the terrible harm he had done:

[14]Afterwards he built an outer wall for the city of David west of Gihon, in the valley, and for the entrance into the Fish Gate, and carried it round Ophel, and raised it to a very great height; he also put commanders of the army in all the fortified cities in Judah. [15]And he took away the foreign gods and the idol from the house of the LORD, and all the altars that he had built on the mountain of the house of the LORD and in Jerusalem, and he threw them outside of the city. [16]He also restored the altar of the LORD and offered upon it sacrifices of peace offerings and of thanksgiving; and he commanded Judah to serve the LORD the God of Israel.

2 Chronicles 33:14-16 (RSV)

Thus, having been grossly unfaithful for most of his life, Manasseh became faithful in the end. That gives us hope for ourselves and for those we know who seem very far from God. The final verdict on Manasseh is brief, but positive. It says he *"slept with his fathers"*.

That is an expression used in the Bible to indicate that a man died as a believer and that he was saved. So, we will see King Manasseh in Heaven. In fact, we shall also see him on the Earth, when Jesus returns and Manasseh is resurrected, so that he can live again on this Earth during the Millennium:

[20]So Manas'seh slept with his fathers, and they buried him in his house; and Amon his son reigned in his stead.

2 Chronicles 33:20 (RSV)

Next came Manasseh's son Amon. He was evil but, unlike his father, he did not repent or change:

21Amon was twenty-two years old when he began to reign, and he reigned two years in Jerusalem. 22He did what was evil in the sight of the LORD, as Manas'seh his father had done. Amon sacrificed to all the images that Manas'seh his father had made, and served them. 23And he did not humble himself before the LORD, as Manas'seh his father had humbled himself, but this Amon incurred guilt more and more. 24And his servants conspired against him and killed him in his house.

2 Chronicles 33:21-24 (RSV)

God's assessment of the reign of King Josiah

We now come to the most faithful King that Judah ever had, the godly child-king, Josiah. He was more faithful, and more wholehearted, than any of his predecessors, even the good ones:

1Josi'ah was eight years old when he began to reign, and he reigned thirty-one years in Jerusalem. 2He did what was right in the eyes of the LORD, and walked in the ways of David his father; and he did not turn aside to the right or to the left. 3For in the eighth year of his reign, while he was yet a boy, he began to seek the God of David his father; and in the twelfth year he began to purge Judah and Jerusalem of the high places, the Ashe'rim, and the graven and the molten images.

2 Chronicles 34:1-3 (RSV)

King Josiah was deeply moved when he came across the Law of Moses and read it in the early part of his reign. He realised how great the need was for repentance and he led the people in that repentance, and in focusing again on the Bible:

19When the king heard the words of the law he rent his clothes. 20And the king commanded Hilki'ah, Ahi'kam the son of Shaphan, Abdon the son of Micah, Shaphan the secretary, and Asai'ah the king's servant, saying, 21"Go, inquire of the LORD for me and for those who are left in Israel and in Judah, concerning the words of the book that has been found; for great is the wrath of the LORD that is poured out on us, because our fathers have not kept the word of the LORD, to do according to all that is written in this book."

2 Chronicles 34:19-21 (RSV)

29Then the king sent and gathered together all the elders of Judah and Jerusalem. 30And the king went up to the house of the LORD, with all the men of Judah and the inhabitants of Jerusalem and the priests and the Levites, all the people both great and small; and he read in their hearing all the words of the book of the covenant which had been found in the house of the LORD. 31And the king stood in his place and made a covenant before the LORD, to walk after the LORD and to keep his commandments and his testimonies and his statutes, with all his heart and all his soul, to perform the words of the covenant that were written in this book.

³²Then he made all who were present in Jerusalem and in Benjamin stand to it. And the inhabitants of Jerusalem did according to the covenant of God, the God of their fathers. ³³And Josi'ah took away all the abominations from all the territory that belonged to the people of Israel, and made all who were in Israel serve the LORD their God. All his days they did not turn away from following the LORD the God of their fathers.

2 Chronicles 34:29-33 (RSV)

The zeal, devotion and faithfulness of King Josiah led to him receiving God's commendation. Look at this passage from 2 Kings. Wouldn't you like Jesus to say something like this about you at the Judgment Seat of Christ?

²⁵Before him there was no king like him, who turned to the LORD with all his heart and with all his soul and with all his might, according to all the law of Moses; nor did any like him arise after him.

2 Kings 23:25 (RSV)

CHAPTER 6

A CLOSER LOOK AT THE VARIOUS TYPES OF PEOPLE WITH WHOM WE MUST BE FAITHFUL

Do not be like your fathers and your brethren, who were faithless to the LORD God of their fathers, so that he made them a desolation, as you see.
2 Chronicles 30:7 (RSV)

10"One who is faithful in a very little is also faithful in much, and one who is dishonest in a very little is also dishonest in much. 11If then you have not been faithful in the unrighteous wealth, who will entrust to you the true riches? 12And if you have not been faithful in that which is another's, who will give you that which is your own? 13No servant can serve two masters, for either he will hate the one and love the other, or he will be devoted to the one and despise the other. You cannot serve God and money."
Luke 16:10-13 (ESV)

Faithful are the wounds of a friend,
but deceitful are the kisses of an enemy.
Proverbs 27:6 (NASB)

The prospect of the Judgment Seat of Christ needs to become a vivid reality to you. It must be real enough to affect your daily life

It's not easy to be faithful, especially over a long period of time. There are so many ways that we can fail God and let other people down. Nevertheless, if we can learn to see the future Judgment Seat of Christ as a reality, then that will help us to be much more faithful, and to remain so to the end.

Accordingly, we may face temptations and we may want to take shortcuts, or let God down, but the thought of one day having to stand before Jesus Christ, face to face, at the Judgment Seat of Christ, will help to bring us back to our senses.

Remembering each day that what we are about to do that day will either bring rebuke or reward at the Judgment Seat of Christ will help to keep us on the right path. Therefore we really need to remind ourselves every day of the Judgment Seat of Christ and what will happen at it:

The faithless will be fully repaid for their ways,
and the good man rewarded for his.
Proverbs 14:14 (NIV)

121

¹⁰Why do you pass judgment on your brother? Or you, why do you despise your brother? For we shall all stand before the judgment seat of God; ¹¹ for it is written, "As I live, says the Lord, every knee shall bow to me, and every tongue shall give praise to God." ¹² So each of us shall give account of himself to God.

Romans 14:10-12 (RSV)

Everything you ever do, however small, is going to be assessed and either rewarded, or not rewarded, at the Judgment Seat of Christ. I have asked God to help me to see that judgment as a very clear reality. I want to become more and more conscious of it every day as I go about my ordinary tasks. One day we will all have to give an individual account to the Lord Jesus Christ for how we used or misused, and invested or wasted, every day of our lives.

When you ponder on what it will be like to meet Jesus face to face at that awesome encounter, do not think of Him as He was when He was with His disciples during His earthly ministry. Instead, think of Him as He is now, as shown in the book of Revelation. When the apostle John saw Jesus as He is now, he fell down at His feet in awe, because seeing Him as He really is came as a huge shock. That was despite the fact that, during His earthly ministry, John had been Jesus' best friend:

¹²Then I turned to see the voice that was speaking to me, and on turning I saw seven golden lampstands, ¹³and in the midst of the lampstands one like a son of man, clothed with a long robe and with a golden girdle round his breast; ¹⁴his head and his hair were white as white wool, white as snow; his eyes were like a flame of fire, ¹⁵his feet were like burnished bronze, refined as in a furnace, and his voice was like the sound of many waters; ¹⁶in his right hand he held seven stars, from his mouth issued a sharp two-edged sword, and his face was like the sun shining in full strength. ¹⁷When I saw him, I fell at his feet as though dead. But he laid his right hand upon me, saying, "Fear not, I am the first and the last, ¹⁸and the living one; I died, and behold I am alive for evermore, and I have the keys of Death and Hades.

Revelation 1:12-18 (RSV)

Jesus is therefore to be feared. The need to face Him on that Judgment Day should concentrate your mind now. That is another benefit that comes from having the fear of the LORD.

Nobody will get away with anything at the Judgment Seat of Christ. Jesus sees everything we ever do.

Nothing we ever do will be overlooked. Jesus is continuously assessing the level of our faithfulness to decide what position and rewards (if any) to award to us in His Kingdom. See my Book Four for much more detail on the Judgment Seat of Christ and about what the Bible says about rewards and rebuke. Do not make the mistake of thinking that there is anything too small for Him to notice or care about:

The eyes of the LORD are in every place,
watching the evil and the good.
Proverbs 15:3 (NASB)

Everything that we ever think, say or do is being recorded in Jesus' infinite memory. He is concerned about every part of your life, especially the private things which nobody else ever sees.

Jesus knows all our real motives – therefore we may as well be totally honest with ourselves

There is no point trying to deceive Jesus or to hide things from Him. He knows exactly what you do and why you do it. He knows whether you are wholehearted or reluctant. Look at the glowing assessment God made of Caleb:

²⁴ But because my servant Caleb has a different spirit and follows me wholeheartedly, I will bring him into the land he went to, and his descendants will inherit it.
Numbers 14:24 (NIV)

Jesus knows exactly how much we care about Him and how loyal we are to Him. Therefore do everything wholeheartedly, as if you were doing it for Jesus, because that is precisely what you are doing. We need to see every task, no matter what it is, as being done for Him:

²³Whatever you do, do your work heartily, as for the Lord rather than for men, *²⁴knowing that from the Lord you will receive the reward of the inheritance It is the Lord Christ whom you serve.*
Colossians 3:23-24 (NASB)

You should resolve, as David did, to live a 'blameless' life. That is to live with integrity and to keep yourself away from corrupt activities and corrupt people:

² I will be careful to lead a blameless life—
when will you come to me?
I will conduct the affairs of my house
with a blameless heart.
³ I will not look with approval
on anything that is vile.
I hate what faithless people do;
I will have no part in it.
⁴ The perverse of heart shall be far from me;
I will have nothing to do with what is evil.
Psalm 101:2-4 (NIV)

Our word must be our bond

For many years I was involved in commercial litigation. I would act as a lawyer for one side or another in commercial disputes. Our client would either be suing or being sued. It would generally be because somebody had failed to keep to the contracts they had agreed. They would have either broken a promise or let some other company down in some way.

Having done so, instead of admitting it, the party in the wrong would generally deny it and seek to get away with it. Those who did that were unfaithful men who did not consider their word to be their bond. Sadly, there are very many people who act in that way.

For that reason, when contracts are entered onto between businesses, one of the jobs of the lawyers drawing up the contract is to give thought to what will happen if one of the parties breaks any of the terms. Even before the contract is entered into, we have to think about, and plan for, somebody breaking the agreement. We even work out in advance what the damages should be.

We also make provisions in the contract for our own client being in breach, not just the other party. That's sad, but necessary, because so few businessmen have any strong sense of honour. Many do not feel any shame at all at the idea of not keeping their word.

For the Christian, there has to be a higher standard. We must consider ourselves bound by our words, regardless of whether it was ever put in writing. We must view our own word as being unbreakable. A hundred years ago, or even fifty, that was how most business was conducted, but no longer. Too few people have enough personal integrity for business to be able to operate on that basis today. It cannot now be based on trust, because so few people can be trusted.

We need to be faithful in all our relationships

That kind of faithfulness and honour, where our word is regarded as our bond, needs to apply not just in business but in every transaction we make and in all our relationships. Look at how Samuel operated as a judge over Israel. He was able to challenge the whole nation to name even a single occasion when he had ever acted unfaithfully. Not one person was able to do so:

[3]*"Here I am; bear witness against me before the LORD and His anointed Whose ox have I taken, or whose donkey have I taken, or whom have I defrauded? Whom have I oppressed, or from whose hand have I taken a bribe to blind my eyes with it? I will restore it to you."* [4]*They said, "You have not defrauded us or oppressed us or taken anything from any man's hand."* [5]*He said to them, "The*

LORD is witness against you, and His anointed is witness this day that you have found nothing in my hand." And they said, "He is witness.

1 Samuel 12:3-5 (NASB)

Would you feel confident enough to stand in front of all the people who have ever known you and challenge them all to point out even one occasion when you have ever acted unfaithfully? Few of us could stand up to that test. We must seek to be blameless, like Samuel, in all our dealings with other people, even in the smallest details.

By contrast, one only has to look at the difficulties faced by the Democratic and Republic parties in the USA when trying to find a presidential candidate, out of a population of over 300 million. One would imagine it would be easy to find thousands of exemplary candidates for that office.

Instead, we see men coming forward, but as soon as the media begin to dig around and investigate their past life, all sorts of things come out, such as drug abuse, adultery, unfaithfulness or sexual harassment. We must be different and go to great lengths to maintain our integrity consistently and over the long term.

Faithfulness to God Himself

Being faithful to God is our greatest duty. He is the main person to whom we must be loyal. God wants us to make a clear and definite choice to follow Him alone and to serve Him with unwavering sincerity. We also need to be faithful in obeying God's Word:

[14] "Now therefore fear the LORD, and serve him in sincerity and in faithfulness; put away the gods which your fathers served beyond the River, and in Egypt, and serve the LORD. [15] And if you be unwilling to serve the LORD, choose this day whom you will serve, whether the gods your fathers served in the region beyond the River, or the gods of the Amorites in whose land you dwell; but as for me and my house, we will serve the LORD."

Joshua 24:14-15 (RSV)

Let your heart therefore be wholly true to the LORD our God, walking in his statutes and keeping his commandments, as at this day."

1 Kings 8:61 (RSV)

Moreover, the prophet Samuel told the people of Israel that they needed to put away all other gods and serve only God. They needed to direct their hearts to Him only and turn away from all other competing attractions. The same applies to us:

[3] Then Samuel said to all the house of Israel, "If you are returning to the Lord with all your heart, then put away the foreign gods and the Ash'taroth from

125

among you, and direct your heart to the Lord, and serve him only, and he will deliver you out of the hand of the Philistines." ⁴ So Israel put away the Ba'als and the Ash'taroth, and they served the Lord only.

1 Samuel 7:3-4 (RSV)

King Saul was not faithful to God. He disobeyed God's commands and failed to seek God's guidance. None of that sounds spectacular or remarkable. Saul did what most of us do. Yet, it was serious enough in God's eyes to cause Him to take the kingdom away from Saul and to give it to David:

¹³ So Saul died for his breach of faith. He broke faith with the LORD in that he did not keep the command of the LORD, and also consulted a medium, seeking guidance. ¹⁴ He did not seek guidance from the LORD. Therefore the LORD put him to death and turned the kingdom over to David the son of Jesse.

1 Chronicles 10:13-14(ESV)

Faithfulness to our husband or wife

Over the past few decades there has been, throughout most of the Western world, a collapse in the sanctity of marriage. Divorce is at epidemic levels. One of the main causes of divorce, after selfishness, is unfaithfulness, where one party, or both, are committing adultery. For Christians that must never happen.

We must stay with our husband or wife through good times and bad, for richer for poorer, in sickness and in health, till death parts us. There must be an absolute determination to do all of that, no matter what happens. We must also resolve never to look at any person in an improper or lustful way. Be like Job. Make a firm decision not even to look at a member of the opposite sex:

¹"I have made a covenant with my eyes; How then could I gaze at a virgin?

Job 31:1 (NASB)

We need to make a decision, as Job did, that we will have eyes for nobody else and that we will not commit adultery, even in our thoughts. We need to honour all the vows we made on our wedding day, no matter what temptations later come our way, as they surely will. The prophet Malachi expresses the strength of God's feelings about divorce very clearly. He says that God hates divorce:

¹³"This is another thing you do: you cover the altar of the LORD with tears, with weeping and with groaning, because He no longer regards the offering or accepts it with favour from your hand. ¹⁴"Yet you say, 'For what reason?' Because the LORD has been a witness between you and the wife of your youth, against whom you have dealt treacherously, though she is your companion and your wife by covenant. ¹⁵"But not one has done so who has a remnant of the Spirit And what did that one do while he was seeking a godly offspring? Take

126

heed then to your spirit, and let no one deal treacherously against the wife of your youth. ¹⁶*"For I hate divorce," says the LORD, the God of Israel, "and him who covers his garment with wrong," says the LORD of hosts. "So take heed to your spirit, that you do not deal treacherously."*

Malachi 2:13-16 (NASB)

Faithfulness to our children and to our parents

Likewise, when we become a parent, we are entrusted with another sacred responsibility, for which God will hold us accountable. This is especially so for fathers. Yet, what we see around us in the West doesn't look much like this. There is a widespread abdication of responsibility by increasingly delinquent and feckless men. Many of them fail to take their duties seriously.

There are lots of men who put their job, or even their hobbies, ahead of their children. Being faithful to a child involves making a solemn commitment to devote ourselves to them. That means spending a lot of time with the child and putting the child's needs first, ahead of what we want.

In particular, it means taking responsibly for the child's spiritual condition. Too many fathers leave these issues to be dealt with solely or mainly by their wives. However, God will still hold fathers primarily accountable for their children's spiritual condition, whether they realise it or not. God has commanded all fathers to teach their children about Him and about the Bible:

⁵ *He established a testimony in Jacob,*
and appointed a law in Israel,
which he commanded our fathers to teach to their children;
⁶ *that the next generation might know them,*
the children yet unborn,
and arise and tell them to their children,
⁷ *so that they should set their hope in God,*
and not forget the works of God,
but keep his commandments;
⁸ *and that they should not be like their fathers,*
a stubborn and rebellious generation,
a generation whose heart was not steadfast,
whose spirit was not faithful to God.

Psalm 78:5-8 (RSV)

The emphasis that God places on the role of the father in bringing his children up to know and obey God flies in the face of our society's attitude and assumptions about fatherhood. Even in better families, it is usually left to the mother to teach the children about God, but that isn't how God wants it.

Therefore we need to get into line with Him, especially those of us who are fathers. See chapter seven of Book One in this series for a more detailed discussion of our duties to our parents. The biblical method of social security is for adult children to look after their own parents in old age.

We are to honour them and care for their practical and financial needs. Therefore start to see yourself and your siblings as having that responsibility. View yourself as being at least one of the people who will care for your parents in their old age.

God will still hold you accountable for how they are treated, no matter how much you might seek to offload that duty onto the State. The only exception would be if you are genuinely incapable of helping them, due to your own health problems or poverty etc. However, we should not be quick to assume that we come into any of those categories.

Faithfulness to our friends and acquaintances

One of the main things we can do to show ourselves faithful to friends is to avoid gossip. Learn to control your tongue. If you are told a secret, then tell nobody. That will eventually transform the way people see you. People who can be fully relied on to keep a confidence are very rare. Aim to become such a person, so that others can trust you completely and confide in you, knowing that you will never reveal a word of what they say.

¹³ A gossip betrays a confidence,
but a trustworthy person keeps a secret.
Proverbs 11:13 (NIV)

The norm however, is to betray other people's confidences and to pass information on to others. We usually do it because we wish to be significant and to be considered to have inside knowledge. Resolve now to build a reputation, for the long term, as one who can be trusted with confidential information. Furthermore, seek to be the kind of friend who tells the truth, gives honest advice, and never engages in flattery:

⁶ Faithful are the wounds of a friend;
profuse are the kisses of an enemy.
Proverbs 27:6 (RSV)

Far too many people are false friends. They say things that they do not really mean. They appear supportive to a person's face but are disloyal to them, and critical of them, behind their backs. Resolve to do the opposite. Tell the truth to your friends' faces, but defend them behind their backs. If so, you will be one of a very small minority. People will eventually notice that and they will seek you out, especially in times of adversity:

¹⁷A friend loves at all times,
And a brother is born for adversity.
Proverbs 17:17 (NASB)

There are friends who pretend to be friends,
but there is a friend who sticks closer than a brother.
Proverbs 18:24 (RSV)

Faithfulness to our employer

Having practiced in employment law for many years, I find it remarkable how many employees resent, despise, or even hate their employer. It seems to be the norm. This is frequently true even amongst Christians. Perhaps this malaise is more widespread in Britain, than elsewhere? However, the reality is that your employer has done you a great favour, simply in giving you a job at all. Presumably, that job is good enough to accept and remain in, otherwise you wouldn't still be there?

Why not start to view your job and your employer differently? Make a decision that from now on you will be appreciative and work diligently, even when nobody is looking. In fact, work hard especially when nobody is looking. The rarest thing for any employer to find in a member of staff is faithfulness. That has always been my experience. Even King Solomon thought so:

Many a man proclaims his own loyalty;
but a faithful man who can find?
Proverbs 20:6 (RSV)

Like the cold of snow in the time of harvest
is a faithful messenger to those who send him,
he refreshes the spirit of his masters.
Proverbs 25:13 (RSV)

Trust in a faithless man in time of trouble
is like a bad tooth or a foot that slips.
Proverbs 25:19 (RSV)

Apostle Paul gives clear instructions on how a servant should relate to their master. They must be faithful, trustworthy and loyal. The same applies to us today in our dealings with employers:

⁹Urge bondslaves to be subject to their own masters in everything, to be well-pleasing, not argumentative, ¹⁰ not pilfering, but showing all good faith so that they will adorn the doctrine of God our Savior in every respect.
Titus 2:9-10 (NASB)

Remind them to be submissive to rulers and authorities, to be obedient, to be ready for any honest work,

Titus 3:1 (RSV)

[5] Slaves, be obedient to those who are your earthly masters, with fear and trembling, in singleness of heart, as to Christ; [6] not in the way of eye-service, as men-pleasers, but as servants of Christ, doing the will of God from the heart, [7] rendering service with a good will as to the Lord and not to men, [8] knowing that whatever good any one does, he will receive the same again from the Lord, whether he is a slave or free.

Ephesians 6:5-8 (RSV)

Resolve to become the most faithful member of staff at your workplace. It won't be very hard because few, if any, other staff will be competing with you for that title. If you do, your bosses will certainly notice. You'll be promoted sooner or later, either there or somewhere else.

If for some reason your current bosses refuse to reward you, God will probably move you to another boss who will. More importantly, Jesus will be so pleased that He will reward you for it Himself, even if your own boss doesn't. Whatever job you do, and whoever you work for, you are a "steward".

That is a person who has been entrusted with responsibilities to look after certain people, property, money or tasks. A steward has a "duty of care". He will be held accountable by his employer for the way in which he discharged his responsibilities. The same applies even if you do not currently have a job. You will have been entrusted by God with specific tasks or duties and He too will hold you accountable and gauge the extent of your trustworthiness, just like any other employer would do:

Moreover, it is required of stewards that they be found faithful.
1 Corinthians 4:2 (ESV)

Please also remember that your duty to be faithful to your employer is not conditional upon him also being faithful to you. It is great if you do happen to have a good and faithful boss, but whether he is or not has no bearing on your duty to be faithful to him. So, you are not merely to be faithful in response, or as your part of a two-way arrangement. Just be faithful to your boss all the time, regardless of how he treats you.

The reason you must be faithful is simply because God wants you to behave in that way, not necessarily because your boss deserves it. The same is true of every other relationship. You are required to be faithful no matter what other people do. They will answer to God for what they do and you will answer to God for what you do.

Therefore don't confuse matters by imagining that there has to be a mutual faithfulness as a pre-condition to you being under any obligation to be faithful yourself. That is not the case. I emphasize that point, because a lot of people wrongly imagine that wrongful behaviour on our own part is justified if the other person has previously treated us wrongly. It isn't.

So, if your boss was to fail to pay you fairly, or on time, or if he was rude or disrespectful, that would not justify you in doing the same back to him. You must not be rude in return, or short-change him with your time or effort. Neither can you steal from him, just because he has stolen from you. Apostle Peter addresses this point in his first letter:

¹⁸ Servants, be submissive to your masters with all respect, not only to the kind and gentle but also to the overbearing. ¹⁹ For one is approved if, mindful of God, he endures pain while suffering unjustly. ²⁰ For what credit is it, if when you do wrong and are beaten for it you take it patiently? But if when you do right and suffer for it you take it patiently, you have God's approval. ²¹ For to this you have been called, because Christ also suffered for you, leaving you an example, that you should follow in his steps. ²² He committed no sin; no guile was found on his lips. ²³ When he was reviled, he did not revile in return; when he suffered, he did not threaten; but he trusted to him who judges justly.

1 Peter 2:18-23 (RSV)

You could, of course, openly question your boss, or even confront him, about his behaviour towards you. But nothing that he does would ever justify you in behaving discourteously, improperly, dishonestly or disloyally towards him. In short, you must be faithful, even if you are the only person who ever operates that way in your workplace.

Faithfulness concerning any responsibilities that are entrusted to us

When King Jehoshaphat, the godly king of Judah, appointed judges this is what he told them:

⁶ He said to the judges, "Consider what you are doing, for you do not judge for man but for the LORD who is with you when you render judgment. ⁷ Now then let the fear of the LORD be upon you; be very careful what you do, for the LORD our God will have no part in unrighteousness or partiality or the taking of a bribe."

2 Chronicles 19:6-7 (NASB)

He wanted them to be aware at all times that God is watching and will hold each one of them accountable for all that they do. The same is true for all of us. Whatever work we do, we are accountable for it, and we are doing it for the Lord. Even if we allow ourselves to forget that, it still remains true. Whether we are managers, or shop floor workers, or have any other kind of job, we need to learn to take every duty very seriously, however small it may seem.

We need to become the kind of person who, when they agree to do something, or are told to, put their whole heart into it. We must remain vigilant and focused until it is done, and done well. Nehemiah, when he was responsible for rebuilding the walls of Jerusalem, appointed men whom he knew to be more faithful than other men:

¹Now when the wall had been built and I had set up the doors, and the gatekeepers, the singers, and the Levites had been appointed, ²I gave my brother Hana'ni and Hanani'ah the governor of the castle charge over Jerusalem, for he was a more faithful and God-fearing man than many.

Nehemiah 7:1-2 (RSV)

This reminds me of my own Dad. He took any responsibility exceptionally seriously and would go very far out of his way to ensure he never let anybody down. If he was asked to do a thing, or if he volunteered to do it, you could guarantee it would be done, not just on time, but early. I never saw him forget anything, or be late, or do a shoddy job. He could always be relied on 100%. When he left the army he was graded as having given 'exemplary service', which is not said of many.

Faithfulness to our colleagues at work and also to customers, clients, patients etc

It's not just with your bosses that you need to be faithful. It's with your colleagues as well, at every level. You owe a duty of care to everybody else at work to be reliable, honest and hard-working. Never take the credit for what others have done. If you are mistakenly praised by a manager for another man's work or input, then say so immediately and redirect the praise.

Always keep your promises and do your tasks faithfully. Do not let your team down. Start to see ordinary, everyday things like that as a part of the process of becoming a mature disciple. If you do, you'll be unusual. Most Christians do not think that their job has got anything to do with being a disciple. However, in God's eyes, it is an essential part of the Christian life, which He takes very seriously.

A Christian employee should be one of the last people to ring in to work to say he is sick. Even if the practice of abusing sick leave is widespread where you work, you must never join in. It lets your colleagues down as well as your company, quite apart from being dishonest. Therefore, even if the whole office does it, including the managers, you must still be the only one who doesn't.

132

Another group to whom we owe a duty of care are the customers, clients, patients etc that we serve in our job. If you are a mechanic working on someone's car, be completely honest, down to the last detail. Do your best standard of work at all times, regardless of whether the customer or client is watching or will ever find out. Also treat every customer well, regardless of whether they are rich and powerful or poor and weak.

The reason to do your best work is not just so that you can avoid getting into trouble. It is because the customer is paying and is, therefore, contractually entitled to your best service. Focus far more on your duty to the customer than on any rights you might have, or think you have. The customer always comes first, not you. If you can understand that, and apply it, then the rest of it will come easily.

Faithfulness to our staff/employees/junior colleagues

If God has put you into a managerial position, or if you have your own business, that doesn't mean you have no boss. God is always your boss and you must report to Him daily. One of the first priorities He will have for you is to treat your staff fairly. Actually they are really His staff, not yours and God is very interested in how you deal with them:

Look! The wages you failed to pay the workmen who mowed your fields are crying out against you. The cries of the harvesters have reached the ears of the Lord Almighty.

James 5:4 (NIV)

God is watching over the people who work for you, or under you, and He hears their cries. So, always pay wages on time. Don't hold them back just to ease your own cash flow. A Christian employer must still pay the wages, even when there is nothing left for himself. I have been in that place, in the past, as most businessmen have, especially when starting out.

Likewise, in dealing with staff, you have a responsibility to treat them fairly and to provide them with the opportunity to grow and develop. Moreover, one of the key duties of every boss is to protect the weak from the strong. In any workplace, unless the boss is vigilant, bullies and tyrants will inevitably emerge amongst the staff, and at every level. Even if you get rid of them, others will always arise.

There will always be some who seek to exploit, dominate and use their colleagues, especially the more timid ones. A good boss always steps in to side with the victim and to resist the bully or manipulator, however difficult or time consuming that may be. That is the duty of every boss, though very few bother even to consider it, let alone do anything about it. A Christian boss must be keenly aware of this and take it all very seriously.

Many bosses choose to turn a blind eye to bullying, domination and manipulation at work. That is because standing up to workplace bullies requires courage and is costly, in all sorts of ways. At the very least, it is emotionally draining and it takes up a lot of time. A good boss will inevitably get abused, undermined and lied about, and especially so if he ever stands up to workplace bullies.

Moreover, few people will recognise the price he is paying, or thank him for what he is doing. Bad staff and workplace bullies will band together to attack and undermine such a boss. You must fully expect that, and be ready for it. Even so, have courage and do your duty.

Use your authority faithfully. Stand up to such people and get all of them out of the business, even if you end up taking a lot of abuse and trouble for it. Be faithful to your good staff and defend them from oppressors and always choose the right course of action, not the easiest one.

Faithfulness to remember and repay those who have helped us

This is an aspect of faithfulness which applies in every relationship. There are bound to be people who, have helped you, given you things or prayed for you. Yet it is a feature of our selfish flesh nature that we tend to take such support for granted. We don't appreciate it enough. Many times we do not even remember it. There are people who have done things for us but we forget them completely. Here is an example of that from the life of Joseph:

⁹So the chief cupbearer told his dream to Joseph and said to him, "In my dream there was a vine before me, ¹⁰ and on the vine there were three branches. As soon as it budded, its blossoms shot forth, and the clusters ripened into grapes. ¹¹Pharaoh's cup was in my hand, and I took the grapes and pressed them into Pharaoh's cup and placed the cup in Pharaoh's hand." ¹²Then Joseph said to him, "This is its interpretation: the three branches are three days. ¹³In three days Pharaoh will lift up your head and restore you to your office, and you shall place Pharaoh's cup in his hand as formerly, when you were his cupbearer. ¹⁴ Only remember me, when it is well with you, and please do me the kindness to mention me to Pharaoh, and so get me out of this house. ¹⁵ For I was indeed stolen out of the land of the Hebrews, and here also I have done nothing that they should put me into the pit."

Genesis 40:9-15 (ESV)

Joseph had helped and encouraged a fellow prisoner while they were in jail together, but when that man got out of prison he forgot Joseph completely and did nothing to help him in return:

²⁰On the third day, which was Pharaoh's birthday, he made a feast for all his servants and lifted up the head of the chief cupbearer and the head of the chief baker among his servants. [21] He restored the chief cupbearer to his position, and he placed the cup in Pharaoh's hand. [22] But he hanged the chief baker, as Joseph had interpreted to them. [23] Yet the chief cupbearer did not remember Joseph, but forgot him.

Genesis 40:20-23 (ESV)

Most of us have played the parts of both Joseph and the cup-bearer in our own lives. We have been unfaithful to others by failing to repay them, or even to thank them. We have also experienced how ingratitude feels when it is shown to us by others. The first step in remedying this fault is to recognise that it exists and to begin to give it thought.

We need to reflect on what we owe to others and start to make an inventory. Then begin to thank people and take opportunities to repay them in whatever way you can when they need your help. Positively seek for opportunities to repay others.

Faithfulness to our enemies

One of the hardest things to learn as a Christian is how to handle your enemies, and defend yourself from them, yet without becoming like them. When dealing with fools or wicked people, they will use lies and dirty tricks and they will conspire with others to undermine you by any means possible. They recognise no moral or ethical boundaries to their behaviour.

In short, they will do whatever they believe they can get away with, regardless of whether it is right or wrong. Such considerations mean nothing to them. When an immature, fleshly, worldly Christian comes up against such opposition at work, or even at church, there is a tendency to operate in the flesh and to "give as good as you get".

They will tend to respond in like manner and hit back at the person wrongly, even to the extent of using the same worldly tactics and methods. They will justify this, if they consider it at all, by saying "*Well, they started it*" or "*They did it to me, so why can't I do it back to them?*"

However, that line of reasoning isn't valid. We cannot fight fire with fire. That is we can't use the same carnal, devious methods that our enemies use. That makes the battle more difficult. We have to realise that other people can be wicked, and therefore anticipate all sorts of deviousness from them, whilst not doing the same in return.

We can certainly be very firm, decisive and assertive. We can also confront people, sack them, give evidence against them and so on. We just can't sink to their level, by sinning in our handling of them. A mature Christian therefore treats his enemies better than most people treat their friends, even while he stands up to them.

CHAPTER 7

SOME MORE OF THE WAYS IN WHICH WE MUST BECOME FAITHFUL

Watch over your heart with all diligence,
For from it flow the springs of life.
Proverbs 4:23 (NASB)

And he did evil, for he did not set his heart to seek the LORD.
2 Chronicles 12:14 (RSV)

"Only take heed, and keep your soul diligently, lest you forget the things which your eyes have seen, and lest they depart from your heart all the days of your life; make them known to your children and your children's children—
Deuteronomy 4:9 (RSV)

Rid yourself of the love of money

One of the main reasons why people act unfaithfully is because they are tempted by the desire for money. The love of money will cause you to do wrong in all sorts of ways:

¹⁰ For the love of money is a root of all kinds of evil. Some people, eager for money, have wandered from the faith and pierced themselves with many griefs.
1 Timothy 6:10 (NIV)

A man who can rid himself of the love of money will be liberated from all that. He will be free to do whatever is right and cannot be bought or controlled by money. Whatever wages you get, be content with them. Never allow yourself to be induced to do wrong in order to get more money.

It is far better to do right, and lose money as a result, than to do wrong in order to keep it. Losing money has only temporary results, but the consequences of doing wrong, or being unfaithful, are eternal. Therefore resolve to change, so that you have no love of money at all:

⁵Make sure that your character is free from the love of money, being content with what you have;
Hebrews 13:5 (a) (NASB)

Moreover, if you should happen to become rich because God blesses you with abundance, do not set your heart on it or grow to depend on it. We need to be open-hearted so that God can give us wealth, or take it away, without us getting

137

agitated about it. If not, then we will always be open to being tempted to do wrong in order to preserve our wealth, even if we did not do anything wrong to acquire it in the first place. That is an easy trap for wealthy people to fall into. The fear of losing what they have can easily cause them to start to compromise and to sin. It also tends to choke the effect of God's Word in their lives:

Put no trust in extortion;
set no vain hopes on robbery;
if riches increase,
set not your heart on them.
                        Psalm 62:10 (ESV)

[18]And others are the ones sown among thorns; they are those who hear the word, [19]but the cares of the world, and the delight in riches, and the desire for other things, enter in and choke the word, and it proves unfruitful.
                        Mark 4:18-19 (ESV)

Rid yourself of selfish ambition

On a similar theme, set out to rid yourself of all selfish or improper ambition. If you don't, then you will always be vulnerable to being tempted to do wrong in order to protect your current position or your promotion prospects. The demons assigned to you will see that selfish ambition in you and they will make full use of it to trip you up. So close off that opening. Then they can't make use of it any longer.

By contrast, godly ambition is fine. You should always aim to do your best, and it is perfectly alright to seek promotion. There is nothing wrong with any of that. However it becomes wrong where your ambition is elevated to the place where it takes priority over your duties to God and to other people, or where your ambitions for yourself in this life mean more to you than your ambitions for the next life.

If any of those things are true of you, then your ambition has become a god or an idol. You have no right to do wrong to others in order to protect, or further, your own career. It is much better for your career to be held back because you do right, than for you to advance it by doing wrong. That may sound obvious, but it's not what most people think, at least, not in my experience.

Most people regularly operate in the flesh, even within churches. In particular, most people would act wrongly, without even hesitating, whenever they see their career as being at stake. That is wrong, and you have to convince yourself of the truth of that, so that you are ready, when the temptation comes, to stand firm.

Also rid yourself of the craving to be approved of or highly esteemed

The desire to be approved of, or to be popular, is another deeply ingrained craving in all of us. It will inevitably affect, or even control, our actions unless we make a determined effort to control and resist it. However, few people do that. Most of us live our lives in a state of fear, dreading disapproval, criticism or ridicule, and making whatever decisions are necessary to avoid these things.

But that will rarely, if ever, cause us to go in the right direction, or to do what God wants. When difficult situations arise you will usually go wrong if your aim is to be approved of by others. Instead, decide that the only approval that really counts is God's. Seek always to do what He wants, regardless of whether anybody else approves, or disapproves, of you for that. This is very hard to achieve. Few even attempt it.

However, if you are willing to do it, you will find it gets easier every time. The first few times where you risk disapproval will be hard, but as time goes by, you will begin to lose your fear of people. Then you will become free to do whatever God wants, without the fear of other people's disapproval influencing your decisions.

Tell the truth every time and be faithful with money

Never give in to the temptation to lie, or to misuse money or property that has been entrusted to you. Resolve always to be a faithful steward and to tell the truth at all times.

⁵A faithful witness does not lie,
But a false witness will utter lies.
> *Proverbs 14:5 (NKJV)*

Make a decision also to be completely honest with other people's money when it is entrusted to you:

¹⁵ They did not require an accounting from those to whom they gave the money to pay the workers, because they acted with complete honesty.
> *2 Kings 12:15 (NIV)*

Aim to gain a reputation for being totally trustworthy with money, and for having complete integrity:

¹³I put Shelemiah the priest, Zadok the scribe, and a Levite named Pedaiah in charge of the storerooms and made Hanan son of Zakkur, the son of Mattaniah, their assistant, because they were considered trustworthy.

They were made responsible for distributing the supplies to their fellow Levites.
Nehemiah 13:13 (NIV)

Never use or manipulate people. Always be direct and straightforward.

Here is another vital principle. You have no right to use any other person. In all your dealings with others you must be open and transparent and pay for all services or goods that you need. If you are willing to reciprocate, then it's alright to seek favours and help from others. But it's only acceptable if it's *mutual.* You must always return the favour later, or be sincerely willing to do so if needed.

It is very wrong to see other people as "resources" to be made use of. There are times when people have rung me up and I know immediately that they are only calling me because they want something. It's not a real friendship. They are solely looking for favours, or the use of my time. But they don't want to pay for it. Neither do they want to return the favour by doing anything for me.

I would be ashamed to ring people in that way, but many are not. They see it as fair game if they can get something from it. Resolve that you will not use other people and that any friendships you have are solely about friendship, not about getting favours on the cheap, or making use of other people in a covert or non-reciprocal way. We must never manipulate others. We must always be straightforward and tell people our real aims and motives. Then they can decide for themselves whether to participate in something.

Never trick people into doing things that you want them to do. The polite word for that is *m*anipulation or control. A blunter word for it is 'witchcraft'. That's what witchcraft really is. It's about trying to manipulate, dominate or control other people, so as to influence them or get them to do what you want, without them realising what you are doing.

So, if you are running a Tupperware business, or selling life insurance, then don't ever invite people to your home or to a function without openly telling them what your aims are. Say *"I've set up a financial services business. Would you like to come to a barbecue I'm having, after which I will give a 20 minute talk about pensions?"* That's OK to say, because it's open and honest.

The person is then made fully aware of your motives and is free to say no. However, it would be wrong if you just invited them to your barbecue without saying why and then took the opportunity to try to sell to them afterwards. Such manipulative behaviour is very widespread. Indeed, it is often taught in courses on how to sell to people, but a Christian must never stoop to such depths.

Always follow your conscience

The Bible is full of principles that guide us in how to approach decisions and situations. Life is so varied that infinite permutations of circumstances can arise. We then have to decide which principles to apply, or which principle comes first on a particular occasion. At such times, we need to be guided by conscience. That is the gift God gives each of us to guide us.

It's like using a compass in a heavy storm, when we can't get directions from anything else. We can ask God and He will guide us through our conscience. We will just know that a certain course of action doesn't *feel* right, even if we can't explain why, and even though it seems there are many good points in favour of it. When that happens, always follow your conscience and never go against it.

Be very careful before you make any vow. God will hold you to your word.

Be careful with your words. Don't make rash promises to God, or anybody else, without proper consideration and reflection. He will hold you to what you say. Therefore avoid making any promise or vow unless you have thought it through and fully intend to honour it. Even then, don't make vows at all, unless you are really sure God wants you to do so:

⁴When you make a vow to God, do not be late in paying it; for He takes no delight in fools Pay what you vow! ⁵It is better that you should not vow than that you should vow and not pay. ⁶Do not let your speech cause you to sin and do not say in the presence of the messenger of God that it was a mistake. Why should God be angry on account of your voice and destroy the work of your hands?

Ecclesiastes 5:4-6 (NASB)

How to decide whether to get drawn in to a dispute which involves other people

This is a vexed question, to which there can be no easy or quick answer. What to do in any given situation will depend on all the specific facts of the case and on a number of relevant principles, one or other of which could loom large. Let's consider first the general problem and then look at some of the different principles that the Bible sets out.

When a conflict arises at work, or in some other setting, such as amongst neighbours, friends or family, it may sometimes be right to get involved and to take sides or speak up. Other times God will want you to stay out of it. It depends on a host of factors. We have to weigh them all up, including, amongst other things, the following series of questions:

141

1) Is there right and wrong on both sides, or just on one side? If there is wrongdoing on both sides, I'd be inclined to stay out of it. If it is only on the one side, I'd be more willing to consider getting involved.

2) How serious is the dispute and how grave could the consequences be? If the dispute is minor, you may be best to keep out of it and only get involved if serious issues are at stake, such as someone's career or reputation or a court case.

3) What are your respective duties to each of the parties? Sometimes you owe no specific duties to either party. Other times you may do so, such as where you are an employee of one of the parties. The greater the duty, the more you ought to be willing to intervene.

4) Are each of the parties wise, simple, foolish or wicked? If both of them are wicked or foolish, there is little point joining in. Nothing will be achieved and harm will come to you for having tried to help. But if one or both are wise, or even simple, that may be different. (See Books Five and Six for more detail)

5) Has the person who needs your help been faithful to you previously and are they generally faithful to others? If not, there would be little point in getting involved, because they would not appreciate your help or reciprocate it. They would not deserve it either.

6) Is anybody's job, reputation, marriage or legal case at stake? If so, a willingness for you to take a risk may be required.

7) Are there frequent conflicts involving this person? Or is this a one-off? If frequent, there may be little point getting involved, as even if you did something on this occasion, another dispute would soon spring up to take its place.

8) Does the dispute properly involve you, or would you be meddling in a quarrel which is not your own, such that you should keep out of it? The Bible warns us not to do that:

He who meddles in a quarrel not his own is like
one who takes a passing dog by the ears.
                    Proverbs 26:17 (RSV)

Keeping away from strife is an honor for a man,
But any fool will quarrel.
                    Proverbs 20:3 (NASB)

9) Is the wronged/innocent party worthy of your support, given that any intervention may involve you putting yourself at risk of hostility? Be aware that people often resent a witness or intervener far more than they resent their original opponent.

10) Is the party who needs your help seeking to use or manipulate you, or any other person? If so, you ought to back off.

There is a time to be diplomatic and to stay out of a conflict, but there is also a time to take risks and get involved

It is usually wrong to get involved in another person's quarrel or dispute, The general rule is that we should stay out of it unless there is a good reason to get involved. But if there is a duty to help, or if our conscience tells us we should, then we must come forward, give evidence, or do whatever else is required of us, even if it is risky to us.

There may be factors which require you to speak up and defend someone, even if it jeopardizes your own position. If so, you need to brace yourself and do your duty. I can think of a particularly heated and protracted dispute which had been going on for some time. It involved parties, who were all well known to me.

Initially I stayed out of it, hoping it would resolve itself without me having to step in or take sides. I knew it would cause problems for me if I did get involved. However the dispute eventually became very nasty and unfair. False accusations were being made by the blameworthy party against the innocent party. Therefore I felt, in the end, that I needed to speak up openly.

The event which prompted it was when the person whom I considered to be at fault rang me up and spoke very unfairly and aggressively about the innocent party. I told them, straightforwardly, that I believed that they were actually the one in the wrong.

Later a meeting took place and again I spoke frankly. It did not resolve the dispute, but I felt that the innocent party needed me to speak out. They were reeling from a series of blows being landed on them and needed to be openly supported. They were being harmed, both emotionally and spiritually. Therefore it was no longer possible for me to remain neutral. Too much was at stake for them and a deep injustice was being done.

So, that was a case where I got openly involved and I think it was right to do so, even though the wrongdoers ended up insulting and resenting me as a result of my having spoken up for the innocent party. But I can also remember a situation about 20 years ago where, very unwisely, I allowed myself to be manipulated into joining in with someone else's dispute at work.

It all ended badly for me and nothing useful was achieved. The person who had enlisted my help was just using me for his own selfish purposes, to advance himself at someone else's expense. I realised that later, but only when it was too late. I had allowed myself to be used by another man in his own private battle with a colleague. It turned out he was no more right than the other person was, and no profound issues of justice were involved.

I misjudged the situation badly and took sides, mainly because I simply preferred him to the other person. I therefore assumed he must be in the right. But I had never looked into it deeply, or weighed it up carefully. I had never prayed about it either, i.e. as to whether to get involved. I just went ahead without seeking God's guidance. That was asking for trouble.

I can recall another occasion, when I was a very young and inexperienced police constable. We received a new shift inspector who was a woman. That was rare in those days. The whole shift felt that she was not very good at her job, and that she had been given accelerated promotion solely due to being female. They were probably right. She was not liked by the shift and the older men in particular bristled at her abrasive style. She lacked people skills, had very little tact, and was not as effective as the other inspectors.

Things got very bad and the atmosphere on the shift declined. Morale was low and, in the end, some of the older constables became insubordinate to her, usually covertly, but sometimes openly. It all went over my head. I was too junior at the time to play any part in it. It got so bad in the end that the Superintendent came in to carry out an enquiry into what was going wrong on our shift.

He questioned us, one by one, in front of the Inspector. I was so naïve that I gave frank, honest answers and told the Superintendent that part of the problem was the Inspector's abrasive manner etc. I said it in front of her, as she was present in the room. It seemed to me that I had been asked a straightforward question and that I therefore needed to answer it truthfully.

However, it achieved no good and my transparency just did me harm. The rest of the shift, having savagely criticised the Inspector behind her back, were shrewd enough to keep quiet and even to be sycophantic, in that formal interview, while she was present.

Ironically, I was the only one to criticise the Inspector openly, even though I was the one who felt the least discontented and who had said the least up to that point. It was purely due to my naivety. I did not realise that that was an occasion when no good could come from my speaking up and that silence was the only wise policy.

Ask God to help you never to compromise and never to betray Him

As with any difficult task, if you are going to succeed, you will need God's help. That is very much the case here. To be faithful to God will require prayer. You need to ask Him to help you never to compromise, even on so called 'small' issues, and never to betray Him.

If you don't pray, then you may have to manage it on your own, which is impossible. Don't even attempt that. Be wise enough to realise that you always need God's help, and especially so where difficult issues are involved and wisdom is needed.

Respond quickly to God's promptings. Never harden your heart or stop listening to Him.

God will speak to you through your conscience to guide you as to what to do in a given situation, especially if you ask Him to do so. When He speaks in this way, it will not be in a loud, clear, unmistakable voice. It will be with a quiet, inner voice which enables you to know, or usually just to feel, that a certain path is right or wrong.

When God speaks through our conscience He does not necessarily explain *why* a thing is wrong, or go into any detail. But He will enable you to know enough to do His will. If you obey that prompting, then more clarity will be given to you later. Then you will more fully grasp *why* God did, or didn't, want you to do the thing in question. Therefore, don't wait till you have that full understanding. Respond to what you do know. Obey your conscience immediately, as it currently stands.

Don't delay or argue with it, just because you don't yet have full understanding. Accept God's promptings quickly and willingly. If you do, then they will get clearer, louder and more frequent, which is exactly what is best for you. Never refuse to listen to, or to obey, your conscience. Never harden your heart towards God, or take liberties with His grace and patience.

If you stop listening to God and stop obeying Him then eventually He may *'hand you over'* and allow you to destroy yourself

The Egyptian Pharoah, with whom Moses dealt, chose to harden his heart repeatedly. He refused to do what he knew to be the will of God. We know this because there was a previous contest between Moses and Pharoah's magicians, Jannes and Jambres. Each time that Moses produced a miracle these occult practitioners did the same, using demonic power. However, there came a point when they could no longer match Moses. When that point came, the magicians, Jannes and Jambres, told Pharoah that what Moses had was from God:

Then the LORD said to Moses, "Say to Aaron, 'Stretch out your rod and strike the dust of the earth, that it may become gnats throughout all the land of Egypt.'" ¹⁷ And they did so; Aaron stretched out his hand with his rod, and struck the dust of the earth, and there came gnats on man and beast; all the dust of the earth became gnats throughout all the land of Egypt. ¹⁸ The magicians tried by their secret arts to bring forth gnats, but they could not. So there were gnats on man and beast. ¹⁹ And the magicians said to Pharaoh, "This is the finger of God." But Pharaoh's heart was hardened, and he would not listen to them; as the LORD had said.

Exodus 8:16-19 (RSV)

So, although he knew that Moses was representing God, Pharoah still chose to 'harden his heart' and to refuse to obey God's instructions. If you read the whole account in Exodus you will see that Pharoah does this repeatedly, at least seven times. After that the position altered. Instead of Pharoah hardening his own heart, we see that God actually began to harden Pharoah's heart for him:

⁸And the LORD said to Moses and Aaron, "Take handfuls of ashes from the kiln, and let Moses throw them toward heaven in the sight of Pharaoh. ⁹And it shall become fine dust over all the land of Egypt, and become boils breaking out in sores on man and beast throughout all the land of Egypt." ¹⁰So they took ashes from the kiln, and stood before Pharaoh, and Moses threw them toward heaven, and it became boils breaking out in sores on man and beast. ¹¹ And the magicians could not stand before Moses because of the boils, for the boils were upon the magicians and upon all the Egyptians. ¹² But the LORD hardened the heart of Pharaoh, and he did not listen to them; as the LORD had spoken to Moses.

Exodus 9:8-12 (RSV)

After this, we see that when God sent a plague of hail, Pharoah again chose to harden his own heart. However, with the next plagues of locusts and the three days of total darkness, it was God who, again, hardened Pharoah's heart for him. We are actually told this directly:

Then the LORD said to Moses, "Go in to Pharaoh; for I have hardened his heart and the heart of his servants, that I may show these signs of mine among them,

Exodus 10:1 (RSV)

The relevance of these passages to us is that there comes a point in our dealings with God where He will, eventually, stop speaking to our conscience and stop trying to get us to listen to Him. This will only come after we have repeatedly and deliberately ignored God's voice, in the form of His written Word, or our

146

conscience, or even the advice of godly people. If so, then at some point, God will 'switch off the transmitter' and stop trying to speak to us. He will then leave us to keep going in the wrong direction that we have chosen, until it ends in disaster.

Therefore do not ever allow that stage to be reached. Who knows how many times, or for how long, God will be patient with you? Perhaps His patience will not run out for several weeks or months, or even years. Or, perhaps today is your final chance to listen to His voice or to obey your conscience before God begins to harden your heart for you, as He did with Pharoah?

Never put God to the test. Never go anywhere near that 'cliff edge'. Obey your conscience today and every day. Obey God's Word today, without delay or argument, and without fudging or compromise. It is not just with Pharoah that God acts in this way. He also did it with the people of Israel:

[11]"But my people did not listen to my voice;
Israel would have none of me.
[12]So I gave them over to their stubborn hearts,
to follow their own counsels.
[13]O that my people would listen to me,
that Israel would walk in my ways!
Psalm 81:11-13 (RSV)

If God is willing to let the Jewish people go their own way and "*give them over to their stubborn hearts*" then what basis is there to assume that He is not willing to do the same with you? Therefore fear Him and do not be presumptuous.

One of the main causes of unfaithfulness is lack of courage. Therefore ask God for the courage to overcome all your fears and to obey Him, even when you are afraid.

I have no statistical data to back up my point, but I have observed from experience that fear is one of the main things which causes people to be unfaithful or to drop their standards. For example a person might know that some practice at work is wrong but they fear to say anything, or are afraid to refuse to take part. They worry that doing so may result in ridicule or unpopularity, or that they may even lose their job.

The list of things that people fear is endless. What frightens you may not frighten someone else and vice versa. But, whoever you are, there will be certain things which you particularly fear. The demons who are involved in your life are well aware of what those particular things are for you. Therefore, they calculate that all they have to do to get you to be unfaithful is to engineer it so that one or more of these things, or people, that you fear are brought into the situation.

They will take care to arrange that, so that you are put under pressure and made to feel afraid. They will then use the thing that you fear, whatever it may be, as a leverage point to unsettle you. They want to get you to lose your nerve, and then to be unfaithful, by doing something which you know to be wrong. The answer, in every such situation, is that we need to have more courage. Lack of courage is perhaps the one most significant feature which causes Christians to let God down and to fail to do their duty.

Conversely, if we have courage, i.e. if we choose to be courageous, then we will be able to go the things that please God, because doing His will requires courage. Look at how God viewed King Jehoshaphat. God praises him in various ways, but especially for being courageous. Moreover, it doesn't just mean courageous in battle, but courageous *"in the ways of the LORD."*

That means having the courage to do God's will, even when that provokes controversy and makes you unpopular. For example, King Jehoshaphat showed courage by getting rid of the 'high places' and the Asherim, i.e. the means by which occultic, idolatrous worship was conducted.

These things were popular with the people. Therefore most kings, even the better ones, left them in place, for fear of getting an adverse reaction from the people. But Jehoshaphat went through with it and tackled the idolatry head on, regardless of the criticism it provoked. He did so because He knew it was what God wanted and he put God's commands ahead of his own welfare:

³ The Lord was with Jehosh'aphat, because he walked in the earlier ways of his father; he did not seek the Ba'als, ⁴ but sought the God of his father and walked in his commandments, and not according to the ways of Israel. ⁵ Therefore the Lord established the kingdom in his hand; and all Judah brought tribute to Jehosh'aphat; and he had great riches and honor. ⁶ His heart was courageous in the ways of the Lord; and furthermore he took the high places and the Ashe'rim out of Judah.

2 Chronicles 17:3-6 (RSV)

Lack of courage causes us to compromise in our preaching and to stay silent when we should speak up

Lack of courage causes people to stay silent when they should speak up. It also causes many preachers to give a compromised, watered down message. They know that telling the whole truth about what the Bible says would cause controversy and tension. It could possibly even lead to them losing their position as a minister. The thought of losing his income, home and pension has caused many a preacher to tone down what the Bible says and to limit themselves to saying what people want to hear, rather than what God wants to be said.

Whoever you are, and whatever the circumstances you might face, the answer is the same. We all need to settle things beforehand, and to make a clear and firm decision, that we will always say and do what is right, regardless of the consequences. It is no good leaving it to the moment of crisis and hoping that at that point you will make the right choice. You won't. You will buckle under the immediate pressure of the situation and give in to your fear.

However, if you settle it all clearly beforehand then, when the moment of testing comes, you will already know very clearly what you must do. The fact that the decision has already been made makes it much easier to carry it out when the crisis comes. It means that you don't have to think quickly on the spot, or make instant decisions, because you have already done your thinking and made your decisions.

Someone might reply to that by saying that if the fear is too strong, and if your courage is too small, then there is nothing you can do about it, just as there is nothing you can do about your height or the colour of your eyes. Some might even say that the amount of courage you have is genetically determined and is just something you are born with. Therefore, they would argue that there is nothing you can do about it if you don't have enough courage.

According to that line of reasoning you can't be blamed if you fail for lack of courage, because it's not your fault. That is not how the Bible presents it. It makes clear that we are very much answerable for our lack of courage. We are also answerable for our failure, in the months or years leading up to that point of severe testing, to have prepared ourselves for it properly.

The point is that, at least in the West, it is rare for any person to begin their life as a Christian and then immediately be thrust into a situation of very severe testing and danger. It is not impossible, especially in certain countries where Christianity is forbidden. However, by and large, God arranges it so that the tests we have to face begin small and then get steadily larger over the years.

Therefore, a faithful person with the right heart-attitude will prepare themselves for larger and larger tests by passing each of the smaller tests which they face along the way. No school will enter a pupil for 'A' level exams before he has taken GCSE exams and a host of other, easier, exams in the years before those. Likewise, God expects you to develop the quality of faithfulness, and to grow your courage, by taking and passing a long series of smaller tests, from the moment you become a Christian.

If you set your heart to pass those earlier tests and sincerely pray that God will give you the courage to face them, then your courage will have grown to the required level when the time comes to face a more severe test. Moreover, the practice you have had will put you in the habit of immediately resolving to be faithful and deciding to be obedient before you ever face the danger.

That way, when danger does come, you will be ready to make the right decisions instantly, before you have had any time to dwell on the danger, or to be talked out of doing what is right. So, you will certainly be held accountable for the hundreds of small challenges and tests of your courage that you take along the way. Therefore, if you really want to be faithful, then you will resolve to learn courage from each of those experiences.

So any failure on your part to handle a severe test later on would really have been caused by your repeated failures to overcome your fear when facing smaller tests in the past. For those reasons, you cannot deny responsibility when your courage fails you in some major crisis. That's because you could have developed your courage to the necessary level, if you had really wanted to and had been determined to pass the earlier test.

A classic example of this is the teenage David, when he volunteered to fight Goliath. He was certainly brave on that day, but it was by no means his first battle. He had, on many occasions, fought smaller battles with bears and lions when he was caring for his father's sheep. It was on those many previous occasions that he learned how to control and overcome his fear.

That was also when he had learned how to use a sling shot. So he perfected that skill too, ready for when he needed it. David had practiced overcoming his fear and so the contest with Goliath was not quite as unfamiliar an experience as it might appear. He knew that he had killed lions and bears before and thus he was confident, with good reason, that he could kill Goliath in the same way.

If you don't resolve now to deal with whatever your current fear may be, and also to seek God's help to overcome it, then it will eventually grow to the point where it controls you and paralyses you. Your fear will then be a snare to you. It will trip you up and trap you every time you have to face a test.

It is not a sin to be afraid. The sin is in giving into your fear and letting it control you.

There is nothing wrong with being afraid. Fear is not sin in itself. It is natural, and even necessary, at times. Indeed, without fear there cannot be any real bravery. A brave person is just someone who has learned how to control their fear and to go ahead despite it, rather than someone who has no capacity to feel it.

A coward is someone who feels exactly the same fear, or even less, but has decided that he is not willing to face up to it. Indeed, for a coward, the fear may well be less, because he is well aware that he has no intention of facing any challenge or taking any risk, whether small or large.

Thus, the dangers he faces are largely academic and theoretical rather than real. However, for a brave person the fear is all the more real, precisely because he knows that he does not have the option of running away and that he will have to face up to it.

By contrast, a coward does not even try to overcome his fear and he does not seek God's help to defeat it. He has already made a clear decision of a very different kind. That is that he will not do or say anything, or make any decision, which would have the potential to cost him, hurt him or upset him. In the end he becomes programmed with a default-setting that guides him on every occasion away from risk, danger or cost and towards the preservation of himself, his property and his reputation.

I have seen this in operation many times and have noted how quickly certain people can be diverted from the right path, merely because they see a risk of danger ahead. As soon as they see it they immediately, and automatically, seek for compromise and a way of escape. They do so as a matter of habit because it has become such a settled policy to avoid personal danger or cost.

They do not even need to think it through when the crisis emerges. They have already pre-programmed themselves to make it their top priority to preserve themselves, and/or their possessions or popularity, rather than be faithful to what God asks of them. For example, I have seen this trait in managers and supervisors within a workplace. Most of them will instinctively choose to overlook wrongdoing, and to 'turn a blind eye', so as to avoid a challenge or a controversy.

They don't want to be put under any personal pressure. Above all, they will avoid any face to face confrontation. Thus, for example, such a manager may face a situation where a nasty, hardened, battle-axe of an employee is causing problems within the office or is bullying or exploiting weaker colleagues.

The duty of that manager is obvious. It is to confront the wrongdoer, stand up for the victim, commence an investigation and disciplinary proceedings and get the wrongdoer out. But they usually don't do so because they already know, without needing to think it over, that doing what is right would be difficult. They don't relish the prospect of tackling the bully or facing a backlash from the bully's supporters. So, they tell themselves that the wrongdoing isn't happening, or that it isn't their responsibility, or that nothing can be done about it.

Then they look the other way and keep on looking the other way. That manager or supervisor is a coward, not because they felt fear, but because they allowed that fear to rule them and to cause them to neglect their clear duty. They chose self-preservation, or even the preservation of their own comfort, peace and well-being, rather than the needs of their junior colleagues and their duty to the business.

Their cowardice manifests itself in their decisions and in the order of their list of priorities. A coward will put himself first every time. By contrast, for a brave person, it is duty that must come first, even though he feels all the same fears, and faces all the same pressures, as the rest of us. Dangerous or challenging situations will inevitably arise from time to time. In fact, God probably causes some of them to happen. At the very least, He makes use of them.

He sees them as tests of your courage and faithfulness and He will watch closely to see how you respond to danger and pressure. One example of this, on a very large scale, is the way that God allowed King Hezekiah of Judah to face the terrible prospect of an invading army. We are told directly that God wanted to see what was in Hezekiah's heart. In other words, God wanted to see what Hezekiah was made of and how he would react in a major crisis, when a large army approached Judah and was likely to invade:

Even in the matter of the envoys of the rulers of Babylon, who sent to him to inquire of the wonder that had happened in the land, God left him alone only to test him, that He might know all that was in his heart.
2 Chronicles 32:31 (NASB)

CHAPTER 8

FURTHER ADVICE ON HOW WE CAN BECOME MORE FAITHFUL

If you will fear the LORD and serve him and hearken to his voice and not rebel against the commandment of the LORD, and if both you and the king who reigns over you will follow the LORD your God, it will be well;

1 Samuel 12:14 (RSV)

[4] For when Solomon was old his wives turned away his heart after other gods; and his heart was not wholly true to the Lord his God, as was the heart of David his father. [5] For Solomon went after Ash'toreth the goddess of the Sido'nians, and after Milcom the abomination of the Ammonites. [6] So Solomon did what was evil in the sight of the Lord, and did not wholly follow the Lord, as David his father had done.

1 Kings 11:4-6 (RSV)

You need to make a firm decision that being faithful is more important than staying alive

Probably the ultimate test of our courage is whether we are willing to die rather than abandon our faithfulness. Resolve now, ahead of time, that being faithful and staying true to what you believe is more important even than staying alive. Then you will be set free from what is probably the demons' best leverage point.

Demons use fear to get you to compromise, to give in, and to let God down. They will whisper into your mind that unless you compromise your faith, or drop your standards, you might lose your job, your home, your business, or even your life. The dread of losing such things causes most of us to panic and to disobey God. We have trained ourselves over many years that, when under pressure, the main priority is self-preservation, i.e. to look after number one.

However, you can reverse that pre-programming. Begin now to train yourself to say that staying faithful to God is more important than getting a pay rise or a promotion. Then you will gradually learn how to see your faithfulness as being far more important than keeping your job or your home or business. Once you've reached that level you will be ready to move up to the next stage, which is to resolve that your faithfulness and loyalty to God are more important than staying alive.

You can build up to that level in stages if you don't feel you can make that jump all in one go. You can then make a firm decision, in advance that, if faced with a crisis, you will stay faithful. Making that decision, now, ahead of time, means that you don't need to pause and think if and when the crisis actually arises, which could be suddenly.

Then you won't be taken by surprise or panic or get 'caught in the headlights'. You will react well to the threat when it comes because your mind was already made up beforehand. It is also because you will have learned to be courageous as a *habit,* by responding to earlier and smaller tests of your nerve and resolve. A classic example of a group of people who made this decision not to compromise, even if it meant death, is the group referred to in Revelation chapter 12.

They are the 'Tribulation saints' who are called upon to face the lies and threats of the antichrist during the period known as the Tribulation. They refuse to give in and worship the antichrist, or his image, because they have decided that they would prefer to die rather than do that. In the RSV it says *"for they loved not their lives even unto death."*

⁹ And the great dragon was thrown down, that ancient serpent, who is called the Devil and Satan, the deceiver of the whole world—he was thrown down to the earth, and his angels were thrown down with him. ¹⁰ And I heard a loud voice in heaven, saying, "Now the salvation and the power and the kingdom of our God and the authority of his Christ have come, for the accuser of our brethren has been thrown down, who accuses them day and night before our God. ¹¹ And they have conquered him by the blood of the Lamb and by the word of their testimony, for they loved not their lives even unto death. ¹² Rejoice then, O heaven and you that dwell therein! But woe to you, O earth and sea, for the devil has come down to you in great wrath, because he knows that his time is short!"
Revelation 12:9-12 (RSV)

They make that choice in a period of intense suffering and persecution which comes about because the Devil knows that the time he has left is very short. The tribulation is only seven years long and the Devil knows that. But so too do the believers who are alive at that time, because the Bible makes that clear. So they wisely choose to give up their lives here and gain eternal life, rather than worship Satan and be lost forever. In their circumstances that is a sensible and logical choice. It is equally so in our circumstances today.

Therefore we must not love our lives so much as to make self-preservation our priority, which is how the world thinks. It is yet another aspect of worldly thinking that we have to reject. Then we too can conquer, as the Tribulation saints will conquer, by not loving our lives, even unto death, or as the NIV translates it, by not loving our lives *"so much as to shrink from death"*:

They triumphed over him
by the blood of the Lamb
and by the word of their testimony;

154

they did not love their lives so much
as to shrink from death.
                    Revelation 12:11 (NIV)

In Revelation chapter two, in Jesus' letter to the church at Smyrna, He actually warns them in advance that a time of persecution is going to come to them. He then urges them to *"Be faithful unto death..."* If they will do so, then He promises them the reward of the *'crown of life'*:

Do not fear what you are about to suffer. Behold, the devil is about to throw some of you into prison, that you may be tested, and for ten days you will have tribulation. Be faithful unto death, and I will give you the crown of life.
                    Revelation 2:10 (RSV)

The fear of the LORD helps you to remain faithful

The Bible regularly tells us to "fear the Lord". It is a major theme and a very important issue. Here is an example. Joshua is speaking to the Israelites as they were about to enter the Promised Land:

[14]"Now therefore fear the LORD, and serve him in sincerity and in faithfulness; put away the gods which your fathers served beyond the River, and in Egypt, and serve the LORD. [15]And if you be unwilling to serve the LORD, choose this day whom you will serve, whether the gods your fathers served in the region beyond the River, or the gods of the Amorites in whose land you dwell; but as for me and my house, we will serve the LORD."
                    Joshua 24:14-15 (RSV)

The phrase *"the fear of the LORD"* is confusing to many people. In particular, its purpose is not clear to them. Basically, the fear of the LORD involves realising who God is and how immense, powerful, and holy He is. It also involves recognising the reality of the fact that He is God and that He judges all people and punishes evil and wrongdoing.

If we are genuine Christians then we will not have to face His wrath at the Great White Throne judgment, provided we remain faithful to Him. However, see Chapter 21 in Book One of this series for an analysis of whether a real Christian can ever lose his salvation and end up at the Great White Throne Judgment and then the Lake of Fire.

However, even if the judgment we have to face is the Judgment Seat of Christ, which is for saved believers, we should still fear it. I am not looking forward to that day. I fear it. I am keenly aware that there are many areas of my life which do not come up to the standard that God wants from me.

155

Although God is patient and is working with me to get me to change, I cannot be complacent or presumptuous or assume that my own sin or unfaithfulness doesn't matter. It does. It will have consequences, especially if I do not take it seriously or repent of it. At the very least, it may involve the loss of rewards that I might otherwise have received. Even worse, it could lead to me being publicly rebuked by Jesus at the Judgment Seat.

I fear that, and very much wish to avoid it. I want Him to praise me and reward me, not to scold me or to tell me what might have been, if only I had obeyed Him. Perhaps the most painful thing of all would be to be told that my unfaithfulness had prevented me and/or others being effective in reaching the lost. I don't want to be told that any men or women went to the Lake of Fire as the indirect consequence of my own disobedience, laziness, selfishness or neglect.

I have not come across many other believers who share that concern, or who are even aware of the concept of the fear of the LORD, let alone gripped by it. It is rare today in the West. However, it is actually something which you should seek for and ask God to produce in you. It is for your own good. Many beneficial things will come from it. A lot of promises are made in the Bible to those who fear the LORD. It is therefore an advantage, not a handicap.

Perhaps the greatest benefit that comes from the fear of the Lord is that it helps us to remain acutely conscious of God at times when we are tempted to sin or to be unfaithful to Him. Our fear of Him can then jolt us back to our senses before it is too late and before we do wrong. Therefore, every day, indeed every moment, we must choose whom we are going to serve. The fear of the LORD will help us to make the right choice:

⁷The fear of the LORD is the beginning of knowledge;
Fools despise wisdom and instruction.
Proverbs 1:7 (NASB)

Stay faithful for the long term - until the day you die

It's hard enough just to begin to be faithful. However, it is much harder to continue. Staying faithful to God, year after year, decade after decade, until the day you die, is very difficult. Few can manage it. The greatest danger is the complacency that can arise after years of having followed the LORD. It is so easy to imagine, having come so far, and having remained faithful until now, that you are immune to temptation.

If you ever assume that, then you will begin to think that you can afford to relax your standards a little and 'cut corners,' or make small compromises. You can't afford to do that. The later stages of a person's life can be the period in which they become most likely to do this, such that they fall into sin and let God down.

156

We must never let that happen to us. The only way to avoid it is to keep relying on God, and to ask for His help in avoiding presumption and in staying vigilant and alert. There is no place for a casual attitude, however well you may have done so far.

Examples of biblical characters who were faithful to begin with, but then compromised and became unfaithful later in life

We have already seen, in earlier chapters, some examples of characters in the Bible who began well but then let God down and became unfaithful later in life. These accounts are in the Bible to bring home to us the danger that we ourselves are in. There is the account of King Uzziah, which we looked at earlier.

He began his reign aged 16 and was faithful for many years but then, due to becoming proud as a result of his fame and success, he became arrogant and disobedient. He usurped the position of the priests and presumed to enter the Temple to offer a sacrifice himself, which he was not authorised to do.

Then there is the sad example of King Saul who began well and with great promise, but who ended up a petulant, self-pitiful, paranoid man. He even consulted a witch rather than seek God's guidance. Saul did all that despite the fact that when he began, he was the best man God could find in all of Israel . He had also operated, for a time, in prophetic gifts.

That ought to sober us. If even he could degenerate so badly, then so can we, if we allow ourselves to drift or to compromise with sin. In addition there is King Solomon. He began very well indeed and had more wisdom than any other man. But even he went astray due to marrying so many wives, many of whom were not Israelites and were worshippers of idols.

Then there is Gehazi, the assistant to the prophet Elisha. He served Elisha for years but then fell into sin and unfaithfulness when he was tempted by the desire for money. He lied to Naaman the Syrian and extracted a financial gift from him, pretending that Elisha had asked for it. As a result of that deception God struck Gehazi down with leprosy.

There is also King Rehoboam, the son of King Solomon. Consider the advantages he had in having a father like that. Yet, we are told that when Rehoboam became established as King he abandoned the law of the LORD and ended up doing evil:

When the rule of Rehoboam was established and he was strong, he abandoned the law of the LORD, and all Israel with him.

2 Chronicles 12:1 (ESV)

157

And he did evil, for he did not set his heart to seek the LORD
2 Chronicles 12:14 (ESV)

Consider also the life of King Asa of Judah. He began well but in his later years he did not maintain the faithfulness with which he began.

One reads of very many bad kings of Judah, and even more so in the Northern Kingdom of Israel. But it is perhaps even sadder to read of kings who began well but who did not keep it up. They failed or let themselves down in the end. One such is King Asa. He began well and was full of zeal for God and did what was right. In particular he took action to stamp out idolatrous worship of false gods and to encourage the people of Judah to serve the one true God:

¹So Abi'jah slept with his fathers, and they buried him in the city of David; and Asa his son reigned in his stead. In his days the land had rest for ten years. ²And Asa did what was good and right in the eyes of the LORD his God. ³ He took away the foreign altars and the high places, and broke down the pillars and hewed down the Ashe'rim, ⁴and commanded Judah to seek the LORD, the God of their fathers, and to keep the law and the commandment. ⁵ He also took out of all the cities of Judah the high places and the incense altars. And the kingdom had rest under him. ⁶He built fortified cities in Judah, for the land had rest. He had no war in those years, for the LORD gave him peace. ⁷And he said to Judah, "Let us build these cities, and surround them with walls and towers, gates and bars; the land is still ours, because we have sought the LORD our God; we have sought him, and he has given us peace on every side." So they built and prospered.
2 Chronicles 14:1-7 (RSV)

King Asa also put his trust in God when it came to military matters. Therefore, with God's help, he was able to defeat armies far larger than his own:

⁸And Asa had an army of three hundred thousand from Judah, armed with bucklers and spears, and two hundred and eighty thousand men from Benjamin, that carried shields and drew bows; all these were mighty men of valor. ⁹Zerah the Ethiopian came out against them with an army of a million men and three hundred chariots, and came as far as Mare'shah. ¹⁰And Asa went out to meet him, and they drew up their lines of battle in the valley of Zeph'athah at Mare'shah. ¹¹And Asa cried to the LORD his God, "O LORD, there is none like thee to help, between the mighty and the weak. Help us, O LORD our God, for we rely on thee, and in thy name we have come against this multitude. O LORD, thou art our God; let not man prevail against thee." ¹²So the LORD defeated the Ethiopians before Asa and before Judah, and the Ethiopians fled.
2 Chronicles 14:8-12 (RSV)

Asa had been inspired by a prophet called Azariah and had embarked on a programme of stamping out idolatry. This was so successful that many of the faithful Jews who were living in the Northern Kingdom of Israel came south to live in Judah:

" ⁸When Asa heard these words, the prophecy of Azari'ah the son of Oded, he took courage, and put away the abominable idols from all the land of Judah and Benjamin and from the cities which he had taken in the hill country of E'phraim, and he repaired the altar of the LORD that was in front of the vestibule of the house of the LORD. ⁹And he gathered all Judah and Benjamin, and those from E'phraim, Manas'seh, and Simeon who were sojourning with them, for great numbers had deserted to him from Israel when they saw that the LORD his God was with him.

2 Chronicles 15:8-9 (RSV)

Asa was so full of faith and zeal that he even confronted his own mother, Maacah, and removed her from her position as Queen Mother, because she got herself involved in idolatry:

Even Ma'acah, his mother, King Asa removed from being queen mother because she had made an abominable image for Ashe'rah. Asa cut down her image, crushed it, and burned it at the brook Kidron.

2 Chronicles 15:16 (RSV)

Nevertheless, despite the great victory he had had over the Ethiopians, who had had an army more than twice the size of his, King Asa let himself down later in his reign. He formed an alliance with the King of Syria and relied on him to help him deal with the threat being made to the Kingdom of Judah from the King of the Northern Kingdom of Israel.

What Asa should have done was to rely on God, as he had done early in his reign in the war against Ethiopia. Instead he put his trust in men and formed an ungodly and unnecessary alliance, which God did not want him to make:

¹In the thirty-sixth year of the reign of Asa, Ba'asha king of Israel went up against Judah, and built Ramah, that he might permit no one to go out or come in to Asa king of Judah. ² Then Asa took silver and gold from the treasures of the house of the LORD and the king's house, and sent them to Ben-ha'dad king of Syria, who dwelt in Damascus, saying, ³"Let there be a league between me and you, as between my father and your father; behold, I am sending to you silver and gold; go, break your league with Ba'asha king of Israel, that he may withdraw from me." ⁴And Ben-ha'dad hearkened to King Asa, and sent the commanders of his armies against the cities of Israel, and they conquered I'jon, Dan, A'bel-ma'im, and all the store-cities of Naph'tali. ⁵And when Ba'asha heard of it, he stopped building Ramah, and let his work cease. ⁶Then King Asa

159

took all Judah, and they carried away the stones of Ramah and its timber, with which Ba'asha had been building, and with them he built Geba and Mizpah.

2 Chronicles 16:1-6 (RSV)

As a result of this disobedience and lack of trust, God sent another prophet, Hanani, to rebuke King Asa. However, Asa's heart had grown proud over the years as a result of all the peace and success he had enjoyed. Therefore, by this stage, he was much less receptive to hear God's voice than he had been when he was younger. Even when he became ill he did not seek God's help, but put his trust solely in doctors to heal him. Evidently, he was no longer as close to God as he had once been:

[7]At that time Hana'ni the seer came to Asa king of Judah, and said to him, "Because you relied on the king of Syria, and did not rely on the LORD your God, the army of the king of Syria has escaped you. [8]Were not the Ethiopians and the Libyans a huge army with exceedingly many chariots and horsemen? Yet because you relied on the LORD, he gave them into your hand. [9]For the eyes of the LORD run to and fro throughout the whole earth, to show his might in behalf of those whose heart is blameless toward him. You have done foolishly in this; for from now on you will have wars." [10]Then Asa was angry with the seer, and put him in the stocks, in prison, for he was in a rage with him because of this. And Asa inflicted cruelties upon some of the people at the same time.

[11]The acts of Asa, from first to last, are written in the Book of the Kings of Judah and Israel. [12]In the thirty-ninth year of his reign Asa was diseased in his feet, and his disease became severe; yet even in his disease he did not seek the LORD, but sought help from physicians. [13]And Asa slept with his fathers, dying in the forty-first year of his reign. [14]They buried him in the tomb which he had hewn out for himself in the city of David. They laid him on a bier which had been filled with various kinds of spices prepared by the perfumer's art; and they made a very great fire in his honor.

2 Chronicles 16:7-14 (RSV)

Before we criticise King Asa, we need to ask whether we are any more faithful than he was

It is easy to be critical of King Asa, but actually the tests of his faith that he faced in the later years of his long reign were very difficult. It is surprisingly hard to remain faithful for long periods of time and to keep on being willing to trust God. It can mean taking risks, even when you have become wealthy and successful and you have grown used to the trappings of power and of being in office. At that stage, when we have more to lose, many of us are less willing to take risks.

I can speak with some experience of how difficult a test that is. I set up a law firm from a standing start when I was in my thirties. At the outset I had no staff, no files, no equipment, no anything. All I had was a burning desire to set up a business which God could use for His purposes. I also wanted to expand the ministry of financial giving, in which I had already been engaged since I was 19.

In the early years of the new firm I faced many different tests and battles which severely stretched my faith. I found it hard. Yet, I found the later years, when the firm was succeeding and prospering, an even more difficult test. In the early years I had no alternative but to trust God, because the firm was small and had no money or strength. But in the end I faced the more difficult test, like King Asa faced, of how to remain faithful, and how to keep on taking risks for God, when I had an abundance of money and when I had a lot of staff working for me.

I will have to find out at the Judgment Seat of Christ how well, or badly, I did. However, what I can say for sure, is that it is much harder to remain faithful to God, to put your trust in Him, and take risks for Him, when you have got power, money and position than it is when you have none of those things.

People might imagine that it must be easy to live the Christian life if you have got power and possessions, but it isn't. Those things actually become a source of temptation in themselves. In one sense they are undoubtedly a blessing from God and a reward for past faithfulness. However, they do also present a real challenge and make it harder, in some ways, to carry on being faithful.

That is one reason why it is wise to ask God not to give you more power, money or influence than you are capable of handling faithfully. You should specifically ask God, in your prayers, not to allow your possessions, power, income, profits, wealth, role or position to become too large for you, such that they might turn your head. Few people ever pray in that way but I really think they ought to. I have done so many times and I believe God has answered my requests.

I could have made even greater profits than I did and made the business even larger, but I don't think it would have been good. To the best of my knowledge, I believe I stayed faithful to the end. I was helped in that test by the fact that God limited my profits and my success to levels that my faithfulness could withstand. I am glad He did.

The faithfulness and unfaithfulness of King Jehu

Next we can look at the life of King Jehu of Israel (i.e. the Northern Kingdom). He had the chance to become the one and only good King that the Northern Kingdom ever had. He began well and showed remarkable zeal and enthusiasm to obey God. He wiped out the evil family of King Ahab and also the wicked practice of Baal worship.

161

In all of that he did well and achieved God's purposes for his life. However, he later allowed himself to become unfaithful. Let's follow him through the stages of his life, starting from the day he was anointed to become King:

[1]Then Elisha the prophet called one of the sons of the prophets and said to him, "Tie up your garments, and take this flask of oil in your hand, and go to Ramoth-gilead.[2] And when you arrive, look there for Jehu the son of Jehoshaphat, son of Nimshi. And go in and have him rise from among his fellows, and lead him to an inner chamber.[3]Then take the flask of oil and pour it on his head and say, 'Thus says the LORD, I anoint you king over Israel.' Then open the door and flee; do not linger." [4]So the young man, the servant of the prophet, went to Ramoth-gilead. [5] And when he came, behold, the commanders of the army were in council. And he said, "I have a word for you, O commander." And Jehu said, "To which of us all?" And he said, "To you, O commander."

[6]So he arose and went into the house. And the young man poured the oil on his head, saying to him, "Thus says the LORD, the God of Israel, I anoint you king over the people of the LORD, over Israel. [7]And you shall strike down the house of Ahab your master, so that I may avenge on Jezebel the blood of my servants the prophets, and the blood of all the servants of the LORD.[8] For the whole house of Ahab shall perish, and I will cut off from Ahab every male, bond or free, in Israel. [9]And I will make the house of Ahab like the house of Jeroboam the son of Nebat, and like the house of Baasha the son of Ahijah.[10] And the dogs shall eat Jezebel in the territory of Jezreel, and none shall bury her." Then he opened the door and fled. [11]When Jehu came out to the servants of his master, they said to him, "Is all well? Why did this mad fellow come to you?" And he said to them, "You know the fellow and his talk." [12] And they said, "That is not true; tell us now." And he said, "Thus and so he spoke to me, saying, 'Thus says the LORD, I anoint you king over Israel.'" [13]Then in haste every man of them took his garment and put it under him on the bare steps, and they blew the trumpet and proclaimed, "Jehu is king."

2 Kings 9:1-13 (ESV)

Jehu knew that it was God's will for him to remove King Joram (the son of King Ahab) and his wicked mother, Jezebel and also to destroy all King Ahab's descendents so that their line could not be resumed. In fact, God had said earlier that this is what would happen. So, he began by removing King Joram:

[21] Joram said, "Make ready." And they made ready his chariot. Then Joram king of Israel and Ahaziah king of Judah set out, each in his chariot, and went to meet Jehu, and met him at the property of Naboth the Jezreelite. [22]And when Joram saw Jehu, he said, "Is it peace, Jehu?" He answered, "What peace can there be, so long as the whorings and the sorceries of your mother Jezebel are so many?" [23] Then Joram reined about and fled, saying to Ahaziah, "Treachery, O Ahaziah!"

²⁴ And Jehu drew his bow with his full strength, and shot Joram between the shoulders, so that the arrow pierced his heart, and he sank in his chariot. ²⁵ Jehu said to Bidkar his aide, "Take him up and throw him on the plot of ground belonging to Naboth the Jezreelite. For remember, when you and I rode side by side behind Ahab his father, how the LORD made this pronouncement against him: ²⁶ 'As surely as I saw yesterday the blood of Naboth and the blood of his sons--declares the LORD--I will repay you on this plot of ground.' Now therefore take him up and throw him on the plot of ground, in accordance with the word of the LORD."

2 Kings 9: 21-26 (ESV)

Then Jehu went and dealt with the despicable Queen Jezebel, the pagan, Baal-worshiping wife of Ahab and mother of King Joram:

³⁰When Jehu came to Jezreel, Jezebel heard of it. And she painted her eyes and adorned her head and looked out of the window. ³¹ And as Jehu entered the gate, she said, "Is it peace, you Zimri, murderer of your master?" ³² And he lifted up his face to the window and said, "Who is on my side? Who?" Two or three eunuchs looked out at him. ³³He said, "Throw her down." So they threw her down. And some of her blood spattered on the wall and on the horses, and they trampled on her. ³⁴ Then he went in and ate and drank. And he said, "See now to this cursed woman and bury her, for she is a king's daughter." ³⁵ But when they went to bury her, they found no more of her than the skull and the feet and the palms of her hands. ³⁶ When they came back and told him, he said, "This is the word of the LORD, which he spoke by his servant Elijah the Tishbite, 'In the territory of Jezreel the dogs shall eat the flesh of Jezebel, ³⁷ and the corpse of Jezebel shall be as dung on the face of the field in the territory of Jezreel, so that no one can say, This is Jezebel.'"

2 Kings 9:30-37 (ESV)

Jehu then proceeded to wipe out all the descendants of King Ahab. He did so on God's instructions, to destroy that family line and prevent them ever regaining the throne:

So Jehu struck down all who remained of the house of Ahab in Jezreel, all his great men and his close friends and his priests, until he left him none remaining

2 Kings 10:11 (ESV)

¹⁵And when he departed from there, he met Jehonadab the son of Rechab coming to meet him. And he greeted him and said to him, "Is your heart true to my heart as mine is to yours?" And Jehonadab answered, "It is." Jehu said,"If it is, give me your hand." So he gave him his hand. And Jehu took him up with him into the chariot. ¹⁶ And he said, "Come with me, and see my zeal for the LORD." So he had him ride in his chariot.

[17]And when he came to Samaria, he struck down all who remained to Ahab in Samaria, till he had wiped them out, according to the word of the LORD that he spoke to Elijah.

2 Kings 10:15-17 (ESV)

After that, Jehu took on all the prophets of Baal and wiped them all out, removing all the leaders of Baal worship from Israel:

[18] Then Jehu assembled all the people and said to them, "Ahab served Baal a little, but Jehu will serve him much. [19] Now therefore call to me all the prophets of Baal, all his worshipers and all his priests. Let none be missing, for I have a great sacrifice to offer to Baal. Whoever is missing shall not live." But Jehu did it with cunning in order to destroy the worshipers of Baal. [20] And Jehu ordered, "Sanctify a solemn assembly for Baal." So they proclaimed it. [21]And Jehu sent throughout all Israel, and all the worshipers of Baal came, so that there was not a man left who did not come. And they entered the house of Baal, and the house of Baal was filled from one end to the other. [22] He said to him who was in charge of the wardrobe, "Bring out the vestments for all the worshipers of Baal." So he brought out the vestments for them.

[23]Then Jehu went into the house of Baal with Jehonadab the son of Rechab, and he said to the worshipers of Baal, "Search, and see that there is no servant of the LORD here among you, but only the worshipers of Baal." [24]Then they went in to offer sacrifices and burnt offerings. Now Jehu had stationed eighty men outside and said, "The man who allows any of those whom I give into your hands to escape shall forfeit his life." [25] So as soon as he had made an end of offering the burnt offering, Jehu said to the guard and to the officers, "Go in and strike them down; let not a man escape." So when they put them to the sword, the guard and the officers cast them out and went into the inner room of the house of Baal, [26] and they brought out the pillar that was in the house of Baal and burned it. [27] And they demolished the pillar of Baal, and demolished the house of Baal, and made it a latrine to this day. [28] Thus Jehu wiped out Baal from Israel.

2 Kings 10:18-28 (ESV)

However, despite all of that initial zeal and dynamic action for the Lord, King Jehu later degenerated and became unfaithful. Like so many others, he started well, but did not finish well:

[29]But Jehu did not turn aside from the sins of Jeroboam the son of Nebat, which he made Israel to sin--that is, the golden calves that were in Bethel and in Dan. [30] And the LORD said to Jehu, "Because you have done well in carrying out what is right in my eyes, and have done to the house of Ahab according to all that was in my heart, your sons of the fourth generation shall sit on the throne of Israel." [31] But Jehu was not careful to walk in the law of the LORD, the God

of Israel, with all his heart. He did not turn from the sins of Jeroboam, which he made Israel to sin.

2 Kings 10:29-31 (ESV)

Some people become unfaithful after they lose their mentor's influence. They can't keep up their faithfulness on their own

One of the reasons why faithful, obedient, God-fearing people sometimes become unfaithful, and let God down in later life, is that they began with the influence and guidance of a godly mentor, but then could not keep up that faithfulness on their own, without that mentor's help. An example of this is King Joash of Judah. He came to the throne when he was only a child and benefitted greatly from the godly influence of Jehoiada, a faithful priest who advised and taught the young king:

¹Jo'ash was seven years old when he began to reign, and he reigned forty years in Jerusalem; his mother's name was Zib'iah of Beer-sheba ² And Jo'ash did what was right in the eyes of the LORD all the days of Jehoi'ada the priest.

2 Chronicles 24:1-2 (RSV)

So, King Joash did what was right for very many years, i.e. while Jehoiada was still alive and able to guide him. But then things changed when Jehoiada died:

¹⁵But Jehoi'ada grew old and full of days, and died; he was a hundred and thirty years old at his death. ¹⁶ And they buried him in the city of David among the kings, because he had done good in Israel, and toward God and his house.

2 Chronicles 24:15-16 (RSV)

¹⁷ Now after the death of Jehoi'ada the princes of Judah came and did obeisance to the king; then the king hearkened to them. ¹⁸ And they forsook the house of the LORD, the God of their fathers, and served the Ashe'rim and the idols. And wrath came upon Judah and Jerusalem for this their guilt. ¹⁹ Yet he sent prophets among them to bring them back to the LORD; these testified against them, but they would not give heed.

2 Chronicles 24:17-19 (RSV)

After Jehoiada died, King Joash unwisely allowed himself to be advised and influenced by unworthy people who were not of the same calibre as Jehoiada. Therefore King Joash went astray, and so did many of the people of Judah. It reached such a point that Zechariah, the son of Jehoiada, tried to intervene to confront King Joash and to get him to see how God saw the situation. However, King Joash did not listen to him. In fact he had him killed, despite all that Zechariah's father had done for him for so many years:

²⁰Then the Spirit of God took possession of Zechari'ah the son of Jehoi'ada the priest; and he stood above the people, and said to them, "Thus says God, 'Why

165

do you transgress the commandments of the LORD, so that you cannot prosper? Because you have forsaken the LORD, he has forsaken you."' ²¹ But they conspired against him, and by command of the king they stoned him with stones in the court of the house of the LORD. ²² Thus Jo'ash the king did not remember the kindness which Jehoi'ada, Zechari'ah's father, had shown him, but killed his son. And when he was dying, he said, "May the LORD see and avenge!"

2 Chronicles 24:20-22 (RSV)

As a result of the unfaithfulness of King Joash, and also in response to Zechariah's prayer, God moved to judge Joash by sending the Syrian army to attack him:

²³At the end of the year the army of the Syrians came up against Jo'ash. They came to Judah and Jerusalem, and destroyed all the princes of the people from among the people, and sent all their spoil to the king of Damascus. ²⁴ Though the army of the Syrians had come with few men, the LORD delivered into their hand a very great army, because they had forsaken the LORD, the God of their fathers. Thus they executed judgment on Jo'ash. ²⁵ When they had departed from him, leaving him severely wounded, his servants conspired against him because of the blood of the son of Jehoi'ada the priest, and slew him on his bed. So he died; and they buried him in the city of David, but they did not bury him in the tombs of the kings.

2 Chronicles 24:23-25 (RSV)

What Joash should have done, following the death of Jehoiada, was to recognise that he was now entering into a new test, i.e. for God to see how well he could do without his mentor. He should therefore have responded to his new circumstances by:

a)   immersing himself in the Bible, so as to obtain guidance from there for himself

b)   carefully selecting other godly people to advise him in place of Jehoiada, instead of being passive and leaving it for advisors to come to him randomly.

One of the hardest things to cope with is success. Few people's faithfulness can survive that

We all know that failure and difficulty are a challenge. However, as we have seen above, in terms of maintaining our faithfulness, success is a much harder test. When a person fails, or suffers, the obvious thing to do is to turn to God for help. But how many of us turn to God when we have been *succeeding* in our job or ministry? If anything, the need for God's help is even greater then, though very few people realise that.

Success, wealth, power, fame, prestige and academic achievement present us with some very strong temptations to pride, self-sufficiency and arrogance. If we yield

166

to such temptations, even once, then we are in grave danger of doing so again and again, until it becomes our undoing. A proud, self-sufficient person is very unlikely to remain faithful to Jesus, or to succeed in the tests that Jesus sets for us.

I spoke to you in your prosperity, but you said, 'I will not listen…….
Jeremiah 22:21 (a)(RSV)

So, if you are fortunate enough to achieve success in any field then see it as your cue to humble yourself, to stay close to God and to pray for His help. Ask Him to provide people and circumstances that will help you to stay humble. Also ask Him to help you to humble yourself and to avoid relying on yourself or trusting in your own ability. Then you will hopefully avoid doing what King Uzziah did, as we saw above. He began well, but success and power went to his head and caused him to stop being faithful:

But when he was strong he grew proud, to his destruction. For he was false to the LORD his God, and entered the temple of the LORD to burn incense on the altar of incense.
2 Chronicles 26:16 (RSV)

You can never afford to become complacent or to cut corners as you get older

On a similar theme, there is a temptation, as you get older, to become casual and to assume that you have now learned how to handle pressures and temptations. You may then begin to loosen your standards and to think that it is safe for you to cut corners slightly, or to compromise a little on ethical issues relating to money, sex, work, relationships, or your use of power. It is precisely when you think you cannot, or will not, fall that you are in greatest danger of falling.

A person who is aware of their weakness, and concerned that they may fall, will take care to avoid tempting situations. But a person who has begun to trust themselves is in great danger. Therefore never trust yourself. Never consider yourself to be above temptation, or immune to falling into any kind of sin, especially the ones that you feel drawn to, or about which you have ever felt tempted to compromise. Those are the very areas where you particularly need to redouble your vigilance, and keep yourself on a short lead. As Malachi puts it, we need to guard ourselves:

So guard yourselves in your spirit, and do not be faithless.
Malachi 2:16(b) (ESV)

Resolve to become more radical, not less, as you get older. Balance is good, but moderation may not be.

It is usually assumed that young people are radical but that as we get older we mellow, moderate ourselves and become more pragmatic, rather than more principled or idealistic. But why should that have to be so? If anything, as we grow older, we ought to aim to become more radical, not less. We should set higher targets for ourselves and aim for greater levels of personal faithfulness.

The more we get to know Jesus, the more we ought to seek to please Him and to honour Him in ways we never even realised existed, or which we never noticed when we were younger. So, following our conversion, when we are only a new believer, Jesus' main objectives for us might be, for example, to give up sexual sin, excessive drinking or drugs.

However, as we get older and gain self-control in those areas, Jesus will turn His eye towards other areas of sin in our lives which might appear less important, but are still crucial if we wish to continue to make progress as a disciple. These areas might include sins such as pride, gossip, over-eating, cowardice, laziness, selfishness and so on.

We need to get all of our thinking, and all our actions, in line with Jesus, and to gain the mastery over every new area of sin that He shines the 'spotlight' on. Instead of considering such things less important, or less urgent, areas in which to obey Him, we should become more radical and less satisfied with ourselves as we grow older.

We never 'arrive' and therefore we never have any basis for being self-satisfied. So you should be just as determined to cut out gossip or pride as a new convert should be to cut out pornography, lying, drunkenness etc. There is no area of sin which is too small for you to care about and to tackle. Neither is there any sin which you can safely indulge in or compromise over. Every sin is toxic and will damage you and your future.

Do not put limits on your faithfulness, such that you only obey God up to a certain point. Go all the way.

A feature which is found in the vast majority of people, even among the best, is that they tend to have limits, beyond which their faithfulness does not go, or does not continue. In other words, even the best of us tend only to be faithful up to a certain point, but no further. We see this feature quite often among the better kings of Judah. The Bible speaks of them as having done what was right and as being faithful.

However, it then points out what they did *not* do, i.e. the things which they did not have the courage or the determination to achieve. An example of this is found in the lives of King Jehoash of Judah and his son, Amaziah and grandson, Azariah. In general, these three kings did what was right, but there were certain things which they did not have enough courage, or strength of will, to do:

In the seventh year of Jehu, Jehoash began to reign, and he reigned forty years in Jerusalem. His mother's name was Zibiah of Beersheba. ² And Jehoash did what was right in the eyes of the LORD all his days, because Jehoiada the priest instructed him. ³ Nevertheless, the high places were not taken away; the people continued to sacrifice and make offerings on the high places.

2 Kings 12:1-3 (ESV)

In the second year of Joash the son of Joahaz, king of Israel, Amaziah the son of Joash, king of Judah, began to reign. ² He was twenty-five years old when he began to reign, and he reigned twenty-nine years in Jerusalem. His mother's name was Jehoaddin of Jerusalem. ³ And he did what was right in the eyes of the LORD, yet not like David his father. He did in all things as Joash his father had done. ⁴ But the high places were not removed; the people still sacrificed and made offerings on the high places.

2 Kings 14:1-4 (ESV)

In the twenty-seventh year of Jeroboam king of Israel, Azariah the son of Amaziah, king of Judah, began to reign. ² He was sixteen years old when he began to reign, and he reigned fifty-two years in Jerusalem. His mother's name was Jecoliah of Jerusalem. ³ And he did what was right in the eyes of the LORD, according to all that his father Amaziah had done. ⁴ Nevertheless, the high places were not taken away. The people still sacrificed and made offerings on the high places.

2 Kings 15:1-4 (ESV)

Kings Jehoash, Amaziah and Azariah, like most of the Kings of Judah, stopped short of demolishing the 'high places' where some of the people used to go to offer false and idolatrous sacrifices. Perhaps they feared the reaction of the people if they went that far, just as modern day politicians will only go so far. They stop short of doing anything which would arouse substantial public outcry or opposition.

We do the same ourselves and set up boundaries, beyond which we will not go, because we think it would be too hard, dangerous, costly or difficult. Sometimes we may even do that unconsciously, without ever saying out loud, even to ourselves, that we are holding back or what it is that we are afraid of.

One of the main reasons why a person sets limits on the extent of their own faithfulness and obedience is that they are not wholehearted. That means that they are generally loyal and willing, but only up to a point. It is usually up to the point where faithfulness begins to cost too much, or is likely to cause more difficulty than they want to face.

The problem with being on God's side, but only up to a certain pre-determined limit, is that there will eventually come a point at which your willingness to obey will be used up. You will then betray God, and even switch sides. That is inevitable if you set any limits beforehand on how much you are willing to endure or how far you are willing to go.

Any such limit, wherever you choose to place it, will inevitably lead to you being brought up to and beyond that point. The demons in your life will make sure of that. So, if you say to yourself: *"I will endure for up to six months, but that's all"*, then you can be sure that a demon will arrange things so that your ordeal lasts longer than six months.

Or, if you were to say: *"I will be honest and do what's right at work, as long as I don't have to lose my job"*, then you can be sure that the demons will engineer some situation that requires you to choose between being faithful to God or losing your job.

Therefore the only safe and sensible policy is total faithfulness, where you are wholehearted and *set no limits at all*. Just resolve to do whatever God asks you to do, no matter what. Then ask Him for the grace to be obedient. That is the only approach that will work. A person who is not wholehearted will inevitably come unstuck and go wrong.

Why not begin to examine yourself in this area and to ask yourself whether, how and where you are doing this and what the boundaries are to your own faithfulness? Ask God to expose these limits or boundaries to you and to help you to break through them and go beyond them.

Imagine the changes that would occur in your life if you were to do this and to become, like King David, a person who is *"a man wholly after God's heart"*. The consequences could be very significant, in terms of what God could then achieve through your life, but also how well you would do at the Judgment Seat of Christ.

The famous nineteenth century evangelist and Bible teacher, D. L Moody, put it very well when he said:

"The world has yet to see what God can do with, and for, and through, and in, and by a man who is fully and wholly consecrated to Him. I will do my utmost to be that man".

CHAPTER 9

WHAT IS 'THE LOVE OF THE TRUTH' AND WHY DOES TRUTH MATTER SO MUCH TO GOD?

"----For this I was born, and for this I have come into the world, to bear witness to the truth. Everyone who is of the truth hears my voice"
John 18:37(b) (RSV)

⁴⁷Jesus saw Nathanael coming to Him, and said of him, "Behold, an Israelite indeed, in whom there is no deceit!"
John 1:47 (NASB)

Behold, you delight in truth in the inward being,....
Psalm 51:6(a) (ESV)

²²Lying lips are an abomination to the LORD,
but those who deal faithfully are His delight.
Proverbs 12:22 (NASB)

⁷ No man who practices deceit shall dwell in my house;
no man who utters lies shall continue in my presence
Psalm 101:7 (RSV)

in hope of eternal life which God, who never lies, promised ages ago
Titus 1:2 (RSV)

For all who do such things, all who act dishonestly, are an abomination to the LORD your God.
Deuteronomy 25:16 (RSV)

Why does truthfulness matter?

Very few people are completely truthful, especially when it is costly. In fact, few people ever think about truthfulness as an issue at all. I cannot remember ever hearing it preached on in any church. Perhaps some preachers feel uncomfortable speaking about something that they know they do not always practice themselves? At any rate, it is a subject that is rarely ever taught about, but which ought to be. God feels very strongly about us being totally truthful at all times, even down to the smallest details. He condemns deceit and falsehood very firmly:

⁷He who practices deceit shall not dwell within my house;
He who speaks falsehood shall not maintain his position before me.
Psalm 101:7 (NASB)

14 Justice is turned back,
and righteousness stands afar off;
for truth has fallen in the public squares,
and uprightness cannot enter.
15 Truth is lacking,
and he who departs from evil makes himself a prey.
The LORD saw it, and it displeased him
that there was no justice.

Isaiah 59:14-15 (RSV)

Moreover, God is continually watching and taking note of everything we say and do. He is aware of all our ways, even those we keep secret. Every lie we ever tell is immediately known about by God:

21 For the ways of a man
are before the eyes of the LORD,
and He watches all his paths

Proverbs 5:21 (NASB)

God detests crookedness, but takes delight in those who are 'blameless'. Remember, that does not mean sinless. It means being sincere, faithful, honest and true.

20 The perverse in heart are an abomination to the LORD,
but the blameless in their walk are His delight.

Proverbs 11:20 (NASB)

Moreover, there will be blessings and rewards for those who are truthful and who live with integrity:

For the eyes of the LORD run to and fro throughout the whole earth, to show his
might in behalf of those whose heart is blameless toward him.........

2 Chronicles 16:9 (a) (RSV)

3 Who shall ascend the hill of the LORD?
And who shall stand in his holy place?
4 He who has clean hands and a pure heart,
who does not lift up his soul to what is false
and does not swear deceitfully.
5 He will receive blessing from the LORD
and righteousness from the God of his salvation.

Psalm 24:3-5 (ESV)

God wants that truthfulness to go very deep inside us. He doesn't merely want us to be superficially honest on the outside, or by appearance, but to be truthful at our very core, i.e. all the way through to the innermost part of us:

172

Behold, you delight in truth in the inward being,
and you teach me wisdom in the secret heart.
Psalm 51:6 (ESV)

Our natural inclination is to be dishonest. That is what our sinful flesh nature will instinctively choose to do.

The heart is deceitful above all things,
and desperately corrupt;
who can understand it?
Jeremiah 17:9 (RSV)

When Jesus said that He is *'the truth'* what did He mean?

One day, when He was speaking to His disciples, Jesus made an unusual claim about Himself. He said He is......."*the way, the truth and the life*"...... For the moment, we need to concern ourselves with the second assertion, i.e. that Jesus is *the truth*. He does not merely say that He *has* the truth, or that He *speaks* the truth. He claims to *be* the truth:

⁶Jesus said to him, "I am the way, and the truth, and the life; no one comes to the Father but through Me.

John 14:6 (NASB)

What does Jesus mean? It would seem that He is saying that, ultimately, He Himself is the source of all truth, and the standard by which all things are to be judged as either true or false. There is nobody else, besides Jesus, who so embodies truth as to be entitled to identify Himself as being *the* truth.

It also means that where we do not know what the truth is in some area of life, or don't know what is right or wrong in a complex situation, the answer is to be found in Jesus. We can ask Him, but we can also look at Him and ask ourselves what Jesus would do in that situation. When Jesus was on trial Pontius Pilate asked Him a very deep question to which Jesus gave no answer.   Pilate asked Him *"What is truth?"*

³⁷ Pilate said to him, "So you are a king?" Jesus answered, "You say that I am a king. For this I was born, and for this I have come into the world, to bear witness to the truth. Everyone who is of the truth hears my voice." ³⁸ Pilate said to him, "What is truth?" After he had said this, he went out to the Jews again, and told them, "I find no crime in him.

John 18:37-38 (RSV)

In fact, the answer was standing right in front of Pilate. Jesus Himself is truth. Everything about Him is whole, complete, consistent, and righteous. He is full of integrity and soundness. That is true of Jesus and also of His Word, the Bible. Given that truth is so important to God, and is the very nature of Jesus, we need to get ourselves into line with Him. Truth and truthfulness must become profoundly important to us as well, even if it makes us the odd one out, and even if it costs us.

If we ever think about truth at all, most of us are satisfied with being generally honest most of the time. We tend to view that as setting the bar high enough. But it isn't. When it comes to honesty we need to put the bar to the very highest setting. We must not settle for anything less than 100% truthfulness 100% of the time.

Anything less than that is compromise and, therefore, is not 'truth'. You can't have 99% truth. If you do, it is just a lie, the same as 50% truth is a lie. Likewise, if you only tell the truth 99% of the time, then that 1% still makes you a liar. So, those of us who feel satisfied and complacent about the issue of truth need to wake up and reassess this whole subject.

God wants us to be incorruptible and totally honest and reliable as witnesses and judges.

We saw in the previous chapter how the prophet Samuel was a completely honest Judge. Nobody in Israel could point to even one corrupt thing that he had ever done. What a testimony! That should be our standard. Most of us will never be judges, but we will probably be witnesses, at some point, whether formally or informally. When we are, we must be completely honest and incorruptible, not just 99% so:

19You shall not pervert justice; you shall not show partiality; and you shall not take a bribe, for a bribe blinds the eyes of the wise and subverts the cause of the righteous. 20Justice, and only justice, you shall follow, that you may live and inherit the land which the LORD your God gives you.
Deuteronomy 16:19-20 (RSV)

To take a bribe does not only mean to do so literally, i.e. to receive money corruptly as a judge or police officer. Any of us can also face the temptation to take a metaphorical bribe by agreeing to help someone who needs us to tell a 'small lie' for them, or to fiddle something for them, in return for some past or future favour. That is just as much a bribe as if money had changed hands. It has caused us to act corruptly.

The problems caused by deception and lies

I have been a police officer, and then I was a solicitor and businessman for many years after that. If I had to say in one word what is the greatest single cause of difficulty within the workplace, I would say it is dishonesty. I mean that in its broadest sense, not just in what we *say*, but in what we *do* and what we *are*. In Great Britain it has now become normal to be dishonest. Things which would have been considered shocking even 20 years ago, let alone 100 years ago, are now commonplace.

The MPs expenses scandal in the House of Commons some time ago, and which is still ongoing, is a prime example. An alarming number of our politicians (not all) were milking the system for all they could get, regardless of right and wrong. The concept of truth probably never entered into the minds of many of those MPs.

They were acting as if there was no God and no day of judgment. They were doing things which would not have been done by the MPs of the 1980s, and certainly not by the politicians of the 1930s or the 1880s. There has been a collapse of integrity amongst the majority of our nation. Genuine honesty is now so rare that the dishonesty of the wider population is accurately reflected in the MPs who represent us.

They are like a mirror, reflecting back at us what we are like ourselves. The public felt a lot of anger when the expenses scandal broke in 2010. However, the reality is that the majority of the British people would have stolen exactly the same, or even more, than their MPs did, if they had been in their position.

The effect of this exponential increase in dishonesty in the Western nations is that there is now no basis for trust. In the past many business deals were done on the basis of a handshake. There was no serious expectation of either party failing to keep their promises. Now that would be wholly unrealistic. Any business which enters contracts anticipates that other people may well break those agreements.

Therefore provisions are made in many contracts to specify in advance what has to be paid if the contract is broken. That said, many people would have no intention of abiding by that provision even when they sign up to it. They would only pay those damages if they could be tracked down and forced to do so. They would not feel honour-bound to pay, in the absence of coercion.

I can say that with some authority because I spent many years in commercial litigation and have seen at first-hand how dishonestly people behave. Even the very word 'honour' now seems outdated and quaint in our culture. It is rarely ever used. It is a concept which was widely understood 100 years ago, or even 50 years ago. It was taken seriously then, not only by businessmen, but by husbands and wives, neighbours, politicians, soldiers, doctors, teachers, lawyers, journalists and so on. That is not the case anymore, at least not for the vast majority of us.

I have an unusual vantage point from which to view what is going on in the world. I have not only got my own experiences to go by, but also those of my staff and of the clients that we acted for. I have observed that people at all levels now seem able to lie effortlessly and without any embarrassment, guilt or anxiety. I have had school teachers lie to me and also lawyers, policemen, medical staff and business people. I have had my own staff, even solicitors, look me straight in the eye and lie to my face. Then, when exposed or challenged, they feel no shame, only resentment at being caught out and thwarted.

When I was a policeman in the 1980s I was shown how to interview witnesses and suspects. I was taught to look at their faces closely as I questioned them and to watch their eyes in particular. When a person told a lie they would feel uncomfortable about it. They would then look away from me, even if only for a split second, at the exact point when the lie was being told. That way you could usually tell quite accurately where the lies were in the story.

That technique still works up to a point, but it is less effective today. It relies on the person having at least some residue of a functioning conscience to make them feel awkward when they lie. But as people's consciences have got weaker, or been entirely switched off, that discomfort factor has been diminishing. Therefore that technique works less effectively today.

I also remember a Solicitor colleague in a previous law firm who said to me one day, quite openly, that if ever her "*own neck was on the line*" she would definitely lie to save herself. I looked surprised and said *"Surely not!"* She replied *"Of course I would, if my neck was on the line."* It was said as if it was obviously the only practical approach. She thought I was odd for being surprised. But what she said isn't right. Telling lies is wrong and will always cause harm, especially to ourselves.

Whenever we lie to try to save our own skin we anger God, which will bring Him into opposition to us. In the short term we might get ourselves out of some tight corner by lying, but if we do that, we are sure to arouse God's opposition. We may even bring His curse upon ourselves, such that we end up with far bigger problems later:

**
³²For the devious are an abomination to the LORD;
but He is intimate with the upright.
³³The curse of the LORD is on the house of the wicked,
but He blesses the dwelling of the righteous.
Proverbs 3:32-33 (NASB)

In the book of Zechariah we are actually told of a specific curse that God Himself deliberately sends out and which attaches to every person who steals or lies. This curse then causes that person to be cut off and to be punished and suffer loss:

³ Then he said to me, "This is the curse that goes out over the face of the whole land; for everyone who steals shall be cut off henceforth according to it, and everyone who swears falsely shall be cut off henceforth according to it. ⁴ I will

176

send it forth, says the Lord of hosts, and it shall enter the house of the thief, and the house of him who swears falsely by my name; and it shall abide in his house and consume it, both timber and stones."

Zechariah 5:3-4 (RSV)

The choice between having God's help, or provoking His opposition, is no small thing. How can it make sense to tell a lie for some short term gain or advantage but put ourselves on an inevitable collision course with God Himself? It would be much better to lose out financially, or miss out on a promotion, than to make God into your opponent.

Remember also that any lie you tell today will be raised with you by Jesus at the Judgment Seat. Moreover, there is good reason to think that it will be exposed *publicly*. (See Book Four in this series, concerning The Judgment Seat of Christ)

Our hearts and consciences become hard and leathery once we start to tell lies, such that it gets easier and easier, until it becomes habitual

Once a person begins to lie, they will do it again in bigger ways, and with increasing frequency. Then lying gets easier, in the following ways:

a) Our conscience is slowly turned down in volume, until it is eventually switched off completely. This is how one gets a hard heart, or a seared conscience. It no longer receives any 'signal' from God about what is right or wrong. When that point comes we are in great danger because our conscience, which is a God-given safety device, has been switched off.

b) We get more imaginative in the lies we tell. They become more elaborate and extensive.

c) We feel more comfortable and less convicted about our sinfulness. Our 'carbon monoxide detectors' are switched off. In the end we become so deeply comatose that we become oblivious to our own dishonesty, and no longer troubled by it.

d) This hard-heartedness can also affect those who purport to be a Christians. It is easy to convince oneself that all is well, no matter how great our sins may be. I am reminded of a man in a church in Northern Ireland who was a dentist. He had murdered his first wife 20 years earlier and got away with it. He subsequently remarried another woman. She was a Christian and knew nothing of his crime. For 20 years he attended church, while continuing to hide his crime. He had no repentance at all and no concept of God's impending judgment for what he had done. That is shocking, but how many of us who purport to be Christians have similarly hard and unrepentant hearts, even if our sins are less spectacular?

The more a person lies, the more they lose their sense of shame and become brass-faced about it

For an honest person, one of the most shameful and humiliating things imaginable would be to be caught out in telling a lie. Even the thought of doing that and being found out and exposed makes me squirm. But that is not how habitual liars see it. It would therefore be highly naive of you to imagine that they would feel any shame at being caught lying. They don't. All they feel is anger at being thwarted or confronted. They feel no shame at what they have done, or even at being caught.

That has been my consistent experience with every liar I have ever come across, in any context, whether they were strangers, work colleagues, church members, or even church leaders. Far from feeling ashamed, a liar feels aggrieved when he is exposed. He acts as if some wrong has been done to him, not by him. I was once involved on the side-lines of a dispute between two couples, watching what was happening and hearing what each side said. The first couple, who were Christians, were consistently telling the truth.

However, the second couple, who were non-Christians, were lying over and over again. At one point the second couple told a clear lie in a letter they wrote. The first couple then pointed out the lie to them and even referred to a specific entry by them on Facebook which proved that they were lying. However, on being caught out, the second couple just replied brazenly: "*So you've been snooping then*". The point was that they:

a)   weren't ashamed, or even embarrassed, at being shown to be lying

b)   spoke as if they had done nothing wrong (in lying)

c)   made no apology and felt no remorse.

d)   even portrayed themselves as having been wronged. They had the nerve to speak as if it was the first couple who were behaving badly, i.e. by checking up on things on Facebook, not they themselves who were acting wrongly by lying.

I can think of another occasion some years ago when I was in a private meeting with 'Rick', the leader of a church that I used to be in. I was the Chairman of the Trustees of that church and was confronting the leader about his improper behaviour, in particular his dishonesty. We were meeting in the presence of two witnesses from the Trustees of the same church, i.e. mature Christians. They had agreed to hear each of us and to try to mediate.

Rick lied repeatedly and brazenly throughout the meeting. I was astonished at hearing him lie, right in front of me. He did it with such a calm face, while looking

178

the two witnesses straight in the eyes. After the meeting was over, the witnesses went home, with no solution having been found. Rick then turned to me and said in a relaxed tone: *"Can't you just let me off the hook?"*

By that he meant that he wanted me to stop holding him accountable and to stop pointing out where he was lying. I said *"Why did you lie to them?"* because I was amazed that he had felt able to do it. I was very naive then and had never previously experienced such blatant dishonesty from a church leader. It would not amaze me today. However, there was not even a flicker of shame or remorse on his face. He just replied: *"Well, I've got to defend myself"*.

He spoke as if he had every right to do whatever was needed to cover his tracks, including lying his way out of trouble. It was an education for me as to how dishonest people can be, even in churches. Above all, it showed how shameless they can be about it. You have to grasp that last point or you will be misled by people's expressions, i.e. the fact that their faces show no trace of embarrassment.

You must not allow yourself to be thrown off course by that. So, don't allow the absence of shame in a person's face or voice to deceive you into thinking that they must therefore be telling the truth. That doesn't follow at all. It is actually quite normal for an habitual liar to be entirely unashamed when caught lying. Jeremiah spoke of this phenomenon:

O LORD, do not your eyes look for truth?
You have struck them down,
but they felt no anguish;
you have consumed them,
but they refused to take correction.
They have made their faces harder than rock;
they have refused to repent.
                    Jeremiah 5:3 (ESV)

Were they ashamed when they committed abomination?
No, they were not at all ashamed;
they did not know how to blush.
Therefore they shall fall among those who fall;
at the time that I punish them, they shall be overthrown,"
says the LORD.
                    Jeremiah 6:15 (ESV)

Each of the people that I have referred to above, the non-Christian couple and Rick, the church leader, had the same feature. They were all willing to tell whatever lies they needed to tell in order to suit their own purposes and to protect themselves. Their approach was entirely amoral. Right and wrong did not even come into it, and certainly didn't matter to any of them. That is why they could be so bold and defiant.

The other key feature is that none of them had any sense of impending judgment. That might be understandable in the case of the non-Christian couple. But it was equally the case with Rick, the church leader. He had no fear of God whatsoever. The idea of facing God in judgment one day, whether at the Judgment Seat of Christ (for believers) or at the Great White Throne (for unbelievers) did not matter to him at all. It made me shudder to think of what judgment lay ahead for him.

I actually felt the fear of God on his behalf, and still do, whereas he was completely immune to it. He had lied so often that it had become normal for him. His heart became progressively hardened until he eventually reached the point where he believed that he would get away with everything, insofar as he was thinking about it at all. He was like the people of Zechariah's day:

11 But they refused to pay attention and turned a stubborn shoulder and stopped their ears that they might not hear. 12 They made their hearts diamond-hard lest they should hear the law and the words that the LORD of hosts had sent by his Spirit through the former prophets. Therefore great anger came from the LORD of hosts.

Zechariah 7:11-12 (ESV)

What is "the love of the truth"?

"The love of the truth" is a technical phrase used in the Bible. It refers to having a heart-attitude which values and pursues the truth for its own sake, not just because we want to avoid getting into trouble for lying. In the verse below, apostle Paul refers to the love of the truth in the context of explaining why so many people will follow the antichrist when he comes.

They will be deceived by him precisely because "*they did not receive the love of the truth*". The truth does not matter to them enough, or even at all. Thus, in the end, God will allow them to lose the very ability to tell the difference between truth and falsehood at all. Then they will become fully deluded, such that they will even follow someone as wicked and deceitful as the antichrist:

8Then that lawless one will be revealed whom the Lord will slay with the breath of His mouth and bring to an end by the appearance of His coming; 9that is, the one whose coming is in accord with the activity of Satan, with all power and signs and false wonders, 10and with all the deception of wickedness for those who perish, because they did not receive the love of the truth so as to be saved. 11For this reason God will send upon them a deluding influence so that they will believe what is false, 12in order that they all may be judged who did not believe the truth, but took pleasure in wickedness.

2 Thessalonians 2:8-12 (NASB)

If we keep on rejecting and despising the truth, there will come a point at which God Himself will respond by deliberately taking away our capacity even to know what is true. The taking away of that faculty will leave us very prone to being deceived. But such deception would still be our own fault, because the very reason we lost the faculty of discernment was that we did not value the truth when we had the chance to see it.

That is we had no regard for the truth in the past, while we were still capable of recognizing it. We need to ask God to help us to develop this quality of absolute truthfulness. We need to love the truth very deeply, such that truth really matters to us, purely for its own sake, not for what it can do for us. If that is our approach, we will be protected from countless problems, and from arousing the opposition of God Himself. More importantly, we will be doing what is right.

As well as loving the truth we must also hate falsehood

We don't often think in terms of a Christian hating anything. But there are actually some things that we have a duty to hate. One of those is falsehood. Most of us are far too laid back and casual about this. We might say that we regard falsehood and falseness as wrong. But many of us don't feel very strongly about it. It doesn't bother us very much and we don't feel motivated to do anything about stopping it. However, we should be bothered and it should concern us very strongly indeed. In fact, like the Psalmist, we should hate it.

I hate and abhor falsehood,
but I love thy law.
    Psalm 119:163 (RSV)

We are supposed to hate all falsehood, wherever we come across it. We are to hate lies, deviousness and manipulation. We are especially to hate the compromising and misrepresenting of God's Word, the Bible and also dishonest preaching. Above all, we are to hate falsehood when we see it in ourselves. All of us have hearts which lie. We even lie to ourselves. In fact, probably most of the lies we tell are told to ourselves.

Therefore we are to hate all kinds of falsehood, deceit, evasiveness, insincerity, manipulation and hypocrisy. We need to confront it zealously, especially within ourselves, and to expose it all and root it out without compromise. And we must not be too easily satisfied that we have completed the job.

We must be entirely without *guile,* as Nathanael was

One of my heroes in the Bible, whom I would most wish to be like, is Nathanael. We rarely hear of him, but he was singled out by Jesus, who especially commented on Nathanael's lack of guile. Evidently, Jesus considered that absence of guile to be remarkable, precisely because it is so rare:

43 The next day Jesus decided to go to Galilee. And he found Philip and said to him, "Follow me." 44 Now Philip was from Beth-sa'ida, the city of Andrew and Peter. 45 Philip found Nathan'a-el, and said to him, "We have found him of whom Moses in the law and also the prophets wrote, Jesus of Nazareth, the son of Joseph." 46 Nathan'a-el said to him, "Can anything good come out of Nazareth?" Philip said to him, "Come and see." 47 Jesus saw Nathan'a-el coming to him, and said of him, "Behold, an Israelite indeed, in whom is no guile

John 1:43-47 (RSV)

In saying that there was no guile in Nathanael, Jesus meant that he was entirely without pretence or hypocrisy. There was 'no side to him', as the saying goes. Nathanael was the type of man who really meant what he said and said what he meant. He did not have hidden agendas or ulterior purposes. If he wanted something he would openly and honestly say what he wanted and why. He would not trick or manipulate people. Neither would he use anybody.

Above all, being without guile means that we are ruthlessly honest with ourselves and about ourselves. A guileless person, when he reads about certain sins or faults in the Bible, or hears them spoken of in a sermon, readily accepts that those sins are to be found in himself. He also knows that the main reason those sins are mentioned at all is to enable us to see the same sins in ourselves.

He then directs his mind to himself and the way in which he exhibits those sins. He does not assume that he is without those sins and that they are only to be found in others. Guileless people are sincere and genuine and have a quality of innocence about them. They are tender rather than hardened and the truth really matters to them. The following two references in the psalms refer to this kind of person:

3 Who may ascend into the hill of the LORD?
And who may stand in His holy place?
4 He who has clean hands and a pure heart,
Who has not lifted up his soul 1to falsehood
And has not sworn deceitfully.
5 He shall receive a blessing from the LORD
And righteousness from the God of his salvation.
Psalm 24:3-5 (NASB)

How blessed is the man to whom the LORD does not impute iniquity,
And in whose spirit there is no deceit!
Psalm 32:2 (NASB)

Another example of a guileless person is Nicodemus

Look now at this lengthy passage from John's gospel where Jesus has a detailed conversation with another man called Nicodemus. He too was very transparent and honest, as Nathanael was. Note the sincere, almost child-like, questions which Nicodemus asks Jesus. He does so despite the fact that he was a prominent man in Israel and a highly educated teacher of the Law of Moses.

His earnestness and unpretentiousness come across very clearly in the simplicity of his questions. He evidently had the love of the truth. He was not trying to justify himself or to impress anybody with his own knowledge or sophistication. He just wanted to understand Jesus better and had no other agenda.

Therefore Jesus took the time to give him a full answer. Jesus was clearly impressed by the humility of Nicodemus and his love of the truth. Therefore he opened up to him. Yet Nicodemus was a Pharisee. Indeed, he was a very senior Pharisee. Some say that he was the most senior teacher of the Law of Moses in all Israel.

The fact that a Pharisee could be a good and honest man might come as a surprise to some. Many of us tend to assume that all of the Scribes and Pharisees were proud and hard hearted, always trying to catch Jesus out rather than to learn from him. That is not the case. Many of them followed Him, as did Nicodemus. Here is the account of his conversation with Jesus:

Now there was a man of the Pharisees, named Nicode'mus, a ruler of the Jews.
² This man came to Jesus by night and said to him, "Rabbi, we know that you are a teacher come from God; for no one can do these signs that you do, unless God is with him." ³ Jesus answered him, "Truly, truly, I say to you, unless one is born anew, he cannot see the kingdom of God." ⁴ Nicode'mus said to him, "How can a man be born when he is old? Can he enter a second time into his mother's womb and be born?"
⁵ Jesus answered, "Truly, truly, I say to you, unless one is born of water and the Spirit, he cannot enter the kingdom of God. ⁶ That which is born of the flesh is flesh, and that which is born of the Spirit is spirit. ⁷ Do not marvel that I said to you, 'You must be born anew.' ⁸ The wind blows where it wills, and you hear the sound of it, but you do not know whence it comes or whither it goes; so it is with everyone who is born of the Spirit."
⁹ Nicode'mus said to him, "How can this be?" ¹⁰ Jesus answered him, "Are you a teacher of Israel, and yet you do not understand this? ¹¹ Truly, truly, I say to you, we speak of what we know, and bear witness to what we have seen; but you do not receive our testimony. ¹² If I have told you earthly things and you do not believe, how can you believe if I tell you heavenly things? ¹³ No one has ascended into heaven but he who descended from heaven, the Son of man.

¹⁴ And as Moses lifted up the serpent in the wilderness, so must the Son of man be lifted up, ¹⁵ that whoever believes in him may have eternal life."

John 3:1-15 (RSV)

The way Jesus answered questions from His critics and enemies was very different from how He answered Nicodemus. Most of the Scribes, Pharisees and Sadducees were hostile to Him. When they asked questions it was not to find an answer or to learn the truth. Truth was not on their agenda. Their aim was to justify their own existing opinions and to discredit Jesus.

They did not care about finding out whether He was telling the truth, or whether they were mistaken. They were determined to maintain their own opinions, regardless of whether they were right or wrong. Indeed, many of the religious leaders were well aware that Jesus really was the Messiah. They knew it because they had seen and verified His miracles.

That was the very reason why they were following Him around, i.e. to check up on Him and find out if His miracles were genuine. However, some of them weren't willing to admit any of that to Him or to the people, or even to themselves. They hated Him even though they already knew He was the Messiah. They didn't like what he was saying, even if it was true, and they weren't willing to change.

With humble and sincere people, Jesus went into detail. But He gave very short answers to the proud and dishonest.

To proud, hard-hearted people such as them, Jesus choose not to go into detail or to give full answers. He would often say things to the crowds standing alongside so as to rebut or condemn the things said by His critics and enemies. But at such times He was really speaking to the crowd, not to the Scribes and Pharisees themselves. When His enemies and critics asked Him questions Jesus frequently chose not to explain Himself or to elaborate on what He was doing.

He tended to give them short answers. He would often just turn to the crowds instead and tell them what was wrong with the Scribes and Pharisees who were standing next to Him. Let's look at a few examples of how Jesus gave them short, abrupt answers, or rebuked them, or even gave no answers at all. It was evidently not an uncommon occurrence:

¹ One day, as he was teaching the people in the temple and preaching the gospel, the chief priests and the scribes with the elders came up ²and said to him, "Tell us by what authority you do these things, or who it is that gave you this authority." ³ He answered them, "I also will ask you a question; now tell me, ⁴Was the baptism of John from heaven or from men?" ⁵And they discussed it with one another, saying, "If we say, 'From heaven,' he will say, 'Why did you not believe him?' ⁶ But if we say, 'From men,' all the people will stone us; for

184

they are convinced that John was a prophet." ⁷So they answered that they did not know whence it was. ⁸ And Jesus said to them, "Neither will I tell you by what authority I do these things."

Luke 20:1-8 (RSV)

They said to him therefore, "Where is your Father?" Jesus answered, "You know neither me nor my Father; if you knew me, you would know my Father also."

John 8:19 (RSV)

³⁷ While he was speaking, a Pharisee asked him to dine with him; so he went in and sat at table. ³⁸ The Pharisee was astonished to see that he did not first wash before dinner. ³⁹ And the Lord said to him, "Now you Pharisees cleanse the outside of the cup and of the dish, but inside you are full of extortion and wickedness. ⁴⁰ You fools! Did not he who made the outside make the inside also? ⁴¹ But give for alms those things which are within; and behold, everything is clean for you.

⁴² "But woe to you Pharisees! for you tithe mint and rue and every herb, and neglect justice and the love of God; these you ought to have done, without neglecting the others. ⁴³ Woe to you Pharisees! for you love the best seat in the synagogues and salutations in the market places. ⁴⁴ Woe to you! for you are like graves which are not seen, and men walk over them without knowing it."

Luke 11:37-44 (RSV)

In the meantime, when so many thousands of the multitude had gathered together that they trod upon one another, he began to say to his disciples first, "Beware of the leaven of the Pharisees, which is hypocrisy.

Luke 12:1 (RSV)

¹⁰ "He who is faithful in a very little is faithful also in much; and he who is dishonest in a very little is dishonest also in much. ¹¹ If then you have not been faithful in the unrighteous mammon, who will entrust to you the true riches? ¹² And if you have not been faithful in that which is another's, who will give you that which is your own? ¹³ No servant can serve two masters; for either he will hate the one and love the other, or he will be devoted to the one and despise the other. You cannot serve God and mammon." ¹⁴ The Pharisees, who were lovers of money, heard all this, and they scoffed at him. ¹⁵ But he said to them, "You are those who justify yourselves before men, but God knows your hearts; for what is exalted among men is an abomination in the sight of God.

Luke 16:10-15 (RSV)

Note the stark contrast between Jesus' direct but helpful response to Nicodemus in John chapter 3 and the way He gave short, sharp answers, or even rebukes, to some of the other Pharisees. God gives revelation, and understanding to those who have the love of the truth but not to people who don't. That is because they don't care about finding out what is true and what is false.

Compare the attitude of Nicodemus with that of some of his fellow Pharisees, as shown in this next passage. His colleagues are criticising Jesus and rejecting His message. By contrast, Nicodemus speaks up publicly in defence of Jesus, right in front of his fellow Pharisees:

37 On the last day of the feast, the great day, Jesus stood up and cried out, "If anyone thirsts, let him come to me and drink. 38 Whoever believes in me, as the Scripture has said, 'Out of his heart will flow rivers of living water.'" 39 Now this he said about the Spirit, whom those who believed in him were to receive, for as yet the Spirit had not been given, because Jesus was not yet glorified.

40 When they heard these words, some of the people said, "This really is the Prophet." 41 Others said, "This is the Christ." But some said, "Is the Christ to come from Galilee? 42 Has not the Scripture said that the Christ comes from the offspring of David, and comes from Bethlehem, the village where David was?" 43 So there was a division among the people over him. 44 Some of them wanted to arrest him, but no one laid hands on him.

45 The officers then came to the chief priests and Pharisees, who said to them, "Why did you not bring him?" 46 The officers answered, "No one ever spoke like this man!" 47 The Pharisees answered them, "Have you also been deceived? 48 Have any of the authorities or the Pharisees believed in him? 49 But this crowd that does not know the law is accursed." 50 Nicodemus, who had gone to him before, and who was one of them, said to them, 51 "Does our law judge a man without first giving him a hearing and learning what he does?" 52 They replied, "Are you from Galilee too? Search and see that no prophet arises from Galilee."
John 7:37-52 (ESV)

Another example of a 'guileless' person is the Samaritan woman who met Jesus at the well.

Another good example of a guileless person who had no pretentiousness and was open to the truth was the Samaritan woman at the well. Jesus meets her in John chapter four. She was not a Jew and she had a lot of sin in her life, as we all do. Yet she had something of that same quality of sincerity, openness and guilelessness that we saw above in Nathanael and Nicodemus. Look at the conversation between her and Jesus when they met at the well.

Note how open and childlike she was and how she took no offence at Jesus, even when He told her frankly of some of the sins in her life. She recognized Him as being a prophet and was wide open to receive information from Him. Therefore Jesus was equally open with her, so much so that He even told her plainly that He was the Messiah. It was a remarkably clear statement, which He made to very few other people, or at least not so directly:

Now when Jesus learned that the Pharisees had heard that Jesus was making and baptizing more disciples than John [2] *(although Jesus himself did not baptize, but only his disciples),* [3] *he left Judea and departed again for Galilee.* [4] *And he had to pass through Samaria.* [5] *So he came to a town of Samaria called Sychar, near the field that Jacob had given to his son Joseph.* [6] *Jacob's well was there; so Jesus, wearied as he was from his journey, was sitting beside the well. It was about the sixth hour.*

[7] *A woman from Samaria came to draw water. Jesus said to her, "Give me a drink."* [8] *(For his disciples had gone away into the city to buy food.)* [9] *The Samaritan woman said to him, "How is it that you, a Jew, ask for a drink from me, a woman of Samaria?" (For Jews have no dealings with Samaritans.)* [10] *Jesus answered her, "If you knew the gift of God, and who it is that is saying to you, 'Give me a drink,' you would have asked him, and he would have given you living water."*

[11] *The woman said to him, "Sir, you have nothing to draw water with, and the well is deep. Where do you get that living water?* [12] *Are you greater than our father Jacob? He gave us the well and drank from it himself, as did his sons and his livestock."* [13] *Jesus said to her, "Everyone who drinks of this water will be thirsty again,* [14] *but whoever drinks of the water that I will give him will never be thirsty again The water that I will give him will become in him a spring of water welling up to eternal life."* [15] *The woman said to him, "Sir, give me this water, so that I will not be thirsty or have to come here to draw water."*

[16] *Jesus said to her, "Go, call your husband, and come here."* [17] *The woman answered him, "I have no husband." Jesus said to her, "You are right in saying, 'I have no husband';* [18] *for you have had five husbands, and the one you now have is not your husband. What you have said is true."* [19] *The woman said to him, "Sir, I perceive that you are a prophet.* [20] *Our fathers worshiped on this mountain, but you say that in Jerusalem is the place where people ought to worship."*

[21] *Jesus said to her, "Woman, believe me, the hour is coming when neither on this mountain nor in Jerusalem will you worship the Father.* [22] *You worship what you do not know; we worship what we know, for salvation is from the Jews.* [23] *But the hour is coming, and is now here, when the true worshipers will worship the Father in spirit and truth, for the Father is seeking such people to worship him.* [24] *God is spirit, and those who worship him must worship in spirit and truth."* [25] *The woman said to him, "I know that Messiah is coming (he who is called Christ). When he comes, he will tell us all things."* [26] *Jesus said to her, "I who speak to you am he."*

John 4:1-26 (ESV)

Moreover, because of the Samaritan woman's openness and willingness to be told the truth, and to respond to it, many more people came to believe. She went out of her way to tell them:

Just then his disciples came back. They marveled that he was talking with a woman, but no one said, "What do you seek?" or, "Why are you talking with her?" ²⁸ So the woman left her water jar and went away into town and said to the people, ²⁹ "Come, see a man who told me all that I ever did. Can this be the Christ?" ³⁰ They went out of the town and were coming to him.

John 4:27-30 (ESV)

³⁹ Many Samaritans from that town believed in him because of the woman's testimony, "He told me all that I ever did." ⁴⁰ So when the Samaritans came to him, they asked him to stay with them, and he stayed there two days. ⁴¹ And many more believed because of his word. ⁴² They said to the woman, "It is no longer because of what you said that we believe, for we have heard for ourselves, and we know that this is indeed the Savior of the world."

John 4:39-42 (ESV)

What is the difference between *guile* and *shrewdness*?

We have looked at what it is to be without guile or to be guileless. What then is the sin of guile and how does it differ from shrewdness, which is a good quality? To be shrewd does not require a person to be cunning, devious, crafty or manipulative. Far from it. A shrewd person is one who can correctly discern the character, intentions and motives of other people. A shrewd person is therefore harder to deceive. He does not overlook, or fail to appreciate, facts or events.

He sees what is really going on and what people are doing and he weighs them up quickly and accurately. However, none of that is sin. None of it requires the shrewd person to have any guile. A person who operates with guile will feel free to trick, manipulate, deceive and exploit other people. He says one thing and means another. He hides his real intentions. He takes advantage of other people's ignorance or lack of discernment. He is insincere and crafty and he uses people.

Therefore guile and shrewdness are very different things and are manifested by very different types of person. We should want very much to be shrewd, but not to use any guile in achieving that shrewdness. The ability to see the deceit and falseness in others does not require us to display those same sinful characteristics ourselves.

We must be totally honest with ourselves when we read the Bible

Many people read the Bible in a superficial way, not really taking it seriously and not being honest with themselves about what it says. That is why most of us can read the Bible, or hear it read or being preached on, and yet be unmoved by it. It's as if we assume that when it's being critical, or speaking about sin, it obviously must be referring to someone else, not us. Or, we just filter it out completely, so that it does not even register.

A dishonest person will make that assumption quite easily. They will not be convicted, even when their own sins or character traits are very clearly what is being spoken about. If we are like that then we are just like the people of Ezekiel's day. They had the prophet Ezekiel in their midst but found it very easy to ignore, and disobey, what God was saying to them through him.

30"As for you, son of man, your people who talk together about you by the walls and at the doors of the houses, say to one another, each to his brother, 'Come, and hear what the word is that comes forth from the LORD.' 31And they come to you as people come, and they sit before you as my people, and they hear what you say but they will not do it; for with their lips they show much love, but their heart is set on their gain. 32And, lo, you are to them like one who sings love songs with a beautiful voice and plays well on an instrument, for they hear what you say, but they will not do it. 33When this comes--and come it will! --then they will know that a prophet has been among them."

Ezekiel 33:30-33 (RSV)

Some of us go to church and even read the Bible, but are not honest enough to really hear what God is saying to us through the Bible. We may like liturgy, or tradition, but not hear what God is saying, because we have a heart that is hard and closed off to Him. Jesus Himself spoke of this when He referred to some of the Pharisees and Scribes. They tend to have a bad name, but many of us are just like they were. We too can be hypocritical, with no love of the truth, and no willingness to be corrected by God, or to respond to His instruction:

5And the Pharisees and the scribes asked him, "Why do your disciples not live according to the tradition of the elders, but eat with hands defiled?" 6And he said to them, "Well did Isaiah prophesy of you hypocrites, as it is written, 'This people honors me with their lips, but their heart is far from me; 7in vain do they worship me, teaching as doctrines the precepts of men.' 8You leave the commandment of God, and hold fast the tradition of men." 9And he said to them, "You have a fine way of rejecting the commandment of God, in order to keep your tradition!

Mark7:5-9 (RSV)

If we want to avoid being hypocrites, as some (not all) of the Pharisees were, then we must develop a rigorous honesty and frankness with ourselves when reading the Bible. We should positively look for God's correction concerning our attitudes and ways. We must have no wish to defend ourselves from the Bible, or to justify or vindicate ourselves.

It is far better to be receptive to whatever God has to say to you, even if He wants to correct or rebuke you. If that is what He is saying to you, it's because you need to hear it, as we all do. Thus, we must never be angry or irritated about what the Bible says to us, as many people were when they heard Jesus tell them the truth about themselves:

²⁵But in truth, I tell you, there were many widows in Israel in the days of Elijah, when the heavens were shut up three years and six months, and a great famine came over all the land, ²⁶and Elijah was sent to none of them but only to Zarephath, in the land of Sidon, to a woman who was a widow. ²⁷And there were many lepers in Israel in the time of the prophet Elisha, and none of them was cleansed, but only Naaman the Syrian." ²⁸When they heard these things, all in the synagogue were filled with wrath. ²⁹And they rose up and drove him out of the town and brought him to the brow of the hill on which their town was built, so that they could throw him down the cliff. ³⁰But passing through their midst, he went away.

Luke 4:25-30 (ESV)

A really honest person will want to find out the full truth of what the Bible has to say to him about his various sins and faults. He will positively seek for the Bible's constructive criticism. By contrast, a superficial person, who does not have the love of the truth, will avoid anyone or anything which confronts him with the truth about himself or his situation.

Instead, he will go looking for preachers and teachers who will flatter him and massage his ego rather than those who will tell him the truth. They did this in Isaiah's day and people still do it today:

⁹For they are a rebellious people,
lying children,
children unwilling to hear
the instruction of the LORD;
¹⁰who say to the seers, "Do not see,"
and to the prophets, "Do not prophesy to us what is right;
speak to us smooth things,
prophesy illusions,

Isaiah 30:9-10 (ESV)

If we have got our doctrine wrong, or have given a false prophecy, we should welcome correction. We must then be willing to alter our opinion or our teaching rather than cling to it stubbornly.

If a person has the love of the truth then, when they realise that they have made a mistake or have got their doctrine or theology wrong, they are pleased to be corrected. They are not proud or stubborn and they don't resent being told that they are wrong. On the contrary, they appreciate the person who has corrected them. They then willingly alter their view, so as to abandon the wrong opinion or doctrine and adopt the correct one.

That is obviously what any sensible person would do. If you are wrong then, surely, it is a good thing to have that error pointed out, so that you can change your view? How could one possibly argue otherwise? Although that is undoubtedly the right approach, the fact is that most of us do not see it that way. The average person, even in churches, resents being corrected or challenged, even when the correction is entirely valid.

Indeed, they resent the correction all the more *because* it is valid. They prefer instead to maintain their existing beliefs, regardless of whether they are right or wrong. In part that is due to pride. However it is also because that person simply does not have the love of the truth. They would prefer to maintain the *appearance* of having been right, rather than change their view so as to actually become right.

Anyone who acts in that way is more in love with their own ego and reputation than with the truth. By contrast, consider two characters in the Bible who were very willing to be corrected. They were also prepared to change their view immediately and without any resentment or stubbornness. The first is the prophet Nathan. King David came to him and said he wanted to build a house (a Temple) for the Lord. Nathan instantly gave his own opinion on this point. He told David to go ahead and that God was with him in that proposed idea:

¹Now when David lived in his house, David said to Nathan the prophet, "Behold, I dwell in a house of cedar, but the ark of the covenant of the LORD is under a tent." ²And Nathan said to David, "Do all that is in your heart, for God is with you."

1 Chronicles 17:1-2 (ESV)

However, later that night God spoke to the prophet Nathan and said that He was *not* actually in support of this and that He did not want David to build the Temple. Instead, God wanted one of David's sons to build it:

³But that same night the word of the LORD came to Nathan, ⁴"Go and tell my servant David, 'Thus says the LORD: It is not you who will build me a house to dwell in.

1 Chronicles 17: 3-4 (ESV)

191

Instead of sulking, taking offense, or feeling embarrassed at having got it wrong, the prophet Nathan immediately went to David. He told him that in fact God did not want him to build the Temple, but wanted his son to do so instead of him:

[11]When your days are fulfilled to walk with your fathers, I will raise up your offspring after you, one of your own sons, and I will establish his kingdom. [12]He shall build a house for me, and I will establish his throne forever.
1 Chronicles 17:11-12 (ESV)

In accordance with all these words, and in accordance with all this vision, Nathan spoke to David
1Chronicles 17:15 (ESV)

Going back to David in this way can't have been easy for Nathan. He was a famous prophet, probably the most senior prophet in Israel, with direct access to the King. A lesser man than him may have been tempted to keep quiet about what God had said, so as to avoid losing face and appearing foolish. At the outset he had given his own honest opinion, i.e. that David should build the Temple.

He genuinely thought that would be God's will. Later when he had discovered that he was wrong, all Nathan wanted to do was to go straight to David to tell him what God actually wanted and to correct the mistake. His own image and reputation did not matter to him, or at least it did not matter in comparison to upholding the truth.

Let's consider a second example, this time from the New Testament. This concerns a very able lawyer called Apollos. He had become a follower of Jesus, but at this point in the book of Acts he only knew the baptism of John the Baptist, not Christian baptism. He was a very eloquent, persuasive man, with all the gifts of an evangelist and was enthusiastically telling people what he knew.

Then one day he met a Christian couple, Priscilla and Aquila. They were not lawyers like him, but they were mature believers. At any rate, they were more mature than he was and they knew the Gospel more fully and accurately than he did. So they corrected Apollos, told him about being baptised in the name of Jesus, and filled in some gaps in his knowledge:

[24]Now a Jew named Apollos, a native of Alexandria, came to Ephesus. He was an eloquent man, competent in the Scriptures. [25]He had been instructed in the way of the Lord. And being fervent in spirit, he spoke and taught accurately the things concerning Jesus, though he knew only the baptism of John. [26]He began to speak boldly in the synagogue, but when Priscilla and Aquila heard him, they took him and explained to him the way of God more accurately
Acts 18:24-26 (ESV)

Like Nathan, Apollos did not take offence, or resist the correction. He humbly accepted what he was told. Then that added knowledge enabled him to increase his effectiveness as an evangelist even further:

²⁷And when he wished to cross to Achaia, the brothers encouraged him and wrote to the disciples to welcome him. When he arrived, he greatly helped those who through grace had believed, ²⁸for he powerfully refuted the Jews in public, showing by the Scriptures that the Christ was Jesus.

Acts 18: 27-28 (ESV)

So, Apollos, though probably more educated, and wealthy, than either Priscilla or Aquila, was willing to be corrected by them. He showed no pride or stubbornness. He loved the truth and positively wanted to be put right wherever he was wrong and to have any gaps in his knowledge filled. He was not aiming to impress anybody and therefore he had no fear of being made to appear wrong or to be lacking in any way.

Why should he, or any of us, fear those things? We are all wrong on many occasions and we all have gaps in our knowledge. Therefore we should never be reluctant to have our errors exposed and corrected. But even if we are reluctant, then we should just force ourselves to accept correction anyway.

I am also reminded of the eminent Bible teacher, the late Derek Prince. One of the reasons God used him so hugely, in a worldwide ministry, was the very fact that he loved the truth far more than he loved himself or his own reputation. He was a major academic, having won a scholarship to Eton and then to King's College Cambridge.

He was also a Fellow of King's College, being qualified to lecture in philosophy and also in Greek. Yet, when he was a young believer, only a few weeks after his conversion, he allowed an old, uneducated, working-class couple in Scarborough, England, to correct him and to tell him about the Holy Spirit. He was not too proud to be taught by them.

Likewise, many years later, when he had become an internationally renowned Bible teacher, Derek Prince made a mistake by teaching that all Christians should have a 'shepherd', i.e. a pastor to whom they 'submit'. This wrong teaching led to what became known as the *'Shepherding Movement'* which quickly became domineering and oppressive.

However, when Derek Prince realised that what he had been teaching was wrong and harmful, he publicly renounced it and told all his listeners that he had been wrong to teach it. That was in the 1970s and from that point onwards his ministry multiplied and became even larger.

I feel that one of the key reasons for his subsequent success is that God was pleased by Derek Prince's humility and love of the truth, which had made him so willing to humble himself and to publicly admit he had been wrong. Accordingly, we must all decide that the truth is what really matters, not how we appear, or what people think of us. Therefore we need to be willing, and even eager, to be corrected whenever our opinions, or understanding of issues are wrong or incomplete.

The average person automatically believes whatever suits their own interests, regardless of whether it is actually true

A key feature of our fallen human nature is that we are self-centred. That has a very adverse effect on the way we behave. However, it also affects the way we handle information. It distorts the way we see and hear things and deflects us away from truth. Thus, the average person is particularly likely to be deceived about anything which has any bearing on themselves.

In short, they will believe whatever it *suits them* to believe i.e. whatever promotes their own interests, regardless of whether it is actually true. These things are not necessarily done consciously. They are usually done by long-established habit. Few people would go so far as to say any of these things out loud. Nevertheless, the average person will rearrange and reconstitute facts within their own minds, so as to be able to:

a) believe the best of themselves

b) see their own actions and motives in the best light

c) see anything favourable to their own interests as obviously true

d) see anything unfavourable to their own interests as obviously untrue

e) see no faults in themselves, but only in others

f) feel automatically entitled to things, without needing any evidence to justify that entitlement

In other words, most of us find it very easy to believe whatever we *want* to believe and to ignore or reject anything which we do not *want* to believe. In doing this, in either direction, there is no honest or rigorous examination of facts or evidence. It is all done instantly and automatically, without the need to analyse anything at all, and irrespective of whether those things are actually true or not.

In my experience that is pretty much the default-setting of the average person. It is rare for anyone, even in churches, to be different from the above. Therefore, if we are to grow as a disciple we have got to get to grips with this self-centred and self-biased way in which most of us have learned to think.

We need to cross examine and challenge ourselves and expose our selfish assumptions whenever they arise. We need to be ruthlessly frank with ourselves and believe things solely because they *are true*, regardless of whether or not it would suit our purposes if it was true.

Every lie will one day be exposed at the Great White Throne Judgment, which is for non-Christians

Every non-Christian will, one day, have to face Jesus Christ at the Great White Throne Judgment. Then, every lie they have ever told will be publicly exposed. All things will be put right and made straight. Any lies that a non-Christian has ever told will be publicly exposed and corrected there. Therefore they will be humiliated, quite apart from the eternal punishment that will then follow.

So, an unbeliever may appear to get away with a lie today, but it is inevitable that it will, eventually, be fully exposed. There is no doubt about that, and no escape from it. It would be like telling a lie today, knowing that it will be exposed as a lie next week by the Headmaster at school assembly, in front of all the staff and pupils of the school. Wouldn't it be stupid to tell such a lie today, knowing it will all come out publicly next week?

Why then does it make any difference if the exposure of that lie might be many years in the future? Why should the timescale matter? It will all still be publicly and humiliatingly revealed, whenever it happens. Perhaps you did not realise that before, but you need to realise it now. Let it act as a brake on your tongue. Let the prospect of it keep you from lying as you reflect on the absolute *inevitability* of being caught and exposed.

Even Christians will have to give an account of their lives at the Judgment Seat of Christ. Therefore it is better to ask for God's correction and judgment now, in this life.

It is not just non-Christians who need to be wary of telling lies. Christians will also have to face Jesus Christ one day in judgment. For them it will be at the Judgment Seat of Christ. The lies told by a Christian might not necessarily be publicly exposed, or punished, though my personal opinion is that they will be. But, at the very least, such lies will cause the loss of some, or perhaps even all, of the rewards that we might otherwise have received. (See Book Four for more details).

Given that you know that you will be judged in the end and that the consequences of that judgment will be eternal, it is much wiser to seek for God's judgment here and now. If you are in a dispute with someone and you are unsure whether your own conduct is right or wrong, or whether it is you or they who are acting in accordance with God's will, then positively ask God to judge between you now. You could do as David did when King Saul was hunting him and seeking to kill him:

May the Lord therefore be judge, and give sentence between me and you, and see to it, and plead my cause, and deliver me from your hand.
1 Samuel 24:15 (RSV)

I do not mean that you should ask for God's punishment upon yourself. Far from it. However, what you can and should do is to ask God to intervene and to do the following kinds of things now, in this life. That is much better than leaving it all to be dealt with later at the Judgment Seat of Christ. You can ask Him:

a) to *expose* any wrongdoing on your own part and make those things very clear for you to see

b) to enable others to see your error or wrongdoing as well and to prompt them to point it out to you

c) to prevent you from doing any wrong to any other person, i.e. ask God to stand in your way

d) to intervene and stop you, or redirect you, if you are handling a situation or person wrongly, unfairly or misguidedly.

e) to expose any wrong motives on your part, even if the things that you are doing are right in themselves

f) to prevent you from going any further in a particular direction if it is wrong, i.e. to close doors so that your way is blocked by Him

g) to expose anything that you believe which is actually untrue, or about which you have been deceived

Why not pray to God along all those lines? Positively ask Him to expose your wrong behaviour, wrong attitudes or wrong beliefs, so as to enable you to change here and now. That way, you may feel some embarrassment or awkwardness now, but in the long term, and especially in eternity, you will gain, because you will:

a) avoid being rebuked (or even punished) for those things at the Judgment Seat of Christ

b) become eligible, instead, to be rewarded for what you go on to do from now on.

CHAPTER 10

HOW WE CAN DEVELOP 'THE LOVE OF THE TRUTH' AND THE CHARACTER QUALITY, AND HABIT, OF TRUTHFULNESS

The LORD is near to all who call upon him,
to all who call upon him in truth.
                    Psalm 145:18 (RSV)

Keep your tongue from evil
 and your lips from speaking deceit.
                    Psalm 34:13 (ESV)

Take heed lest your heart be deceived, and you turn aside and serve other gods
and worship them,
                    Deuteronomy 11:16 (RSV)

"......... and he who is dishonest in a very little is dishonest also in much"
                    Luke 16:10 (b) (RSV)

[16] These are the things that you shall do: Speak the truth to one another; render
in your gates judgments that are true and make for peace; [17] do not devise evil
in your hearts against one another, and love no false oath, for all these things I
hate, declares the LORD."
                    Zechariah 8:16-17 (ESV)

Do not lie to one another, seeing that you have put off the old nature with its
practices
                    Colossians 3:9 (RSV)

So put away all malice and all guile and insincerity and envy and all slander.
                    1 Peter 2:1 (RSV)

You have to make a clear decision to cut out all lies, without exception or compromise and then keep watch over your heart

I have come to the conclusion that the only way for a person to change the habit of a life time and stop being a liar is to come off it "cold turkey". Lying has to be stopped 100% and overnight. Lies are something that we learn to rely on and which we get used to. Therefore, they seem natural.

There is no safe level, or acceptable number, of lies that can be continued with after we become a Christian. They *all* have to go, however small they may seem to you. You have to declare to yourself *"No more lies, whatsoever, to anybody, any time"*. Moreover, you need to mean it, because if you say that, you will certainly be tested on it:

²³Watch over your heart with all diligence,
for from it flow the springs of life.
²⁴Put away from you a deceitful mouth
and put devious speech far from you.
²⁵Let your eyes look directly ahead and
let your gaze be fixed straight in front of you.
                        Proverbs 4:23-25 (NASB)

Why not do as Job did? Make a promise to yourself that you will not tell any lies at all to anybody. This is how Job put it:

as long as my breath is in me,
and the spirit of God is in my nostrils;
⁴ my lips will not speak falsehood,
and my tongue will not utter deceit.
                        Job 27:3-4 (RSV)

Go further and do as King David did. He resolved to walk with integrity of heart and not to set before his eyes anything that is base. He said that second point because we can easily be tempted into sin as a result of what we see. This is very true of men, so many of whom have a problem with pornography. I have been very surprised by whom I have had to counsel about this. It is a widespread problem. Therefore resolve not to look at it. Better still, set your computer to block it, as when it is set for a child:

".... I will walk with integrity of heart
within my house;
I will not set before my eyes
anything that is base...."
                        Psalm 101:2(b)-3(a) (RSV)

You have responsibility for the condition of your own heart. *"It is your most important stewardship"*, as the Bible teacher, Chuck Missler, often says. What he means is that if you can guard and preserve your own integrity, and remain honest in all things at all times, then all other areas of your life will go well. If you don't take that stewardship of your own heart seriously enough, then the rest of your life will end up in a mess.

It has to be all or nothing. You must decide to cut out all lies, no matter what the circumstances and no matter what the cost. You also need to ask for God's help to achieve this new lifestyle of truthfulness and to deal with the repercussions which it will inevitably produce. Ask Him to help you. Also ask Him to expose, and remove from your life, anything that would tempt you to lie. That is how seriously you need to take this:

⁷Two things I asked of You,
Do not refuse me before I die:
⁸Keep deception and lies far from me,
Give me neither poverty nor riches;
Feed me with the food that is my portion,
⁹That I not be full and deny You and say,
"Who is the LORD?"
Or that I not be in want and steal,
And profane the name of my God.
Proverbs 30:7-9 (NASB)

It would be far better to stay poor if becoming rich caused or required us to become a liar, either in getting the riches, or in keeping them. If that fact doesn't seem real to you and the awfulness of dishonesty still doesn't resonate with you, then ask God to change your heart attitude. Ask Him to give you His attitude to truth and to enable you to value it as He does, so that you become a modern day 'Nathanael'.

God promises to grant us anything we ask for, provided it is in accordance with His will. Therefore if there is one prayer you can be sure He will be delighted to answer, it is a heart-felt prayer to help you to become an entirely honest person and to give you the love of the truth. He will not refuse that request, if you really mean it, because it is undoubtedly His will for you to become such a person.

Having said that, neither will He do it all for you. If it is up to you to decide that you want the love of the truth and to be determined to choose truth over lies every time. God will not do that for you, but He will help you to change, if you really want Him to.

Then turn that decision to be truthful into an ingrained habit, so it becomes instinctive, without needing to think

Having made a genuine decision to eliminate all lying, no matter how small or seemingly justified it may be, you then have to take steps to turn that decision into an ingrained habit. That means sticking at it for a long enough period of time to enable you to adjust. It also means praying for God to give you the love of the truth. As soon as you make that your aim, you will find that you have to make a stand on all sorts of small issues, day after day.

Eventually, the habit of truthfulness will be solidly formed in you. It then becomes automatic and instinctive for you to come out with the truth when under sudden pressure, rather than tell a lie. Your reflexes will be changed, so that truth becomes your default-setting. All of that is possible, if you really want it. Any Christian can become totally honest if they truly want to be. The sad reality though, is that very few people do want to be. Few even consider this issue at all, let alone resolve to change their ways.

Succeeding in the future at the Day of Judgment matters much more than succeeding today.

Every lie will have to be accounted for, whichever judgment we go to. That is the one day of your life that matters more than any other. How a Christian is assessed at the Judgment Seat of Christ is the ultimate priority, after salvation itself. That assessment and its consequences are eternal.

What could possibly be above that? Therefore resolve never to allow the habit of dishonesty to tarnish the assessment that Jesus makes of your life. (See Book Four in this series which deals with the Judgment Seat of Christ)

Being truthful means swimming against the tide and refusing to compromise

If you seriously set out to become totally honest from now on then it will frequently mean swimming against the tide. You will stand out from the crowd and your honesty will not be liked or appreciated by everybody. That is putting it mildly. Many will actually hate and despise what you're seeking to do. It will lead you into all sorts of conflict, trouble and costly choices.

Telling the truth all the time is not easy, and it never will be easy, until after Jesus returns. Until then, you will usually be the odd one out, not only at work, or school, or among your neighbours. You will even be the odd one out among many Christians, and even among some church leaders. That is how rare real truthfulness is. It is rare even within the church, where deception, and especially self-deception, are now commonplace.

Peer pressure is real and very powerful, both outside, in the world, and also inside the church. There is a strong pressure on all of us to fit in and not to rock the boat by objecting to things that those around us have decided are good. However, if you follow your conscience, or if you stand up for what the Bible says, then you will find that you regularly end up as the odd one out.

It is inevitable, because the majority of people, even within churches (in the West) are not following either the Bible, or their consciences, but the standards of the world. (See Book Seven)

You will find yourself in positions where you believe a certain thing is wrong, but all of the people around you, including leaders in the church, may agree unanimously that it's right. At least they may say that is 'acceptable' or 'can be justified'. However, where that happens, you must always follow your conscience rather than following the crowd, even if it means that you stand entirely alone:

"Do not follow the crowd in doing wrong. When you give testimony in a lawsuit, do not pervert justice by siding with the crowd,

Exodus 23:2 (NIV)

Such situations are very difficult and painful to deal with and they can also be costly to you. But you still need to brace yourself and insist on listening to your conscience and on following God's Word, even if that puts you out on a limb as the only person who thinks as you do. That is very hard to handle, but the alternative is far worse. That is to fit in with current orthodoxy and to go along with whatever those around you are saying or doing.

The problem with just following the crowd and fitting in with the world's standards is that you will then end up disobeying, or even opposing, God, simply to win the approval and acceptance of those around you. That is a tragically foolish bargain. Therefore, never be willing to call evil things good or good things evil. Always insist on staying true to what the Bible says. Also always obey what your conscience says about how to apply the Bible in practice:

Woe to those who call evil good and good evil, who put darkness for light and light for darkness, who put bitter for sweet and sweet for bitter!

Isaiah 5: 20 (RSV)

Truthfulness will inevitably make you unpopular with some people

Refusing to tell lies can make you very unpopular. I vividly remember my first day on patrol as a police constable in November 1983. I was put with my designated 'tutor constable', whose task was to teach me the practicalities of how to do the job. He had to accompany me all the time for my first 10 weeks in the police. As we sat in the police car he said to me, at the start of my first day: *"Let's get one thing straight - whatever I write in my pocket book, that's what you will write in yours."*

I knew immediately what he meant, and that I needed to take a firm stand, there and then. Basically, he was saying that no matter what I saw or heard, my evidence would have to be whatever he said it was. He was insisting that I did not contradict him or write anything different. I knew what he meant and I also knew that it would lead to problems.

Therefore I replied, as politely and deferentially as I could, that I would be happy to be guided by him as to how to write up my evidence, *so long as it was all true.* When he heard that last point he became furious. He went back to the police

203

station at lunch time and began to spread the news to the entire station, of over 100 officers, that I was a menace and that I was not safe to be with!

He told people that I could get them into trouble because I would just write down whatever I saw and heard. He believed I could even get people the sack, for revealing that they were doing wrong, breaking rules, or telling lies. A large proportion of the station then 'sent me to Coventry', or it seemed so to me. Very few people spoke to me for months and most were wary of going on patrol with me.

It was a very painful time indeed. It's one thing to look back on it all now, but it was agonising at the time, especially as I was so young and inexperienced. However, I'm not sure what else I could have done. I had to make a stand, or my integrity would have been compromised. If I had buckled to the pressure I would soon have ended up writing something false in my pocket book.

Moreover, it wouldn't have ended there. I would then have had to copy that false evidence from my pocket book into witness statements and reports for senior officers to look at. I would then have had to sign those to certify they were true. I simply couldn't have done it, and I knew that.

Even worse, I would, eventually, have ended up in a Court, having to testify on oath, in front of Judges, Magistrates and juries, that what I had written in my statement and my pocket book was the truth, the whole truth, and nothing but the truth. I would then have had to stick to that false or incomplete story and look the judge and jury in the eye when cross examined about it.

I knew I just wouldn't be able to go through with any of that, even if I had wanted to. I would never have had a single night's sleep during my years in the police if I'd allowed myself to be compromised in those ways. Also, my personal witness as a Christian would have been ruined.

How could I ever look another officer in the eye and tell him what the Christian Gospel is if both he and I knew that I was a liar? My testimony as a Christian would have become worthless. That was how I saw it, and I think I was right to see it that way. Though He allowed me to suffer for a while, God later honoured me for the stand that I took. He also had pity on my sad plight and solved it all for me.

Four months later the Coal Miners' strike began, in March 1984. I suddenly found that I was sent out in carrier vans, every day, for very long shifts on the miners' picket lines. I had to spend 10 or 12 hours a day with 6-12 other officers cooped up in a van. Moreover, because we were doing a lot of overtime, I got to spend sustained periods of time with officers from other shifts too.

They were the ones who had heard bad reports about me, but who had never really met me. It put an end to my enforced isolation. They were all forced to get to know me and, as they did, their wariness of me diminished and then disappeared. In the end, I was fully accepted by all of them. However, I had to suffer for four months beforehand, due to the stand I had taken.

Another much smaller problem came up a year or so later, when a group of us were sent in a carrier van to police a football match. We got back from it at a certain time, say 6.30pm. However, the Sergeant told us all to write in our pocket books that we had got back later, at about 7.00pm, so as to claim an extra 30 minutes worth of overtime.

That would have been OK if we could have openly said that we actually got back at 6.30pm, but that we were being awarded that extra time as a bonus. I'd have been happy to do that, provided it could be done legitimately and openly. However, that was not what the Sergeant meant.

So I announced, in front of the whole carrier van of police officers, that I was going to write down that I had got back at 6.30pm. That meant they all had to do the same, even the sergeant. They had no choice. They all therefore lost the extra 30 minutes overtime pay. As you might imagine, that went down badly, but nothing like as badly as the first time I took a principled stand.

They must have been getting used to me by then, because nothing came of it. I found after that that I had fewer problems. I suspect that, in part, that was because some officers modified their behaviour whenever they were with me. Therefore, there was nothing improper for me to see or write about. All our evidence was true.

That, in itself, shows something important. The clear and resolute stand that I took saved me, in the end, from witnessing all sorts of wrong things that would otherwise have happened in front of me. It modified other officers' conduct. So, it worked to my advantage and, I believe, to the advantage of the police force and the public.

It is more important to have a good name than to be successful or rich

It is more important to preserve our good name and reputation than to be rich or successful. However, how many of us actually believe that? It cannot be very many, or we would not behave as we do. Yet the Bible says that it is true:

A good name is to be chosen rather than great riches,
and favour is better than silver or gold.
Proverbs 22:1 (RSV)

205

Note that it says that a good name is to be "chosen" rather than great riches. That is because it frequently is a choice. We may find that the opportunity arises for us to have one, or the other, but not both, and we need to choose between them. Don't be confused by the reference to 'great riches'. It is not only talking about the very wealthy. When it comes to wealth, all figures are relative. Therefore we all face this dilemma, however much, or little, money we may have.

It may be that for a particular man, even a few pounds would be enough 'riches' to entice him to choose to surrender his good name. If he does so then he is a fool, and well on the way to becoming wicked. For one thing, wealth obtained by dishonest means will not last. It will evaporate away later and will also lead us into other problems and traps:

A fortune made by a lying tongue
is a fleeting vapour and a deadly snare.
Proverbs 21:6 (NIV)

When the Bible speaks of having a 'good name' and of receiving 'favour', as we saw above, it does not only mean the opinions of other people. Their views do come into it, and they do matter, primarily in terms of whether or not you are a good witness or ambassador for Christianity. That's the main thing that matters when it comes to what people think of you. People could choose either to believe the Gospel, or to reject it, based on what they think of *you*.

So your reputation really does matter, if only for that reason alone. However, what the verse is really talking about is God's view of you. The crucial question is whether He is pleased, or displeased, by your life and by the choices you make. What could matter more than that? How could any purely temporary financial gain (for a maximum of about 70 years) be worth losing your eternal life?

Even if you didn't lose that, how could it be worth losing your eternal reward at the Judgment Seat of Christ? How much does having a good name matter to you? If you are a Christian then it ought to matter a lot. The people around you, at work and elsewhere, are very observant and discerning. They will notice if your life doesn't match up to what you say you believe.

If there's a mismatch, you will have no credibility from then on in sharing the gospel with anybody. Moreover, your reputation is the key to your promotion prospects, not only at your place of work, but in every context, including your service for God. You therefore need to guard your good name and never do anything to jeopardize it.

Whenever we are tempted to dishonesty, we need to pause and think of our reputation and what the proposed lie might do to it. The people around you will notice, and remember, any lie you ever tell and they won't allow you to forget it. That is true even where they themselves are much bigger liars than us.

Their hypocrisy is irrelevant, because they are not claiming to be a Christian. If you are claiming to be one, then they will judge you by a very different standard than they apply to themselves. But that is actually fair enough. They have a valid point. Why should they take your faith seriously if you don't take it seriously yourself, such that you are willing to do the same things as they do? You gain the respect of non-Christians by being different from them and standing out, not by being the same and fitting in.

Lies are natural to the Devil and to demons. They lie all the time

Lying comes naturally to us. It flows out of our sinful flesh nature. It also comes naturally to Satan and to his demons. They are compulsive liars and lie continuously. Even if a demon says something which contains some true facts, there will always be a false twist to it, which renders it false overall. Therefore, whenever we lie we are following the example of the Devil and his demons. We are showing that the Devil is our real father:

⁴⁴"You are of your father the devil, and you want to do the desires of your father He was a murderer from the beginning, and does not stand in the truth because there is no truth in him Whenever he speaks a lie, he speaks from his own nature, for he is a liar and the father of lies.

John 8:44 (NASB)

Lies are a demon's main weapon

See Books Seven and Nine for more details on how demons use lies as a device to control and manipulate us. They use lies on a daily basis to get us to believe what *they* say, instead of believing the truth. Believing those lies causes a huge amount of disruption and damage in our lives. In addition to lying to us, the demons also want to get us to lie to other people. They will tempt and lure you into becoming a liar and to make it habitual.

Our flesh nature is deceitful enough already, but the added influence of a demon whispering into our ear can lead to us going further than we would ever have gone by ourselves. The tendency to lie, especially where it has become habitual or addictive, is a strong sign of demonic involvement in your life.

Why do the demons want us to lie?

There are many reasons why a demon wants to get you to lie, and why they put so much effort into getting you to do it. Firstly, if they can get you to become a liar, then it brings God's curse upon you, as we saw earlier, in Zechariah chapter five. That then turns God Himself into your opponent. That suits the demon very well.

It means they can get God to oppose you in ways that they are not capable of themselves.

Therefore, merely by luring you into lying, they can bring about serious damage in your life and in your walk with God. They also want us to lie because of the havoc that it causes in our marriage, relationships, career and church and because it ruins our credibility as a witness for Jesus Christ.

Lying is habit-forming and addictive. You can't just lie occasionally.

Lying is addictive. If you continue lying then it will become a settled habit. You can't set a limit on how often you'll lie, or on what level of seriousness of lies you are willing to tell. If you are prepared to lie at all, to any degree, then you will, inevitably, end up lying more and more. Eventually you will find that you lie almost all the time. You can't just remain at a certain level.

That's another reason why you have to come off it cold turkey and resolve to tell no lies at all. Then you will find yourself getting more and more truthful, until that too becomes a habit, just as lying used to be. Eventually you will come to love the truth for its own sake, quite apart from the many benefits it brings.

What if telling the truth is costly or painful?

We have already seen that there is a price to pay when you tell the truth and sometimes a very high price. There's no denying that it brings trouble. However, the cost of *not* telling the truth is always very much higher. The price you pay for telling the truth is generally limited and short term. However, the cost of lying is unlimited and long term.

Indeed, whether we are a Christian or not, it is eternal. For an unbeliever, it leads to the Lake of Fire. For a Christian, it will lead to the loss of some, or perhaps all, of the rewards we would otherwise have received at the Judgment Seat of Christ. Either way, those are really tragic consequences. And they are both eternal.

"The truth, the whole truth and nothing but the truth."

The above phrase comes from the wording of the oath which is used in Courts and Tribunals every day. But what does it mean? It is actually a carefully constructed phrase which forbids any kind of deception when a person gives evidence. It means that the witness is swearing to tell:

a) **"the truth"** - i.e. that everything they say will be *true*

b) **"the whole truth"** - i.e. that they *will not leave anything out.* Omitting something could alter the effect and impact of the evidence and make it untrue overall, even if no direct lie is told. In other words, it is to prevent the witness lying by the things he chooses *not* to say.

c) **"and nothing but the truth"** - this is to prevent someone telling all of the truth, and leaving nothing out, but then *adding something untrue on top of it,* i.e. lying by adding a lie to what would, otherwise, be the truth.

Must we always tell the whole truth?

The famous wording of the oath is clearly appropriate for use in *Courts,* because it is absolutely comprehensive and watertight. But it is not necessarily the right way to operate in our day to day lives. We do not always have a duty to tell the whole truth. We are not always under a duty to say all that we know, or all that is on our minds. To do so would sometimes be very unwise. Note the approach that Nehemiah took:

12And I arose in the night, I and a few men with me. I did not tell anyone what my God was putting into my mind to do for Jerusalem and there was no animal with me except the animal on which I was riding. 13So I went out at night by the Valley Gate in the direction of the Dragon's Well and on to the Refuse Gate, inspecting the walls of Jerusalem which were broken down and its gates which were consumed by fire. 14Then I passed on to the Fountain Gate and the King's Pool, but there was no place for my mount to pass. 15So I went up at night by the ravine and inspected the wall. Then I entered the Valley Gate again and returned. 16The officials did not know where I had gone or what I had done; nor had I as yet told the Jews, the priests, the nobles, the officials or the rest who did the work.

Nehemiah 2:12-16 (NASB)

Nehemiah was heading to Jerusalem on a mission to rebuild the wall of the city. He knew that his project was going to come in for a lot of opposition from the enemies of God's people. Therefore, although Nehemiah told no lies, he did not tell other people everything that God had told him to do. He kept some of it to himself.

Nehemiah's approach would be inappropriate in a criminal Court, or even in a civil court, where the system is based on finding out exactly what the whole truth is. That objective means that the Court must insist on total, unlimited frankness and for nothing at all to be held back. Justice is at stake. However, that is not always the case in our day to day lives, where we may be entitled to withhold certain facts, provided that doing so does not amount to a lie.

Nevertheless, in some situations, not mentioning something could amount to a lie.

However, there can be circumstances where to leave out, or fail to mention, some fact would amount to misleading someone and in a dishonest way. That can apply even where there is no Court involved and nobody is giving evidence. Our conscience has to guide us. In any given situation we have to decide whether we can, with integrity, choose *not* to say something. It is impossible to create a hard and fast rule, because every situation turns on its own facts.

You must therefore ask God to guide you in those specific circumstances. Then use your conscience to gauge what is right on that occasion. The more inherently honest and sincere a person is, the more they will tend to assume that total frankness and transparency are needed. However, that is not always wise, and it can sometimes be naive to think that way, depending on the facts.

We have to ask ourselves whether the person is entitled to be told the whole truth

A good question to ask oneself, when seeking to decide how much one is obliged to disclose, is whether the other person is *entitled* to be told the whole truth. They may, or they may not be. If they are a police officer, judge, tax official or officer of the Court, the likelihood is they would be entitled to 100% of what you know, without leaving anything out. However, if the other person is a work colleague, friend, relative, neighbour etc, they may not be entitled to know everything, or indeed anything at all.

It all depends on their position and yours, and also on any duties that may, or may not be, owed by you to them as a result. Imagine that a friend of yours has confided in you, but then another friend of both of you asks what you have been discussing. You have no duty to answer that question. It would be legitimate to fob them off by saying "*Oh we were just chatting about this and that*". Failing to give an answer would be no lie, because there was no duty to answer them at all.

We don't always have to answer the questions people ask us

One of the things that has caused me difficulty for many years is knowing what to do when asked a difficult question where I am not yet entitled, or willing, to reveal the truth, but where I may not tell a lie either. Often the only solution is to sidestep the question. Politicians have to learn how to do this and it does not necessarily signify that they are dishonest. Often it's for very good reasons.

The point is that we do not always have a duty to give people an answer. It depends on the circumstances, on who is asking the question, and on whether they have any right to receive an answer. Often they do not. Realising this fact has been a great benefit to me. I had previously felt obliged to give an answer all the time and that caused me many difficulties. Here is an example of Jesus brushing aside a question which had not been asked sincerely, and was only intended to trap Him:

19The scribes and the chief priests tried to lay hands on Him that very hour, and they feared the people; for they understood that He spoke this parable against them. 20So they watched Him, and sent spies who pretended to be righteous, in order that they might catch Him in some statement, so that they could deliver Him to the rule and the authority of the governor. 21They questioned Him, saying, "Teacher, we know that You speak and teach correctly, and You are not partial to any, but teach the way of God in truth. 22"Is it lawful for us to pay taxes to Caesar, or not?" 23But He detected their trickery and said to them, 24"Show Me a denarius. Whose likeness and inscription does it have?" They said, "Caesar's." 25And He said to them, "Then render to Caesar the things that are Caesar's, and to God the things that are God's." 26And they were unable to catch Him in a saying in the presence of the people; and being amazed at His answer, they became silent.

Luke 20:19-26 (NASB)

Nevertheless, it's also possible to lie without saying any words at all, by choosing not to give information to those who are entitled to it.

Sometimes a clear duty to speak does exist, for example because you are acting in some fiduciary capacity, i.e. a position of trust. If so, then you must speak. To fail to do so would then be dishonest, whereas it would not be so if there had not been a duty to speak. It could therefore be a lie to say nothing, where your silence could be reasonably taken to mean something, so as to convey a false impression.

Let's imagine that at 12:00 noon you send an email saying, truthfully, that £x would be a fair price for some shares, or for a house. Then at 3.00pm some event occurs that changes everything, such that the value has suddenly gone up or down. Must you send another email to say *"Ignore my previous email"*?

It may be that you must, depending on your role and the position of the other person in relation to you. You would have to ask yourself: *"Do I owe this person a duty of care? Would my silence now be misleading? Is the other person professionally represented or not?"* It may turn on questions such as those, and many others.

What about "nothing but the truth"?

It is hard to imagine any circumstances, other than in warfare, where it would be appropriate to add facts that are not true. We can sometimes withhold true facts, but we may not add false ones. So, if we need to fob a person off or get them to stop asking questions, without indirectly betraying that some secret is being withheld, you may need to think of creative ways of changing the subject, as Jesus often did. But you still cannot lie in doing so, unless, as stated, there is a war on and you are being questioned by the enemy.

What about exaggeration?

Exaggeration is very common, but it is still lying. and it is a trait which can easily become a habit. It can be like the thin end of a wedge. Exaggeration is often seen as a more acceptable form of lying. It isn't. It's actually dangerous, because if it isn't eliminated, it can undermine your conscience and, gradually, lead you into telling much more explicit lies. I knew a church leader some years ago whom I'm calling Rick. I have referred to him earlier. He was particularly prone to exaggeration. He actually became well known for it.

People used to excuse Rick and speak of it as "*just his way*" and that he was "*evangelastic*". But it's actually very wrong. Exaggeration can easily escalate to the point where you aren't just being a little rough and ready with figures, but increasingly wide of the mark. Therefore, make a decision never to exaggerate. It is wrong in itself, but it is also wrong because of what it leads to.

It is far better to make a firm decision that you will always just say exactly what you mean and no more. Do not allow yourself to embroider a story. Then, if you find that exaggeration is still is a habit, make a further promise to yourself that whenever it happens you will always immediately correct what you've said. Do it there and then, in the presence of whoever else is there.

That correction repairs the damage, but the discomfort and embarrassment you will feel at having to correct yourself in front of others will help to put yourself off doing it again. It would be like getting an electric shock every time you exaggerate. Your sinful flesh nature doesn't like being embarrassed. Therefore you will quickly learn not to risk doing it again, provided you know that you really will force yourself to correct any exaggeration publicly. It's a good way to cure yourself of this habit.

Are we allowed to be tactful and diplomatic?

What about saying things which are not true just in order to be kind or diplomatic? For example, what if someone asks you whether you like their dress? In a situation like that you are entitled to ask yourself *"What is this person really asking?"* It is likely that what they really mean is *"Please reassure me"*.

If so, you can honestly do so, whatever your real view, because it wasn't really a request for information, but for reassurance. However, there could conceivably be a situation where you knew someone's dress was a problem or that it would cause them humiliation if you were to say nothing. If so, it may actually be your duty to speak the truth. If so, then your task would be to do so as gracefully, and kindly, as possible.

Honesty in all our relationships

Truth is also needed is in our personal relationships, not just where we are dealing with money or property. People can be distressingly false with each other. It is possible to be false without telling direct lies about facts and figures, or without even using any words at all, simply by misrepresenting your true feelings.

For example it is commonplace for people to pretend to be someone's friend to their face, but to be very disloyal behind their backs. It is a form of falseness which may involve words, but which doesn't have to. It involves being dishonest about your real feelings, intentions or affiliation.

That sort of falseness is distasteful to have to witness and painful to experience. Yet it's happening millions of times every day in Great Britain alone. It sickens me, and I feel sure it sickens God. Resolve to yourself that you will never act in that way. Never allow yourself to have two faces. Commit yourself to be true and real in every relationship you have. Never pretend to be, or to feel, anything which isn't real.

Honesty in business or at work

God also hates to see trickery and falseness in our business dealings:

A false balance is an abomination to the LORD,
but a just weight is His delight.
Proverbs 11: 1(NASB)

God detests cheating and every kind of scheme to swindle other people, whether they are our customers, colleagues or competitors. God loves it when our weights and measures are genuine and we don't 'short-change' people. Many times I have been in a shop or market stall and the assistant has handed me back my change, but it is 50 pence or a pound too little.

213

When I raise the matter it is quite apparent from their reaction, and from the look on their face, that they were fully aware, and that the 'error' was intentional. They were just waiting to see whether I would notice. Sometimes they look brazen, or even resentful, about it. They don't even mind that you know what they were up to. Amazing though it sounds, God finds time to concern Himself with every such incident. He notices, and it all matters to Him very deeply.

Sometimes in a workplace a person offers to tell a lie to "assist" you. He may even offer to do it expecting to be rewarded, or to be considered loyal, because of his willingness to lie for you. But I don't want staff who are willing to lie for me. I'm not even willing to lie for myself, so I'd hardly want them to do it on my behalf.

A person's willingness to lie for their boss may impress others, but not me. Besides being inherently wrong, a practical point to bear in mind is that if a man is willing to lie *for* you, he will be equally willing to lie *to* you later, whenever the need arises. Such a man cannot be trusted.

Many a time I have interviewed staff who have offered to pretend to be ill so that they can get time off from their current employer to come to a second interview. They somehow imagine that that will impress me. The moment they offer to do that I cancel the second interview.

If he is willing to lie to his current employer, then I know full well that he won't hesitate to lie to me later. And, if he's as open as that about it, he obviously doesn't even consider it to be wrong. That means his conscience is already badly seared. Therefore he will be dishonest across the board, not just in relation to lying to employers.

Honesty with money

With money, nothing less than 100%, meticulous accuracy and honesty is needed. Resolve not to take anything that is not yours, however small. Don't compromise, even at a microscopic level. If you do, you will inevitably find that the level of your dishonesty will start going up and up, until you are eventually embezzling large sums.

Every embezzler always begins by taking little bits of money, here and there, never large sums. If you harden your heart repeatedly with the little amounts, then your heart will, one day, let you down when it faces the temptation to take large sums. Therefore, win the honesty battle over the pennies, and there will never be any battles over major sums.

Honesty in our use of power or authority

Many people, at all levels, abuse their position of authority in order to use, control or manipulate other people. Some do it purely for the pleasure of asserting themselves, feeling a sense of importance and drawing attention to their position of power. They get pleasure simply out of having power over someone, even if they are only in a lowly role or responsibility. In fact, that is where it most often occurs. Those with only a small amount of authority are the ones most likely to behave proudly.

That abuse of authority is a form of dishonesty, because it is the misuse of a position for an illegitimate reason. Our employer did not put us into an intermediate managerial or supervisory role so that we could get a thrill out of lording it over someone else. He put us there to serve the legitimate purposes of the business, and for no other reason. So, misusing a position or role is not much different from misusing a car or a piece of property for a purpose of which we know our employer would not approve.

Honesty in preaching and in teaching the Bible

Some might imagine that this point would not even need to be made. They assume that if a man is sufficiently mature and motivated to preach or teach the Bible then he would surely never lie, exaggerate, dodge issues or be misleading. If only that was true. At any rate, it has not been the case for a large number of the men whom I have heard preach. I have heard countless men treat the Word of God in an extraordinarily careless manner and say things which are plainly not correct.

In doing so, some have actually been fully aware that what they were saying was wrong, but they did not care. Others have been unaware of their errors, but only because they did not care enough about the truth, to take the trouble to find out. So, for a variety of reasons, they misrepresent God's Word and give people a false impression of Him.

I would never want to be in that position. Everything I say is what I sincerely believe to be the true meaning of God's Word, after much study. On many occasions, where I have felt unsure of the meaning I have either explicitly said so, or I have left it alone for the time being and spoken or written on some other topic instead.

That is the right approach. We must never take a cavalier or reckless attitude towards God's Word. When a man who stands up to teach, the responsibility placed upon him is very heavy, and so will be the judgment that comes upon him if he is not sincere and careful. Note what James tells us:

215

Let not many of you become teachers, my brethren, for you know that we who teach shall be judged with greater strictness.

James 3:1 (RSV)

Nevertheless, I have heard a great many men make careless, or even reckless, statements while preaching, for which they have no biblical mandate or authority. They present their own opinions and preferences as if they were God's, and as if God's Word supported what they say, when it clearly doesn't. I would classify that as dishonesty, and of the most grievous kind. Indeed, can there be any more serious subject matter about which to lie or exaggerate, or even to risk making errors, than God's Word?

Perhaps the main reason why so many men behave like that when preaching is because they feel no fear while handling God's Word. But we should. It is such a heavy and serious matter that it should actually make us tremble, for fear of misrepresenting God and misleading people about Him or His will. No less a person than Isaiah tells us that God wants us to tremble at [His] Word:

All these things my hand has made,
 and so all these things are mine,
 says the LORD.
But this is the man to whom I will look,
 he that is humble and contrite in spirit,
 and trembles at my word.
                    Isaiah 66:2 (RSV)

Likewise, the Psalmist tells us that he trembles at both the prospect of God's judgment and the responsibility of dealing with His Word:

My flesh trembles for fear of thee,
 and I am afraid of thy judgments.
                    Psalm 119:120 (RSV)

Rulers persecute me without cause,
 but my heart trembles at your word.
                    Psalm 119:161 (NIV)

An example of a preacher who was not honest in handling God's Word

In spite of all that, the mishandling of God's Word, and even outright dishonesty while preaching and teaching, are far more common than most of us would ever imagine. I can think of a particular leader, some years ago, who gave a series of talks on the subject of the gifts of the Holy Spirit. He was a 'cessationist'. That is he believed that the gifts of the Holy Spirit ceased in the first century AD and are no longer in operation.

The Bible never says any of that. Nor does it even hint at it, to the slightest extent. In short, there is no biblical basis for saying it. It is a teaching which is based solely on what men have said, i.e. church tradition. So, this leader made a series of assertions, for which he had absolutely no biblical mandate. He could not point to even one verse or passage which expressly supported his position. That is because there aren't any.

Nevertheless, that fact did not prevent him from setting out many quite irrelevant passages and speaking of them as if they supported what he was saying. I could see that those verses did not prove his point, or even support it. Many of them did not even relate to this issue at all. They had other meanings and were therefore being misused.

He wanted people to think that those passages supported his theological stance, but they manifestly didn't. I can see two main possibilities. At worst, he was being intentionally misleading. At 'best' he was being sloppy and careless with God's Word and was bandying it about without a proper sense of reverence for what he was handling.

I actually questioned him twice during the talk, because the meeting was a kind of seminar, where that was possible. However, he dodged both my questions, either because he could not, or would not, answer them. Yet, at the same time, he did not withdraw or modify any of his claims.

I was told later by another person that someone else had also questioned him in an earlier seminar and that he had, likewise, given them no straight answers. He had sought instead just to fob off the questioner and to avoid answering them, rather than be put under pressure, or have his errors, or his ignorance, exposed. What then should that leader have done?

Firstly, he ought not to have claimed that God's Word supported his stance when it doesn't. That is he should not have twisted the meaning of verses that he was quoting from, to make them appear to be saying that the gifts of the Holy Spirit were only intended for a minority of people and, at any rate, only for the first century.

Secondly, on being questioned, he should have given honest, clear, straight-forward answers, even if that caused an upset or made himself look foolish or under-prepared. For example, he should have said: *"I don't really have any answers to that question, because. I don't fully understand this subject."*

Or he could have said: *I haven't really studied the Bible for myself on this point. I have merely read what some other men have said and am stating their conclusions, without really knowing how, or why, they arrived at them. Indeed, I actually just downloaded most of this sermon from the internet."*

He could even have said: "*What I am saying is the traditional stance of my denomination. I don't really know why, or how, to justify any of it from the Bible. It's just what I have always heard other men say and therefore I'm passing it on.*" Needless to say, he didn't make any of those candid statements. Neither have I ever heard any other preacher say anything similarly honest.

However, they should say such things, or something equally explicit, if it describes their actual position, which it frequently does. Men don't want to look foolish or to be diminished in the eyes of others. But isn't it far better to be thought to lack competence but to be honest, than to be thought competent but to lack honesty? I would say so.

More to the point, it doesn't matter, even if the audience does think you lack knowledge. What matters, above all, is that you are honest in your handling of God's Word. Your fear of God needs to outweigh, and therefore displace, any fear that you may feel about your audience or concern for your reputation.

Moreover, if any leader is willing to be completely open and honest, and to handle God's Word with the utmost care and reverence, then God would respond by increasing their knowledge anyway. It is precisely to such people, who "*tremble at [His] Word*", that God looks, and to whom He will give revelation and insights.

When lies are used as weapons or to gain a competitive advantage

Although God is calling us to live lives of absolute truthfulness, the reality is that most of the people around us, and maybe even we ourselves, use lies as weapons. They are used routinely:

a) to damage and undermine others who may be rivals, competitors or personal enemies.

b) to gain assets, positions or any kind of competitive advantage for oneself.

c) to avoid detection or criticism

d) to cause strife, division and mistrust between other people. People often create discord deliberately, so that a particular person can be kept isolated and prevented from working together with others. Such cooperation might be a threat to the wrongdoer. In other words, they tell lies about the people they work with in order to "*divide and rule*".

See Book Six, which is about identifying and dealing with wicked people, for further detail on these issues and the tactics which devious people use. Deception is an important part of the 'armoury' of the average unbeliever, whether he is only a fool or a fully-fledged wicked person. The people around us use lies as weapons and devices and they do so routinely, on a daily basis.

A high percentage of what we are told by our colleagues, bosses, staff, acquaintances, and even friends, is untrue, whether in whole or in part. That is not merely a possibility, but a virtual certainty. The real question is not *whether* one is being lied to, but *by whom*, and *on what issues*. Frequently it comes in the most unexpected ways and from the people one least suspects. Accordingly, we need to be on high alert for such lies. That said, our first duty is to root out deception from our own lives and to 'unilaterally disarm'.

That means that we cease to use lies as a weapon ourselves. However, while doing so, we must also recognise that most other people will be continuing to tell lies to us, whether small or large, and whether rarely or frequently. Their lies will inevitably keep coming and we need to become equipped to identify those lies and to protect ourselves from their effect.

Winning without lying

God wants us to be overcomers. He wants us to succeed in life, to win our battles, and to overcome the problems that we come up against. So it's true that God wants His people to be winners. However, for success to be real it has to be achieved without resorting to deception, deviousness or manipulation, and also without using other people.

In other words, for a Christian, success is only real if we achieve it in a righteous *manner*, by operating in line with God's standards and principles. If we don't, then any supposed 'success' that we might achieve would count for nothing. God would not view it as success, but as failure. It would therefore be 'burned up' and counted as 'dross' at the Judgment Seat of Christ. No reward would be given to us for it.

On the contrary, we would be rebuked, at the very least, and probably punished as well. In other words, your achievements would only be viewed as a success in your own eyes, and possibly in the eyes of the people around you, but not to God. However, succeeding in God's eyes, and by His criteria, is the only form of success worth having, and the only type that will last.

The things we achieve for God, in accordance with His principles, and in response to His promptings, will last forever. We will be rewarded for them and those rewards, whatever form they take, will last for eternity. We will be allowed to keep them. However, anything achieved by deception, or by cheating, will not last. They will probably disappear or be taken from us, even in this life, but even more so in eternity:

Bread obtained by falsehood is sweet to a man,
but afterward his mouth will be filled with gravel.
Proverbs 20:17 (NASB)

The need to be truthful is one of God's main ways of guiding you - it makes it easier to decide what to do, because it automatically rules out every dishonest option, thus narrowing the choice.

We all struggle at times to know God's will and to get clear guidance from Him as to what steps we should take in complicated or difficult situations. However, one of the clearest forms of guidance God has given us this general principle of truthfulness, in whatever situation we face. The fact that we know that we are always meant to be truthful is a kind of permanent guidance.

This applies in all types of problems or circumstances. So when you face a thorny problem, and have to choose between two or more courses of action, you may well find that some of your options can be ruled out automatically. That is because they would involve an element of dishonesty, compromise, or something squalid or underhand.

Your conscience therefore tells you that one or more of the options would be wrong, or at least questionable. If so, then there is your ready-made guidance. You already know which way to go, or at least which way *not* to go, even without any specific guidance from God.

It is a kind of "standing order" as the Police say. The Chief Constable issues certain orders which always apply. He expects every officer to be aware of them, without needing to be told on each and every occasion. Accordingly, as Christians, one of our main 'standing orders' is that we should always act with integrity:

The integrity of the upright will guide them,
But the crookedness of the treacherous will destroy them.
Proverbs 11:3 (NASB)

Whenever you need guidance let integrity, and the need to maintain your honour and your reputation for honesty, be your guide. So, if a man is selling some goods so cheaply that you suspect they may be stolen, you don't even need to ask God for specific guidance as to whether to buy them from him on this occasion. You already know the answer will be no. The principle of integrity provides you with ready-made guidance:

Righteousness guards the one whose way is blameless,
but wickedness subverts the sinner.
Proverbs 13:6 (NASB)

220

Likewise, if we have integrity we will be secure. We may not necessarily end up as the biggest, or the best, or the richest, but at least we cannot be accused of any wrongdoing. That is what counts most to God. Thus our reputation, especially before God, will be secure, whereas other men's reputations may crumble, as they will be found out:

He who walks in integrity walks securely,
but he who perverts his ways will be found out.
Proverbs 10:9 (NASB)

As we have seen, a 'blameless' man is not sinless. It just means that he is sincere, earnest and godly and has a genuine desire to do God's will. His righteous life will, in itself, be a protection and will keep him from scandals and disasters:

O LORD, who shall sojourn in your tent?
Who shall dwell on your holy hill?
² He who walks blamelessly and does what is right
and speaks truth in his heart;
who does not slander with his tongue
and does no evil to his neighbor,
nor takes up a reproach against his friend;
⁴ in whose eyes a vile person is despised,
but who honors those who fear the LORD;
who swears to his own hurt and does not change;
⁵ who does not put out his money at interest
and does not take a bribe against the innocent.
He who does these things shall never be moved.
Psalm 15:1-5 (ESV)

Who shall ascend the hill of the LORD?
And who shall stand in his holy place?
⁴ He who has clean hands and a pure heart,
who does not lift up his soul to what is false,
and does not swear deceitfully.
⁵ He will receive blessing from the LORD,
and vindication from the God of his salvation.
Psalm 24:3-5 (RSV)

Many of the people who are ruined in financial collapses fail because they made dishonest decisions, or took excessive risks, or over-extended themselves. They did so in ways which their consciences could easily have told them were wrong at the time. But they pressed on regardless, in pursuit of success, and put aside any feelings of uneasiness that they may have had. That is a sure way to end up in ruin.

The hardest form of truth - being honest with yourself

It is very rare to find people who are willing to be brutally honest with themselves. Most people cannot even see the issue here. The point is that the person to whom we lie the most is ourselves. Our own hearts lie to us and we justify ourselves automatically:

"The heart is more deceitful than all else and is desperately sick; who can understand it?
Jeremiah 17:9 (NASB)

All the ways of a man are clean in his own sight,
But the LORD weighs the motives.
Proverbs 16:2 (NIV)

We are highly skilled at telling lies to ourselves and believing them, when even the most naive person, if he was standing nearby, would recognise it as a lie. We operate a hypocritical double standard. We judge ourselves, and our own motives, and actions extremely generously, without any inner debate or questioning of ourselves. Therefore, we give ourselves the benefit of the doubt, and are quick to justify our actions and excuse our failures.

We frequently block out, and therefore do not hear, any thought which contradicts, or even questions, our own actions or attitudes. It is exceptionally rare for a person who has been in a conflict or argument to sit down and say privately to themselves: *"Now let's examine my own actions and attitudes here. Am I out of order myself? How must my actions and words appear to others?"*

Those are obvious questions and we ought to ask them of ourselves daily. But most of us very rarely do so, if ever. If we did ask such questions we would then come to see ourselves as others see us. That would be a major revelation. It would also transform the way we live.

These points are completely obvious. We can see them clearly in the lives of the people around us. We just struggle to see them in ourselves. Even if we can see it in principle, and recognise the concept in abstract terms, we do not carry it over and continue to see this when we are actually in the heat of a conflict situation. Even those who can see that this point applies to them find it very hard to actually put it into practice while in an argument or crisis.

At such times, even if we know these things are true, we will tend to 'revert to type' and behave in a self-deluding way. This is an area where enormous personal growth is available to us if we can learn to cross examine ourselves. That is especially true if we can learn to do this even in the middle of a tense situation, where we are in an argument with another person, or even being mistreated by them.

This blindness about our own faults also arises within family life, and between husband and wife. It happens in the workplace too. In each of these contexts, we are required to live at close quarters with other people. Their ways and attitudes may, therefore, get on our nerves. But, at the same time, we are usually blind to our own faults and selfish ways, because what we do seems so normal and so obviously right.

That is why we need to begin to ask ourselves searching questions about how we must seem to other people and whether there is anything unfair, selfish or annoying in what we say or do. But to learn to ask ourselves obvious questions like that is like learning to speak in a foreign language. It is alien to us because it runs entirely against the grain of our sinful nature.

To begin to operate that way will require us to do what is contrary to our nature and the opposite of the habits we have learned. Likewise, at work, if your boss criticizes or challenges you then, instead of assuming that such a criticism is obviously unfounded, unfair, ridiculous etc, stop and ask yourself: *"How do my actions appear to other people? What can be done to improve my style, manner, technique, method etc?"*

Also, it's essential to ask God to help you to see what others can see in you and in your behaviour. If not you are bound to fail because being honest and objective about yourself is extremely hard to do, even with God's help, let alone without it. In such situations pray something like this:

"Lord, please help me not to react hastily or selfishly, or to do what my flesh nature wants. Help me to calm down and humble myself. Help me to see this situation, and my part in it, as you see it and as others see it. Help me to be objective, fair, honest, unbiased and rational, even when evaluating my own actions. Please also open my eyes to see anything bad about myself that I'm currently blind to."

That is an unusual prayer. God doesn't get many prayers as sincere as that, so it will touch His heart. It is the sort of prayer that He delights to answer. God will pour out self-knowledge to a person who asks for it genuinely, and is not just seeking justification and vindication, but to truly see themselves as they really are. That's the key. Your prayer must be sincere.

Have you ever been in a situation where a friend or colleague asks you what you think of the rights and wrongs of a conflict they are engaged in? Have you ever tried to answer them, only to discover that they were not seeking an honest answer, but just your support and affirmation? Your prayer must not be like that.

Don't just ask God so that He can agree with you and take your side. Ask God with a real willingness to be corrected, and even to be rebuked. The more honest and open you are, the more gracious and polite He can afford to be. However, if you don't approach it that way then you leave God with only two options:

a) to leave you in ignorance and self-delusion or

b) to get some other person to speak to you. However, they are not going to be anywhere near as gracious as God would be in the way they tell you about your faults.

Though you may not realise it at the time, if you are in a position where you are not listening to God, then it is much better for you if He chooses option (b) above. Therefore He will make sure to send people into your life who will tackle you and tell you the truth about yourself. It was a revelation to me when I began to realise that such people, though they didn't know it, were all working for God. They were giving me some very blunt messages that I needed to hear.

As I look back at over 34 years as a Christian, I can see many such people whom God clearly sent my way to point out my faults and failings. God often uses bosses for this. They are one of His favourite types of 'sub-contractor' or 'agent' that He engages to do such tasks for Him. God uses our bosses to correct us because they have the right, and the need, to tackle us. It is also because we are obliged to listen to them and cannot ignore them.

God will also use older Christians, and parents, even non-Christian parents. We need to become willing and even eager to listen to all such people. In fact we need to go to them and seek out their honest views and to reassure them that we really do *want* them to be frank. You need to emphasize that. If not, people will tend to go easy on you, for fear of causing offence.

So, go looking for constructive feedback and criticism. Ask for it. Then it makes it so much easier for God's 'messengers' to speak the truth to you. As well as that, go straight to God and ask Him to speak to you directly, not just through other people. If you ask for that He will correct you in all sorts of ways that are far easier to take than being corrected or rebuked by others. God will speak to you through:

a) the Bible - as you read it certain passages or words will 'leap out at you'. Some character in the Bible will be acting in a certain way and the Holy Spirit will whisper the thought into your head "*He's making the same mistake you make*" or "*His attitude is wrong, but so is yours*".

b) other people saying things in passing - even where they aren't speaking directly to you. God will cause certain words or phrases to resonate with you. It could be something in a book or on the TV or radio. God will make it go 'fluorescent' or somehow make it resonate in your mind as being applicable to you.

c) speaking directly into your mind or your spirit - this is similar to what has been said above. You may be just getting on with your work when God will plant a thought in your mind. It will contain some truth about you, your motives, or your shortcomings.

Whenever God chooses to speak to you, and whatever method He uses, the crucial thing is to be open to it. Don't brush Him aside or forget what He says. Be teachable and willing to listen. He will then speak to you more clearly and more often. However, the moment you start to become willing to listen to God's voice the demons who hang around with you will seek to join in.

They too will seek to plant thoughts in your mind. The only difference is that the thoughts that they put into your head are lies. So, you'll need to learn to discern the difference between God's authentic voice and the false whisperings of demons.

That requires you to be alert to weigh up both the *tone* and *content* of whatever thought comes in to your mind. Is it constructive, wholesome, consistent with Scripture, and in line with all of God's ways and principles? If so, it will probably be God's voice. However, if it is destructive, condemning, contrary to Scripture or clashes with one or more biblical principles, then it is demonic.

Once you start to analyse your own thoughts in this way it will become progressively easier to tell the difference. It's largely common sense. For example, if someone claiming to be from your bank rang up asking you to reveal your personal PIN number, you'd quickly realise something was wrong. At least you should realise it. Some naïve people don't, and just hand over the information.

Learning the real truth about yourself is bound to be a long and uncomfortable process of discovery. Coming to terms with what sort of person you really are, "warts and all", is a vital first stage to the project of changing. That's what God is really after. It requires this rare quality of being honest with yourself, no matter where that takes you, or what it costs. Make it your aim to cooperate with God as He seeks to build that level of honesty in you.

If you'll compromise on truth what else will you compromise on?

You may think I'm over-emphasising the importance of truth and focusing on it too strongly. I don't think so. It is at the centre and it holds everything together. That's why apostle Paul, in Ephesians chapter 6, refers to the *"belt of truth"*. It holds all the rest of our 'armour' in place:

[10]Finally, be strong in the Lord and in his mighty power. [11]Put on the full armour of God, so that you can take your stand against the devil's schemes. [12]For our struggle is not against flesh and blood, but against the rulers, against

the authorities, against the powers of this dark world and against the spiritual forces of evil in the heavenly realms. [13]Therefore put on the full armour of God, so that when the day of evil comes, you may be able to stand your ground, and after you have done everything, to stand.

[14]Stand firm then, with the belt of truth buckled around your waist, with the breastplate of righteousness in place, [15]and with your feet fitted with the readiness that comes from the gospel of peace. [16]In addition to all this, take up the shield of faith, with which you can extinguish all the flaming arrows of the evil one. [17]Take the helmet of salvation and the sword of the Spirit, which is the word of God. [18]And pray in the Spirit on all occasions with all kinds of prayers and requests. With this in mind, be alert and always keep on praying for all the Lord's people.

Ephesians 6:10-18 (NIV)

A soldier's belt holds together all the rest of the kit that he wears and also provides a place to which he can attach ammunition and other equipment that he carries. It keeps it all in place. Likewise, truth, if we really love it and value it, will hold all the other parts of our lives together and keep us on the right path. If instead we are casual about truth, and willing to compromise on it, then every other part of our lives will become distorted and fall apart.

CHAPTER 11

THE COMPLICATIONS THAT ARISE WHEN WE TELL THE TRUTH, AND A LOOK AT SOME EXCEPTIONAL SITUATIONS WHERE WE COULD LIE

[1]Truly God is good to the upright, to those who are pure in heart.
Psalm 73:1 (RSV)

The sum of thy word is truth;
and every one of thy righteous ordinances endures forever.
Psalm 119:160 (RSV)

[2]Blessed is the man to whom the LORD imputes no iniquity,
and in whose spirit there is no deceit.
Psalm 32:2(RSV)

[9]"The heart is more deceitful than all else and is desperately sick; who can understand it?
Jeremiah 17:9 (NASB)

Then the LORD said to me, "The prophets are prophesying falsehood in My name. I have neither sent them nor commanded them nor spoken to them; they are prophesying to you a false vision, divination, futility and the deception of their own minds
John 14:6 (NASB)

[9]The coming of the lawless one is by the activity of Satan with all power and false signs and wonders, [10]and with all wicked deception for those who are perishing, because they refused to love the truth and so be saved. [11]Therefore God sends them a strong delusion, so that they may believe what is false, [12]in order that all may be condemned who did not believe the truth but had pleasure in unrighteousness.
2 Thessalonians 2:9-12 (ESV)

Are there ever any exceptions when it's OK to lie?

This is the sort of question which few people ever ask themselves. It only arises if you love the truth so strongly that the question of exactly how truthful we are meant to be starts to become an issue. The average person never feels the need to ask this question. He lies, exaggerates or compromises, whenever it is necessary in order to protect himself or his own interests. It's just not a problem in his view. However, if you are truly serious about committing yourself always to tell the truth, then extreme or complex situations will arise from time to time which really test you to the limit.

Sometimes situations arise for me where I suspect that even the prophet Daniel might wonder what to do for the best. Having said that, there can be certain extremely unusual circumstances where telling a deliberate lie can become the right thing to do. Admittedly, it is very rare indeed. Nevertheless, there are some examples of this in the Bible which we ought to examine, for completeness, so that we have looked at honesty from every angle.

The lie told to Pharoah by the Egyptian midwives to save the lives of Israelite boys

We read in the book of Exodus of how the Israelites went to Egypt at the time of Joseph. They were welcomed by the Pharoah of that time. However, four centuries later they had grown into a nation of about two million people and the Pharoah of that time was very hostile to them. Therefore he even gave orders that any boys born to Israelite women were to be killed. He ordered the Egyptian midwives to put them to death deliberately and only to allow baby girls to live:

[15] Then the king of Egypt spoke to the Hebrew midwives, one of whom was named Shiphrah and the other was named Puah; [16] and he said, "When you are helping the Hebrew women to give birth and see them upon the birthstool, if it is a son, then you shall put him to death; but if it is a daughter, then she shall live."

Exodus 1:15-16 (NASB)

No doubt some midwives carried out these orders. However, these two particular midwives, Shiphrah and Puah, refused to do what Pharoah had ordered. It was impossible for them to openly oppose Pharoah or to refuse his orders. So, they lied to him and told him that the Israelite women gave birth so quickly that the boys were born before they could get to them. The clear implication is that that was not true. It was only said to mislead Pharoah and to obstruct his wicked plans:

[17] But the midwives feared God, and did not do as the king of Egypt had commanded them, but let the boys live. [18] So the king of Egypt called for the midwives and said to them, "Why have you done this thing, and let the boys live?" [19] The midwives said to Pharoah, "Because the Hebrew women are not as the Egyptian women; for they are vigorous and give birth before the midwife can get to them." [20] So God was good to the midwives, and the people multiplied, and became very mighty. [21] Because the midwives feared God, He established households for them.

Exodus 1:17-21(NASB)

Some have argued that perhaps what the midwives said was true and that the boys were saved purely because the Israelite women gave birth quicker than Egyptians women. However, that cannot be the case. Firstly, it is inherently unlikely. Secondly, there would be no need for God to reward any of the midwives if this was the explanation.

They would have done nothing to reward. Therefore we are faced with the inescapable fact that God is praising and rewarding the actions of these Egyptian midwives. When faced with the choice of killing Israelite babies or lying to Pharoah, they chose to lie.

Misleading Pharoah was the only way that they could have saved those children. If they had told the truth, then the Israelite baby boys would have had to die. In that context, when dealing with questions from a wicked man, and where the lives of children were at stake, God evidently deemed it right and proper for those midwives to lie to Pharoah. That creates an ethical and theological complication, but it is one that we cannot get away from. It is plainly there in the Scriptures. Moreover, it is not the only example:

The lie told by Jehu in order to trick the followers of Baal so that he could destroy them

There was a King of the Northern Kingdom of Israel called Ahab who was exceptionally wicked. He also had a remarkably wicked wife called Jezebel. Between them they dragged Israel down to their level and led the people into sin and idolatry on a huge scale. Under Ahab's reign, Baal worship flourished and expanded rapidly. Therefore God declared through the prophet Elijah that He would destroy the whole house and lineage of King Ahab.

Elijah's grim prophecy was all fulfilled in due course. In particular, let us look at what was done by a man called Jehu. He was actually anointed on the instructions of the prophet Elisha to be the next King of Israel, precisely in order that he could wipe out the whole family line of Ahab and all that he stood for:

⁴ So the young man, the servant of the prophet, went to Ramoth-gilead. ⁵ And when he came, behold, the commanders of the army were in council. And he said, "I have a word for you, O commander." And Jehu said, "To which of us all?" And he said, "To you, O commander." ⁶ So he arose and went into the house. And the young man poured the oil on his head, saying to him, "Thus says the LORD, the God of Israel, I anoint you king over the people of the LORD, over Israel. ⁷ And you shall strike down the house of Ahab your master, so that I may avenge on Jezebel the blood of my servants the prophets, and the blood of all the servants of the LORD. ⁸ For the whole house of Ahab shall perish, and I will cut off from Ahab every male, bond or free, in Israel. ⁹ And I will make the house of Ahab like the house of Jeroboam the son of Nebat, and like the house of Baasha the son of Ahijah.

2 Kings 9:4-9 (ESV)

Jehu then proceeded to wipe out every member of Ahab's family, so that none of them could ever claim the throne of Israel again. That sets the context and brings us to the main point I am making, which is that Jehu then set about wiping out all of the followers of Baal. They were occultic and idolatrous and had led many of the people to forsake God and worship Baal.

In the process of doing this Jehu told a lie in order to trick the followers of Baal so that he could gather them all into one place and destroy them. He did it by pretending to be a follower of Baal himself. He commanded all the priests and other followers of Baal to gather in one place and declared that he would be an even bigger follower of Baal than King Ahab had been:

[18] Then Jehu assembled all the people and said to them, "Ahab served Baal a little, but Jehu will serve him much. [19] Now therefore call to me all the prophets of Baal, all his worshipers and all his priests. Let none be missing, for I have a great sacrifice to offer to Baal. Whoever is missing shall not live." But Jehu did it with cunning in order to destroy the worshipers of Baal. [20] And Jehu ordered, "Sanctify a solemn assembly for Baal." So they proclaimed it. [21] And Jehu sent throughout all Israel, and all the worshipers of Baal came, so that there was not a man left who did not come. And they entered the house of Baal, and the house of Baal was filled from one end to the other. [22] He said to him who was in charge of the wardrobe, "Bring out the vestments for all the worshipers of Baal." So he brought out the vestments for them. [23] Then Jehu went into the house of Baal with Jehonadab the son of Rechab, and he said to the worshipers of Baal, "Search, and see that there is no servant of the LORD here among you, but only the worshipers of Baal." [24] Then they went in to offer sacrifices and burnt offerings.

Now Jehu had stationed eighty men outside and said, "The man who allows any of those whom I give into your hands to escape shall forfeit his life." [25] So as soon as he had made an end of offering the burnt offering, Jehu said to the guard and to the officers, "Go in and strike them down; let not a man escape." So when they put them to the sword, the guard and the officers cast them out and went into the inner room of the house of Baal, [26] and they brought out the pillar that was in the house of Baal and burned it. [27] And they demolished the pillar of Baal, and demolished the house of Baal, and made it a latrine to this day.

2 Kings 10:18-27 (ESV)

So, Jehu told a direct lie in order to lure the followers of Baal into his trap. He said it while intending to do the very opposite. It is clear that God approved of

Jehu's actions. At any rate, God rewarded Jehu and said nothing to indicate that He did not approve of the lie:

And the LORD said to Jehu, "Because you have done well in carrying out what is right in my eyes, and have done to the house of Ahab according to all that was in my heart, your sons of the fourth generation shall sit on the throne of Israel."

2 Kings 10:30 (ESV)

Let us now consider how God viewed Jehu's lie and why God did not disapprove of him for telling it:

a) Jehu had been anointed as King of God's people, Israel, i.e. the Northern Kingdom. It was therefore his duty to do God's will and to fight against God's enemies.

b) The followers of Baal were God's enemies.

c) Jehu was commanded to make war against the whole house of Ahab and to wipe out his line and try to reverse the harm that Ahab had caused. This necessarily involved wiping out the followers of Baal. They were like cancer cells within the nation of Israel.

d) The only way to destroy them was to lure them into a trap. That could only be done by deceiving them, because they would never come willingly to be destroyed.

e) In short, Jehu was waging war on God's behalf. Therefore it was legitimate to tell a lie in the pursuit of a war objective.

So, it was legitimate, on that very specific occasion, for Jehu to deceive the followers of Baal. But that does not provide any general authorisation to us to tell lies, not even if done in order to pursue God's objectives. If we could do so at all, it would only be if we were in equally exceptional circumstances. Let us now consider another unusual example:

Rahab of Jericho telling a lie about where the Jewish spies were hiding

Rahab (the harlot) lived in Jericho at the time when the Israelites were leaving the wilderness and entering into the land of Canaan to take possession of it. Their leader, Joshua, sent two spies ahead to the city of Jericho, to do reconnaissance and bring back information. Rahab was not an Israelite. She was a Canaanite.

However, she knew that God was going to destroy Jericho and give the land to His people, the Israelites. So she chose to cooperate with God. She therefore

231

sheltered the two spies in her house and told a lie to the men of Jericho (Canaanites) who were searching for them. She said they had left earlier, which was not true:

¹Then Joshua the son of Nun sent two men as spies secretly from Shittim, saying, "Go, view the land, especially Jericho " So they went and came into the house of a harlot whose name was Rahab, and lodged there. ²It was told the king of Jericho, saying, "Behold, men from the sons of Israel have come here tonight to search out the land." ³And the king of Jericho sent word to Rahab, saying, "Bring out the men who have come to you, who have entered your house, for they have come to search out all the land." ⁴But the woman had taken the two men and hidden them, and she said, "Yes, the men came to me, but I did not know where they were from. ⁵"It came about when it was time to shut the gate at dark, that the men went out; I do not know where the men went. Pursue them quickly, for you will overtake them." ⁶But she had brought them up to the roof and hidden them in the stalks of flax which she had laid in order on the roof. ⁷So the men pursued them on the road to the Jordan to the fords; and as soon as those who were pursuing them had gone out, they shut the gate.
Joshua 2:1-7 (NASB)

Rahab's motives for telling that lie are set out later in Joshua chapter two:

⁸Now before they lay down, she came up to them on the roof,
⁹and said to the men, "I know that the LORD has given you the land, and that the terror of you has fallen on us, and that all the inhabitants of the land have melted away before you.
¹⁰"For we have heard how the LORD dried up the water of the Red Sea before you when you came out of Egypt, and what you did to the two kings of the Amorites who were beyond the Jordan, to Sihon and Og, whom you utterly destroyed.
¹¹"When we heard it, our hearts melted and no courage remained in any man any longer because of you; for the LORD your God, He is God in heaven above and on earth beneath.
¹²"Now therefore, please swear to me by the LORD, since I have dealt kindly with you, that you also will deal kindly with my father's household, and give me a pledge of truth,
¹³and spare my father and my mother and my brothers and my sisters, with all who belong to them, and deliver our lives from death."
¹⁴So the men said to her, "Our life for yours if you do not tell this business of ours; and it shall come about when the LORD gives us the land that we will deal kindly and faithfully with you."
¹⁵Then she let them down by a rope through the window, for her house was on the city wall, so that she was living on the wall.
Joshua 2:8-15 (NASB)

So, a promise was made to Rahab that in return for her help (the lie she told) and for continuing to keep the secret, the invading Israelite army would not harm Rahab or her family,. They agreed not to attack anybody within Rahab's house. She was told to hang out a scarlet cord to identify where she and her relatives lived.

However, note what God then does and how He deals with Rahab. Far from punishing her, He rewards and protects her when the city is destroyed. God told Joshua to march around the city walls for seven days, at the end of which God promised to cause the walls of the city to collapse:

⁴"Also seven priests shall carry seven trumpets of rams' horns before the ark; then on the seventh day you shall march around the city seven times, and the priests shall blow the trumpets. ⁵"It shall be that when they make a long blast with the ram's horn, and when you hear the sound of the trumpet, all the people shall shout with a great shout; and the wall of the city will fall down flat, and the people will go up every man straight ahead."

Joshua 6:4-5 (NASB)

The Israelites did as God said and He knocked down the entire walls of the city, except for one short stretch of wall in which Rahab's house was built. People used to have houses actually on and within the city walls.

¹⁵Then she let them down by a rope through the window, for her house was on the city wall, so that she was living on the wall.

Joshua 2:15 (NASB)

²²Joshua said to the two men who had spied out the land, "Go into the harlot's house and bring the woman and all she has out of there, as you have sworn to her." ²³So the young men who were spies went in and brought out Rahab and her father and her mother and her brothers and all she had; they also brought out all her relatives and placed them outside the camp of Israel. ²⁴They burned the city with fire, and all that was in it. Only the silver and gold, and articles of bronze and iron, they put into the treasury of the house of the LORD. ²⁵However, Rahab the harlot and her father's household and all she had, Joshua spared; and she has lived in the midst of Israel to this day, for she hid the messengers whom Joshua sent to spy out Jericho.

Joshua 6:22-25 (NASB)

The old city wall of Jericho is completely destroyed, right down to the base, for its entire length, except for one small section where part of the lower section of the wall still remains. That was where Rahab lived. The point is that it was God who destroyed that wall and it was God who preserved the part of the wall which Rahab lived in. But why would God do that to reward a woman even though she had told a lie?

233

Indeed, we have to go further than that and face the fact that He was rewarding her *because* she had told a lie to protect the Israelite spies. It doesn't even end there. Look at what is then said in chapter 11 of the letter to the Hebrews. It lists a 'hall of fame' of individuals whose faith was very great and who did exceptional things for God. Guess who's in there - it's Rahab:

[30]By faith the walls of Jericho fell down after they had been encircled for seven days. [31]By faith Rahab the harlot did not perish along with those who were disobedient, after she had welcomed the spies in peace.
Hebrews11:30-31(NASB)

So, not only did God reward Rahab, He even praises her actions in Hebrews Chapter 11 and describes her behaviour as 'faith'. What's the explanation? It is that Rahab faced a situation of war where God's chosen people the Israelites, were in great need and two of Joshua's best men, the spies, were in mortal danger.

If they had been caught by the search party they would have been killed. Plus, they wouldn't have been able to bring the information back to Joshua. So, it was a life or death situation for them. And, on top of that, it involved the protection of God's chosen people. In that very narrow and highly unusual context, what Rahab said and did was right. Indeed it was noble and brave.

So, again we can say that there are some extremely exceptional circumstances where to tell a direct lie is right. But we must always remember how very rare such circumstances are. So far, in my own life, I don't think I have ever come across any such circumstances.

However, God also rewarded Betsy Ten Boom for doing the very opposite of what Rehab did.

Let's look now at a similar situation where another person chose to handle it very differently from Rahab. Yet, God still honoured her for it, and came to her aid. It involves Betsy Ten Boom, the sister of Corrie Ten Boom, of the famous Dutch family. They risked their lives to shelter Jewish refugees in their home and to help them to escape from the Nazis. So, we have a roughly similar situation.

God's people, the Jews, were in danger and needed to be hidden and protected. However Betsy Ten Boom was a remarkable person. She was extraordinarily sincere and had decided, years before, that she would never tell a lie. It became for her an unbreakable principle.

One day some German soldiers came unexpectedly to the door and burst in to the house to search it, looking for Jews. There was a family of Jews hiding in a chamber under the floor. They had gone down through a trap door hidden under the table.

A German soldier asked *"Are there any Jews hidden in this house?"* Betsy Ten Boom had no time to think, or even to pray, about what to do. So, she just acted on instinct, in accordance with the ingrained habits she had built up over many years. She blurted out *"Yes, they are hiding underneath the table"*.

I don't think God wanted Betsy to say that. She didn't need to say it. She had no duty to say it. Indeed, the Germans had no right even to be there, let alone to ask that question. Moreover, their purpose in asking it was abominable. They were seeking to kill God's people, the Jews, which is the very reason why the Ten Boom family were hiding them. So, Betsy's family were horrified at what she had just said.

However, God's heart was evidently touched by Betsy's sincerity. So He honoured it, and her, and intervened. God must have planted a thought into the German soldier's mind, because he immediately got the wrong end of the stick. He assumed Betsy was making fun of him and that she couldn't possibly have meant what she had just said.

He mistakenly took it as sarcasm, which is the exact opposite of what it actually was. He therefore became red-faced. He felt that if he looked under the table everybody would laugh at him. So, he turned and left the room. The Germans then searched the whole of the rest of the house, i.e. everywhere *except* under the table, but they found nothing.

It all ended happily. That group of Jews who had been under the table all survived the war. God preserved all their lives. In part, I expect He did so in honour of what Betsy had just done, due to the strength and sincerity of her conviction. God covered up for Betsy and saved her, and the Jews, from the consequences of her own honesty.

However, we must face the fact that He will not always do so. As we have seen, there is often a heavy price to pay for being truthful. But He did intervene on that occasion. Thus we have two very similar situations handled in totally opposite ways by two women, Rahab and Betsy Ten Boom. Yet God honoured both of them.

What about using deception in a war?

Ever since God established the separate nations of the earth, at the time of the Tower of Babel, nations have gone to war with each other. Sometimes they have been justified in doing so, at least the non-aggressor, which is defending itself. In warfare soldiers kill each other. Since the twentieth century, they also kill civilians.

You will have your own view of this, but mine is that warfare can be justified in certain circumstances. That means that killing can be justified, where it is essential in pursuit of a legitimate war. If that is so, then it must follow that one is also entitled to use deception as a weapon of war, i.e. to trick and mislead the enemy so that its performance is impaired.

Such deception may save the lives of your own men. It may also cost the lives of the enemy's men. However, it would be justified, in my view, provided that the war itself is justified. So, to reduce it to a phrase we could say that if you're morally entitled to kill a man, then you may be entitled to lie to him. Thus we have another exception where we may be entitled to tell a lie.

An example of this would be where the Allies sought to trick Hitler into believing that the invasion of France would come at Calais. In fact it came at Normandy. That process of deception saved many lives. Hitler insisted on keeping a number of German Panzer divisions tied down at Calais, even after the Normandy invasion had begun, because he was so convinced by our elaborate deceptions.

These involved fake tanks, aircraft and other military equipment being stockpiled near Dover and fake radio messages being broadcast by fake divisions which did not even exist. It was all done so that the Germans would think that the real invasion would come at Calais.

The problems caused for those who have 'scruples' - is it possible to be too honest?

Is it ever possible to be too honest? Sometimes it is, in a certain sense. Problems can arise for honest people which are the result of inexperience, lack of wisdom and the inability to handle delicate, finely balanced situations. We can find that both honesty and wisdom are needed in combination, but that we have only got honesty, not wisdom.

This problem affects very few people, because not many are honest enough for their honesty to become their problem. Usually it's the other way round. However, there is a small minority of people who spend a lot of their time and energy fretting over what they can and can't say and do, i.e. in terms of truthfulness.

This problem is called '*scruples*'. It means the burden borne, and the problems experienced, by those people who think very deeply about their duty to be truthful. For them lying is not an option. However, such people still have to manage to get through their lives as best they can without upsetting people, causing turmoil, betraying secrets and mishandling fiduciary responsibilities.

Achieving all of those objectives is far from easy. One of Mrs. Thatcher's cabinet ministers was a man called Sir Keith Joseph. He struggled a great deal with questions of conscience. He used to go back and forth in his mind, questioning himself about the rights and wrongs of his proposed actions and whether they could be justified ethically. Such things mattered to him enormously and he was tormented by it all.

In fact, many feel that he would have become leader of the Conservative Party in 1975, rather than Margaret Thatcher, had it not been for the way he agonized over the ethics of the decisions he had to take and the duties he had to fulfil. He suffered in ways which 99% of other politicians never did because his conscience was so highly developed and so important to him.

I sympathized with Sir Keith Joseph because I too have often struggled to know how to handle complex situations where I don't feel comfortable in my conscience with *any* of the options available to me. In some ways I have envied those who did not share my problem with scruples. I have known many people who found it easy to brush aside such concerns, without any difficulty, let alone torment. Yet, I would still not choose to be otherwise.

Such difficult pressure points are one of the inevitable side effects of having the quality called the love of the truth. At least they are until you reach a very high level of wisdom and maturity, which I haven't yet managed to arrive at. However, it is far better to have the love of the truth, and therefore to face these difficulties, than to be without these problems, but not have the love of the truth. In other words, it is a price worth paying.

When your heart is more honest than your head is wise.

The more you love the truth, the more of a problem this issue of scruples can become. The essence of the problem is that you have a heart which is currently more honest than your head is wise. That has been my problem on many occasions. God has put me into many situations as a police officer, and then as a solicitor and supervisor of other solicitors, where my integrity was more advanced than my wisdom.

There is a mismatch, like where one muscle is bigger than its counterpart. You know you have to be totally honest, and you have committed yourself to be so. But you aren't yet sufficiently mature, wise or discerning to know how to achieve this without getting into excruciatingly tight corners, of the kind that the prophet Daniel would have been able to see coming and avoid.

"Be not righteous over much" - the day when I was corrected by Inspector Bell

When I was in my first year as a police officer I struggled with knowing how to be a Christian in an overwhelmingly non-Christian workplace. Sometimes I behaved too rigidly and legalistically. I was so afraid of doing something dishonest that I didn't allow myself to go anywhere near doing so. That meant I was sometimes overly strict and inflexible with myself, in ways that a wiser person would have avoided.

For example, on one occasion I just needed to photocopy one sheet of paper for private use but I felt unable to use the photocopier at the police station. Therefore, when the shift ended, I walked all the way into town to copy it at the post office instead. On reflection, I don't think I needed to be quite as rigid as I was. I could have just asked and used the Police Station photocopier. That would not have been wrong, for just one sheet, if permission was given.

However, I didn't feel at the time that even the Inspector could validly give me such permission, given that it wasn't his own paper or copier. I would be less rigid today and would accept that an Inspector had got the authority to permit me to do something like that. That was the sort of stance I took on that and various other issues.

One day a senior officer called Inspector Bell corrected me. He wasn't on my shift and so I only knew him at a distance. I assumed that I knew more than him about the Bible and that he wouldn't understand the issues I was facing. However, on one occasion some ethical situation arose and he took me completely by surprise when he suddenly quoted the Bible to me, from the book of Ecclesiastes. He said:

"Be not righteous over much; neither make thyself over wise: why shouldest thou destroy thyself?"
Ecclesiastes 7:16 (KJV)

It was a word in season for me. His quoting of that verse helped me to realise that even in things which are as profoundly important as honesty, truth and righteousness, it is possible to 'go over the top' and to become unbalanced and unwise.

At what point does the quality of the love of the truth turn into the error of excessive scruples?

As we have seen, the essence of the problem of scruples is that you have a highly developed sense of the importance of honesty in all things at all times, but you don't yet have the wisdom and discernment to know how to handle every tight

238

corner. Jesus always made things look so easy. When He was put on the spot by an awkward question He always had a brilliantly inspired answer to give.

It stopped people in their tracks and got Him off the hook. That ability would be marvellous to have and would make life so much easier. But what are we meant to do if we *don't have* a brilliant mind, which can think at the speed of light and instantly come up with the perfect reply or solution?

It is not too difficult to handle extreme 'black and white' situations, where it is very clear that something is, or is not, dishonest. But what about the issues which are much more finely balanced? For example, what about telling the truth where it would mean betraying a confidence, or causing collateral damage to an innocent third party?

In such situations it is as if one is called upon to distinguish between light grey and pale grey, rather than black and white. The reality is that we can only learn to distinguish light grey from pale grey by:

a) studying the Bible thoroughly, and over many years, until you have a very good knowledge of God's ways and principles

b) praying to God regularly for His guidance on difficult points

c) being determined always to do what is right, and to pay the price if necessary, rather than just do whatever is expedient or easy

d) being willing to risk making mistakes, and to learn from them, over a long period of time

e) being determined always to obey your conscience, even in the early years, when your wisdom is too small and undeveloped to enable you to avoid these difficulties

If the truth really matters to you, and if you are willing to persist for long enough, and to learn from your mistakes, then God will eventually give you a much higher level of discernment. Then you will know how to handle very finely balanced ethical issues, which were previously way beyond you.

Be truthful in your use of the Bible and see every verse in its entire context. Refuse to twist any verse to suit your own purposes or interests

When we read the Bible, and especially if we teach it to others, we are under a solemn duty to be careful and truthful in the way we interpret its meaning. That means that we need to read every verse in its full and proper context and refuse to twist any verse to suit our own purposes. Instead of adjusting the meaning of a verse to suit our opinions we need to change our opinions to get into line with what the Bible says. This may sound obvious, but it is not what many of us do.

We take liberties with the Bible and ignore what we see on the page. We also read things into a verse which aren't there, so as to get the Bible to fit in with our opinions and traditions. That is wrong. Every Christian must show the utmost reverence towards God's Word. That includes taking great care to find its *real* meaning, rather than imposing on it a meaning of our own making, which is more to our liking.

Every verse of the Bible needs to be interpreted in accordance with what the whole of the rest of the Bible says. Therefore if you are taught that a verse has a particular meaning, but that meaning is contradicted by some other passage, then what you have been taught cannot be the correct interpretation. The Bible is fully consistent with itself. That is why the proper context for any verse is the whole of the rest of the Bible.

That puts you under a duty to know the whole Bible and to be vigilant to check everything that you are taught to make sure that it is biblical. That means that it is consistent with what the rest of the Bible says. As we shall see in Book Three, every verse of the Bible is true, but only the whole Bible, i.e. the sum of God's Word, is the truth:

The sum of thy word is truth;
and every one of thy righteous ordinances endures forever.
Psalm 119:160 (RSV)

Therefore you need to study all of the Bible to be able to say that you have got the whole truth. The responsibility is on you to make sure you get that. So, being a disciple involves accepting the challenge of seeking to become familiar with the whole Bible. Without that you will always be at risk of being deceived or mistaken about the meaning of any particular passage.

People twist the Bible's meaning for a variety of reasons, but if you have the love of the truth you will be vigilant to resist that. You will always want to know the real and true meaning, even if that contradicts your own opinions, or your denominational traditions, and even if it requires you to admit that you were wrong previously.

That last point is the hardest for many people. There is a pride in us which hates the idea of having to admit that the way we have always interpreted a passage, or the belief we have held about a particular doctrine, was wrong. People feel that such an admission would diminish them in the eyes of others and they are not willing to risk that. As a result, many of us stubbornly hold onto a wrong belief, or refuse even to consider an alternative belief, simply because to do so could involve loss of face.

This is a particular problem for many church leaders. It means that they are deliberately, or at least negligently, holding onto error and rejecting truth merely for the sake of maintaining their own image and prestige. Imagine how seriously God views that kind of failure to love the truth and how He will judge it.

How to develop the love of the truth and strengthen your conscience

We have spoken of the vital importance of having the love of the truth. But what if you don't yet have it, or if you only have it to a limited extent? The answer is that it can be developed or grown. That's because the love of the truth is a character quality. It's not an attribute that you inherit genetically from your parents, like being tall or having blue eyes or blond hair.

Those are features that you can't do anything about. You either have them or you don't. They can't be developed and you can't just decide to have those things. That's the crucial difference - you can decide to develop the love of the truth. It is entirely a matter of choice and depends on your own free will.

So that's the good news - everybody is capable of developing the love of the truth, if they want it. But that's the problem. Most people don't want it. At any rate, it doesn't matter much to them, if indeed it matters at all. Therefore they certainly aren't willing to pay what it costs to develop it.

That brings us to the bad news, which is that there is a cost involved for those who love the truth. Moreover, it can be a very high one in terms of inconvenience, trouble, financial loss and even danger. Those are the disadvantages which you will have to accept if you want to have the love of the truth. There's no point thinking otherwise, because it's a fact. Being genuinely honest will cost you.

However, the advantages and benefits that come from having the love of the truth, are infinitely larger. Moreover, they are eternal, whereas the costs and downsides are only temporary. Therefore, any wise person will choose to develop the love of the truth, no matter what it may cost them in the short term.

Let's now turn to how this character quality of the love of the truth can be developed. That is what practical steps do you need to take to develop the love of the truth, or to increase it, if you know that you need more of it? I will list a number of steps and then try to explain how to take them:

1. Recognise your need for the love of the truth, or for more of it, and for a stronger, better-informed conscience.

2. Make a decision of your will that you are going to seek for both of these and that you will do so with all your heart and strength, not just mildly.

241

3. Pray and ask God to help you to develop these, whilst recognizing that He will not do it all for you. It is primarily your choice to develop them, though His help is crucial. Moreover, His help must be sought persistently, not just as a one-off prayer.

4. Study the subject of judgment and learn all you can about it from the Bible, in particular the Judgment Seat of Christ, which is for saved Christians.

5. Ask God to make the prospect of judgment more real to you, so that it stops being mere theory and becomes something tangible, which is frequently on your mind.

6. Ask God to give you the fear of the LORD, and in large measure.

7. Do a Bible study on the fear of the LORD.

8. Resolve to tell no more lies at all, to anybody, anywhere.

9. If you do ever tell a lie, by lapsing back into the habit, then correct it immediately, every time. The embarrassment of doing so will help to prevent you lying again.

10. Resolve not to exaggerate.

11. Likewise, if you ever do exaggerate, then correct yourself, there and then, in front of people. The discomfort of doing that will put you off repeating it and will help to cure the habit.

12. Also, whenever you tell a lie, however small, confess it to God and repent. Take it very seriously.

13. Ask God to strengthen your conscience and to speak to you more clearly and more often.

14. Listen to your conscience every time, no matter how small the issue may seem, or how much it costs. The more you respond on each occasion, the louder your conscience will become when subsequent issues arise, and vice versa.

15. Help your conscience to become more informed by reading the whole Bible, over and over again, in daily readings and also by more intensive Bible study. This will greatly sharpen your sensitivity as to right and wrong.

If you will do all these things, and keep on doing them, you will assuredly change. God will respond and fully keep His side of the 'bargain', provided He sees that you are taking seriously the need to become truthful. The effort must come from you, but God's heart will be touched, and He will help you, if He sees that you really mean business and are determined to change.

CHAPTER 12

WHAT IS REALLY MEANT BY FORGIVING OTHERS AND WHAT DOES IT INVOLVE?

[12] There is only one lawgiver and judge, he who is able to save and to destroy. But who are you to judge your neighbor?

James 4:12 (ESV)

[11] 'Give us this day our daily bread.
[12] 'And forgive us our debts, as we also have forgiven our debtors.

Matthew 6:11-12 (NASB)

Anyone who hates his brother is a murderer, and you know that no murderer has eternal life abiding in him.

1 John 3:15 (RSV)

Do not say, "I will do to him as he has done to me;
I will pay the man back for what he has done."

Proverbs 24:29 (RSV)

The duty to forgive people rather than judge them – first of all we have to realise that we are not authorised to judge anybody

We can see from the above passages that we are commanded not to judge other people. Instead, we are told to forgive them, and that very serious consequences will follow if we don't. In short, God will not forgive us unless we are willing to forgive others. That puts a heavy duty upon us in what can frequently be a difficult and painful area.

In particular, it also makes it essential that we know exactly what forgiveness is. Then we can make sure that what we do meets the biblical definition of forgiveness and that we are not missing the mark, either by doing too little, or trying to do too much.

Some people set the bar too low and therefore assume that they are being forgiving when, in fact, they aren't. Probably a larger number make the opposite error and set the bar too high. Then they assume that forgiveness is far too hard for them to achieve. In fact, they are trying to do more than merely 'forgiving' the other person and are going farther than the Bible actually requires of us.

Therefore, in this chapter, we will examine the vital link between *not judging* people and *forgiving* them. These two commands go together and need to be understood as a combined package. We will also look at exactly what forgiveness is, how it works, why it matters, and how to actually forgive people, and avoid bitterness, in practical terms.

We shall also look carefully at what forgiveness *isn't* and what it *doesn't* involve. We need to do this because forgiving others is such a badly misunderstood subject. It gets mixed up with, or mistaken for, many other things which are closely related to forgiveness, but are actually separate and distinct.

For many years, I personally found it hard to define forgiveness, i.e. to know exactly what was being required of me. I was not helped by any of the preaching I ever heard in any church. If anything, the few sermons that I did hear on forgiveness tended to add to the confusion. They also promoted a general feeling of failure and that forgiveness of others is too difficult for most of us to achieve.

When people come to the conclusion that forgiveness is too difficult, or even impossible, it is often because they are wrongly defining it. In particular, they are probably including within its definition some or all of these other things, such as mercy, grace, reconciliation and the resumption of trust and friendship.

Admittedly, they are all linked to forgiveness, and often accompany it, but they go beyond forgiveness and are not part of its basic definition. So, when a person says, *"I have tried to forgive, but it's impossible. I just can't do it"*, the chances are that what they really mean is that they can't be *reconciled* with the wrongdoer.

Or, they may mean that they can no longer *trust* the wrongdoer, or that they still feel *violated* or *angry* or *hurt*. But the point is that a person can validly and genuinely forgive a wrongdoer and yet still continue to feel any or all of the following things:

a)   hurt and emotionally upset

b)   wounded, violated or traumatized

c)   anger (which must not be confused with holding a grudge or feeling bitterness or rage – see below)

d)   distrustful and wary

e)   unreconciled and unwilling even to attempt reconciliation, at least for the time being

f)   unable to relate to the wrongdoer or to have fellowship with them or work alongside them

g) unwilling to give them another chance, at least for now, for fear that they will do it again

Many people have been put under condemnation by misinformed preachers, or have made themselves feel condemned, for being unable or unwilling to forgive. Yet the real issue is often their inability or unwillingness to do something else, which is not actually a part of the definition of forgiveness at all.

So, when people speak of forgiveness, or even when the Bible speaks of it, we always need to ask what the context is and work out exactly what is being referred to, or required of us. Sometimes what is meant is just the narrowest, most basic definition of forgiveness. Then again, at other times, it may be that what is being spoken of is the same basic forgiveness plus some other related concept(s) alongside it, or together with it.

We therefore need to be able to identify, at any given time, exactly what the Bible is referring to, or commanding us to do. Then we can be clear as to what we must do, so that we do not attempt to do more than is required of us in the circumstances we face.

The narrowest, most basic definition of forgiveness – to 'recuse yourself', as a Judge does when he feels he is the wrong person to try a case.

If you want to buy a car, you are well aware that you can get them at varying levels of specification, even for the same model. You can have a car which is at the bottom of the manufacturer's range and is not much more than a chassis with wheels and an engine. Or, you can have the same model, but at the top of the range, with various extras such as air conditioning, alloy wheels, satellite navigation, leather seats etc.

They are both a car. Indeed, they may even be the same model of car, but one is basic and the other has a number of extra features. It is a little bit like that when we speak of forgiveness. In one situation we might mean basic forgiveness, at its narrowest definition. On another occasion we might mean an enlarged or wider definition, with extra features included.

Our starting place, therefore, is to try to identify the narrowest, most basic, definition of forgiveness, when it is looked at without any added features. I would say that at its lowest and simplest level, forgiveness essentially means that we *'step aside'* and *'hand the person over to Jesus'*.

That is we *leave their judgment to Him*, so that He can judge them, and possibly even punish them, instead of us seeking to do any of that to them ourselves, which we are neither qualified, nor authorized, to do.

247

When writing this chapter I asked God to help me to explain the connection between the command not to judge others and the command to forgive people. I also asked for help in explaining this process of 'stepping aside' and 'handing over' to Jesus the judgment of someone who has wronged us.

Finally, I asked Him to give me an analogy, so as to make clear exactly how it all works and what is the minimum that we have to do in order to 'forgive'. I believe He gave me one and that it may be helpful. The analogy is to think of a judge who realises that he is not the right person to hear a particular case.

It could be because, for example, the defendant is a personal friend or even an enemy. Or, he could be a neighbour or colleague or a relative of his. That judge therefore realises that he cannot give that defendant a fair trial, or that it would be unsafe, or even corrupt, for him to try to involve himself in that man's case.

When a judge is in that situation he will contact the court office and ask one of the clerks to remove that defendant's case from his own list and put it onto the list of some other judge instead. When a judge does that, so as to prevent himself from hearing a case that is unsuitable for him to hear, we say that he has *'recused'* himself.

That means he has rejected himself as the judge, due to being unsuitable to handle that case. Or you could say that he has 'objected to himself' being the judge. By taking that sensible precautionary step he makes sure that he himself is not the judge of that particular case and that it is transferred to someone else, who is more suitable to deal with it.

I would suggest to you that when we are commanded to 'forgive' others, the Bible is often speaking of forgiveness in its narrowest sense. If so, then what we are being commanded to do is effectively to *'recuse ourselves'*. That is to stop seeing ourselves as the right person to judge and punish whoever it is that has wronged us.

Then we are required to hand their 'case' over to Jesus and let Him judge, and perhaps punish, the wrongdoer while we play no further part in any of it. Most of the time, unless the context, or the precise words used, indicate a wider or larger meaning, then that is all that we are being required to do. It should be a comfort to us to realise that, because when it is defined very narrowly in this way, forgiveness is exclusively a decision of the will and thus much easier to achieve.

At its most basic level, forgiveness is purely a decision of the will, not an emotion or feeling

Indeed, basic forgiveness, without the involvement of any other added features, is achievable by all of us, and on every occasion. That is because it is a pure *decision*. It does not involve anything further or wider or deeper than simply deciding to step aside and leaving the judgment of that person to Jesus. In particular, it need not involve our emotions, over which we have no direct control. That is why God never commands us what to *feel*, but only what to *do* or *say*.

Our speech and our actions are always within our power to control and to alter, whereas our emotions and feelings aren't. Realising that one simple fact might enable you to make a breakthrough and to discover that forgiveness, at least by its narrow definition, is possible after all. Indeed, it is always possible, no matter what the circumstances are.

That said, there are some times where we see characters in the Bible going further than the basic definition of forgiveness. We see them showing mercy and grace to the wrongdoer, being reconciled to him, working together with him and re-establishing trust and close personal friendship etc. But, where such things occur, they are going beyond what we are ordinarily commanded to do. That is because there may be circumstances where God would want us to go further than basic forgiveness.

However, if He does, we need to realise that we are doing something additional, which goes beyond the narrow definition of forgiveness. If we mistakenly think that the command to forgive always includes being able to do *all* of these other things, and to their fullest extent, then we are likely to become confused and also discouraged by the size and difficulty of the task.

Therefore, the reality is that we can obey the basic command to forgive without necessarily going so far as to do any of those additional things. When you realise that, it can be tremendously liberating. You suddenly discover that you are actually capable of forgiving people, even those who have wronged you very badly, and even those who are continuing to wrong you.

So, if you find that you are not presently able to go further than basic forgiveness, i.e. recusing yourself, it is *not* necessarily a sign that you have not genuinely forgiven the wrongdoer. It could be that, in your circumstances, all that God is asking of you, at least for the moment, is basic forgiveness, without any of those other things.

Of course, it could also be that you are not genuinely forgiving the person. But we are not entitled to arrive at that conclusion based solely on the fact that you do not currently feel able to go beyond basic forgiveness. We would need to know quite a lot more about the facts of the situation in order to say whether God is requiring you to go any further than that at present and, if so, what exactly you should do.

So, the starting point for real forgiveness, as narrowly defined, is realising that you are not the one who has been appointed to judge the world. That judicial appointment has already been made. The position has been given to Jesus Christ and He will, one day, fully perform that role.

When you grasp that the judging, sentencing and punishing of other people is what Jesus alone is going to do, and that He really will do it, then you will also realise that you don't need to and, secondly, that you are not authorized to do so. It's all going to be dealt with by Him, and only by Him. Nobody else is either worthy to do it, or capable of it, whereas He is.

Moreover, you can be fully confident that He will judge every person, including the one who has wronged you. Grasping that last fact is vital, because it helps you to 'step aside' and let Jesus handle the wrongdoer's 'case'. You can be sure that the wrong done to you is not being forgotten about, or ignored, and that justice really will be done.

Furthermore, when Jesus judges people, nothing will be overlooked, mishandled or misunderstood, whereas they would be if you or I were the judge. There is therefore no need for you to bring forward the Day of Judgment for the wrongdoer by seeking to handle his case yourself now.

More importantly, it would be *wrong* for you to try to form a judgment of him, and to punish him now, before the appointed time. You are not capable of it and you have no right to attempt it. Only Jesus can properly judge the wrongdoer. We are therefore commanded to leave it all to Him and not to interfere or usurp His position:

Never take your own revenge, beloved, but leave room for the wrath of God, for it is written, "vengeance is Mine, I will repay," says the Lord.
Romans 12:19 (NASB)

There is only one lawgiver and judge, he who is able to save and to destroy. But who are you to judge your neighbor?
James 4:12 (ESV)

Let's remind ourselves that Jesus, and only Jesus, is authorised to conduct the final judgments

Let's look more closely at these final Judgments that are going to be conducted by Jesus. We know that He will judge the whole world, one at a time, and face to face. That includes the person who has wronged you. However, you need to realise that it also includes you because, so far as some other people are concerned, *you* are the wrongdoer. At least, you are *their wrongdoer*, so far as *they* can see.

Therefore you are the one that they are commanded to forgive. Holding that sobering fact in mind is very helpful. It provides us with a more balanced

250

perspective on this whole subject of forgiveness, as we begin to turn our minds to the question of how and why we should forgive the man who has wronged us.

Remember that somewhere in your neighbourhood there are people who may be trying to come to terms with their duty to forgive *you*. The more you can keep that fact in mind, the easier this issue of forgiveness will become, and the more it will make sense. At any rate, here are a few sample passages which deal with what Jesus will do when He judges us all, both Christians and non-Christians, i.e. the saved and the unsaved:

At the set time which I appoint
I will judge with equity.
Psalm 75:2 (RSV)

But thou, terrible art thou!
Who can stand before thee when once thy anger is roused?
Psalm 76:7 (RSV)

Then the trees of the forest will sing for joy before the LORD;
For He is coming to judge the earth.
1 Chronicles 16:33 (NASB)

And He will judge the world in righteousness;
He will execute judgment for the peoples with equity.
Psalm 9:8 (NASB)

Before the LORD, for He is coming,
For He is coming to judge the earth.
He will judge the world in righteousness
And the peoples in His faithfulness.
Psalm 96:13 (NASB)

³¹because He has fixed a day in which He will judge the world in righteousness through a Man whom He has appointed, having furnished proof to all men by raising Him from the dead."
Acts 17:31 (NASB)

¹⁶on the day when, according to my gospel, God will judge the secrets of men through Christ Jesus.
Romans 2:16 (NASB)

So, Jesus is the only one in the whole universe who is authorised to judge human beings. The role of Judge has been assigned to Him, and only to Him. It is not for us to do it, either now or later. Realising that is the vital starting point in considering this whole subject of avoiding judging others and engaging instead in forgiveness, i.e. *basic* forgiveness.

251

As we saw, that essentially amounts to stepping aside, or recusing ourselves, and leaving the judging to Jesus. Given all of that, you might then ask why we have courts in this world in which people get judged here and now by human judges. Are they wrong to do that? The answer is no, because any person who is appointed by the State to be a judge is actually put there by God.

A human judge, who has been officially and validly appointed, as opposed to illegitimately self-appointed, has been temporarily delegated a tiny portion of Jesus' authority to judge. So, unless of course he is corrupt, which, sadly can be the case in some countries, a human judge in a court of law is not doing anything wrong. When he does his job he is not disobeying Jesus' command not to judge others.

In fact, he is doing God's will by providing a legitimate foretaste of God's justice and punishment where it is needed. That is entirely different from each of us illegitimately judging our fellow men, when we have not been appointed by God to do so. Indeed, each of us are directly commanded not to judge others:

10 But you, why do you judge your brother? Or you again, why do you regard your brother with contempt? For we will all stand before the judgment seat of God. 11 For it is written, "As I live, says the Lord, every knee shall bow to Me, and every tongue shall]give praise to God." 12 So then each one of us will give an account of himself to God. 13 Therefore let us not judge one another anymore, but rather determine this—not to put an obstacle or a stumbling block in a brother's way.

Romans 14:10-13 (NASB)

5 Therefore do not go on passing judgment before the time, but wait until the Lord comes who will both bring to light the things hidden in the darkness and disclose the motives of men's hearts; and then each man's praise will come to him from God.

1 Corinthians 4:5 (NASB)

We are commanded to forgive others – it isn't optional

We are commanded not to judge others. On top of that, we also have a positive duty to forgive them. Moreover, we are not merely advised to do so. We are commanded to forgive. It is stated very clearly and on many occasions, for example:

37"Do not judge, and you will not be judged; and do not condemn, and you will not be condemned; pardon, and you will be pardoned.

Luke 6:37 (NASB)

[31]Let all bitterness and wrath and anger and clamor and slander be put away from you, along with all malice. [32]Be kind to one another, tender-hearted, forgiving each other, just as God in Christ also has forgiven you.

Ephesians 4:31-32 (NASB)

[21]"You have heard that the ancients were told, 'you shall not commit murder' and 'Whoever commits murder shall be liable to the court.' [22]"But I say to you that everyone who is angry with his brother shall be guilty before the court; and whoever says to his brother, 'You good-for-nothing,' shall be guilty before the supreme court; and whoever says, 'You fool,' shall be guilty enough to go into the fiery hell.

Matthew 5:21-22 (NASB)

[14]"For if you forgive others for their transgressions, your heavenly Father will also forgive you. [15]"But if you do not forgive others, then your Father will not forgive your transgressions.

Matthew 6:14-15 (NASB)

Moreover, it is assumed by God that we will obey these commands to forgive others. In what has come to be known as "the Lord's prayer", which really ought to be called 'the disciples' prayer', Jesus shows us the manner, style and attitude that we need to have when praying to God. We are not meant to say this prayer by rote, as most people seem to do, but to see it as a model or precedent.

At any rate, the point is that in praying for God to forgive us, Jesus assumes that we have already forgiven others, i.e. at least stepped aside and left their cases to be judged by Him. It is taken as a given. Or you could say that it is treated as a combined package of events. That is He links together our forgiveness of others with God's forgiveness of us.

In this instance, what Jesus is referring to goes beyond basic, narrowly-defined forgiveness. It also includes a duty to release others from their debts to us, i.e. the guilt of their sins, in the same way that we want God to release us from our debts to Him, i.e. the guilt of our sins:

[11] 'Give us this day our daily bread.
[12] 'And forgive us our debts, as we also have forgiven our debtors.
Matthew 6:11-12 (NASB)

But Jesus goes further than just telling us to forgive others, or to release them from their guilt or debt to us. He also states that unless we forgive others, God will not forgive us. That is a very worrying statement, but it is clearly what He said:

[25]"Whenever you stand praying, forgive, if you have anything against anyone, so that your Father who is in heaven will also forgive you your

transgressions. [26]"But if you do not forgive, neither will your Father who is in heaven forgive your transgressions."

Mark 11:25-26 (NASB)

So, that is clearly the command. We have to forgive others. That therefore makes it all the more essential that we know what exactly we must do and how exactly we are meant to do it, in practical terms. We have to ask, what is real forgiveness and how can we be sure that we have achieved it in our own particular circumstances? We shall therefore examine forgiveness more closely in the pages below and try to answer these questions fully.

In particular, we shall need to look further at the definition (or definitions) of forgiveness and get very clear on what it does, *and doesn't*, include. How else can we know whether we have obeyed the command to forgive others unless we know exactly what forgiveness involves, and how far we have to go?

How many times are we supposed to forgive people?

The apostle Peter asked Jesus a question which must have occurred to most of us - how many times are we expected to forgive people? Is there a limit? What if they just carry on sinning against us, again and again? Jesus answered Peter by telling him a story:

[21]*Then Peter came and said to Him, "Lord, how often shall my brother sin against me and I forgive him? Up to seven times?"* [22]*Jesus said to him, "I do not say to you, up to seven times, but up to seventy times seven.* [23]*"For this reason the kingdom of heaven may be compared to a king who wished to settle accounts with his slaves.*

[24]*"When he had begun to settle them, one who owed him ten thousand talents was brought to him.* [25]*"But since he did not have the means to repay, his lord commanded him to be sold, along with his wife and children and all that he had, and repayment to be made.* [26]*"So the slave fell to the ground and prostrated himself before him, saying, 'Have patience with me and I will repay you everything.'*

[27]*"And the lord of that slave felt compassion and released him and forgave him the debt.* [28]*"But that slave went out and found one of his fellow slaves who owed him a hundred denarii; and he seized him and began to choke him, saying, 'Pay back what you owe.'* [29]*"So his fellow slave fell to the ground and began to plead with him, saying, 'Have patience with me and I will repay you.'*

[30]*"But he was unwilling and went and threw him in prison until he should pay back what was owed.* [31]*"So when his fellow slaves saw what had happened, they were deeply grieved and came and reported to their lord all that had*

happened. ³²"Then summoning him, his lord said to him, 'You wicked slave, I forgave you all that debt because you pleaded with me.

³³'Should you not also have had mercy on your fellow slave, in the same way that I had mercy on you?' ³⁴"And his lord, moved with anger, handed him over to the torturers until he should repay all that was owed him. ³⁵"My heavenly Father will also do the same to you, if each of you does not forgive his brother from your heart."

Matthew 18:21-35 (NASB)

The above parable about waiving the debts (sins) of others, in the same way that we want God to forgive our sins, is alarming. I say that because Jesus concludes it by saying that God the Father will do the same with us as the King did to the man who failed to forgive. But the King in the story responded harshly. He did not merely re-impose the financial debt. He also handed the man over to be punished by "the torturers".

My understanding of that is as follows. We are commanded to forgive other people, at least in the narrow sense of stepping aside and leaving it to Jesus to judge them. Possibly, we may be required to go even further than that, by releasing them from their debt or guilt towards us.

However, if we will not do these things, then God will respond by allowing demons greater and greater access to us. They will then create additional difficulties for us until, under all of that pressure, we eventually come to realise our duty to forgive others and release them from their debts or guilt, just as we want God to release us from ours.

That point about the 'torturers' actually matches our experience in practice. A person who is in a state of unforgiveness, i.e. one who still wants to judge the wrongdoer themselves, and will not release them, will have a very difficult time, especially if they are bitter and vengeful. All sorts of other things will begin to go wrong for them.

That may seem unfair, given that they were wronged in the first place. Even so, it is what we have seen happen in our own lives, and in other people's lives, when there is unforgiveness and bitterness. Part of the rationale behind all of this is that we ourselves have been forgiven many things. Indeed, God's forgiveness of us is broadly defined and goes well beyond the narrow definition of forgiveness, which is the minimum that is required of us.

Therefore, what right do we have to withhold even the narrowest form of forgiveness from others, and yet seek it ourselves, and in the widest possible sense, for our own sins? Quite apart from the unfairness of that, there is also the fact that we are not authorised to judge anybody in the first place.

'Forbearance' - the duty to tolerate each other and to put up with each other's sins, faults and irritating ways

Forbearance is another concept which is closely linked to forgiveness but is still separate and distinct. Sometimes we become alienated from others, or do not get on with them, not necessarily because they have wronged us or harmed us, but simply because we do not like them. We are all very different and our ways, habits, mannerisms etc can be very irritating.

If this is not dealt with promptly, and in the right way, it can produce relationship problems, the effects of which are not much less than if we had been wronged. Moreover, if people do not get on, or if they irritate each other, they can eventually get to the stage where they do start to do actual wrong to each other, such that they really would have a need to forgive and be forgiven. Therefore, we also have a duty to show forbearance.

This is an aspect of forgiveness, albeit usually not at the fullest level, because it also applies even where people have not wronged us. It means to be patient and to put up with each other's sins, faults, weaknesses, annoying habits and minor acts of rudeness. Forbearance involves being slow to anger and tolerating such things, rather than reacting carnally to them. That is how God wants each of us to be, if we claim to be Christians:

12Put on then, as God's chosen ones, holy and beloved, compassion, kindness, lowliness, meekness, and patience, 13forbearing one another and, if one has a complaint against another, forgiving each other; as the Lord has forgiven you, so you also must forgive. 14And above all these put on love, which binds everything together in perfect harmony. 15And let the peace of Christ rule in your hearts, to which indeed you were called in the one body. And be thankful.
Colossians 3:12-15 (RSV)

I therefore, a prisoner for the Lord, beg you to lead a life worthy of the calling to which you have been called, 2 with all lowliness and meekness, with patience, forbearing one another in love, 3 eager to maintain the unity of the Spirit in the bond of peace.
Ephesians 4:1-3 (RSV)

Let all men know your forbearance. The Lord is at hand.
Philippians 4:5 (RSV)

If God was short-tempered, touchy, irritable, resentful, easily offended and prone to holding onto grudges, as we often tend to be, then none of us could relate to Him at all. He would be able to find far more to object to in us than we can legitimately object to in each other. Thankfully, that is not how He is. He is gracious and slow to anger. That involves Him being patient with us and putting up with our many faults, bad habits and selfish ways:

256

³ If you, O Lord, should mark iniquities,
O Lord, who could stand?
                                Psalm 130:3 (ESV)

⁸ The LORD is gracious and merciful,
slow to anger and abounding in steadfast love.
⁹ The LORD is good to all,
and his mercy is over all that he has made.
                                Psalm 145:8-9 (ESV)

So, forbearance is a *part* of what forgiveness is about. It primarily concerns the lesser things which are at the 'shallow end' of what we are called upon to forgive. It basically means putting up with it when people behave selfishly, foolishly, rudely or thoughtlessly. Yet, forbearance is still very important because it is likely that more relationships are undermined or destroyed because of minor irritations and personality clashes than by major situations, where one person has been seriously wronged by another.

The little pin pricks may be trivial in themselves, but they may mount up over time and their eventual consequences can be major, if we are not willing to practice the art of forbearance. However, if we can develop forbearance and make the effort to put up with things and get along with people that we don't naturally like, then everybody will benefit.

This has not been an area of strength for me. I find I am too easily irritated by others and so I need to work at this much harder. God wants us all to make a bigger effort to get along with other Christians, and to be slow to anger. We are to tolerate their faults, and also their habits and ways, even where they are not necessarily at fault, but are merely different from us:

Behold, how good and pleasant
it is when brothers dwell in unity!
                                Psalm 133:1 (ESV)

God also wants us to encourage those who fail and lift up those who fall, whether it is into sin or other problems or mishaps. We should be willing to do that for them, because that's what He does with us:

The LORD upholds all who are falling
and raises up all who are bowed down.
                                Psalm 145:14 (ESV)

When disagreements arise over questions of doctrine or practice we also need to be very selective about the issues over which we ought to take a stand. We should not get into a conflict situation over every difference of opinion. Otherwise we could end up contending with others unnecessarily, when no vital issue of principle is at stake:

But avoid stupid controversies, genealogies, dissensions, and quarrels over the law, for they are unprofitable and futile.

Titus 3:9 (RSV)

Do not contend with a man for no reason,
when he has done you no harm.

Proverbs 3:30 (ESV)

Try to see other people as God sees them

A good technique, when irritated by people, and where we want to avoid the problem escalating or continuing, is to try to see people the way God sees them. God isn't irritated by people's accents, opinions or mannerisms or by their peculiar ways. He looks at people more deeply and sees the value and also the potential inside them.

In particular, He is keenly aware that that person, whom we may find irritating, is someone for whom Jesus died and who could be saved if they would just repent and turn to Him. Even between fellow Christians there can be, and frequently is, friction, and tension. This can spoil relationships, not only for the two people concerned, but for a whole church.

Apostle Paul came across this in the church in Philippi. Two good women, both of whom were devout and hard working for the church, just did not get along with each other. Paul urged them to 'agree' with each other and he asked the rest of the church to help them to do so:

²I entreat Euodia and I entreat Syntyche to agree in the Lord. ³Yes, I ask you also, true companion, help these women, who have labored side by side with me in the gospel together with Clement and the rest of my fellow workers, whose names are in the book of life. ⁴Rejoice in the Lord always; again I will say, rejoice. ⁵Let your reasonableness be known to everyone. The Lord is at hand;

Philippians 4:2-5 (ESV)

We are never to take vengeance by or for ourselves - we are to leave that to God

Forgiving others, even at its narrowest definition, also means that we must not do anything to take vengeance. We must never seek to 'get even' with people, or to 'pay them back' for what they did to us. We are to *"leave room for the wrath of*

God". That is we are to leave it to Him to punish people, which He certainly will do:

When he was reviled, he did not revile in return; when he suffered, he did not threaten; but he trusted to him who judges justly.
1 Peter 2:23 (RSV)

not returning evil for evil or insult for insult, but giving a blessing instead; for you were called for the very purpose that you might inherit a blessing.
1 Peter 3:9 (NASB)

[17]Never pay back evil for evil to anyone Respect what is right in the sight of all men. [18]If possible, so far as it depends on you, be at peace with all men. [19]Never take your own revenge, beloved, but leave room for the wrath of God, for it is written, "vengeance is mine, I will repay," says the Lord. [20]"but if your enemy is hungry, feed him, and if he is thirsty, give him a drink; for in so doing you will heap burning coals on his head." [21]Do not be overcome by evil, but overcome evil with good.
Romans 12:17-21 (NASB)

When King David was a young man he spent a number of years on the run from King Saul, who was persecuting him unjustly and seeking to kill him. However, David refused to take matters into his own hands or to take vengeance. Instead he asked God to intervene and judge between himself and King Saul:

[12] May the Lord judge between me and you, may the Lord avenge me upon you; but my hand shall not be against you.
1 Samuel 24:12 (RSV)

Seeking vengeance would also amount to usurping Jesus' unique role as Judge. It would mean we were punishing people ourselves, instead of leaving them for Jesus to deal with. He wants us to leave it to Him to punish people, not to do it now, for ourselves:

Do not say, "I will repay evil";
wait for the Lord, and he will deliver you.
                    Proverbs 20:22 (ESV)

since indeed God deems it just to repay with affliction those who afflict you,
2 Thessalonians 1:6 (RSV)

So, although *we* are not authorised to take vengeance, Jesus *is* authorised to do so, and He will, i.e. with all those who do not repent and do not believe in Him. We can be very sure of that. Moreover, there are circumstances in which it may even be appropriate for us to look forward with some sense of anticipation to the Day of Judgment, when Jesus will take that vengeance on our behalf. The taking of vengeance, so long as it is done only by Jesus, is a right and proper aspect of God's justice. Thus it is something good, for which we can give thanks, and even rejoice:

10 The righteous will rejoice when he sees the vengeance;
he will bathe his feet in the blood of the wicked.
11 Men will say, "Surely there is a reward for the righteous;
surely there is a God who judges on earth."
Psalm 58:10-11 (RSV)

8 Let the floods clap their hands;
let the hills sing for joy together
9 before the LORD, for he comes
to judge the earth.
He will judge the world with righteousness,
and the peoples with equity.
Psalm 98:8-9 (RSV)

For example, if a person's child has been murdered, then at the Day of Judgment, the murderer will be punished for it unless, of course, he has become a Christian in the meantime and been forgiven. However, if he has not repented and been forgiven by God, then it would not necessarily be wrong for the relatives of that victim to want God's Judgment to come, and even to take satisfaction, and achieve a sense of closure, from that Judgment when it takes place.

That is a valid way to think in relation to an unrepentant person. It is not necessarily inconsistent with having forgiven the other person, at least at the most basic level, i.e. having stepped aside and left it to Jesus to judge them. However, the position is different in relation to a wrongdoer who has, like us, repented and been saved. Such a man is forgiven, just as we are, and will not be punished. We shall examine this issue in some detail below.

If appropriate, Jesus will punish those who have harmed us. It is not necessarily wrong for us to take comfort from that fact.

When we forgive a wrongdoer it does not mean that he will never be judged. It is simply that they won't be judged *by us*. Jesus will actually judge unrepentant, unsaved people with a devastating severity, on a scale far greater than anything we could do to them:

35 'Vengeance is Mine, and retribution,
In due time their foot will slip;
For the day of their calamity is near,
And the impending things are hastening upon them.'
36 "For the LORD will vindicate His people,
And will have compassion on His servants,

When He sees that their strength is gone,
And there is none remaining, bond or free.
                              Deuteronomy 32:35-36 (NASB)

Say to those with anxious heart,
"Take courage, fear not.
Behold, your God will come with vengeance;
The recompense of God will come,
But He will save you."
                              Isaiah 35:4(NASB)

[5]This is a plain indication of God's righteous judgment so that you will be considered worthy of the kingdom of God, for which indeed you are suffering. [6]For after all it is only just for God to repay with affliction those who afflict you, [7]and to give relief to you who are afflicted and to us as well when the Lord Jesus will be revealed from heaven with His mighty angels in flaming fire, [8]dealing out retribution to those who do not know God and to those who do not obey the gospel of our Lord Jesus. [9]These will pay the penalty of eternal destruction, away from the presence of the Lord and from the glory of His power, [10]when He comes to be glorified in His saints on that day, and to be marvelled at among all who have believed--for our testimony to you was believed.
                              2 Thessalonians 1:5-10 (NASB)

It is not necessarily inappropriate for a wronged party to take comfort from, and even look forward to, the fact that Jesus' judgment will come upon the wrongdoer. In part, it is the very fact that we know that that is going to happen which can make it possible for us to step back and to leave the judgment, and even the taking of vengeance, for Him to deal with instead of us.

Therefore we need not necessarily feel guilty or hypocritical about the fact that we want Jesus' judgment to come upon a person who has done something wrong. It does not necessarily mean that we are being unforgiving. In itself it is consistent with 'stepping aside' and letting Jesus be the one who judges.

However, what if the wrongdoer has repented and been saved and forgiven by God? In those circumstances it would no longer be right to desire that they be punished. In such a case, everything has changed. The wrongdoer, if he truly has been saved, has now had all his sins washed away. That includes his sins(s) against you.

Moreover, he now has all the righteousness of Jesus Christ, because it has been imputed or transferred to him, just as was done for you when you were saved and forgiven. We might object that it would be unfair for that wrongdoer to be 'let off' by Jesus. We might see it as an injustice and feel aggrieved that he is no longer going to get what he deserves.

In one sense that is an understandable emotion. However, we ought to think very carefully indeed before saying that we want everybody to get what they 'deserve'. If God did that, then He would also have to give *us* what *we* deserve, not just other people. But that would be a place in the Lake of Fire, not forgiveness and mercy.

The point is how can we say that God should forgive us for *our* sins, including what we did to harm person Y, but then demand that justice and vengeance be shown to person X for the harm *they* did to us? Surely it has to be either both, or neither, of us that can receive God's mercy? We can't say that it should be shown to us, but not to person X.

If we did claim to be entitled to insist on justice as against person X then what if person Y, whom we have wronged, was to demand, in like manner, that God punish us? That is the dilemma we face. If we want to receive forgiveness we must also be willing to give it.

Likewise, if we are going to demand justice and retribution for others then we would have to accept that those things should be dispensed to us as well, which would not be a good idea. It certainly wouldn't get my vote. If the wrongdoer meets God's conditions, as we did, and receives His forgiveness, we cannot any longer look for God to take vengeance upon him.

We have to accept the whole package, i.e. receiving forgiveness ourselves and also giving it to others. Otherwise, we have not really understood the Gospel. Let us now attempt to define forgiveness more fully and enlarge upon some of these other related concepts that have been mentioned.

A closer look at what forgiveness consists of

To forgive another person, *in the narrowest sense* of the word, requires us to recognise and accept the following things:

a) that a wrong has been done to you and, perhaps, that harm has been caused.

b) that it has been done by person X (or group X)

c) that all wrongdoing will be fully dealt with by Jesus, either at the Judgment Seat of Christ (for Christians) or the Great White Throne Judgment (for non-Christians).

d) that only Jesus is legitimately qualified for the role of judging person X or group X.

e) that for you to attempt to judge and/or punish that person or group now would be premature, illegitimate and unauthorized. It would involve usurping Jesus' role.

f) that due to your inadequate knowledge and understanding, person X would never get a 'fair trial' from you. You would never be able to take fully into account the multitude of relevant facts, his various motives, and any other aggravating or mitigating factors. You just don't have enough wisdom or computing capacity for a job like that. It would be worse than if you had just wandered into the Old Bailey, sat in a Judge's chair and started to try a case. Doing that would be unthinkable. None of us would even dream of it. Yet that is the equivalent of what we would be doing if we refused to forgive others and tried to judge them ourselves.

g) that we have to make a decision to hand the case over to Jesus. We can, and must, step aside and leave it all to Him. He will then deal with everything in His own time, either now, or later, or both.

These points summarize the main things we need to do if we are to forgive someone effectively. But the above list sounds quite different from most people's idea of what forgiveness involves. Forgiveness is not a well understood concept, even amongst Christians. There is a lot of confusion and misunderstanding about it, due to poor teaching, or no teaching at all.

It is also caused by demonic deception which obscures the biblical understanding of forgiveness and promotes various other garbled definitions instead. The Devil does not want forgiveness to be properly understood or practiced. He tries particularly hard, therefore, to distort our understanding of this subject.

CHAPTER 13

SOME COMMON ERRORS AND AREAS OF CONFUSION ABOUT WHAT FORGIVENESS IS, AND HOW AND WHY WE ARE TO DO IT

[17] "You shall not hate your brother in your heart, but you shall reason frankly with your neighbor, lest you incur sin because of him. [18] You shall not take vengeance or bear a grudge against the sons of your own people, but you shall love your neighbor as yourself: I am the LORD.

Leviticus 19:17-18 (ESV)

[10]If you forgive anyone, I also forgive him. And what I have forgiven--if there was anything to forgive--I have forgiven in the sight of Christ for your sake, [11]in order that Satan might not outwit us. For we are not unaware of his schemes.

Corinthians 2:10-11 (NIV)

Repay no one evil for evil, but take thought for what is noble in the sight of all.

Romans 12:17 (RSV)

Most people misunderstand what forgiveness is. They then reject it, or fail to achieve it, because their definition is wrong

Many of us have such an inaccurate understanding of forgiveness that we reject the very idea as being unrealistic. We can't accept the unbiblical concept that we mistakenly have in mind when the word 'forgiveness' is used. Therefore we don't even try to do it. Others do attempt it, even repeatedly, but because their definition of forgiveness is wrong, they don't succeed.

Therefore they become discouraged and give up. They may never realise that the things they were trying to do were not necessarily what God means by forgiveness. They could have succeeded, and still could succeed, if they only understood correctly what God actually wants them to do in their particular circumstances.

God is the most sensible, practical, reasonable and realistic person in the whole universe. Therefore, if the very idea of forgiveness seems to you to be absurdly idealistic, impractical, and even impossible, then that indicates that you have probably misunderstood what you are being commanded to do.

God would not command you to do something which is impossible. Neither would He say anything unrealistic or impractical. So, if we feel that He is being unrealistic, that should prompt us to look again at the definitions of the words we are dealing with.

Why is forgiveness preached on so rarely?

Probably the main reason why so few Christians understand forgiveness correctly is that there is so little teaching on it. It is either taught poorly by church leaders, who don't know what it really means, or it is not taught at all. The latter is the normal position. When did you ever hear a useful, practical and biblical sermon on *what* forgiveness is and *how* and *why* you should forgive others? I haven't heard one in the last 25 years at least. Indeed, I don't think I have ever heard one.

Why is that? Perhaps one reason is that forgiveness is difficult, even if correctly defined, and probably impossible if wrongly defined. Thus many preachers find, in their own personal experience, that forgiving others has not been a success. So, because few men want to discuss their own failures or difficulties, the whole subject is avoided.

Another probable reason is that the subject of forgiveness is a difficult one for church members to listen to. Thus, if a church leader is the kind of man who wants to be liked, as many are, then he will avoid teaching on any subject which is controversial, or makes people feel uncomfortable. He won't want to say anything which has the potential to remind them of their grievances and get them stirred up.

However, perhaps the main reason that forgiveness is not preached on is that many leaders just don't understand it themselves. That is probably because they too have not been properly taught about it. There are very few good books on the subject of forgiveness and preachers themselves have not heard any good biblical sermons on it, which they can copy or download.

What forgiveness does *not* mean, and does *not* involve:

Contrary to what millions of people assume, forgiveness does *not* mean, or involve, any of the following:

a) telling yourself that no real wrong was ever done to you by person X or that you are over-reacting, being over-sensitive or even imagining things

b) saying that person X was right to do what he did to you

c) excusing or covering up for person X

d) sympathizing with person X

e) telling yourself that it was all your own fault, not the wrongdoer's fault

f) being soppy and wet about what happened and making yourself into a 'doormat' to be walked on.

g) resuming or continuing a close relationship with the wrongdoer, as if nothing had ever happened

h) being able to make all the pain go away, such that you no longer feel upset or angry about it and have made yourself 'get over it'

i) forgetting the wrong done to you, how it made you feel, and the harm it did

j) believing that the wrongdoer should not have to be punished and should not be required to repay what he has taken, or pay compensation for the damage or injury caused

k) letting the wrongdoer 'get away with it', such that it would be considered wrong for you to go to the police or appoint a lawyer to sue them

l) being reconciled with the wrongdoer, such that you are on friendly terms with them, and would be happy to have them round to your house, go out for a drink, or even just engage in 'small talk' with them. In fact, forgiveness and reconciliation are totally separate and different concepts. The former does not require, or imply, the latter. Forgiveness is something you decide to do on your own. It does not require the wrongdoer's cooperation, apology or repentance or for him to reciprocate in any way. He need not necessarily even be aware that you have forgiven him. However, reconciliation has to be mutual. It can't happen unless the wrongdoer firstly acknowledges his fault, apologizes, repents and, above all, stops wronging you.

m) feeling able to trust the wrongdoer. Again, it is foolishness to think that forgiveness implies or requires that trust has to be resumed. Nevertheless, a lot of people do assume that, which is one reason why they wrongly conclude that it is impossible to forgive. Actually, the Bible never even tells us to trust people who haven't wronged us, let alone those who have. Accordingly, there is no requirement to trust the wrongdoer in order to prove to God, or to others, that we have genuinely forgiven him. A wrongdoer has to earn your trust, over a period of time, just as anybody else does, even if they aren't a wrongdoer. Furthermore, it is perfectly reasonable that you wait two or three times longer to trust a wrongdoer than a stranger who has never yet wronged you. In short, they have no right to receive your trust, and you are not under any duty to trust them, or anybody else, for that matter.

Nevertheless, many people, even within the Church, assume that forgiveness does involves some or all of (a)-(m) above. But it doesn't, or at least it doesn't necessarily involve any of them. The word 'forgiveness' has had its meaning distorted, like the word 'gay'. We must therefore recapture and reinforce the correct meaning of the word, because if we don't, a great many people will continue to believe that forgiveness is impossible to achieve.

There are also other words which mean similar things as forgiveness. They may even include forgiveness as a component element within them. But they still have their own, separate and distinct definitions

As we saw, people often confuse words like *reconciliation* with forgiveness, as if they were the same thing. There are other words as well which have their own separate and distinct definitions. Yet they are frequently assumed to be the same as forgiveness, or at least to be required, or implied, by forgiveness. We shall look at a few more of these words and examine what they do actually mean and how they are different from forgiveness, even if they often go together with forgiveness, or follow on afterwards.

a) peace

It is by no means always necessary, in order to forgive a person, that you must also be at peace with them. Sometimes forgiveness will lead to peace, but sometimes it will not. The two things do not necessarily have to go together in order for forgiveness to be valid. Moreover, peace requires the voluntary cooperation of *both parties*, not just the one doing the forgiving. We actually need to look more closely at the word 'peace' and distinguish between two of its definitions, because it has more than one:

i) irene

This is a Greek word, from which we get the girls' name, and is the basis for what most of us think of, at least in the West, when we hear the word peace. It means the absence of hostility or conflict, such that we are not at war, or actively engaged in a dispute, or otherwise struggling, against some other person or group. It is possible to have genuinely forgiven a person and yet not be at peace with them, in the sense of *irene* peace. You might still need to be a witness against them in a criminal trial, or give evidence against them in a workplace disciplinary hearing.

Or you might feel it necessary to contact the local council to pursue a complaint against them because of their abusive behaviour, or for parking across your driveway, and so on. The list of possibilities is endless. Yet, each of these things, which clearly show that we are *not* at peace (irene peace) are entirely consistent with us having truly forgiven the other person. There is no contradiction or inconsistency, because forgiveness does not necessarily require that we be at peace (irene) with the other person. It may lead to irene peace, or it may not. They, or you, might be unwilling or unable to be at irene peace. Nevertheless, you can still validly forgive them.

268

ii) shalom

This is a Hebrew word which is also translated as 'peace' in English. However, it does not mean the same as the Greek word 'irene'. Shalom peace is much deeper and wider than the mere absence of hostilities or conflict. Shalom means a complete wholesomeness, integrity, prosperity and sense of well-being at the deepest level. So, if a person does not forgive another person, and is holding a grudge and feeling vengeful, they will not have shalom peace within themselves.

However, a person may have genuinely forgiven the wrongdoer but still not be experiencing shalom peace (or not yet) because they are still grieving or feeling wounded, violated or traumatized. They may even feel righteous indignation or anger. Such feelings may be felt, such that there is no shalom type peace, but it does not necessarily mean that the injured party is disobeying Jesus' command to forgive.

He might well have obeyed that command, and genuinely handed the whole matter over to God and/or to the civil or criminal authorities. However, he is still reeling from the shock of what happened, trying to come to terms with it, and gradually getting his emotions back under control.

That process of re-establishing your equilibrium may well take a long time, but it does not necessarily indicate that there is a lack of forgiveness. Of course, it could be that there is unforgiveness, but we cannot just assume it. The issue of whether we have recovered our shalom-type peace is an entirely separate question from the question of whether we have genuinely forgiven the wrongdoer.

I emphasize this because some people have felt guilt, or have been put under pressure, or falsely accused of being unforgiving, simply because they have not yet recovered their composure and their shalom-type peace. Such accusations come from one or more of the following sources:

- other people who don't understand the true definition of forgiveness and wrongly assume that it requires us to be fully at peace etc. They might foolishly say that a person who has not yet calmed down and is "*still going on about what happened to them*" is a nuisance and is causing problems by being 'unforgiving'.

- ourselves, because we too misunderstand, or wrongly define, forgiveness. Therefore we may feel convinced that we have not achieved it, or never can achieve it, because we still feel some emotional turmoil.

- demons, who whisper lies into our minds and tell us that we are being unforgiving and are disobeying what Jesus said. They don't say that in order to induce you to become obedient to God's Word. They just want to increase your wretchedness and misery by making you feel guilt, shame and hopelessness. The truth is that you could actually achieve real forgiveness if you only knew its correct definition. Indeed, you may already have done so, but the demons have convinced you that you haven't.

b) mercy

The word *mercy* is obviously linked to forgiveness. However, it is not the same thing. Perhaps the simplest and best definition of mercy is that it is where person A (who is usually in a position of power, strength or authority) chooses not to do, or give, to person B what they deserve. The point, for our present purposes, is that even when we genuinely obey Jesus' command to forgive, it does not necessarily mean that we must *also* show mercy.

Mercy is a separate and additional step to take. It goes beyond forgiveness. So, person A might truly forgive person B by handing the matter over to God and/or leave it to the civil/criminal authorities to deal with, and he may seek no vengeance or retribution for himself. Yet, he might also, at the same time, choose not to show mercy.

For example, he would be doing nothing wrong if he chose to tell the Police that he wants person B to be prosecuted. Alternatively, person A might freely choose to say to the Police: *"Please don't press any charges against person B. I want to drop the matter and I don't want to see his life blighted by receiving a criminal record."*

If person A said that, they would be showing mercy. Another word for that is *clemency*, although we mainly use that word in the context of a person who is in a position of authority and chooses not to exercise their power. Yet another word which we use for showing mercy is '*magnanimity*'. This is the kind of mercy that is shown by the victor to the loser in a war, or indeed by the victor, or stronger party, in any kind of dispute.

Therefore, at the end of World War Two, Churchill's advice to the Allies was that they should show magnanimity to the Germans, unlike what happened at the end of World War One. That war culminated in what most felt was a punitive, vengeful and even oppressive treaty. Magnanimity is what we can choose to show when we have been wronged, but now have the upper hand, and the wrongdoer lies prostrate at our feet.

In those circumstances, to choose not to seek for justice, but instead to stay one's hand and demand less than one is entitled to, is magnanimous. Magnanimity goes beyond forgiveness. Therefore a person can truly forgive, at least in the basic, narrow sense, without also choosing to be magnanimous in the way that they handle their victory.

It may, or may not, be right to show mercy, in any of its various forms, but the point is that it is something different from, and *additional to*, forgiveness. In other words, person A may have genuinely forgiven person B for the assault or theft or whatever, but still feel that it is necessary and appropriate for justice to take its course. Therefore they choose to go to the police rather than show mercy by not going to them.

Remember the crucial point about what forgiveness is at its most basic level. It primarily means handing the case over so that someone else can be the judge and carry out any sentence. One can do that completely sincerely without also being under a duty to refrain from helping the prosecution, or civil action, or workplace disciplinary action, which then follows.

If forgiveness involves handing the case over, which it does, then how can anybody say that in order to truly forgive we must choose not even to hand it over, but rather that we should feel obligated to drop the matter entirely? That would be to extend the meaning of forgiveness illegitimately and to turn it into something much bigger and wider than what the Bible means by the word.

Therefore, if person A merely hands the case over to the Police (and/or to God) and seeks no personal vengeance, then he has already fulfilled the basic meaning of forgiveness. God might, or might not, want person A to go even further and to show mercy *as well*. However, if that is what God wants, then God would be asking person A to *show mercy*, not to forgive, because he has already done that.

God does not get confused about the words He uses. Neither does He say one thing when He means another. Therefore, forgiveness means forgiveness. Mercy means mercy. Peace means peace and so on. They are all distinct words in their own right, with their own definitions, and are not inter-changeable synonyms. To do one of them does not necessarily require us to do any or all of the others as well.

c) grace/graciousness

We saw that mercy is *"not giving people what they do deserve"*. Grace is the other side of the same coin. It basically means *"giving people what they don't deserve"*. Therefore, extending the points made above, we can imagine various factual situations where it would be right, and indeed essential, to forgive, but not necessarily appropriate to show grace.

So, if a person has wronged us, and we have genuinely forgiven them, God might, or might not, want us to go further and show grace to them. Or, God might want us to show grace in a particular way, but not necessarily in some other way.

271

Alternatively, God might want us to show grace up to a certain point, but not beyond that point.

Therefore, if we choose not to help a person who has wronged us, or choose not to give them a favour, or privilege or gift, it would not necessarily mean that we have not genuinely forgiven them. Showing such grace towards them might, or might not, be wise or appropriate. That is it may, or may not, be God's will in those circumstances.

You cannot make a general rule. Even less can you equate forgiveness with grace and therefore accuse another person, or even yourself, of being unforgiving, merely for choosing not to go beyond forgiveness and show grace to a particular person in a particular situation. It does not necessarily follow.

However, what if a person was so full of bitterness and the desire for vengeance that they were revelling in their decision to withhold grace from the wrongdoer and taking pleasure from withholding it? If so, then their heart-attitude would obviously be wrong. It might even indicate that they had not truly forgiven the wrongdoer. Nevertheless, the point is that the giving, or withholding, of grace is a completely separate, stand-alone issue. Like mercy, it goes beyond the duty to forgive and is distinct from it.

d) forgetting

By this I mean forgetting the wrong done to you, no longer feeling upset, and ceasing to think about the person who did the harm. 'Forgetting' is another much misunderstood word, which is frequently confused with forgiving. Therefore, if person A can't, or can't yet, forget what was done to him by person B, or the feelings it produced, it does not necessarily mean that he has not genuinely forgiven person B.

The command to forgive others does not extend to also forgetting what they did or how it made you feel. If Jesus had wanted to command that we forget all about the offence as well, then He would have said so, but He did not. One reason why God did not command us to forget all about the wrongs done to us, or to forget the way we felt as a result, is because He knows that we often aren't capable of doing that. God can choose to forget, but we can't necessarily manage to do that.

At any rate, we can't do it purely as an exercise of our will. We sometimes need time for our feelings to heal and become less raw. That is very significant, because God never gives us any command *to* feel, or not feel, a particular *emotion*. He only gives commands in connection with the exercise of our *will*. It is always expressed in terms of what we should say or do, not how we should feel in our emotions.

You might respond to that by saying that He commands us not to be angry. However, when He makes that command, what God means is that we are not to *speak* or *act*, or *react*, towards other people with sinful, fleshly, unrighteous anger. Those are all things we can control and decide to do or not to do. He is referring to circumstances where the expression of anger would be carnal, and thus sinful. He is not referring to godly anger, or righteous indignation, such as Jesus demonstrated when He expelled the money changers from the Temple.

At any rate, the point is that all of God's commandments have to do with what we say, do and even think, as an exercise of our will. We are accountable for what we choose to do or say, but not necessarily for how we feel. Accordingly, we are never commanded not to feel grief, sadness, hurt or shock or not to feel that we have been violated. There is no sin in feeling any of those things.

Therefore our inability to forget the wrong done to us, or to alter our feelings, is not disobedience. It is not, in itself, even evidence, let alone proof, that we have not genuinely forgiven someone. That said, what if the real reason why we are failing to forget a wrong done to us, or to stop feeling as we do, is because we are deliberately, and repeatedly, choosing to remind ourselves of it?

We may even be reminding the wrongdoer of it, because we get pleasure from bringing it up in conversation and from making the other person feel guilty about it. Then, that would be a sign that we have not genuinely forgiven the person. As with everything else, we have to approach this difficult subject with balance. We also need to have regard to our real motives, which may not necessarily be what we say they are.

e)   **trusting the wrongdoer**

It may, or may not, be appropriate to *trust* a person who has previously wronged you. It depends entirely on the circumstances and on the role, responsibility or property which you are considering entrusting or re-entrusting to them. It could be very unwise, or even dangerous, to trust them again.

It may also be impossible, or a breach of your professional duty to do so, because you have to bear in mind the needs of others who might be adversely affected if the wrongdoer was to act wrongly, or let you down, again. The point is that whether it is right or wrong to trust the person again is an entirely separate issue from the duty to forgive him.

It is perfectly valid to forgive and yet still not feel able to trust the person. Or, you might feel that it is possible, and appropriate, to do both. However, if that is the case, you are going beyond forgiving them and are adding a further dimension.

f) giving the wrongdoer another chance

This is linked to the issue of whether or not we feel able to trust the wrongdoer again. However, it is also a separate point in itself. It is possible to give a person another chance, even if we don't yet trust them, and even if we actually expect them to let us down again. The point is that the issue of whether or not to give them another chance goes beyond forgiveness.

So we can genuinely forgive a person and yet not feel that it would be wise or safe to give them another chance. It is a matter of individual judgment, such that another Christian might be willing to give them another chance, whereas you are not. Yet, you could both be right.

A classic example of this is the crisis that arose in the Book of Acts when John Mark (better known to us as Mark, the writer of the second gospel) deserted apostle Paul and let him down when under pressure. Later on, Mark evidently said that he had repented and wanted to rejoin the team, but that led to an argument.

Paul's personal stance was that he was not willing to give Mark another chance. However, Paul's partner, Barnabas, felt that Mark should be allowed to have another go and to work with them again. They could not agree on this, so Paul and Barnabas split up and went their separate ways. Barnabas therefore took Mark with him and Paul took Silas:

36 And after some days Paul said to Barnabas, "Come, let us return and visit the brethren in every city where we proclaimed the word of the Lord, and see how they are." 37 And Barnabas wanted to take with them John called Mark. 38 But Paul thought best not to take with them one who had withdrawn from them in Pamphyl'ia, and had not gone with them to the work. 39 And there arose a sharp contention, so that they separated from each other; Barnabas took Mark with him and sailed away to Cyprus, 40 but Paul chose Silas and departed, being commended by the brethren to the grace of the Lord. 41 And he went through Syria and Cili'cia, strengthening the churches.

Acts 15:36-41 (RSV)

That episode had a happy ending. Mark genuinely changed and turned into a mature, reliable worker. Indeed, in the end, God honoured him by allowing him to write the second gospel, for which he got the material from apostle Peter, with whom he became very close:

She who is at Babylon, who is likewise chosen, sends you greetings; and so does my son Mark.

1 Peter 5:13 (RSV)

More to the point, Mark was eventually accepted, trusted and welcomed back by Paul to work alongside him:

Aristar'chus my fellow prisoner greets you, and Mark the cousin of Barnabas (concerning whom you have received instructions—if he comes to you, receive him),

Colossians 4:10 (RSV)

Mark's dramatic and total rehabilitation is an encouragement to us all to believe that even where people fail badly, or behave badly, there is always the chance to repent and change and eventually become a success. The question is who was right, Paul or Barnabas? The short answer is probably that they both were. At any rate, Paul did not act wrongly by refusing to let Mark rejoin the team. He clearly felt it would be unwise and even unsafe.

In making that decision, Paul was not failing to forgive Mark, or acting in a way that was inconsistent with genuine forgiveness. It was up to Paul to decide what was best and whether or not it would be wise to go beyond forgiving Mark, by choosing to give him another chance. Barnabas saw it differently and was willing to take the risk. That was his personal choice. Happily, it turned out to have been an inspired one.

That said, it may well have had more to do with the simple fact that Mark was a cousin of Barnabas and therefore he possibly chose to give him more leeway than he would have given to a non-relative. The point is that in choosing not to go as far as Barnabas was willing to go, Paul was not sinning. In particular, he was not failing to forgive.

g) being reconciled with the wrongdoer and starting or resuming a friendship with him

You will see the pattern by now and realise that this is going even further than trusting the wrongdoer and/or giving him another chance. To be *reconciled* may mean that we are resuming a full personal relationship involving trust, friendship, closeness and even intimacy and the sharing of confidences. Clearly, that goes way beyond merely forgiving the person. Therefore, whether to be reconciled is an even bigger decision.

The point, for our purposes, is that we have absolutely no duty to be reconciled to every wrongdoer. Reconciliation is not required in order for us to be able to say that we have genuinely forgiven them. I emphasize that because this issue has caused a great deal of confusion and stress for people who are trying hard to forgive a wrongdoer.

They may mistakenly assume that unless they are willing to be fully reconciled, and feel entirely comfortable about resuming a close personal relationship, then they have not genuinely forgiven the person and are even being disobedient to Jesus' command to forgive.

That is plainly wrong and is a particularly unhelpful thing to say to a person who is struggling to deal with a wrong done to them. Reconciliation may, or may not, be achieved at some later point. It depends on a host of circumstances, in particular the *attitude* and subsequent *conduct* of the wrongdoer and whether he has genuinely repented, apologized and changed.

If he hasn't done all of those things, then there would be no valid or meaningful basis for reconciliation. It could even be foolish to attempt it. So, as with all the other words, we need to see reconciliation as another separate, stand-alone issue, over and above forgiveness. It may or may not be appropriate, or possible, even in the long term.

An example illustrating basic forgiveness, but then adding further elements on top of that

It may assist our understanding of how forgiveness works in its narrower and broader senses, to present a simple illustration. Imagine that you have loaned your lawnmower to your next door neighbour. However, you then discover that he has misused it, either carelessly or deliberately, and caused serious damage to it, rendering it useless.

Perhaps it has cost you £200 and he is not sorry for what he did, or bothered about how you feel. Moreover, he is refusing to repay you for the lawnmower, even though he is well able to do so. Let's examine that scenario and see how you might forgive that person and what else you might, or might not, also do, over and above forgiving him.

I have deliberately kept the example mundane and homely because, for most of us, the things we have to forgive are not spectacular things like murders or armed robberies. They are usually smaller injuries, offences and rudenesses which occur in ordinary, day to day life. To begin with, we can say for sure that you have a clear duty to forgive your neighbour *in the basic, narrow sense*.

That is you would have to step aside, recuse yourself and leave it to Jesus to judge him for what he has done to your lawnmower and his subsequent refusal to repay you, or even to apologise. That is always your duty and you are expressly commanded to do that.

However, it might, or might not, be possible, or even appropriate, for you to go further than that and do any or all of the other things which we have looked at, each of which go beyond basic forgiveness. So, it may be that God *also* wants you to do some or all of these things. Alternatively, He might not.

276

What is more, even if He does want you to do them, it may be that He only wants you to do so up to a certain point, rather than to the fullest extent possible. Let's therefore look at each of these possible extra steps that you could take:

a)   to be at *peace* with your neighbour in the sense of not being angry with him, or in terms of not going to see a lawyer and suing him for the damage he did. Alternatively, you could actually choose to sue him and yet still have genuinely forgiven him, in the narrow sense of handing the judgment over to Jesus and, in the meantime, to the civil courts which God has put in place. You can do that provided you are not seeking to exact any vengeance of your own, and are refusing to allow yourself to hold a grudge or nurse any bitterness or hatred towards him.

b)   to show *mercy* towards him by not requiring him to get what he deserves, for example by choosing not to make him pay for the damage. You might, or might not, choose to show such mercy to him, depending on the circumstances. Conversely, you might choose not to be merciful, and to insist, instead, on obtaining redress. That decision would not necessarily be inconsistent with forgiving him, in the narrow sense. In other words, if you choose to show mercy by letting him off, it would be something you were doing in addition to forgiving him, rather than being an integral part of the act of forgiveness in itself.

c)   to show *grace* towards him by causing or permitting him to receive some benefit or privilege which he does not deserve. You might do that, for example, by allowing him to continue to borrow your new lawnmower, despite what he did to the previous one. You would be under no duty to show such grace towards him. It goes beyond basic forgiveness and it may, or may not, be wise. It would depend on all sorts of other factors such as the attitude he shows, whether he later apologizes, and what his circumstances are. It could even be that God wants you to give him an unusually large amount of leeway, because He wants you to try to build a relationship with that man so that you can perhaps reach him, or his family, with the Gospel. So, God might, or might not, want you to let him use your new lawnmower in future. But, either way, He will always want you to forgive him, i.e. in the narrow sense.

d)   to *forget* the wrong done to you. Again, this is not required for genuine forgiveness, i.e. in the basic, narrow sense. It is a quite separate matter, which goes well beyond basic forgiveness. It may, or may not, be wise, or even possible, for you to forget what he did. There could be circumstances, for example if the damage was purely accidental, where you might feel it right, and feel able, to put the harm done to you entirely out of your mind. Then you could forget all about it, and treat your neighbour as if nothing had ever happened. Or, the circumstances could be such that you would not feel that that was appropriate, or even possible. For example, he might have done the damage recklessly, or even spitefully, and he could be wholly unrepentant. He could even be mocking you and laughing about what he did. It entirely depends. So, not forgetting the wrong done to you does not mean that you have not genuinely forgiven him. Likewise,

277

if you do manage to forget it, you have gone a long way beyond what is required of you for basic forgiveness.

e)   to *trust* him, either with your tools, or in some other way. Forgiving your neighbour does not oblige you to trust him, either now or in the future. Indeed, it might be very unwise, or even downright foolish, to trust him. He could be entirely unworthy of any trust, either in that area, or any other. God would, very probably, not want you to trust him, because the Bible does not tell us to trust others. On the contrary, the usual default-setting is that we should be cautious. Even so, He still commands you to forgive him, at least in the basic sense, but the resumption of trust is not required in order for genuine forgiveness to occur.

f)   to be *reconciled* with him, such that you are back on friendly terms and in a full relationship, as if nothing had ever happened. Again, this may or may not be either appropriate or possible. As we have seen above, it depends on all sorts of other factors. What we can say for sure is that the issue of whether you have, or have not, become reconciled has nothing to do with whether you have genuinely forgiven him in the basic, narrow sense of the word.

One reason why forgiveness is so badly misunderstood is that demons work hard to make sure that we misunderstand it. Their focus on this area shows how important it is.

As you consider the issue now, does it occur to you that it is odd that we are so prone to misunderstanding words like forgiveness, but understand other words very easily? For example, have you ever met anybody who does not understand words like 'refrigerator' or 'temperature' or even more complex words like 'democracy' or 'unemployment'?

In fact, I would go so far as to predict that if a survey was carried out, it would reveal that even the offside rule in football (soccer) is more widely and accurately understood than the meaning of the word 'forgiveness'. I would suggest that one explanation for this widespread lack of understanding is that the demons work hard to ensure that there is confusion about any word or concept which really matters.

They know which things would cause the biggest problems for the Church if they are not understood correctly. The demons don't mind at all if you accurately understand refrigerators, the offside rule, and even democracy. So, they don't bother to cause any sabotage in those areas. However, the demons know the huge significance of forgiveness.

It not only affects your relationships with other people, especially within the Church. It also has a major bearing on your effectiveness as a Christian, right across the board. It also affects the ability of the wider Church to function properly and to be a witness to the unsaved world around us. Most importantly of all, it even has a bearing on God's willingness to forgive you.

It would therefore be hard to think of many things which could be more important than forgiving other people. The demons can't stop you from reading the Bible or from seeing that the forgiving of others is required of you. However, what they can very easily do is to render your efforts to forgive others ineffective by getting you *to define* forgiveness differently from how God defines it.

In particular, they want you to see it as being something bigger, wider and more difficult than it really is. If they can achieve that, then the chances are that you will:

a) consider it impossible to forgive others

b) therefore not even attempt it

c) attempt it but fail, or at least believe you have failed, because you are trying to go further than God actually commands, and to do things which are over and above what He asks of us

d) see forgiveness as something which has to be achieved at the level of your feelings when God sees it as taking place at the level of your will, i.e. a pure decision, or choice

e) conclude that your attempts to forgive are not working and therefore give up on it and lapse back into unforgiveness, bitterness, and even hate

f) avoid preaching to others on the subject of forgiveness, because you are discouraged and confused about it yourself, and find it hard to put into practice. That reluctance to teach others about the subject then compounds the problem of ignorance and confusion even further

As stated earlier, we don't seem to have any equivalent difficulty understanding other words that are in common usage, or even the less common words. We don't add extra layers of complexity to the meaning of those words, or mix them up with other things. Therefore, the fact that forgiveness is so widely and seriously misunderstood, and that our efforts to implement it are so profoundly ineffectual, shows how much effort the demons are putting in to sabotaging our thinking.

That in itself should help to persuade you that forgiveness is an exceptionally important issue and one which warrants a great deal of extra attention. The demons consider the derailing of our attempts to forgive each other to be of vital strategic importance to their war aims. Therefore, understanding it correctly, and achieving it in practice, must be equally important to ours. Accordingly, we should make at least the same effort to define its meaning correctly as the demons make in trying to obscure it.

Why does God make our forgiving others a pre-condition to Him forgiving us?

I believe that God has two main reasons for requiring us to forgive others, i.e. at least in the narrow, basic sense, before He will forgive us. They are as follows:

a) For us to judge and punish people ourselves is to usurp the role of Jesus, which is presumptuous. If you think God is being overly sensitive about that, just imagine the reaction you would get from one of the judges at The Royal Courts of Justice on the Strand if you went into his court room and sat down in his chair. Would you accuse him of being over-sensitive if he sent for the ushers and had you thrown out?

b) If we won't forgive others and insist instead on judging them, and even punishing and taking vengeance against them, ourselves, then it shows that we haven't properly grasped the fact that we too are sinful. We are each guilty of the same, or similar, things as that wrongdoer whom we are refusing to forgive. If we won't, or can't, see that then it may mean that our own repentance is insincere or inadequate. How can we, in our own sinful state as wrongdoers, cry out to God for mercy and forgiveness if we haven't understood that the person who has wronged us is in an identical situation to our own?

At the very least, an unwillingness to forgive others may be evidence that you have not genuinely grasped the extent of your own sinfulness and your own need for repentance. Conversely, a genuine willingness to forgive others is powerful evidence that you have. Therefore, the fact that you have an ongoing attitude of unforgiveness and bitterness towards others calls into question the adequacy, and even the genuineness, of your own faith and repentance.

God is looking for truth and sincerity. Therefore it follows that this test of our genuineness, i.e. the question of whether we are willing to forgive others, will be very significant to Him. Accordingly, let's make sure we pass this test. Let's forgive others, at least in the basic, narrow sense. Ideally, let's try to go farther than that, if we can, and if it is appropriate. Then, without any hypocrisy, we can ask God to do the same for us.

The harm that unforgiveness and bitterness can do

There are many harmful consequences that follow if we will not forgive others. One major problem is the ongoing emotional effect that it has on us. If the many wrongs done to us are not forgiven and handed over to Jesus to judge (and punish if need be) then they won't go away. Instead, they will fester within us and grow into a 'tumour' of bitterness.

That build-up of unresolved grievances will have a very damaging effect on us. We know that from our own experience. There is even a nasty chemical reaction within us when we feel pent up anger which is not properly dealt with and has no outlet. When that reservoir of accumulated grievances isn't dealt with it turns into bitterness. That then flares up into fresh anger (i.e. of the carnal variety, not righteous anger) every time we remember what was done to us.

Sometimes we remind ourselves of the grievance by 'nursing' it and forming a grudge. We get the sense of grievance out, from time to time, to dwell on it and think about it again and again. Every time we do that we cause another dose of damaging chemicals and hormones to be produced within ourselves. These then linger in our system, doing physical harm to us, as well as emotional and spiritual damage.

In fact, these chemical responses are the cause of many literal cancers. I was speaking to a throat and mouth cancer specialist some time ago. She sees a regular pattern among her patients. Many of them are heavy-drinking men who are also embittered and angry, and have been so for years. Cancer appears to be one of the end results of all that.

I recall a very unfortunate woman whose son was brutally murdered in the 1960s by the 'Moors Murderers', Ian Brady and Myra Hindley. For decades the mother held on to all of her bitterness and campaigned for the murderers never to be released from prison. She would often appear on TV saying "*I will never forgive them for what they did*".

One really can understand her reaction and sympathize deeply with her. Who wouldn't? Her 12 year old son had been tortured and killed by two sadistic people who had done it all purely for 'fun' and showed no remorse. Yet, despite the appalling injustice of it all, the undeniable fact is that she caused severe additional damage to herself by holding on to all the bitterness, instead of handing it all over to Jesus.

One could see in her face, and hear in her voice, what her unforgiveness was doing to her. She eventually died, never having managed to forgive the killers, and never having got free of her own bitterness. The final 40 years of her life were blighted by it. By contrast, another man had a daughter who was killed by an IRA bomb at Enniskillen.

He decided, to forgive the men who did it. He was a mature Christian and had an accurate understanding of what forgiveness really is. His life from then on was totally different to that of the mother of the Moors murderers' victim. He still had to bear all his grief, but he was capable of carrying on living his life.

So, he still suffered all the sadness and loss, but the point is that those things did not destroy him, because he refused to let them do so. The same effect is seen, in either direction, in our own lives. We can choose to allow the bitterness to remain. If so, we will be harmed by it. Or, we can let it go, hand it over to Jesus (i.e. forgive the person in the narrow, basic sense) and have peace of mind.

Bitterness, rage and hate will also create major obstacles to your own progress, i.e. spiritually and otherwise. You will not be able to grow as a Christian, or serve God as you should, if you are harbouring such feelings. They prevent us from being of any use to God and create boundaries, beyond which we cannot go until we deal with them.

However, that can only be done by forgiving. There is no other way. There is no form of counselling or psychological technique or medication which can achieve what real forgiveness achieves. If we refuse to forgive the wrongdoer, the initial wrong done to us can end up having an exponentially increased impact upon the whole of the rest of our lives, even in eternity.

It seems unfair, in a sense, but that is the way it is and we have no alternative but to face that fact. A wise person will therefore do whatever is needed to remove from his life anything which hinders his own spiritual progress, regardless of whether it seems 'fair' to him. In particular, we need to prevent any *"root of bitterness"* from developing:

See to it that no one fail to obtain the grace of God; that no "root of bitterness" spring up and cause trouble, and by it the many become defiled;
Hebrews 12:15 (RSV)

Unforgiveness makes us hard and sour. It also causes us to lose our sense of proportion and perspective. If so, we may become unjust to others, as the indirect, but foreseeable, result of the original wrong done to us. We are not to blame for that original wrong, but we are answerable for our reactions to it.

Thus a wrong can be endlessly multiplied in its effect, i.e. in the harm it causes, if we fail to forgive. Conversely, forgiveness, especially if it is done early, puts a stop to that chain of causation. It prevents the escalation of harm that would otherwise have resulted.

What is the difference between 'anger' and 'rage'?

We have seen above how so many important biblical words and concepts are seriously misunderstood. We shall now look at two more, i.e. *'anger'* and *'rage'*.

The first, anger, is not necessarily sinful. Indeed, it can be entirely justified and even righteous, depending on the circumstances and the way in which the anger is handled and expressed:

26Be angry, and yet do not sin; do not let the sun go down on your anger, 27and do not give the devil an opportunity.

Ephesians 4:26-27 (NASB)

The classic example in the Scriptures of righteous anger, or righteous indignation, is the occasion when Jesus drove the corrupt and irreverent money changers out of the Temple:

And they came to Jerusalem. And he entered the temple and began to drive out those who sold and those who bought in the temple, and he overturned the tables of the money-changers and the seats of those who sold pigeons; 16 and he would not allow anyone to carry anything through the temple. 17 And he taught, and said to them, "Is it not written, 'My house shall be called a house of prayer for all the nations'? But you have made it a den of robbers." 18 And the chief priests and the scribes heard it and sought a way to destroy him; for they feared him, because all the multitude was astonished at his teaching.

Mark 11:15-18 (RSV)

What Jesus did on that occasion was obviously not sinful. That has to be the case, because He never sinned in any way at all. The anger He showed was righteous. Those men were dishonouring God. Moreover, they were doing so in the Temple, of which Jesus was the rightful Lord. So, He had every right to throw them out and He was not over-stepping the mark or exceeding His proper authority.

Moreover, the way in which He manifested His anger was equally righteous. That is He never lost His self-control. Everything He did to the money changers was what He intended to do. That is He did not "*lose His temper*" or "*go too far*" or "*lash out*" or say things which he later regretted.

That is the essential difference between anger and rage. Anger is an emotion which is potentially righteous. It is capable of being felt by our 'new man' or 'spirit' or 'new nature'. (See Book Seven for a fuller explanation of these terms.) Our new man or human spirit, which is what we are meant to operate in, and through, is capable of feeling anger and of expressing it and acting upon it.

So, whilst ever we continue to operate solely in or through our new man/spirit we will do all of this in a righteous, godly, sinless manner. That's because our new man, i.e. our human spirit which is brought back to life when we are born again, is capable of feeling anger, but is incapable of sin.

However, if we are, instead, operating in, or through, our 'old man' or 'flesh' or 'sinful nature' or 'Adamic nature' (see Book Seven) then we will act sinfully and express or manifest our anger in a sinful or 'carnal' way. A person who is acting in that way will do the following kinds of things:

a) raise their voice, or even shout

b) lose their temper, i.e. lose their self-control

c) lash out in words, or even physically

d) say hurtful, wounding, insulting things which they may well regret later

e) seek to get even with, or hit back at, the other person, i.e. as opposed to dealing firmly, but calmly, with the situation and simply doing what is appropriate and necessary, but no more

Perhaps it will assist if we look at some practical examples from my own past experience. If you are a police officer, as I was, and are dealing with an offender who has done something very wrong, you might feel a sense of anger at their conduct and its consequences. However, you must never allow that to affect the way you do your job. You must remain calm, measured and professional and not allow your interrogation of that prisoner to become intemperate.

Neither can you ever let your judgment become clouded by your feelings. Likewise, if you are a manager or proprietor dealing with a particularly nasty episode of misconduct, bullying or theft on the part of an employee, you could feel anger (in your spirit) but you must conduct the investigation and/or disciplinary hearing(s) with complete self-control at all times.

I am not discussing hypothetical or theoretical situations here. I have had to do both of the above things on many occasions. I am not saying that I always achieved it, but what I was aiming for was to do my job, get to the truth, and then take whatever action was justified by the facts. That could include prosecuting an offender, or sacking an employee, or perhaps giving a lesser sanction such as a warning, or suspending the person, pending further enquiries etc.

In such situations it is absolutely essential that you maintain complete self-control throughout. I actually found that it helped if I deliberately lowered my voice and spoke more quietly and slowly than I would usually do. Then, if you decide to charge the person and recommend prosecution, or if you decide to sack them, you are making those decisions while acting in, or through, your spirit, with the help of the Holy Spirit, rather than through your old man or flesh.

The same considerations apply in all sorts of other situations, not just the ones described above. So, for example, you might need to take a faulty item back to a shop, or speak to a motorist who parks across your driveway, blocking your access. If so, your duty is to handle that situation with self-control, in and through your spirit, not your flesh.

You must also avoid any intemperate speech or conduct. Accordingly, we can, and sometimes must, handle situations which require us to make decisions about another person, or to confront them about their behaviour, but at the same time we can and must also:

a) forgive them, in the narrow sense of not purporting to take Jesus' proper place as their ultimate Judge

b) where appropriate, show mercy and grace to them, to the extent that it is right to do so

c) possibly even go further than that and seek to make peace with them, be reconciled, resume trust and friendship etc, where those things are feasible and appropriate

d) conduct ourselves temperately and with self-control, recognizing our own feelings, and even feeling anger where that is legitimate, but without any form of rage, railing or lashing out

Illegitimately judging other people brings God's judgment upon ourselves.

There is another good reason to forgive others. It is that when we judge other people (in the wrong sense of that word) we bring God's judgment upon ourselves. Moreover, He has said that He will use the same standards, or criteria, to judge us as we have used to judge others. So, if we are merciful and forgiving with others, then God will be merciful and forgiving with us. But if we are harsh, strict and unyielding, then He will be like that with us:

[1]"Do not judge so that you will not be judged. [2]"For in the way you judge, you will be judged; and by your standard of measure, it will be measured to you.
Matthew 7:1-2 (NASB)

"Blessed are the merciful, for they shall obtain mercy.
Matthew 5:7 (RSV)

What if the wrongdoer is unrepentant and unconcerned?

For many of us, this is the hardest thing to bear - seeing the wrongdoer walking around, carefree and not even showing any concern, let alone repentance, for what He has done. He may even taunt us about it and laugh about the harm he did to us. That is much harder to handle than when the wrongdoer recognises the wrong he did and is sorry for it.

In addition to the original wrong done to you, there is the fresh insult every day of seeing the wrongdoer's brazen face, knowing that he feels no remorse and that he seems to have got away with it, i.e. that there is no justice, or at least not at present.

Perhaps the police are refusing to deal with it. Or, the people around you, even in the church, may seem not to care about the wrong done to you. They may even be more sympathetic towards the wrongdoer than they are to you, as the victim. That is often the case. In these circumstance it is as if a fresh wound is created, or at least opened up, every day.

So, in addition to forgiving the original wrong, we also have to keep forgiving each fresh violation, day by day. That is very hard, but it is still possible, because what you are being commanded to do is actually quite narrow and is entirely a matter of your will, which is always under your control. It is not about your feelings or emotions, which you are not necessarily able to control.

Remember that what we are commanded to do is basic forgiveness, i.e. narrowly defined. Therefore it does not necessarily involve going any further than simply stepping aside, 'recusing yourself', and leaving everything, including any new offences caused by the wrongdoer's lack of remorse, to be judged by Jesus. It does not necessarily mean doing anything beyond that, or at least not to begin with. More could be required of us later.

So, whatever state our emotions might currently be in, we can always choose, purely as an exercise of our will, to step aside and leave the judging for Jesus to deal with. That basic act of forgiveness is all we are being required to do, until or unless God asks us to go further than that. Moreover, we are always capable of it. We just don't always choose to do it.

Dealing practically with the fresh violation you feel when you see that the wrongdoer is brass-faced and feels no shame

The same principles apply as with the original wrongdoing. So, along with the difficulties that come from the original wrong, you have the extra ordeal of facing the wrongdoer and seeing him, large as life. Perhaps he is even attending the same church as you, despite showing no apparent repentance. It may be that nobody thinks it matters, or is willing to confront him about it on your behalf.

Jesus is still the one who will judge these additional, ongoing offences. It is all going to be dealt with by Him, just as the original wrong will be. We can still step aside and leave each new violation to Him, in just the same way. We can hand it

286

over to Jesus each day, tell Him how we feel, ask Him to deal with it and then go on to forgive the wrongdoer as a decision of our will.

If need be, we can do this over and over again, as many times as it takes, even *"seventy times seven"*, as Jesus said. That said, we also need to be realistic. So, if the wrongdoer's brass-faced attitude is offending you, why not consider altering your daily routines, or travel times, or the place where you sit, so as to avoid coming into any further contact with him, or at least minimizing the contact?

There is no reason why you shouldn't do that. It is not inconsistent with genuinely forgiving, and it may well be a big help. However, if the avoidance of further contact isn't possible, for practical reasons, we just need to keep on forgiving. We should also ask God to help us to do so, and also to help us at an emotional level to deal with our feelings, even though those are not directly involved in the decision to forgive.

Those feelings may not be what forgiveness is about, but they still matter to us, and they also matter to God. He created us with emotions and it is possible for us to have feelings, even very strong ones, without degenerating into unforgiveness, or into any other form of sin, as a result.

Forgiveness is not done for the benefit of the wrongdoer. Therefore, it does not require their repentance before we can forgive them (though it does help a lot)

We must remember this crucial point, which may help some people who are struggling to forgive. It is that we do not forgive people for *their* sake, so that they can benefit. It is done, primarily, for *our own* benefit. So, it is not something we are doing to help the wrongdoer.

Furthermore, it does not require his repentance as a precondition. It is done to help ourselves and also, above all, to obey God. The wrongdoer may also benefit indirectly from our forgiveness, provided he repents and is willing to receive forgiveness from you and from God.

However, other than that, he will not usually benefit. In any case, even if he does benefit, he is not to be seen as the focal point of the situation, either from your perspective or God's. It is not about the wrongdoer and it is not being done for his sake. On the contrary, his indifference to our forgiveness, and to any mercy or grace that we show to him, will probably only make his own eventual judgment a stricter one.

So, when we struggle to forgive, we need to keep reminding ourselves that it is something we are trying to do for our own benefit. It is for the sake of our own health, both emotional and physical, and also to protect ourselves spiritually. Above all, though, it is an issue of obedience.

Don't allow the wrongdoer to harm you even further by preventing you from forgiving

Given all these factors, and there are some more that we shall look at below, we must not allow the wrongdoer's unrepentant attitude to prevent us from achieving forgiveness. That would be to allow the wrongdoer to compound the original wrong which he did. So, do not allow anybody to have so much influence over you that they can determine whether, or when, you forgive them. It is not up to them.

It is up to you, because your forgiveness of them is primarily being done for your benefit, not theirs. And, of course, it is being done in order to obey God's command. Therefore you must not allow anybody else to be in control of whether or not you obey God. So, be in sole control of your own life. Don't allow the wrongdoer to retain any ongoing power or influence over you, either in this area, or in any other. Of course, this is much easier said than done, but it still remains the right thing to aim for.

CHAPTER 14

HOW TO FORGIVE PEOPLE IN PRACTICAL TERMS – SOME ADVICE ON WHAT TO DO AND HOW TO GO ABOUT IT

²¹Then Peter came and said to Him, "Lord, how often shall my brother sin against me and I forgive him? Up to seven times?" ²²Jesus said to him, "I do not say to you, up to seven times, but up to seventy times seven.

Matthew 18:21-22 (NASB)

Refrain from anger, and forsake wrath!
Fret not yourself; it tends only to evil.
Psalm 37:8 (RSV)

Bless those who persecute you; bless and do not curse them.
Romans 12:14 (RSV)

See that none of you repays evil for evil, but always seek to do good to one another and to all.
1 Thessalonians 5:15 (RSV)

How to actually forgive, in practical terms

Where forgiveness is proving to be difficult, you would always be well advised to begin with prayer. You might find that although basic forgiveness is a decision made by your will, you somehow feel unable to achieve forgiveness on your own, solely by willpower. The very fact that it can be difficult is what makes it essential to seek God's help. Without Him we may not always be able to bring ourselves to do it.

Moreover, we may not be able to overcome the feelings of bitterness, or even rage, that we might be experiencing. So, begin by telling God exactly how you feel, without any pretence, and without hiding anything, because He knows anyway. The reason for telling Him is not so that He can be better informed. It is so that you can recognise the reality of your position and begin to seek His help.

God knows all about your feelings anyway, but it will help you if you express it all to Him, preferably out loud. It will also help you to be real and to identify exactly what the wrong is, or at least what you believe it to be. It may also help to spell out to yourself exactly what it is that you are seeking to achieve.

For example, are you still trying to get to the stage of even basic forgiveness, where you 'recuse yourself' and hand the case over to Jesus? It could be that you are struggling to get rid of intense feelings of bitterness, which are overwhelming you? Or it could be that you have got beyond that stage and are now seeking for the grace to go further and become capable of being reconciled with the wrongdoer, or of working alongside him again.

If you spell all of this out, purely for your own sake, it will help you to define your current position and your objectives more clearly. It will also help you to avoid confusing yourself about what your duty is and what exactly it is that you are struggling to achieve. It could be that setting this out, in plain words will cause you to realise that you are trying to go too far too fast and that you are actually going beyond what Jesus has commanded you to do.

Ideally, write it all down on a piece of paper, so that you can see your own thinking and force any error or confusion to come to the surface. It will probably be staring up at you from the page. Then, you will be better placed to ask God to give you the ability to forgive the wrong, at least in basic terms, or even to go further than that, if that seems appropriate.

It may be that you feel so low, and so damaged by the actions or words of the wrongdoer, that you do not even feel capable of praying for the ability to forgive them. If so, go back a stage. Ask God to help you even to be *"willing to be willing"*. God is totally realistic about us and He is very practical. He knows that we are frail, weak and sinful.

He also knows our difficulties in the area of forgiveness, because He is our Creator and He made our emotions as a valid and essential part of us. He created us with emotions because we need them, but also because He has emotions Himself and we are made in His image and likeness. So, the point is that God really does understand that we feel things, as well as merely thinking or deciding and He knows that we find those feelings hard to handle at times.

In addition to that, Jesus was, and still is, a man. Therefore He knows exactly how you feel from first-hand experience. He felt very similar feelings Himself. The difference is that when He felt violated or traumatized He reacted in a totally sinless way, whereas we usually don't. So, for all those reasons, He really does understand you, and He also sympathizes. He will therefore honour an honest prayer, perhaps along the following lines:

"The truth is I'm not yet willing to forgive, even in the narrow, basic sense of the word. However, I want to be obedient, so I want to get to a place where I could become willing to do so. Therefore, please help me to change my heart attitude, so as to become willing to forgive person X".

God strongly desires to answer a sincere and unpretentious prayer like that. You can be sure that He will readily respond to it by changing you on the inside and by giving you the grace that you need to take difficult decisions and steps. Therefore pray like that, and continue doing so, for as long as it takes.

Pray directly for the wrongdoer himself. In doing so, you are showing grace towards them and you will therefore receive God's grace in return. Plus it will soften your own heart.

Another very helpful approach, which can help to get you to the place where you become capable of forgiving, or even to be 'willing to be willing' to do so, is just to begin to pray in general terms for the overall benefit of the person who has wronged you. It is possible to do this as a sheer exercise of your will, before you have managed to forgive them at all, even in the narrow sense.

It is something which you can make yourself do, even while your emotions are very raw. For example, pray for God to bless the wrongdoer, and their family and to bring him to a place of repentance and salvation. Also you could ask God to forgive the wrongdoer, even if you do not yet feel able to forgive him yourself.

There is nothing hypocritical about that. It is good preliminary ground-work and will help to make your own forgiveness of the wrongdoer achievable. The point is you cannot control how you *feel*, but you can control what you *say and do*.

Thus you can pray like this for the general benefit of the person who has harmed you, even if you are still unable to forgive them and/or if you keep falling back into unforgiveness and bitterness. If you pray for the person who has wronged you, or is still wronging you, then it has the following beneficial results:

a) It changes you on the inside. It also gradually alters your attitude to the wrongdoer.

b) It also brings emotional healing such that, eventually, it will bring you up to a place where you can manage to forgive.

c) It changes the way God deals with you. When God sees you praying for the wrongdoer and showing such mercy and grace towards him, then God will show equivalent mercy and grace towards you, as we saw above.

God is also particularly pleased when He sees us doing something from sheer obedience, as an exercise of our will, even when we do not feel like doing it. He knows how we feel inside. Therefore, that sacrifice on our part makes our obedience all the more precious to God. Accordingly, one can see that praying for one's enemies and persecutors is not idealistic, unrealistic or silly.

It is actually hard-headed common sense and it is entirely in your own interests to do it. In short, if you show grace towards others, you will receive God's grace towards you in return. That is a certainty. Part of that grace will be that He will give you the ability to forgive others in circumstances where you are currently struggling to do it.

Forgiveness is primarily something we do rather than something we feel

Many people struggle and get confused because they don't realise, or they keep forgetting, that forgiveness is primarily something we *do*, not something we *feel*. To a very large extent, feelings follow actions. Thus, merely by the physical act of speaking the words of forgiveness and doing tangible things such as praying for the wrongdoer, your feelings will eventually come into line with what you are saying and doing.

It is important to remember this when you feel you just can't bring yourself to forgive someone, or where the bitterness won't go away. If you, nonetheless, force yourself to speak out the words of forgiveness and to pray for the wrongdoer, you will find that your feelings towards him will gradually alter.

What was initially unthinkable will start to become thinkable. After that, it will become possible and, eventually, it will be achieved. If you don't realise that forgiveness is sometimes only possible if it is done in stages, and that it is primarily a decision, not a feeling, you could waste years of your life just waiting forlornly for your feelings to change.

However, they won't. If anything, the bitterness usually gets more intense as time goes by. So, it is a major error to imagine that you must feel like forgiving before you can actually forgive. That is not true. The truth is that most of us won't ever feel like forgiving. Why would we? It doesn't work that way. We are sinners, with a flesh nature, to which forgiving others does not come naturally.

Moreover, we are still living in this sinful world, surrounded by other sinners who don't believe in forgiveness either. We are not yet glorified, or even fully sanctified, so why should we expect forgiveness to be easy or to be something that we would ever 'want' to do. It's not a question of *wanting* to forgive, but of *choosing* to do so. That choice need not have anything to do with our feelings.

Ask God to help you to see your own faults too, and even how you may possibly have contributed to the wrong that was done to you

Another very helpful thing to do is to ask God to reveal to us what our own faults and sins are. All of us tend to under-estimate our own sinfulness. We don't realise the degree to which, and the ways in which, we have, ourselves, wronged God and wronged others. Sometimes (not always) the truth is that we were, in some way or another, at least partly to blame for the wrong that was done to us.

We may even have provoked it in some way that we did not realise or have forgotten about. We can therefore be greatly helped if we ask God to bring our own faults to the surface and to expose them. That revelation will help us to be able to forgive the wrongdoer, because we will realise, all the more clearly, how we are also a wrongdoer.

We may even see that we have partly caused, or contributed to, the wrong that was done to us. Or we might discover that we have wronged others in similar ways. Regrettably, the truth is that most of us are largely blind to our own faults. We either don't see them properly or we don't see them at all.

Sometimes, (not always) we may be operating hypocritically, wrestling with our inability to forgive person X, whilst being oblivious to the damage *we* have done to him and/or to someone else, perhaps person Y or Z. If we could see the incident that hurt us from the perspectives of any or all of those others, then our own grievance may suddenly appear different and less one-sided.

This is not always true, but it often is. I can think of one situation I know of where Person A was speaking of the way they had been mistreated by Person B. Those who heard this account, and who knew the background facts, were well aware that Person A was seriously deluded. They were convinced that they had *"done nothing wrong"*, but we all knew that they had.

It possibly wasn't our place to say so, but if Person A had asked God, He would have revealed the fuller picture to them. That would have enabled them to see how, in fact, the mess they were in was partly caused by their own selfishness, pride, stubbornness etc.

What's more, if Person A had really wanted to know the truth, they could have asked any of us and said: *"Tell me the truth - did I contribute to the problem in any way with wrong behaviour or wrong attitudes of my own?"*

Had Person A done that, we could have explained things to them gently. That would have made it so much easier for them to forgive the wrong (a real one) which had been done to them by person B. They would have seen the whole episode more clearly and fairly and in its proper context.

When and how does God judge and punish?

One day Jesus will judge all of us, either at the Judgment Seat of Christ or at the Great White Throne. However, He will also judge wrongdoers in various other preliminary ways, long before those final Judgments occur. God uses human governments to judge wrongdoers here and now. He also uses the police, lawyers, judges, magistrates, prisons, civil courts, local councils etc etc. All of these bodies, are used by God to punish wrongdoers, albeit only to a limited extent.

God puts them in place for that very purpose, to maintain order, restrain crime and punish the wicked, pending the final Day of Judgment. These organisations are all God's agents. That's why we are commanded to pray for them, and all the more so in countries where those institutions are inefficient or even corrupt. They are doing God's work, or at least they are meant to be, even if they don't realise it.

Therefore, where they exist, we can allow God to use institutions like the police or civil courts to deal with the person who has wronged us, even ahead of the final Judgment. That is not inconsistent with our forgiving them. So, we could go to the police about a crime, or even sue someone, but still genuinely forgive them.

There is not necessarily a contradiction in any of that. Sometimes it's the very fact that we can hand it all over to the police, or to a court, that makes it possible for us to forgive the wrongdoer. It brings justice forward, at least in part, so that we don't always have to wait to the very end of this age in order to be vindicated or to see justice done.

I emphasize this because some people think that if they do go to the police or take part in a civil case, as the Claimant or as a witness, then that must mean they are not properly forgiving the other person. That could be true, in some situations, but it is not necessarily so in all cases. On the contrary, forgiveness involves handing things over to God to deal with.

Therefore that can, sometimes, also include handing it over to God to deal with right now by making use of the very institutions which He has set up to punish people on His behalf. Those courts or prisons etc are a part of Jesus' role as Judge of the world. They are a small foretaste of what the final Judgments are going to be like.

He will conduct those final hearings Himself, in person. However, for now, Jesus chooses to operate, in part, through various human agencies. So a Christian need not feel precluded from using those. Jesus gave those institutions to us for our benefit, and we are meant to use them, where it is appropriate.

Admittedly, it is not always right to go to the police or to lawyers. Much will depend on your real motives and heart attitude. But it may well be right to go to those people for help. Doing so is not necessarily inconsistent with the idea of forgiving the wrongdoer and does not necessarily mean that you are disobeying God or being vindictive.

One important question to ask yourself is whether you are motivated by vindictiveness or by a genuine wish to seek for justice. It may not always be easy for you to tell what your own motives are. You may need the guidance of others to help you decide whether or not to take a matter to the police, or to pursue a civil claim, or just to let the matter drop. There is no obviously right answer, which is always appropriate. It depends on all sorts of factors and circumstances.

Handing things over to be judged by God because there are no human courts or institutions which we can go to

Sometimes there is no human court that we can go to. The wrong done to us may not even be a crime. Thus it may be something that the police cannot help us with. If so, we may need to just hand the situation over to God and ask Him to decide who is right and to deal with any wrong done to us. David adopted that approach in his dealings with King Saul who was persecuting him maliciously:

May the LORD therefore be judge, and give sentence between me and you, and see to it, and plead my cause, and deliver me from your hand."
                                                                    1 Samuel 24:15 (RSV)

David could not appeal to the King for help or justice, because the man persecuting him was *the King* himself. So he trusted in God to judge who was right and to do justice in their dispute. However, even while doing that, David refused to hit back at King Saul for himself, or to kill him. Saul recognized that fact and knew that it made David a better man than he was:

¹⁷He said to David, "You are more righteous than I; for you have repaid me good, whereas I have repaid you evil. ¹⁸And you have declared this day how you have dealt well with me, in that you did not kill me when the LORD put me into your hands. ¹⁹For if a man finds his enemy, will he let him go away safe? So may the LORD reward you with good for what you have done to me this day. ²⁰And now, behold, I know that you shall surely be king, and that the kingdom of Israel shall be established in your hand. ²¹ Swear to me therefore by the LORD that you will not cut off my descendants after me, and that you will not destroy my name out of my father's house." ²²And David swore this to Saul. Then Saul went home; but David and his men went up to the stronghold.
                                                                    1 Samuel 24:17-22 (RSV)

What about disputes with fellow Christians?

What we have been looking at has mainly been about disputes with unbelievers. But what if the wrongdoer is a Christian, or claims to be? Apostle Paul tells us not to bring law suits against fellow Christians but, instead, to seek to resolve matters via the local church. Let's look firstly at what Paul says:

¹Does any one of you, when he has a case against his neighbor, dare to go to law before the unrighteous and not before the saints? ²Or do you not know that the saints will judge the world? If the world is judged by you, are you not competent to constitute the smallest law courts? ³Do you not know that we will judge angels? How much more matters of this life? ⁴So if you have law courts dealing with matters of this life, do you appoint them as judges who are of no account in the church? ⁵I say this to your shame Is it so, that there is not among you one wise man who will be able to decide between his brethren, ⁶but brother goes to law with brother, and that before unbelievers? ⁷Actually, then, it is already a defeat for you, that you have lawsuits with one another. Why not rather be wronged? Why not rather be defrauded?

1 Corinthians 6:1-7 (NASB)

Apostle Paul is referring to situations within the very carnal church at Corinth. Some church members at Corinth were taking each other to the world's courts to deal with grievances, rather than resolving them internally within the local church. Paul disapproves of this and urges them not to engage in litigation with fellow Christians. Such disputes should be resolved within the church. That is the biblical way.

It would be good for us if Christians did handle disputes that way. However, the problem is that what we have come to know as church is very different from what used to happen in the first century. See Book Eight for more detail on what a real biblical church is meant to be like. It differed from what most churches do today in just about every conceivable way.

If we are to resolve disputes within a church, rather than via secular courts, it would require us firstly to have a proper, biblically structured church. Then it would be well placed to do all of the things it is meant to do. Sadly, we have very few biblical churches, i.e. of the type that existed in the book of Acts and for the first three centuries afterwards.

Regrettably, the man-made, traditional, hierarchical, clergy-orientated church structure which is in operation in most churches today prevents us even attempting to do things in the correct, biblical way. The structure itself makes it all impossible. Thus, whereas apostle Paul (and Jesus) envisaged such disputes being resolved within the local church, there are very few churches today which are set up in such a way as to make any of that possible, or which would even have the courage to attempt it.

For most Christians today, the idea of taking a dispute to the local church for it to be resolved there is wholly unrealistic. It would probably not be dealt with at all and, if it was even attempted, it would only be fudged or swept under the carpet. In 99% of churches that I know of the leaders would be horrified if anybody did what Paul instructed us to do.

Most leaders would do anything they could to avoid tackling such disputes and they would not permit you to bring a matter to the whole church. Nevertheless, let's look at what Jesus says about how we are meant to resolve conflict in the church:

¹⁵"If your brother sins, go and show him his fault in private; if he listens to you, you have won your brother. ¹⁶"But if he does not listen to you, take one or two more with you, so that by the mouth of two or three witnesses every fact may be confirmed. [17]*"If he refuses to listen to them, tell it to the church; and if he refuses to listen even to the church, let him be to you as a Gentile and a tax collector.*

Matthew 18:15-17 (NASB)

The Matthew chapter 18 procedure

This is Jesus speaking of how a dispute should be dealt with, as between two genuine Christians, not between two unbelievers, or even a Christian and an unbeliever. So, the first problem, before we even get to examining the problems caused by unbiblical church structure, is that it would be futile to expect this procedure to work unless all the parties are real Christians. If even one party is just a worldly, lukewarm, unrepentant 'churchgoer', it almost certainly wouldn't work.

Jesus speaks of dispute resolution as a progression, taking place in stages. Let's therefore look at the four stages that are involved in handling a dispute biblically. Then we can be aware of what we all ought to be doing, even if current church structures and practices make it virtually impossible to operate in that way. There may yet be a day when biblical church structure will be reintroduced. If so, the Matthew 18 approach to resolving conflict would become possible again. Until then, I don't think it is. Even so, here is what we are supposed to do:

a) The offended/wronged Christian goes to see the Christian whom he believes is the wrongdoer. It is to be handled privately, one to one, and face to face. The innocent party then explains what the sin is. Hopefully, the one who has done wrong will listen, repent and apologize. If so, the matter is resolved quickly and privately.

b) If the wrongdoer will not listen, or will not respond constructively, then the wronged Christian should go back to see the wrongdoer again. But this time he is to take some witnesses with him. Then he is to try again to discuss the offence, hopefully with more success. The witnesses can listen to both parties and may also be able to help to mediate between them. If that doesn't work, then the witnesses can at least try to decide what the real position is. They can also attempt to get one, or both, parties to see what they did wrong.

c) If that, in turn, fails, then the Christian who believes he has been wronged is to take the matter before the whole local church. This further escalation means that the dispute is now being openly discussed between all the members of the local church. However, if we want to see this correctly, as it was in Paul's day, we must not visualize a church of hundreds of people meeting in a big, formal building. That isn't biblical. Picture instead a small group of 20-70 people, meeting in a house or barn or school hall, all of whom know each other intimately. That is the correct biblical context in which this "Matthew 18 procedure" for resolving disputes is to be conducted. More to the point, it is the only context in which it is likely to be effective.

d) If even that fails, then the local church should no longer consider the wrongdoer to be a part of them. In short, the wrongdoer is to be expelled. This is difficult for us to understand today unless we correctly visualize the kind of church structure Jesus was speaking of. Indeed, expelling a person from a church, at least in Great Britain, is technically and legally difficult. That is because churches which wish to be registered as charities, and thus receive tax relief and other advantages, must make their services *"open to the public"*. Therefore, so far as the law is concerned, nobody can actually be prevented from attending public worship meetings.

That would not be the case if our churches today met in homes or barns or farm outbuildings, as they did in the first century. Then the provisions of Matthew 18 would be workable. The point is that what the New Testament means by a church is very different from what most of us now think of as a church. When most of us think of a church we tend to see, in our mind's eye, something which:

i) is big in numbers and meets in a large and formal building. Therefore it is very far from being a suitable setting in which to discuss a private dispute between two individuals.

ii) has at least one paid senior leader and perhaps several assistant paid leaders. Each of these has a church-based career, which would be put at risk if they were to upset people. Thus they frequently have too many vested interests at stake to be able to operate fearlessly and honestly.

iii) is full of cautious, fearful, self-centred people, such that disputes are not faced up to and addressed. Instead, disputes are generally swept under the carpet and dodged.

iv) As we have seen, is a registered charity, for tax purposes, and therefore that church can't prevent a person from attending its public services, even if it wanted to, which it probably wouldn't.

Accordingly, given the unbiblical way in which most churches are structured and led today, the procedures commanded by Jesus are not possible to implement. It is pretty much as simple as that. The context and setting that we have today are not what Jesus was referring to. Indeed, they are almost the exact opposite, in virtually every respect.

A very bad experience I once had in trying to put Matthew 18:15-17 into practice

A wronged believer might seek to carry out Jesus' commands, but he will not get very far. The structure of most churches will not allow him to do what Jesus said. Even if he tried it, he would be thwarted by the system itself and by the leaders. I speak from personal experience of this. Some years ago I went to see 'Rick', the leader of the church I was then part of. I was actually the Chairman of the Trustees of that church and he was the main full time, paid leader.

I had become increasingly concerned about the way Rick was operating. He was getting a well-deserved reputation within the town for being worldly, carnal and dishonest. However, I got absolutely nowhere in trying to raise these issues. The entire system obstructed me instead of helping me. My own experience on that occasion of attempting each of the stages of Matthew 18 was as follows:

a) Stage One

When I spoke to the leader privately, one to one, he rejected what I had to say to him, even though it was all true and fully documented. Instead of facing the real issues, Rick attacked me for raising them. He then set about telling lies about me within the church to prevent me from being able to take matters any further.

He deliberately 'got in first' to stop me being listened to or believed by other people. He did it all very craftily, partly because he was so dishonest, but also because he had had a lot of practice at handling such complaints and challenges. He had already had substantial previous experience at doing this with others who had tried to complain before.

b) Stage Two

I saw the leader him again, this time with two witnesses present. But he lied brazenly, in front of them, about what was happening. Amazingly, when the two witnesses left, Rick then openly admitted to me that he had been lying to them about it. When I asked why he had lied to them, he just shrugged his shoulders and said: "*Well, I had to defend myself*".

Unfortunately, the two witnesses were of no use at all. They were concerned only with trying to smooth things over and were not sufficiently robust or vigorous. Indeed, they weren't robust at all, as Rick knew very well. If they had been, he would never have allowed them to get involved. So, they did not actually want to tackle anything, for fear that it would create some unpleasantness or controversy for themselves. Thus they may as well not have been there at all.

299

c) Stage Three

I wasn't even permitted to implement stage three and bring it to the whole church (over 200 people). The leadership team didn't want me to, despite it being commanded in Matthew 18. I now know why. Some of them were behaving very carnally and dishonestly themselves. They didn't, therefore, want any of these facts about the leader, or themselves, to come out.

Had such information been allowed to come out to the membership, a lot of people, who already had growing concerns of their own, would have been able to see the wider picture. They would have 'joined the dots together' and realised that there was a consistent pattern of behaviour and of covering things up. The leaders as a whole were not willing to risk any of that becoming known.

I was by no means the first to tackle Rick. There had been several people beforehand with similar concerns. Many had already left the church quietly in the past, without any of the other members getting to know why they had left or the matters which they had raised before leaving.

Instead, on each occasion, false explanations for these departures were given out by Rick. They always seemed to make sense. He found a way, every time, to put the blame on those who had left and the members always believed him. Moreover, the leaders also used to make earnest sounding pleas to the remaining members not to 'gossip' or not to 'believe anything said about an elder' etc.

It was all said very insincerely, just to stop people asking questions. However, it worked. These deliberate lies and tactics prevented the wider membership from believing, or even speaking to, those who had expressed concerns. I didn't realise any of this till later. Then, when my turn came, I thought I was the first, and only, one ever to have any concerns. So did all the others who had tried to tackle Rick before I did.

d) Stage Four

The leaders had already skipped stage three, and they completely avoided stage four as well. Rick himself remained a member of the church and he even continued as the leader. Nothing was done to confront him or to expose him. Instead of the elders discussing his misconduct with the whole membership of the church, Rick himself spoke to two leaders of separate churches in the town. However, they were both his friends.

He then arranged for them to see me to discuss my concerns or, more accurately, to pacify me and get me to be quiet. Just like the two people from within the church who had acted as witnesses/mediators, these two external leaders had no real wish to deal with anything. They were not willing to do anything robust or decisive, which might cause them to get their hands dirty. In particular they were nor willing to confront Rick about any of his behaviour. All they wanted was to *"resolve matters amicably"*.

However, what they really meant by that was just meant to sweep it all under the carpet and stop it from being spoken about any longer. There was not just a lack of appetite to tackle the real issues. They were absolutely determined not to tackle any of it, and to prevent me from doing so either.

In their own way, these two external leaders were kindly people. To a certain extent they meant well, albeit in a weak and misguided sort of way. However, they were never going to be willing to grasp any nettles or tackle anything head on. Their only aim was to calm things down.

Above all, they wanted to protect the interests, and the career, of Rick, their fellow leader, no matter what he may have done. It was more like trade unionism, where a couple of shop stewards are protecting a fellow shop steward, regardless of whether he is right or wrong.

I actually put that point to one of the external leaders, i.e. that they were acting like a trade union for leaders, rather than as a church. He smiled nervously and agreed with me, but then shrugged, as if to say *"What else can we do? We've got to stick together"*. I had put my finger right on the truth and he couldn't deny it.

I was so naive at that time that all of this deceit, evasion and scheming was shocking to me. I could hardly bring myself to believe that leaders in our own church, and other churches, could act so wrongly, and without any apparent concern about what Jesus thought of them. They seemed to have no fear of God and no wish to do what Jesus said in Matthew 18.

Neither did they want to cooperate with me to enable me to do what Jesus said. Had I not been such an assertive and professionally qualified person, I would never have even got past stage one. It was exceptional to have got that far. Nobody before me had ever done so. Many others had tried to tackle this leader before me, but they had all achieved even less than I did.

In the end it had a very sad ending. Rick wasn't able to keep up appearances much longer after his clash with me. Within a year or so, he had totally given up church leadership, left his wife, and found another woman. Also one of the other members of the senior leadership team, whom I will call 'Peter' left his wife as well. He was the main one who had opposed me and who had so stridently obstructed my questions about the leader.

It also came out later that Peter himself had been having an affair, for a long time, even while he was on the senior leadership team. It then made sense as to why Peter had shouted me down when I had raised the issue of the senior leader's carnal lifestyle. It was all too close to home for him. In particular, he didn't want to allow this Matthew 18 process to lead to any questions being asked about himself.

So, all the attempts that various church leaders had made over many years, to cover things up achieved nothing good. It just caused more damage and even more people got hurt. It would be good if I could say that my experience was exceptional and that this kind of thing doesn't happen elsewhere, or to anybody else.

Sadly, I can't say that. It is actually close to being the norm. I have since come to learn, from many other people, that they have had very similar experiences all over the country. It is by no means a merely local problem.

In fact, several years later, I left another church as a result of the leader's behaviour. I did so because it came to light that that leader's character was also seriously flawed. His conduct was controlling, manipulative and deceptive. However, this time, once I had realised what was going on, I did not even attempt to implement the Matthew 18 procedure.

I took no steps to do anything about it, other than to telephone the deputy leader of the church to say that we were leaving. I also wrote a private letter to the leader, and his deputy, explaining my concern. Again, it got me absolutely nowhere. The leader just sent back a brazen and evasive reply ignoring all my points. The deputy leader of that church did nothing to assist either.

He just got annoyed with me for being "*unhelpful*" and for writing a "*critical letter*", even though it was private and was sent only to the leader and to him. As was the case when I tackled Rick, they both saw the person who was raising the concerns as being the problem, not the person about whom those concerns were being expressed. That is a very typical response.

On this second occasion I largely kept out of it, having learned my lesson the previous time. However, three other families who were members of that second church made a valiant attempt to deal with the issues. It lead, curiously, to two leaders from another local church being invited in, supposedly to "mediate".

It was all remarkably similar to what had happened in my own case, some years earlier. In the same way as before, all that these two external "mediators" wanted to achieve was to smooth things over and to get people to be quiet. Again, there was no attempt to genuinely address any of the character issues, or behavioural problems, in the life of that leader.

This second episode happened years later, in a different church, and in a different town. Yet, the techniques, used and the attitudes and approach adopted were all startlingly familiar. I have set out the brief facts of those two separate church disputes for two reasons:

a) Firstly, to enable me to explain the issues of forgiveness which arose out of it, i.e. my own need to forgive the leaders who had wronged me, plus the other leaders. Their half-hearted intervention had served only to cover things up. They obstructed the proper Matthew 18 process, rather than helping to implement it.

b) Secondly, to consider why it is so difficult even to discuss, let alone resolve, disputes within a church. If it isn't operating in a biblical way then genuine, meaningful attempts to deal with disputes between Christians are usually impossible. The unbiblical structure, and the worldly and carnal model of leadership, which has now become the norm, will not permit it. Moreover, that obstruction is generally deliberate, not accidental. Allowing such things to be openly discussed and dealt with within a church is too dangerous in their view. Far too much is at stake for them personally, in terms of careers, salaries, houses and pensions, not to mention ego and pride. Therefore they simply don't let it happen.

My experiences of reaching a place of being able to forgive abusive and dishonest church leaders

After the futile experience of trying to address issues within the first church, both my wife and I were traumatized, and far more so than we realised at the time. Moreover, the sense of violation and trauma lasted for at least three years, and probably more. This emotional reaction came from several factors which we experienced:

a) other church members avoiding us and disapproving of us, without ever asking us any questions, or checking anything with us. They simply believed everything that the leaders told them, as I had previously done myself, when other people had left the church.

b) being undermined and lied about by the elders, so as to harm our reputation and prevent people listening to us.

c) being deliberately obstructed by other leaders within our own church, so as to prevent the Matthew 18 procedure from being used effectively.

d) being betrayed and abused by Rick, the senior leader, and also other leaders within that church.

e) being let down by the external leaders from other churches in the town. They had supposedly been brought in to investigate matters, but never had any genuine intention of actually doing so. Their real aim was only to smooth things over, not to grasp any nettle or confront any person or issue. They saw me and my wife as dispensable and viewed our departure as preferable to allowing a scandal to come to light. Therefore they did nothing at all to defend us. They sought only to defend the leader's career, and to preserve only his reputation, not ours.

f)   being effectively driven out of our own church, where we had been for seven years, and had many genuine friendships, simply for having tried to address our (valid) concerns in a biblical way.

g)   being lied about by the senior leader

It was all very painful and we took far longer to get over it than I ever expected. Our initial reaction was to want to speak at length to anybody who would listen and to show how justified we were and how we had been wronged. But it did no good. It was a futile waste of time and energy. People just weren't interested.

At any rate, they didn't want to get involved or to rock the boat, especially after seeing what had happened to us for speaking out. The other members of the church basically didn't seem to mind whether the leadership was corrupt or not, provided they could have a quiet life.

Of course, the problem was hugely compounded by the fact that we were operating outside of the church structure and leadership framework envisaged by Jesus when He gave the command set out in Matthew 18. So, all of our speaking about it was unproductive. It achieved nothing other than us letting off steam.

That said, it may actually have created more trauma for us when we realised that the people to whom we thought we could turn weren't interested. They had no wish to help us. What I found most hurtful of all was the willingness of so many people to believe any lie told about us. They never questioned any of it, or checked any of it with us.

I suppose that was partly because the lies were coming directly from the mouth of the leader. They assumed that what he was saying must, therefore, be true. Even so, it wounded us badly and we felt violated. It took us about three years for our emotions to calm down. That isn't unusual. I have noticed from speaking to others that that's how long such things usually seem to take, especially when there is no proper biblical structure in place.

What made it worse was that once we left the first church, which we'd been in for seven years, we found it impossible to find any other good church to go to. That was partly because our own eyes had been opened. We therefore went from one extreme to the other. Having been absurdly naive and trusting, we then became extremely wary of other church leaders, even the better ones.

Sadly, that wariness was not solely based on our imaginations. Indeed, on the whole, it was actually well-founded.   Once God had opened our eyes to this problem within the churches, we saw falseness, ambition, pride, domination, control and manipulation almost everywhere we went. It seems that such features are now widespread among most of the leadership of churches in Great Britain.

That is partly due to the carnal condition of the churches and their leaders, but also the institutional and hierarchical nature of church structure. For many men, church leadership has become a career rather than a ministry. That is why so many of them are *hirelings* rather than shepherds.

All in all, it meant we couldn't settle in any local church for some years, until we had calmed down from the emotional trauma of the experience. When the second crisis came and we left another church for similar reasons, we suffered much less hurt. But that was only because while we were in that church we had remained at a distance, due to our wariness. We didn't allow the leaders of that second church to get close enough to us to do much harm.

As it turned out, that was a wise and fully justified policy. Three other couples we knew did get badly hurt, as we had been earlier, because they made a futile, and very naïve, attempt to tackle the issues. But we avoided it the second time. We just left quietly, without trying to deal with any of it. We knew that those three couples would be unsuccessful, and that the leader would not listen to them, or feel any remorse. Sadly, that proved to be the case.

As for dealing with the need for forgiveness from both these episodes, we just had to work it all out by ourselves. Time gradually helped to deal with the wounds. We also learned how to hand the whole dispute over to God for Him to deal with it all. Thus, we no longer felt the need to talk about it or to prove our innocence to everybody.

We also learned how to pray for all the leaders concerned. We genuinely prayed for God to bless, restore and rebuild the ministries of the leaders who had lied about us. We also asked Him to forgive them, rather than judge them, and to hold nothing against them on our account. It helped us to pray in those ways and it may, perhaps, have helped them too.

Should a Christian ever sue a fellow believer in a civil court or tribunal?

As we saw earlier, apostle Paul made a powerful statement about this in his first letter to the Corinthians. On the face of it, what he says seems quite clear and conclusive:

[1] When one of you has a grievance against another, does he dare go to law before the unrighteous instead of the saints? [2] Or do you not know that the saints will judge the world? And if the world is to be judged by you, are you incompetent to try trivial cases? [3] Do you not know that we are to judge angels? How much

more, then, matters pertaining to this life! ⁴ So if you have such cases, why do you lay them before those who have no standing in the church? ⁵ I say this to your shame. Can it be that there is no one among you wise enough to settle a dispute between the brothers, ⁶ but brother goes to law against brother, and that before unbelievers? ⁷ To have lawsuits at all with one another is already a defeat for you. Why not rather suffer wrong? Why not rather be defrauded? ⁸ But you yourselves wrong and defraud--even your own brothers!

1 Corinthians 6:1-8 (ESV)

Paul is effectively saying that if two genuine Christians, both of whom are *"brothers"*, are in a genuine, biblical church, then they should not sue each other. Instead, they should follow the Matthew Chapter 18 procedure which was laid down by Jesus, as set out above. The point is that if a church is led in a biblical way, by proper elders, who take their responsibilities seriously, then this approach can succeed, because real and meaningful discipline will result for the wrongdoer.

Moreover, there will be scope for real vindication, and perhaps even genuine redress, for the wronged party. The dispute will be tackled on an increasingly open basis, until eventually it is heard by the whole local church. Then, if the wrongdoer will not repent and put things right, he may be expelled from the church. To a real believer, in a biblical church, that sanction would matter. It would create a real and meaningful incentive to operate honestly and properly.

When Paul tells us not to sue fellow believers, I believe he means when both are real Christians and members of a biblical church, which is capable of resolving disputes. The problem today is that virtually none of the conditions which apostle Paul assumed to exist are actually applicable in our churches. Most or all of the necessary features are missing or inapplicable:

a)   There are many non-Christians who are long standing members of churches, despite the fact that they are not genuinely 'regenerate'. They may not necessarily be repentant and may not even genuinely believe. Many are just 'churchgoers', i.e. 'religious' people. They like the liturgy, tradition or culture of church, but they aren't real Christians and they aren't born again.

b)   The churches as a whole are not biblical (see Book Eight). Most are led by one man, who is paid, and views himself as belonging to a special class called 'clergy', rather than being led by a group of unpaid 'elders'.

c)   They are not small groups meeting in a house, barn or school, with 20-70 people, who know each other intimately. Most churches meet in specially designed buildings with perhaps hundreds of people, who don't know each other well, or even at all. Many people who attend churches, even those who go regularly, do not even know the names of many of the others there, let alone know them intimately. Therefore they cannot even hope to accurately assess the true nature of their characters.

d) Instead of existing to preach the authentic Gospel and make genuine disciples, most churches today (in the West) exist for other purposes. Church leadership is seen as a career by many leaders. If so, their main aim is to keep the church going, remain firmly in control, avoid controversy, and preserve their own salary and pension. That may sound cynical, but it is true far too much of the time, even for many of those men who began their ministries with high ideals.

The net effect of all this is that what Paul said in 1 Corinthians 6:1-8 and what Jesus said in Matthew 18: 15-17 cannot effectively operate in the churches that most of us attend today in the West. Can you imagine going to the leader of any church you know, whether he be a priest, vicar, or pastor, and telling him that one of the people in the church has wronged or defrauded you?

He would be most unlikely to want to get involved. But even if, somehow, he did, can you imagine him agreeing, if the dispute couldn't be resolved, to take it in the end to the 'whole church'? When and how could that ever be done? The members as a whole would not be willing or able to tackle it.

More importantly, the leader(s) would not be willing to let them try in any event. That said, you wouldn't even want it yourself, because you know it would be a shambles and that nothing useful would be achieved by it. What would actually happen, 99% of the time, is that issues would be dodged, fudged, or otherwise glossed over, so as to avoid confrontation or the need for any decision to be made.

That has always been my experience when I have tried it, and I have heard the same from many others. Accordingly, the idea of not suing a fellow Christian, even if you can be sure he really is genuinely born again, is not realistic. Paul was speaking of a context and setting which he knew, and regularly experienced, in all the churches he founded or taught at.

However, that is something which we do not have in most churches today, at least in the West. Therefore, we have to operate according to the facts as they really are and the context which we are actually in. Much of the time, the person with whom we are in dispute may not be a genuine Christian. Moreover, we are probably not in a genuine biblical church, which meets in homes, where everyone is known, and which is led by biblical elders.

Therefore the prohibition Paul spoke of would not apply, at least not in my view. That may be a revelation to some people. It may even set some people free, who have been harmed by others but wrongly believe they are forbidden by the Bible to do anything to seek redress.

I remember a problem I dealt with some years ago where a man in the church, who was a school teacher and worship leader, had loaned money to a young Christian woman who was getting married. It was to help her to cover the costs of her wedding and was a significant sum to this man. Let's call him 'Samuel' and the young woman 'Sybil'.

Samuel came to me long after the wedding because Sybil and her new husband were doing nothing to repay him. He felt frustrated and betrayed, but he also felt trapped by apostle Paul's words in 1 Corinthians 6. He believed that that passage prevented him from doing anything to force Sybil, or her husband, to repay him. He asked for my advice, as both a Solicitor and a Christian. I advised him that we could, and should, take a firm line.

Therefore I wrote a strong letter to Sybil and her husband and said that if they did not repay him then I would take on Samuel's case and sue them myself, free of charge. It worked! They paid up immediately, which proved that their non-payment up to that point was not due to any inability to pay. They just didn't *want* to pay and they had actually relied on Samuel's sincerity in taking 1 Corinthians so seriously, and therefore not being willing to force them to repay.

They knew what the Bible said on this point and were making capital from it for themselves. They thought apostle Paul's letter put them in the clear, such that they would never have to pay up. I thought it was an absolutely appalling attitude, and a clear sign of apostasy. However, they miscalculated on that particular occasion.

What about reporting a fellow believer to the police or giving evidence against them in a criminal case?

The thing which Paul prohibited in 1 Corinthians 6 was civil litigation against fellow Christians. He wasn't speaking about how we should deal with criminal offences i.e. where a Christian has committed a crime and another Christian is a witness or the injured party. This is an entirely different type of situation.

There is no reason, in principle, why a Christian should not report such a crime to the police or offer to be a witness. It is not what 1 Corinthians 6 is referring to. The first point to make is that a crime is entirely different from a civil dispute. In the eyes of the law, in the United Kingdom, all crime is committed against the Queen. It is against the State in other jurisdictions.

So, even the direct victim of a crime is technically only a witness. It is the Crown, or the State, which is actually pursuing the offender and which decides whether to prosecute. Realising that fact changes everything. The prosecuting authorities, whoever they may be, have all been put there by God so as to keep order and punish wrongdoing.

That is what God wants them to do, whether they, or those accused of crimes, are believers or not. If that is so, then it must follow that for a Christian to cooperate with the State in bringing a prosecution, is effectively to help God to pursue His objectives. That is one of the reasons why He appointed rulers and authorities in every nation:

¹ Let every person be subject to the governing authorities. For there is no authority except from God, and those that exist have been instituted by God. ² Therefore whoever resists the authorities resists what God has appointed, and those who resist will incur judgment. ³ For rulers are not a terror to good conduct, but to bad. Would you have no fear of the one who is in authority? Then do what is good, and you will receive his approval, ⁴ for he is God's servant for your good. But if you do wrong, be afraid, for he does not bear the sword in vain. For he is the servant of God, an avenger who carries out God's wrath on the wrongdoer. ⁵ Therefore one must be in subjection, not only to avoid God's wrath but also for the sake of conscience

Romans 13: 1-5 (ESV)

I emphasize all that this because I once heard of a situation where a family were put under pressure by a church leader not to go to the police when one of their own children was sexually molested by a 17 year old boy from another family in the church. They were told that it would not be right to involve the police in a "*church matter*". Paul's words from 1 Corinthians 6 were then quoted in support of that argument. However, the church leader was wrong.

He had no right to counsel the parents of the victim in that way. They were free to go to the police. Indeed, arguably, they even had a duty to go, so as to protect other people's children. At any rate, it was solely their decision, not the Pastor's, as to whether or not to involve the police. It was a matter of conscience and depended on all the facts of the case and on the circumstances and personalities of the people concerned.

I once had to give evidence in a criminal prosecution against a fellow member of a church. The story began when I gave a job to a woman who went to a church of which I used to be a member. The job didn't last long because she turned out to be lazy, dishonest and manipulative. So I got rid of her after only one month. She did not get through her probationary trial period.

To my surprise, some years later, I was contacted by the Benefits Agency. They questioned me about this lady and it turned out that she had been claiming unemployment benefits while working for me. In fact she denied to them that she had ever worked for me at all. She did the same with several other employers too. Therefore a number of managers from different companies were called as witnesses, together with me, to give evidence against her in a criminal trial.

Though I found it all very sad, I had no hesitation in signing a witness statement to testify against her. I also went to the trial, though she pleaded guilty at the last minute. Therefore I did not, in the end, need to give my evidence verbally. I believe it was my civic duty to give evidence for the prosecution. It would have been entirely wrong for me to fail to do so merely because she was a Christian, or claimed to be.

One important point to note is that I was not giving evidence for my own sake. If I had, then it would have been my own decision as to whether to do so. However, it was not my case at all. This was a prosecution by the state-appointed authorities, whom God had put in place to do justice. Christians are just as subject to their authority as anybody else is. Thus, we are all under the same duty to assist a prosecution by providing evidence, whether the accused is a Christian or not.

At any rate, we are free to do so. That said, one is not always obliged to go to the police to report every crime or offence that you believe may have been committed by a fellow believer. That would be to define the duty much too highly. It is a matter of conscience and requires wisdom, based on all the facts, to know whether to report a crime or not. The point is simply that one is not prevented from doing so by what Paul said in 1 Corinthians 6.

By the way, I am speaking of the situation in a country, the United Kingdom, which has honest judges and a largely honest police force. I recognise that that is not the case in every country and that some people will need to bear in mind the quality and level of integrity of the police and legal system when deciding whether, and if so, to what extent, to go to them and/or cooperate with them. It may be futile, or even dangerous, to try to use any of those institutions.

What if you are in a position of authority yourself, but in a work context, rather than a church?

Let's change the subject now and consider how you should act if you are, yourself, in a position of authority as a manager, or as the proprietor of a business. What if you have staff who have done wrong and need to be disciplined or even dismissed? How can that be handled, vigorously and effectively, whilst at the same time maintaining an attitude of forgiveness, and even mercy and grace, rather than one of seeking personal vengeance?

If you are in such a position of authority, then you are going to have to do what is necessary to fulfil your managerial duties. Sometimes that has to mean punishing or dismissing the person. Even so, you still need to do it with the right attitude. On many occasions I have had to dismiss members of staff for various types of misconduct. Sadly, some of those were Christians, or claimed to be.

When that occurs there can be a temptation to abuse one's position and to try to *teach the person a lesson'* or to *'get even'*. That desire for revenge, if it arises, has to be firmly resisted. We must do what is needed, but we must take no pleasure in it. This is a difficulty which most of us never have to encounter, but it is a real problem for those who do have to face such issues. Most managers make the opposite mistake of dodging the confrontation and doing nothing about the misconduct.

A minority may go the other way and tackle wrongdoers, but in a vengeful, abusive way, such that they then become part of the problem themselves, due to their carnal response. To achieve a balance, whereby you act decisively and firmly, and yet without being vengeful or abusing your own position, is surprisingly hard. Therefore it's rare for managers even to attempt it, let alone succeed in it.

Another problem that one encounters in management is the giving of references for former staff. If you have had to discipline, or even dismiss, an employee and then they get offered a job elsewhere, even years later, you will find that the prospective employer writes to you seeking a detailed reference. These reference requests present a difficulty in terms of the issue of forgiveness. One needs to:

a) tell no lies and avoid misleading the new employer and yet also

b) avoid the temptation to take revenge on the ex-member of staff by giving an unfairly harsh reference, or even an accurate one, but where one's real underlying motive is to hit back at them by revealing the truth, but in a vengeful way

This problem arose for me some time ago. An ex-member of staff, whom we will call Josephine, had claimed to be a Christian. She worked for me several years ago and had been a major disappointment. She was lazy, had a poor attendance record and was two-faced. In the end I saw through her and was very glad when she left voluntarily. Her departure prevented me from having to sack her.

Then, some years later, I got a letter asking for a reference and sending a detailed questionnaire. If I filled it in truthfully she wouldn't get the job, because I would have had to be very critical. I couldn't lie about her but, at the same time, I didn't want to harm her. So I just didn't reply.

The new employer chased again so I said I didn't want to fill in their form, without explaining why. Then Josephine contacted us herself, pleading for a reference. She said she had split up with her partner (not her husband) and was wanting to move area and start again. She made no mention of her past misconduct, and gave no apology.

Even so, I decided to write a very brief reference letter, just giving the most basic details of salary and start/end dates, etc. I was telling no lies, but trying to avoid doing her any harm, if I could avoid it. My aim at such moments is to do what is right, and yet to make sure that I do nothing to hit back or take revenge. One's

311

aim must be to remain professional and honest, yet with forgiveness, and even mercy and grace, when those are possible and appropriate.

That said, there are times when it becomes one's duty to be much more frank. That could arise where the ex-employee was so bad that one is obliged to feel concerned for the welfare of the prospective employers and/or their staff. Even so, one still needs to take no pleasure from revealing the truth about that person. We must limit ourselves solely to doing our duty, and not indulge in the taking of any kind of vengeance.

Continue to pray for those who have done you harm, even long afterwards

We are commanded to pray for the people who do us harm and abuse us:

¹⁴Bless those who persecute you; bless and do not curse.
Romans 12:14 (NASB)

There have been many people who have done me harm over the years. To the best of my knowledge, I believe that I do not feel any bitterness towards them. For many of them I have continued, over the years, to pray for their salvation. If you have been wronged and yet you freely choose to forgive them and even to become an intercessor for that person, it gives you a special standing with God.

He is more inclined to hear such a prayer and to answer it, precisely because it is unselfish. The very motivation for it, and the ability to do it, has obviously come from the Holy Spirit, not from yourself. You therefore have a special status when you pray for the people who have done you harm. It will cause your prayer to be heard. Such a prayer could be said to be the *"prayer of a righteous man"*:

.... the prayer of a righteous man is powerful and effective
James 5:16(b) (NIV)

To understand why God would give such weight to the prayer of a wronged person who is pleading with Him for mercy for the wrongdoer, consider a legal illustration. Imagine that a Judge, at the end of a criminal trial, is hearing pleas in mitigation on behalf of the wrongdoer. The Judge would hear a speech from the wrongdoer's own defence lawyer and perhaps also read reports from his social worker, probation officer, doctor, psychiatrist etc.

The Judge would listen carefully to all of them. However, it is fair to say that he would be likely to be rather guarded about placing too much weight on what any of them might say. He would be keenly aware that it is their job to speak up for the Defendant.

So the Judge would probably filter their words carefully and be slow to accept their recommendations. However, what if the victim himself was to stand up in court and ask to say a few words on the Defendant's behalf? What if the injured party said:

"I know that this young man did wrong when he robbed me, but I personally would prefer him not to go to prison, but to a drug rehabilitation unit and to resume his education as well. Would you please consider allowing that to be the sentence, instead of sending him to prison?"

One can easily imagine a Judge, on hearing the injured party speak in that way, listening very attentively and placing a great deal of weight on their plea for mercy. Likewise, when we pray for someone who has wronged us, and ask God to forgive them, bless them, and not to judge them for what they did to us, we will find that God is a very willing listener. He will take such a prayer extremely seriously.

An example of a prayer of this kind is found in Paul's second letter to Timothy. He refers to certain fellow believers who let him down by failing to stand by him when he was put on trial. They deserted him because they feared for themselves. But even as he writes about it to Timothy, Paul suddenly breaks off to utter a short prayer within the letter. He asks that God will not hold those people responsible for what they failed to do for Paul, i.e. that God will not charge them with it at the Judgment Seat of Christ:

At my first defense no one took my part; all deserted me. May it not be charged against them!

2 Timothy 4:16 (RSV)

Consider what a great opportunity that therefore gives you to do good by asking God to forgive, save and generally show mercy and grace, to those who have done you harm. You may well see men and women in Heaven who only had their eyes opened to understand the Gospel due to your unselfish prayers on their behalf. How wonderful would that be?

Nobody has the *right* to demand forgiveness from us. It is simply that we have a *duty* to forgive them. We sometimes come across people who do wrong to us, and are caught, but then speak and act as if they have an entitlement to be forgiven. Such a person may even begin to see themselves as being wronged if they are not forgiven, or rather excused.

Therefore they may get angry and say something like: *"I've said I'm sorry. Why don't you get over it?"* I once heard of a person who had been badly treated by a Christian and that the wrongdoer then told them that it was their *duty* to forgive him. That is technically true, but it was not his place to say it. The fact that he did say it was compelling evidence of his own impertinence, falseness and lack of real remorse.

I was also told of another situation where a church leader misbehaved sexually and then announced that people were obliged to forgive him. What he actually meant by that was that was that he wanted to be 'let off' and spared from the consequences of his actions. That is not the same thing as forgiveness and, again, it was not his place to say what the duty of those people was, given that he himself was the wrongdoer.

Or a person may feel aggrieved because you are continuing to investigate, or complain about, something they have done. I spoke earlier in this chapter of a church leader called Rick, whom I had to tackle some years ago, when I was the chairman of the trustees of a certain church and of how I tried, forlornly, to implement the Mathew 18 procedure. I had met the leader in the presence of witnesses, during which he blatantly lied to them. Then he said to me after they had left: *"Can't you just let me off the hook?"* He also added later: *"Why don't we draw a line under all of this?"*

However, there was no repentance on his part. He simply wanted to avoid being held accountable for his actions. For him, 'drawing a line under all of this' was not something that one does after having dealt with all the issues. It is what one does *instead of* dealing with things. He said these things as requests, but also as complaints.

He saw my continued questioning of him, and my unwillingness to drop the matter, or to be fobbed off, as if that was a wrong on my part. Like the other leader above, who was guilty of sexual sin, he felt aggrieved at being held accountable for his actions and wanted to be "let off". He spoke as if he had some kind of entitlement to be forgiven. But he hadn't.

None of us actually have any right to be forgiven, or indeed any inherent, God-given right to anything whatsoever. The correct way to put it is that other people have a duty to forgive us. But that is done in order to obey God. It does not create any corresponding right on our part to be forgiven, least of all to demand to be forgiven.

This is not mere theological hair-splitting. It has a major bearing on how we operate, which is why I give a fair amount of attention to the error of human rights based thinking, and the growing attitude of entitlement, within Book Five in this series. Please refer to that for a fuller discussion of the significance of those errors, which have been adopted by very many churches.

Moreover, any person who is assertively demanding to be forgiven or asserting a right to be "let off" is demonstrating by that attitude that they have not adequately or genuinely repented. If they had, their principal concern would be about the welfare and feelings of their victim, not about obtaining forgiveness for themselves. So, the more demanding they are, the more unrepentant they must be.

Nevertheless, the wrongdoer's bad attitude does not take away your duty to obey God by forgiving them. However, it is a factor which you can validly bear in mind in assessing the genuineness or otherwise of their repentance/apology and whether it would be appropriate to be reconciled and resume relations with them, or to avoid them.

In the story I referred to above, about my dealings with Rick, the carnal and dishonest church leader, the position was more complicated than is usually the case. I was a private individual who had been wronged by him and I therefore had a duty to forgive him. However, at the same time, I was also the Chairman of the Trustees of that church.

Therefore, given that role, I also had a duty to investigate and deal with his misconduct, or at least to attempt to do so, because I never actually succeeded. Usually you will only have one or the other of those roles, not both. Nevertheless, it serves to illustrate the problems that arise when a wrongdoer has a misguided sense of entitlement to be forgiven.

We do not necessarily need to become able or willing to trust a person whom we have forgiven

We alluded to this earlier, but it is worth elaborating on. We are not under any duty to trust the person whom we have forgiven. To be wary of that person, or even to directly expect them to wrong you again, or to lie to you, or to take advantage of you, is not an indication that you have not properly forgiven them. The Bible never tells you to trust those whom you have forgiven. Indeed, far from telling us to trust wrongdoers, the Bible never actually tells us to trust anybody at all.

On the contrary, we are to be cautious with all of the people that we do not know. That means anybody who has not yet proved, by their consistent faithfulness and reliability, that they are worthy of trust. Trust has to be earned, and over a sufficiently long period of time to be sure that it is warranted.

That applies to the people we meet outside in the world, but also to those who claim to be Christians, and even to those who really are Christians, unless and until they have proved their trustworthiness over a period of time. Even then, any trust that we do show, even to those people, is neither absolute nor unconditional. We are only to trust them up to a point, the precise level of which will depend on all the circumstances.

To do otherwise, or to go further than that, would be evidence of your naivety, not the genuineness of your forgiveness. How then can it be that some people think that a willingness to trust the wrongdoer is essential in order to prove that one's forgiveness of him was genuine? The Bible never says that, or even implies it. Indeed, it tells us to do the direct opposite, even with those who have never wronged us, let alone those who already have.

Therefore, if you have been wronged and now feel wary of that person and don't trust them enough to take any chances with them, or perhaps even to have any dealings with them at all, please do not allow yourself to be told that that, in itself, proves that you are being 'unforgiving'. At least, do not allow that accusation to be made on that basis alone. The likelihood is that you are simply showing common sense by being wary. If so, you should continue to be so, until it is proved that you don't need to be.

What if the wrongdoer is your parent?

Some people struggle with bitterness towards a parent who has wronged them, perhaps long ago. The wounds from that can be especially deep, because a parent has a unique position, from which they can do terrible harm. Thankfully, I have no personal experience of any mistreatment by my parents. So, I have nothing to forgive.

However, those who have had bad experiences and choose to harbour bitterness towards a parent rather than forgive them, do great additional harm to themselves. The bitterness causes serious problems in itself, which is bad enough. However it also prevents the person from honouring their father and mother, as God commands us all to do in the fifth commandment:

12 "Honor your father and your mother, that your days may be prolonged in the land which the LORD your God gives you.
Exodus 20:12 (NASB)

There are specific blessings that come from honouring our parents, even if we feel they have harmed us. That being so, there are all the more reasons to forgive our parents and to seek to be reconciled with them, where possible, while they are still alive. However, even if the parent is dead, you can still make a decision to forgive them and to honour them.

Their death does not take away the need to forgive them, or the ability to do so. Indeed, that is true of any person who has died. You can still tell God that you forgive that person, and release them to Him, and you should do so. You will benefit from it.

316

Forgiveness within marriage

Possibly one of the stupidest lines ever spoken in a film was in *'Love Story'* where one character says *"Love is never needing to say you're sorry"*. On the contrary, love means *regularly* having to say you're sorry. However, the reverse side of the coin is that love also means endlessly needing to *accept* such apologies and being willing to grant forgiveness to one's spouse. If not, then marriage cannot survive.

Perhaps the main reason why so many marriages today end in divorce is because of a chronic, ongoing failure to forgive. It eventually creates a vast reservoir of bitterness, which has been made from a multitude of small incidents of rudeness or thoughtfulness, each of which could, and should, have been *dealt with at the time*.

The two relationships in which one gets to know another person's sins and weaknesses in the closest detail are those of husband and wife and employer and employee. In both you get to see the other person as they really are. That is mainly by virtue of spending so much time with them, but also because you get to see them at times of great stress and pressure.

If we want our marriage to work we have to learn how to repent and apologize and also how to do so early and often, so as to prevent and/or minimize the harm that is caused by unforgiveness and bitterness. However, it is equally important to learn how to receive apologies and be a good 'forgiver' and a 'non grudge-holder'.

It is grievous to see how many married couples there are where one, or both, of them is holding onto a catalogue of complaints and will not accept apologies or let go of past grievances. They may have a long list of grudges, resentments and bitterness, some of which relate to events or words from years, or even decades earlier.

We would gain enormously from making a conscious decision to let those long lists of grievances go now, however belatedly. We should write them off and then ask God to help us not to take them back.

Our forgiveness of somebody else can be the key which opens the door for them to come to faith

One of the greatest benefits of our forgiveness of another person is that it can open the door for that person to become a Christian. Not only can forgiveness influence others and even soften their hearts. It also has the effect of prompting God to intervene and to open their eyes. Consider the experience of Saul of Tarsus, who became the apostle Paul. He hated Christianity at first and did all he could to oppose it.

Then, one day he came across Stephen, who became the first Christian martyr. Saul of Tarsus was holding the coats of those who stoned Stephen to death for speaking about Jesus. He saw Stephen die. He also saw and heard the manner in which he died, in particular the way he prayed for God to forgive those who were stoning him:

58When they had driven him out of the city, they began stoning him; and the witnesses laid aside their robes at the feet of a young man named Saul. 59They went on stoning Stephen as he called on the Lord and said, "Lord Jesus, receive my spirit!" 60Then falling on his knees, he cried out with a loud voice, "Lord, do not hold this sin against them!" Having said this, he fell asleep.

Acts 7:58-60 (NASB)

There is good reason to believe that one of the ways that God answered Stephen's prayer was by forgiving and saving Saul of Tarsus. Instead of punishing him, God then used Saul as a mighty instrument to do more for the sake of the Gospel than Stephen could ever have done. It did not happen immediately.

Saul continued to attack the church for a while longer, but it is quite likely that, even as he was doing so, he was coming under God's conviction. Indeed, it is probably because of that very conviction that Saul tried so hard thereafter to resist the Gospel. But God eventually broke down his resistance and made him into the great man that we know as Paul:

1Saul was in hearty agreement with putting him to death And on that day a great persecution began against the church in Jerusalem, and they were all scattered throughout the regions of Judea and Samaria, except the apostles. 2Some devout men buried Stephen, and made loud lamentation over him. 3But Saul began ravaging the church, entering house after house, and dragging off men and women, he would put them in prison.

Acts 8:1-3 (NASB)

1Now Saul, still breathing threats and murder against the disciples of the Lord, went to the high priest, 2and asked for letters from him to the synagogues at Damascus, so that if he found any belonging to the Way, both men and women, he might bring them bound to Jerusalem. 3As he was traveling, it happened that he was approaching Damascus, and suddenly a light from heaven flashed around him; 4and he fell to the ground and heard a voice saying to him, "Saul, Saul, why are you persecuting Me?" 5And he said, "Who are You, Lord?" And He said, "I am Jesus whom you are persecuting, 6but get up and enter the city, and it will be told you what you must do." 7The men who travelled with him stood speechless, hearing the voice but seeing no one.

Acts 9:1-7 (NASB)

10Now there was a disciple at Damascus named Ananias; and the Lord said to him in a vision, "Ananias." And he said, "Here I am, Lord." 11And the Lord said to him, "Get up and go to the street called Straight, and inquire at the house of Judas for a man from Tarsus named Saul, for he is praying, [12]and he has seen in a vision a man named Ananias come in and lay his hands on him, so that he might regain his sight." [13]But Ananias answered, "Lord, I have heard from many about this man, how much harm he did to Your saints at Jerusalem; [14]and here he has authority from the chief priests to bind all who call on Your name." [15]But the Lord said to him, "Go, for he is a chosen instrument of Mine, to bear My name before the Gentiles and kings and the sons of Israel;

Acts 9:10-15 (NASB)

Imagine how you will feel one day, on getting to Heaven, and discovering that some of your decisions to forgive people had, like Stephen's, opened the door for others to believe in Jesus Christ and be saved. That alone would make it all worthwhile.

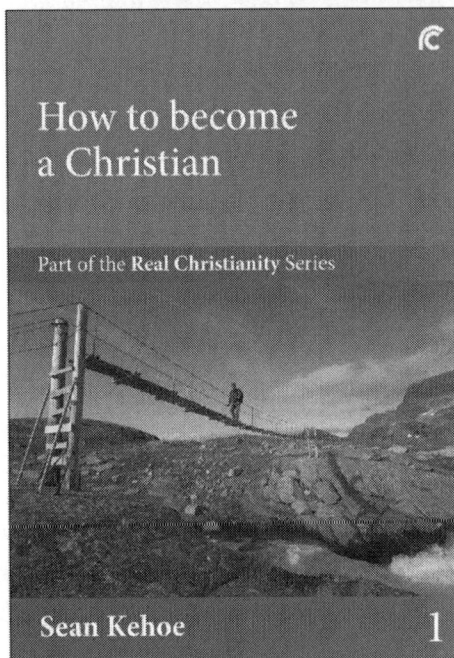

How to become a Christian

Part of the **Real Christianity** Series

Sean Kehoe

1

How to become a Christian

Sean Kehoe

Book 1 in the Real Christianity series seeks to explain the full, authentic Gospel, or "good news", as it is set out in the Bible. Tragically, much of the Church has reduced it to *"God loves you and wants you to love Him."* That is very true, but it isn't the Gospel. It leaves out many essential 'ingredients' such as our sin, God's holiness, His impending judgment, Hell, the Lake of Fire and our urgent need to repent. Each of those things, which we might call "the bad news", have been edited out by most preachers in the hope that it would make the Christian message more attractive and also to avoid offending people. Therefore we have ended up with a false, watered down, man made gospel which does not bring salvation. Ironically, such compromise does not actually attract people anyway.

Indeed, it is counter-productive, because the good news only makes sense if someone has told you what the bad news is. Therefore, because they have not heard any of that, many see no reason to repent or believe. So, this book frankly explains the real Gospel, firstly for your sake, but also to enable you to witness to others more effectively and authentically. It has been written in the clearest possible way, using plain English and avoiding religious jargon. It can be read by an absolute beginner but will also help mature Christians and leaders who want to understand and share the Gospel more accurately.

All of the books in this series, plus audio MP3s, can be ordered online from **www.realchristianity.com**.

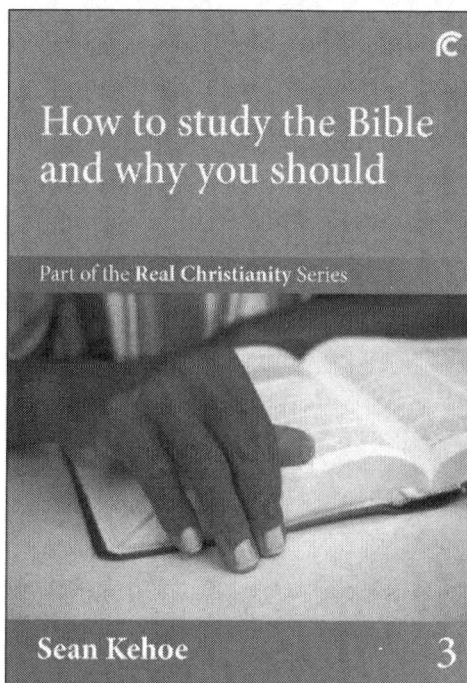

How to study the Bible and why you should

Sean Kehoe

Book 3 in the Real Christianity series explains how to study the Bible more effectively. Even in Evangelical and Pentecostal churches, which were once known for their devotion to God's Word, the Bible is now widely neglected, misunderstood and even ignored. To read the Bible properly does require some skill but, more importantly, that you approach it diligently and with the right heart attitude and method. Many of us find it difficult because nobody has shown us how. Even worse, some have been taught wrong ways, which then handicap them. This book looks at the right way to interpret the Bible, known as the 'golden rule'. That is to take the Bible literally unless the words used, or the context, plainly indicate that we should do otherwise, such as where a figure of speech is used.

It also looks at the main errors in people's thinking, which undermine faith and promote unbelief, namely 'scepticism', 'liberalism' and 'allegorism' or the 'allegorical approach'. The author has a very high view of Scripture and would urge you to take it literally and seriously, with a determination to understand it, act upon it, and be changed by it. The Bible is utterly unique. It is God's Word to us. No equivalent book has ever been, or ever will be, written. The author also advises on Bible translations, recommending those which take a literal 'word for word' approach, rather than 'dynamic equivalence', or even paraphrasing, which often take liberties with God's Word. He is convinced that every determined person, provided they can read and write, is able to gain a balanced understanding of the whole Bible for themselves, whoever they are, and regardless of ability or education

All of the books in this series, plus audio MP3s, can be ordered online from **www.realchristianity.com.**

Real Christianity

Book 4

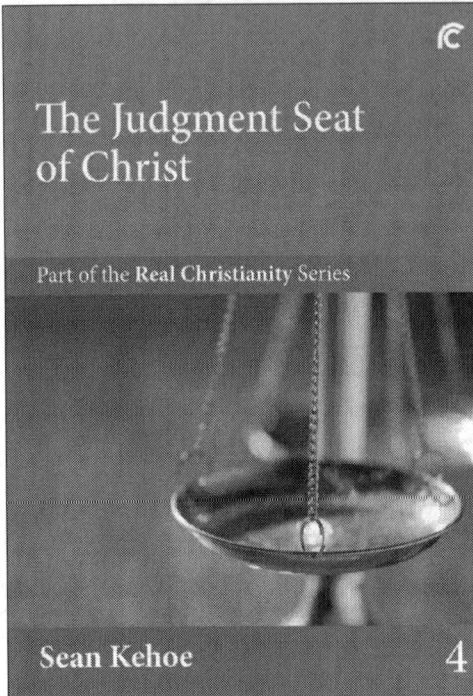

The Judgment Seat of Christ

Sean Kehoe

The Judgment Seat of Christ

Part of the **Real Christianity** Series

Sean Kehoe 4

Book 4 in the Real Christianity series looks closely at a subject which most churches ignore and which is, therefore, very little known or understood. It is the judgment which awaits Christians, at the 'Judgment Seat of Christ'. On that momentous day our whole lives, from conversion onwards, will be evaluated in a face to face meeting with Jesus Christ Himself. He will either reward and congratulate us, or rebuke us and leave us empty handed. N.B. This is not to be confused with the Great White Throne judgment, for the unsaved, at which they will be condemned. One would imagine that this hugely important issue would be taught thoroughly and be a regular topic of conversation. Yet it is rarely even mentioned in most churches.

The author explains what it is and why it matters. In particular, he focuses on what each of us can do now to improve Jesus' assessment of us and to increase the rewards, and praise, which He gives us on that Day. The author also looks very closely at the criteria for this judgment, and identifies at least 30 different issues on which we will be assessed. If we address these things now, while we have time to change, we can alter the outcome of that judgment. We are meant to see life as a test, and to be motivated by the prospect of rewards. Indeed, that is why Jesus Himself told us about them and urged us to seek for them. So, contrary to what many imagine, we are actually supposed to seek for rewards, and also for a high place in Jesus' Millennial Kingdom and in the eternal state thereafter.

All of the books in this series, plus audio MP3s, can be ordered online from **www.realchristianity.com**.

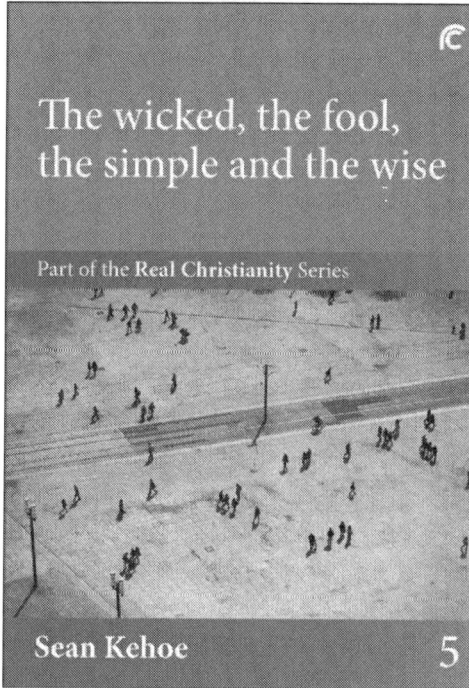

The wicked, the fool, the simple and the wise

Part of the **Real Christianity** Series

Sean Kehoe

5

The wicked, the fool, the simple and the wise

Sean Kehoe

Book 5 in the Real Christianity series looks at the four broad character types in the Bible - the wicked, the fool, the simple (or naïve) and the wise. God says a lot about all of these, and urges us to become wise. Yet, we hear very little about it in most churches. If people think about this at all, they tend to take it for granted that they are wise. But that is a problem, because God thinks very few people are wise, even within churches, and that most Christians are actually simple, or naïve. So, the author's first task is a delicate one. It is to convince you that you probably aren't wise. Then he seeks to explain why you should seek to become wise and how that can be achieved, by diligent study of the whole Bible and by spending time with those who are wise, or at least wiser than you.

He also emphasises that wisdom is available to everyone, not just the academically clever or educated. Indeed, they are often the most foolish of all. If you doubt that the pursuit of wisdom is crucial, look at the first eight chapters of Proverbs, in which God makes that same point over and over again. He does so because most of us aren't wise, but desperately need to become so. Admittedly, ceasing to be naïve, or foolish, will require a lot of time, effort, diligent study and a willingness to be brutally honest with ourselves. However, it is truly worth all of that effort. More importantly, it is what God commands us to do, which ought to settle it.

All of the books in this series, plus audio MP3s, can be ordered online from **www.realchristianity.com.**

Real Christianity

Book 6

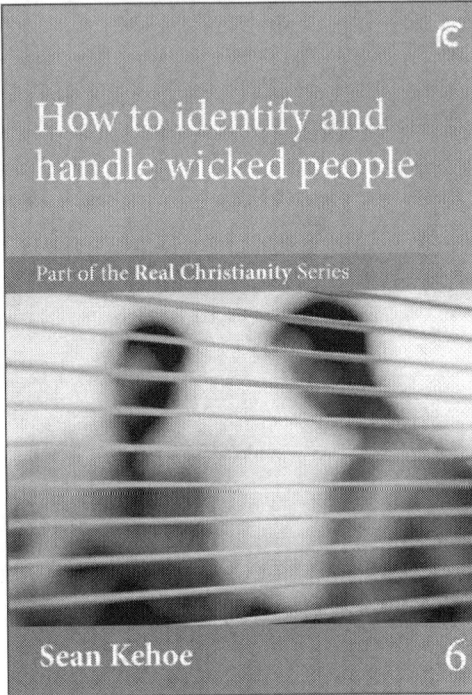

How to identify and handle wicked people

Sean Kehoe

How to identify and handle wicked people

Part of the **Real Christianity** Series

Sean Kehoe   6

Book 6 in the Real Christianity series looks at yet another subject which is rarely even mentioned, let alone taught, in most churches. It is about how to identify and handle wicked people. The author has much experience in this field, and from many angles, having spent three years in the police and then 25 as a lawyer and as a businessman and employer. He also practised in litigation and employment law and was also active in politics for many years. Thus he is able to write about many of the things which the wicked do and how they go about it. His view is that 'the wicked' are far more numerous than most of us imagine, and, crucially, that they include many people who appear to be entirely ordinary. Moreover, he maintains that the wicked are also to be found, in large numbers, inside churches, not just among unbelievers.

Indeed, it is often the leaders of churches whom God regards as the most wicked of all, if they become dishonest, manipulative, or unfaithful. That is partly because they have greater knowledge and are thus more accountable, but also because they do such terrible damage to God's people. The book seeks to define this group known as 'the wicked', and then to describe their techniques. It also gives many detailed examples of their malice, deviousness and schemes from real life situations. The aim is to help you identify the wicked earlier, and then to handle them better, both in practical terms, but also spiritually. That is, we not only need to know what to do about the wicked, but also how to pray about, and even against, them.

All of the books in this series, plus audio MP3s, can be ordered online from **www.realchristianity.com**.